Mallorca
& Menorca

THE ROUGH GUIDE

KT-239-986

There are more than seventy Rough Guide titles covering
destinations from Amsterdam to Zimbabwe

Forthcoming titles include
China • Jamaica • South Africa • Vietnam

Rough Guide Reference Series
Classical Music • Jazz • The Internet • World Music

Rough Guide Phrasebooks
Czech • French • German • Greek • Italian • Spanish

Rough Guide credits

Text Editor:	Paul Gray
Series Editor:	Mark Ellingham
Editorial:	Martin Dunford, Jonathan Buckley, Samantha Cook, Jo Mead, Alison Cowan, Amanda Tomlin, Annie Shaw, Catherine McHale, Lemisse al-Hafidh, Vivienne Heller, Al Spicer
Production:	Susanne Hillen, Andy Hilliard, Judy Pang, Link Hall, Nicola Williamson, Helen Ostick
Cartography:	Melissa Flack and David Callier
Finance:	John Fisher, Celia Crowley, Catherine Gillespie
Marketing and Publicity:	Richard Trillo, Simon Carloss (UK); Jean-Marie Kelly, Jeff Kaye, Andrew Rosenberg (US)

Acknowledgements

With special thanks to Maria Peterson for all her help with the Spanish and for discovering all sorts of important information; Dave Robson for his assistance with Spanish wine; Chez Woodhead for her motoring and motivating; Guillem Riera-Palou for his advice on Catalan; Beryl Whitehead for her gourmet expertise; Roger Spalding for his historical insights; and Ruth Rigby because I forgot to thank her in an earlier book.

Further thanks are due to June Parker; the tourist offices in Palma, Maó and Ciutadella; Euan Pinkerton; Juan Marí Tur; the Hotel Formentor; the Hotel Sol Palas Atenea; Rob Duckett; Earl and Chris Pick; and Jules Brown. Not to mention Cathy and Emma Rees.

At Rough Guides, I'm very grateful to Paul Gray for his thorough and extremely helpful editing; Melissa Flack and David Callier for the maps; Kate Berens and Gareth Nash for proofreading; and Martin Dunford and Mark Ellingham for encouraging and supporting the whole project.

This book is dedicated to my mother and to all her friends at Aspley Evangelical Church, whose kindness I will not forget.

This first edition published 1996 by Rough Guides Ltd, 1 Mercer Street, London WC2H 9QJ.

Distributed by the Penguin Group:
Penguin Books Ltd, 27 Wrights Lane, London W8 5TZ.
Penguin Books USA Inc., 375 Hudson Street, New York 10014, USA.
Penguin Books Australia Ltd, 487 Maroondah Highway, PO Box 257, Ringwood, Victoria 3134, Australia.
Penguin Books Canada Ltd, 10 Alcorn Avenue, Toronto, Ontario, Canada M4V 1E4.
Penguin Books (NZ) Ltd, 182–190 Wairau Road, Auckland 10, New Zealand.

Printed in the United Kingdom by Cox and Wyman Ltd (Reading).

Typography and original design by Jonathan Dear and The Crowd Roars.
Illustrations throughout by Edward Briant.

272pp. Includes index.

A catalogue record for this book is available from the British Library.

ISBN 1-85828-165-2

Mallorca
& Menorca

THE ROUGH GUIDE

Written and researched by
Phil Lee

THE ROUGH GUIDES

List of maps

MAP SYMBOLS

▰▰▰	Motorway	🏛	Country mansion
═══	Main road	♙	Monastery
━━━	Minor road	◆	Prehistoric site
▥▥▥	Steps	▲	Mountain peak
- - - -	Footpath	⌇	Cliff
━━━━	Railway	◠	Cave
++++	Tram line	⌁	Lighthouse
───────	Waterway	☼	Viewpoint
— —	Ferry route	ⓘ	Tourist office
━ ━ ━	Chapter division boundary	⊠	Post office
✕	Airport	★	Bus stop
◉	Hotel	⊠	Gate
△	Campsite	✛	Church (town maps)
⚲	Church (regional maps)	▨	Park
♜	Castle	⬚	Beach

Contents

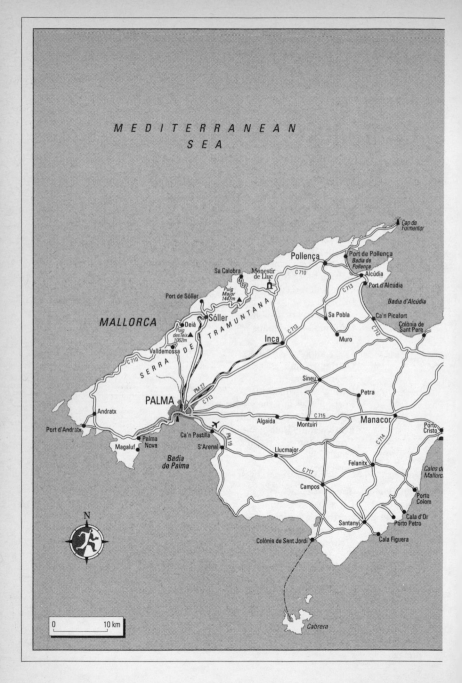

MEDITERRANEAN SEA

Cap de Formentor

Port de Pollença
Badia de Pollença
Pollença
Alcúdia
Port d'Alcúdia

Sa Calobra
Monestir de Lluc

C 710

C 713

Badia d'Alcúdia

Port de Sóller

Puig Major 1447m

Sa Pobla

Ca'n Picafort

Colònia de Sant Pere

MALLORCA

Deià

Sóller

SERRA DE TRAMUNTANA

C 713

Inca

Muro

C 712

Puig des Teix 1062m

Valldemossa

C 710

SERRA DE

PM 27

C 713

Sineu

Petra

PALMA

C 713

Andratx

Algaida

Montuïri

C 715

Manacor

Porto Cristo

Port d'Andratx

Ca'n Pastilla

S'Arenal

PM 19

Llucmajor

C 714

Magaluf

Palma Nova

Badia de Palma

Felanitx

Cales de Mallorca

C 717

Campos

Porto Colom

N

Santanyí

Cala d'Or
Porto Petro

Colònia de Sant Jordi

Cala Figuera

Cabrera

0   10 km

A MAP OF

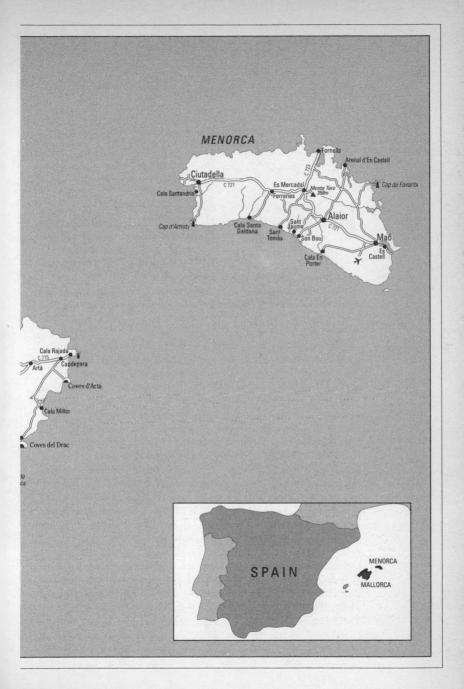

MENORCA

Fornells
Arenal d'En Castell
Ciutadella
C 723
Cala Santandria
C 721
Es Mercadal
Cap de Favaritx
Ferreries
Monte Toro
358m
Cap d'Artrutx
Cala Santa
Galdana
Sant
Jaume
Alaior
C 721
Sant
Tomàs
Son Bou
Maó
Cala En
Porter
Es
Castell
Cala Rajada
C 715
Capdepera
Artà
Coves d'Artà
Cala Millor
Coves del Drac

SPAIN

MENORCA

MALLORCA

Introduction

F ew Mediterranean holiday spots are as often and as unfairly maligned as **Mallorca**. The largest of the Balearic Islands, an archipelago to the east of the Spanish mainland which also comprises Menorca, Ibiza and Formentera, Mallorca is commonly perceived as little more than sun, sex, booze and high-rise hotels – so much so that there's a long-standing Spanish joke about a mythical fifth Balearic island called *Majorca* (the English spelling), inhabited by an estimated four million tourists a year. However, this image, spawned by the helter-skelter development of the 1960s, takes no account of Mallorca's beguiling diversity.

Until well into this century, Mallorca was a sleepily agrarian backwater, left behind in the Spanish dash to exploit the Americas from the sixteenth century onwards. Mass tourism has reversed the island's fortunes since World War II, bringing the highest level of disposable income per capita in Spain, but the price has been profound social transformation and the disfigurement of tracts of the coastal landscape. In fact, the spread of development is surprisingly limited, essentially confined to the Bay of Palma, a thirty-kilometre strip flanking the island capital, and a handful of mega-resorts notching the east coast. Elsewhere, Mallorca is much less developed than many other parts of Spain. **Palma** itself, the Balearics' one real city, is a bustling, historic place whose grandee mansions and magnificent Gothic cathedral defy the expectations of many visitors. To the east of the capital stretches **Es Pla**, an agricultural plain that fills out the centre of the island, sprinkled with ancient and seldom visited country towns. On either side of the plain are coastal mountains. In the northwest, the rugged **Serra de Tramuntana** hides beautiful cove beaches, notably Cala de Deià and Platja de Formentor, and deep sheltered valleys. Crisscrossed with footpaths, the range is ideal hiking country, particularly in the cooler spring and autumn. Tucked away here too are a string of picturesque villages, such as Orient and Fornalutx, and a pair of intriguing monasteries at Valldemossa and Lluc. The gentler, greener **Serres de Llevant** shadow the coves of the east coast and culminate in the pine-clad

Catalan and Castilian

Since the death of Franco and the subsequent federalization of Spain, the Balearics have formed their own autonomous region and asserted the primacy of their language, Catalan (*Català*). On Mallorca and Menorca, it's spoken, with only slight local variations, as the dialects *Mallorquín* and *Menorquín*. The most obvious sign of this linguistic assertiveness is the recent replacement of Castilian (Spanish) street names by their Catalan equivalents. In speech, though, the islanders are almost all bilingual, speaking Castilian and Catalan with equal fluency, and you'll find no shortage of people with perfect English or French either. In this book we've given the Catalan for everything to do with the islands – from town, street and beach names through to topographical features and food – as this is mostly what the visitor encounters. There are exceptions, and in these cases we've provided the Castilian equivalent, usually in brackets after the Catalan.

headlands and medieval hill towns of the island's northeast corner. There's a startling variety and physical beauty to the land, which, along with the mildness of the climate, has drawn tourists to visit and well-heeled expatriates to settle here since the nineteenth century, including artists and writers of many descriptions, from Robert Graves to Roger McGough.

Smaller, flatter **Menorca**, next door, has escaped character assassination, principally because the development has been more restrained. Here on the most easterly Balearic, resorts and villa-villages are spread around the coast, with ready access to pristine coves and the rolling agricultural scenery of the interior. The resorts have been kept at a discreet distance from the two main towns, the island capital of **Maó**, with its magnificent harbour, and the beguiling old port of **Ciutadella**, arguably the prettiest settlement in the Balearics. Menorca's other claim to fame is its liberal smattering of **Bronze Age remains**, most notably the cone-shaped stone heaps known as *talayots* and, unique to the island, the mysterious, T-shaped megaliths called *taulas*.

Practicalities

Access to Mallorca and Menorca is easy from Britain and northern Europe, with plenty of charter flights and complete package deals, some of which drop to absurd prices out of season or through last-minute booking. From mainland Spain, both ferries and flights are frequent and comparatively inexpensive. The islands have one airport each, conveniently situated on the outskirts of Palma and Maó, and two ferry ports apiece – Palma and Port d'Alcúdia on Mallorca, Maó and Ciutadella on Menorca. From these points of arrival, the rest of each island is within easy striking distance by car, and to a large extent by public transport as well; it only takes an hour or so to drive across Menorca, while from one corner of Majorca to the other is a three- or four-hour trip.

The main constraint for travellers is accommodation. From mid-June to mid-September rooms are in very short supply on both islands. If you go at this time, you're well advised to make a reservation several months in advance or to book a package. Out of season on Mallorca, things ease up and you can idle round, staying pretty much where you want. Two or three weeks are sufficient to see most of the island; on a shorter visit, head for Palma and the northwest coast. Bear in mind also that six of Mallorca's monasteries rent out renovated cells at exceptionally inexpensive rates – it's well worth sampling at least one. On Menorca, most tourist facilities close down from November to April – the best bases are Maó, Fornells and Ciutadella, each of which has a small cache of all-year hotels and *hostals*.

Climate

There's little significant difference between the climates of Mallorca and Menorca. Spring and autumn are the ideal times for a visit, when the weather is comfortably warm, with none of the oven-like temperatures which bake the islands in July and August. It's well worth considering a winter break too – even in January, temperatures are usually high enough during the day to sit out at a café in shirtsleeves. Both islands see occasional rain in winter, however, and the Serra de Tramuntana mountains, which protect the rest of Mallorca from inclement weather, are often buffeted by storms, while Menorca, where there's no mountain barrier, can be irritatingly windy.

Palma climate table

	J	F	M	A	M	J	J	A	S	O	N	D
Highest recorded temp. (°C)	22	23	24	26	31	37	39	37	35	31	26	24
Average daily max. temp. (°C)	14	15	17	19	22	26	29	29	27	23	18	15
Average daily min. temp. (°C)	6	6	8	10	13	17	20	20	18	14	10	8
Lowest recorded temp. (°C)	-3	-4	-1	1	5	8	12	11	4	1	1	-1
Average hours of sunshine per day	5	6	6	7	9	10	11	11	8	6	5	4
Average no. of days with rain	8	6	8	6	5	3	1	3	5	9	8	9

Part 1

Basics

Getting there from Britain

As far as **scheduled flights** are concerned, your choices are limited to a couple of direct flights a day to Mallorca and a handful of daily services to both islands via Barcelona. A full fare on a scheduled flight to either Mallorca or Menorca costs around twice the average charter price, but scheduled tickets on special offer or with certain restrictions can be reasonably good value, especially as the departure times of scheduled flights are often more sociable than those of charters.

It's also worth considering buying a **package holiday** (see p.5) – even if you've no intention of using the accommodation provided, package prices, especially at the last minute, can be so low that they represent a reasonable deal for the flight alone.

Each island's **airport** is a short hop from its capital – Palma in Mallorca, and Menorca's Maó.

Charter flights

There are frequent **charter flights** from London and almost all of Britain's regional airports to Mallorca throughout the year, and to Menorca from May to October. For an idea of current prices and availability, contact any high street travel agent or a specialist operator. The widest selection of ads for London departures is invariably found in the classified pages of the London listings magazine *Time Out* or in the *Evening Standard*; for both London and regional departures, scan the local newspapers and the travel pages of the weekend broadsheets. You could also browse the personal sections of local papers for individuals trying to sell unwanted tickets on a private basis. Otherwise, the operators and agents listed in the boxes on pp.4 and 5 are a good starting place.

The principal disadvantage of charter flights is the **fixed return date** – a maximum of four weeks from the outward journey. Some return charters are, however, good value even if you only use half, but for more flexibility you'll probably want to buy a ticket for a scheduled flight.

Scheduled flights

Spain's national airline, **Iberia**, is the main operator of **scheduled flights** from Britain to Mallorca

The easiest and cheapest way to reach Mallorca and Menorca from Britain is to fly, which takes around two hours from London, and two and a half hours from Manchester. More arduous is the long drive to the east coast of Spain, where regular car ferries depart for both islands from Barcelona and, further south still, for Mallorca from Tarragona, Valencia and Dénia. If you do decide to drive, it's worth considering the ferries linking Plymouth with Santander and Portsmouth with Bilbao, both of which shave many hours off the driving time. The train journey from London to Barcelona takes around 24 hours.

By air

Hundreds of aircraft, mostly **charter** planes, shuttle back and forth between Britain and Mallorca and Menorca during the summer season, and, although the charters are heavily subscribed by package-tour operators well in advance, there are usually spare seats for independent travellers once these package firms have taken their allocation. Excellent deals are available, with tickets averaging around £150 return – though you can pay up to £50 less. As a general rule, prices are at their highest during July and August. On these flight-only deals, waiting until the last minute to book won't gain you much advantage: you won't save much (if any) cash and you may have to be prepared to fly from any UK airport at any time of the day or night.

Airlines

British Airways, 156 Regent St, London W1R 6LB; 146 New St, Birmingham B2 4HN; 19–21 St Mary's Gate, Market St, Manchester M1 1PU; 64 Gordon St, Glasgow G1 3RS; 32 Frederick St, Edinburgh EH2 2JR (all enquiries ☎ 0345/222 111).

British Midland, Donington Hall, Castle Donington, Derby DE4 2SB (☎ 0345/554 554).

Iberia, 27–29 Glasshouse St, London W1R 6JU (☎ 0171/930 7259); plus local telephone services around the country including Edinburgh (☎ 0131/225 9257) and Cardiff (☎ 01222/373 404).

Discount flight agents

APA Travel, 138 Eversholt St, London NW1 (☎ 0171/387 5337). *Spanish flight specialists.*

Campus Travel, 52 Grosvenor Gardens, London SW1W 0AG (☎ 0171/730 3402); 541 Bristol Rd, Selly Oak, Birmingham B29 6AU (☎ 0121/414 1848); 61 Ditchling Rd, Brighton BN1 4SD (☎ 01273/570 226); 39 Queen's Rd, Clifton, Bristol BS8 1QE (☎ 0117/929 2494); 5 Emmanuel St, Cambridge CB1 1NE (☎ 01223/ 324 283); 53 Forest Rd, Edinburgh EH1 2QP (☎ 0131/668 3303); 166 Deansgate, Manchester

M3 3FE (☎ 0161/833 2046); 105–106 St Aldates, Oxford OX1 1DD (☎ 01865/242 067). *Student/ youth travel specialists, with branches also in YHA shops and on university campuses all over Britain.*

Council Travel, 28a Poland St, London W1V 3DB (☎ 0171/437 7767). *Flights and student discounts.*

STA Travel, 86 Old Brompton Rd, London SW7 3LH; 117 Euston Rd, London NW1 2SX; 38 Store St, London WC1 (all ☎ 0171/361 6161); 25 Queens Rd, Bristol BS8 1QE (☎ 0117/929 4399); 38 Sidney St, Cambridge CB2 3HX (☎ 01223/366 966); 75 Deansgate, Manchester M3 2BW (☎ 0161/834 0668); 88 Vicar Lane, Leeds LS1 7JH (☎ 0113/244 9212); 36 George St, Oxford OX1 2OJ (☎ 01865/792 800); and branches in Birmingham, Canterbury, Cardiff, Coventry, Durham, Glasgow, Loughborough, Nottingham, Warwick and Sheffield. *Worldwide specialists in low-cost flights and tours for students and under-26s.*

Travel Bug, 597 Cheetham Hill Rd, Manchester M8 5EJ (☎ 0161/721 4000). *Large range of discounted tickets.*

Union Travel, 93 Piccadilly, London W1 (☎ 0171/493 4343). *Competitive airfares.*

and Menorca. They operate one direct flight a day from London Heathrow to Palma, as well as a one-stop service from Heathrow (twice daily in summer, once in winter), which takes around five hours to either Mallorca or Menorca via Barcelona. *Iberia* also run a daily service from Manchester to Palma via Barcelona, again with a journey time of around five hours. Their principal competitor is **British Midland**, who operate direct services from Heathrow (daily) and from East Midlands (once or twice weekly) to Mallorca. *British Midland* can also provide good connections through to Mallorca via Heathrow from several other British airports: Edinburgh (1 daily; 6hr), Glasgow (1 daily; 6hr), Leeds (1 daily; 6hr) and Teesside (1 daily; 6hr). **British Airways** do not have scheduled flights to either island, but they do fly to Barcelona from a wide range of regional airports, including Birmingham, Edinburgh, Glasgow and Newcastle. If you choose this routing, *BA* will ticket you through from Barcelona to

Menorca or Mallorca, but it's usually cheaper to book the final leg of your journey separately with *Iberia* (for more information on flights to the islands from the Spanish mainland, see p.15).

Scheduled tickets at the cheapest **prices** carry almost as many restrictions as charter flights. Usually they are only valid for one month, need to be booked a minimum of fourteen days in advance, require you to stay at least one Saturday night, and don't allow for cancellation or change. *Iberia*'s "Economy Class" return ticket from London to Mallorca, on which the above restrictions apply, costs around £250 in the summer, £155 in the winter, whereas a "Club Class" ticket without restrictions will set you back £388 return. Similarly, *British Midland*'s "Diamond Euro Class" return to Palma (with no restrictions) costs £388 from Heathrow and an incredible £616 from Edinburgh; its restricted "Economy Class" return fares from London begin at £125 in the off-season, increasing to £155 mid-season, and £165 in the high season (£195, £210 and £225 from Edinburgh). Look out also for the **special offers** which the scheduled airlines sometimes run on their "Economy Class" tickets – in 1995, for example, *Iberia* reduced their midsummer fare on the direct Heathrow–Palma flight to £150 return. *Iberia* also have competitive rates for fly-drive (see p.4), and sell the least expensive **open-jaw tickets**, whereby you fly into one island and return from the other, with an inter-island flight as part of the arrangement – London–Palma–Maó–London costs about £280 in summer, £220 in winter (remember, in the height of the season, to book your inter-island flight well ahead of time).

Packages

Few places on earth provide the **package tourist** with as many choices as Mallorca and Menorca, but unfortunately for the islands' reputations it's the ugly high-rise hotels – along with the drunken antics of some of their clientele – that have grabbed most of the media attention.

However, there are also plenty of countrified villas and apartments, genteel pensions and ritzy hotels on offer, from companies such as *Magic of Spain* and *Mundi Color*, as well as walking holidays around the islands' lesser-known beauty spots.

High street travel agents will help you trawl through a wide range of packages, some of which are excellent value. If the price is right, it can also be worth booking a package simply for the flight – with a reasonably comfortable hotel laid on for a night or two at each end of your trip, if you want it (there's no compulsion to stick around at your hotel for the full period of your holiday). Packages are especially worth considering in the height of the season when island accommodation can be very hard to find through independent means; and the last-minute deals advertised in travel agents' windows can work out almost cheaper than staying at home.

To give yourself a general idea of prices, you could start by looking at the *Thomson*

Package tour operators

Alternative Mallorca, 60 Steinbeck Rd, Leeds LS7 2PW (☎0113/278 6862).
All-in and accommodation-only packages at a wide range of prices in lesser-known parts of Mallorca, as well as walking holidays, and courses in bird-watching and painting.

Eclipse, First Choice House, Peel Cross Rd, Salford, Manchester M5 2AN (☎0161/742 2222); 272 Argyle St, Glasgow G2 8QW (☎0141/248 4776).
Standard-issue hotel packages at reasonable prices.

Exodus Expeditions, 9 Weir Road, London SW12 OLT (☎0181/675 5550).
Week-long walking holidays (Oct–early May) in the Serra de Tramuntana for around £460, including flight and pensió accommodation.

Globespan, Colinton House, 10 West Mill Rd, Colinton Village, Edinburgh EH13 0NX (☎0131/441 1388).
Seven- and fourteen-night hiking holidays (Sept–May), including self-catering accommodation but not flights.

Ilkeston Co-op, 12 South St, Ilkeston, Derbyshire DE7 5SG (☎0115/932 3546).
A wide range of package holidays, often at extraordinarily cheap prices, plus bargain-

basement charter flights to both Mallorca and Menorca, especially from Birmingham and East Midlands airports.

Individual Travellers Spain, Bignor, Pulborough, West Sussex RH20 1QD (☎0179/886 9485).
Deluxe farmhouses, villas, cottages and village houses on both Mallorca and Menorca.

Magic of Spain, 227 Shepherd's Bush Rd, London W6 7AS (☎0181/748 7575).
Upmarket hotel and villa holidays, often in out-of-the-way places, on both Mallorca and Menorca.

Mundi Color, 276 Vauxhall Bridge Rd, London SW1V 1BE (☎0171/828 6021).
Quality hotel package holidays across Mallorca.

Thomson, Greater London House, Hampstead Rd, London NW1 7SD (☎0171/707 9000).
The largest UK package-tour company to both Mallorca and Menorca, with separate brochures on all manner of holidays to suit most budgets, available at any high street travel agent. Vacations in villas and apartments, family-owned hotels and luxury hotels, as well as city breaks in Palma.

---

brochures in any travel agent. Prices per person for seven nights in a self-catering **apartment**, including the return flight, start at around £120 in the low season and rise to £220 in July and August. In one of *Thomson's* **villas** – most of which have their own private swimming pool – a package, including the return flight and a rental car, starts at about £230 per person for seven nights. *Thomson's* **hotel** holidays begin at about £185 in the low season (£316 in August) for a week in a standard high-rise with half-board, whereas a week in a top-flight hotel in the low season will set you back about £350 per person B&B (£560 in August). By comparison, *Magic of Spain* offers a week's half-board in a comfortable, medium-sized hotel for £400 per person (£560 in high season), and spacious villas for two to six people, with car rental and private pool, for £309 per person per week (£539). *Mundi Color* send their customers to some of the finest hotels on the island, such as *La Residencia* in Deià (7 nights B&B from £700) and the *Mar i Vent* in Banyalbufar (7 nights B&B from £360).

Packaged **activity holidays** are another option, with **walking** in Mallorca an especially popular pastime. The best hiking is in the Serra de Tramuntana mountains of northwest Mallorca, and going with a guide makes sense as the available hiking maps are not wholly reliable. *Globespan*, for example, specializes in this type of holiday in Mallorca, running over twenty different hikes with an average length of around 12km. Based in Port de Pollença, their seven-night package (Sept–May only), including three or four guided walks and self-catering accommodation, but not flights, costs as little as £99 in November, increasing to a maximum of £186 at the end of May.

By train

Travelling by **train** from London, it can take as little as fifteen hours to reach **Barcelona**, where there are regular ferries to Palma and Maó (see p.16). The journey is fairly comfortable provided you've **reserved a seat**, which needs to be done well in advance in summer. You may also want to reserve a **couchette bed** on the overnight leg from Paris.

On the hourly *Eurostar* trains from Waterloo station through the **Channel Tunnel**, the first leg of the journey takes you to the Gare du Nord in Paris in three hours. In Paris you change trains

Train information

British Rail, European Information Line (☎0171/834 2345).

Eurostar, EPS House, Waterloo station, London SE1 8SE (☎0345/881 881 or 01233/617 575).

Eurotrain, 52 Grosvenor Gardens, London SW1W 0AG (☎0171/730 3402).

Wasteels, Victoria station, London SW1V 1JT (☎0171/834 7066).

Bus information

Eurolines, *National Express*, 164 Buckingham Palace Rd, London SW1W 9TR (☎0171/730 0202).

and stations (you want Gare Austerlitz, about 40 minutes away on the Métro) for the long haul south to Barcelona. There are two services daily: the *Talgo* train, which can handle the change in the gauge between the French and Spanish systems, leaves Paris at 9.15pm and arrives in Barcelona at 8.20am; the slower service leaves Paris at 9.39pm, with a change of trains early in the morning on the Franco-Spanish border, reaching Barcelona's Estació-Sants station at 12.20pm. In Barcelona, the Estació Marítim for ferries to the Balearics is at the foot of Las Ramblas, in the heart of the city and a short taxi ride (or twenty-minute walk) from the train station. It's also possible to begin your train journey to Barcelona at London's Charing Cross, using the **Dover–Calais ferry** to get to Paris, though this increases the journey time to about 24 hours.

The **price** of a standard rail ticket from London to Barcelona via the Chunnel (available from some travel agents, major train stations, and from *Eurostar*) fluctuates with the seasons and in accordance with restrictions similar to those of an airline ticket. To get the cheaper fares, you need to be away on a Saturday night and book at least fourteen days in advance. A sample fare in March within these restrictions costs £95 return to Paris (for fourteen days), plus £254 return from Paris to Barcelona on the *Talgo* (including compulsory sleeping accommodation), £128 return on the slower train. Fares are far more economical if you use the Dover–Calais ferry, with a return costing £158 – £141 if you're under 26 (bookable through *Eurotrain*, *Campus Travel* or *Wasteels*).

By bus

The main **bus route** between Britain and Spain connects London with Barcelona (from where you can reach the Balearics by ferry – see p.16) via Calais, Perpignan and Girona. Bus services are operated by *Eurolines* in Britain, with departures from London's Victoria station daily except Tuesday and Sunday from July to mid-September, three times weekly the rest of the year. *Eurolines* sell tickets, including through-transport to London, at all British *National Express* bus terminals, and through many travel agents. The one-way **fare** from London to Barcelona is £68, £121 return, and there's also a **youth fare** (for under-25s) of £61 single, £109 return.

The journey time from London to Barcelona is around 26 hours, long but just about bearable if you take enough to eat, drink and read. There are stops for around twenty minutes every four to five hours, and the routine is also broken by the cross-Channel ferry (included in the cost of a ticket). A small amount of French currency is useful for coffees and snacks. The Barcelona bus terminal is on Avgda Vilanova, some 3km north of the Balearic ferry dock, which is in the town centre at the foot of Las Ramblas.

By car

The traditional route **by car** to Spain involves taking a ferry across the Channel and driving through France, for which you should allow at least two days – unless, that is, you can manage to drive non-stop. You can book your vehicle onto a **cross-Channel ferry** or **hovercraft** through a travel agent or direct with the company. As a rough guide, a low-season return fare on *P&O's* **Dover–Calais** ferry costs around £100 for a driver and average-sized car, plus about £25 per extra passenger, increasing to around £200 for driver and vehicle in the summer. Dover–Calais is the obvious – and fastest – choice, but you could also travel **Dover–Boulogne** or **Ramsgate–Dunkerque**. If your starting point is to the west of London, or if you simply want to cut down on driving time through France, it may well be worth **crossing to Normandy or Brittany** via one of the other south coast ports: potentially useful routings are Newhaven to Dieppe, and Portsmouth, Weymouth or Poole to Le Havre, Caen or Cherbourg. For details of ferries from mainland Spain to the Balearics, see p.16.

Via Le Shuttle

Taking **Le Shuttle's** drive-on/drive-off service through the Channel Tunnel, rather than a cross-Channel ferry, cuts a couple of hours off the journey time to Spain. *Le Shuttle* operates trains 24 hours a day, carrying cars, motorcycles, buses and their passengers, and taking 35 minutes between Folkestone and Calais. At peak times services operate every fifteen minutes; during the night they run hourly. **Fares** vary with the season and the time of day you travel, with standard returns beginning at £136 from October to March and increasing to a maximum of £310 on July and August weekends between 6am and 6pm. Tickets cover the car and all its passengers.

Via Santander or Bilbao

Although they're expensive, the direct car and passenger ferry services from England to northern Spain greatly reduce the driving time to Barcelona. *Brittany Ferries* sail from **Plymouth to Santander** twice weekly from March to early November, with a sailing time of 24 hours, and from **Portsmouth**

Ferry companies and Le Shuttle

Brittany Ferries, Millbay Docks, Plymouth PL1 3EW; New Harbour Road, Poole BH15 4AJ; Wharf Road, Portsmouth PO2 8RU. Nationwide reservations and enquiries on ☎ 0990/360 360. *To Santander, Cherbourg and Caen.*

Hoverspeed, International Hoverport, Dover CT17 9TG (☎ 0130/424 0101). *To Boulogne and Calais.*

Le Shuttle, information and ticket sales on ☎ 0990/35 35 35.

P&O European Ferries, Channel House, Channel View Road, Dover CT17 9TJ;

Peninsular House, Wharf Road, Portsmouth PO2 8TA. Nationwide enquiries on ☎ 0990/980 111, reservations on ☎ 0990/980 980. *To Calais, Cherbourg, Le Havre and Bilbao.*

Sally Line, Argyle Centre, York St, Ramsgate, Kent CT11 9DS (☎ 0184/359 5522); 81 Piccadilly, London W1V 9HF (☎ 0171/409 2240). *To Dunkerque.*

Stena Sealink Line, Charter House, Park St, Ashford, Kent TN24 8ZX (☎ 0123/364 7047). *To Calais, Cherbourg and Dieppe.*

to Santander once weekly for the rest of the year. This latter is a thirty-hour trip, as is *P&O's* twice-weekly ferry service from **Portsmouth to Bilbao**. From Santander it's about nine hours' drive to Barcelona, from Bilbao about eight.

Ticket **prices** vary enormously according to the season and the number of passengers carried. As an illustration, a return with *Brittany Ferries* would cost around £330 for two adults and car in low season, £574 in peak season, including pullman seats for sleeping. Two-berth cabins are available from £104 return in low season, £142 in high season. Tickets are best booked in advance, either directly with the company or through any major travel agent.

Freewheelers (☎0191/222 0090) is a Newcastle-based **lift-sharing** service, which can arrange lifts from all over the UK for Spain. It is free to drivers and costs passengers a few pounds in fees plus any arrangements with the driver.

Getting there from Ireland

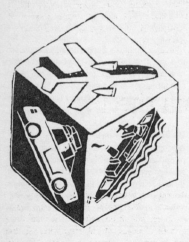

Summer charter flights direct to Mallorca and Menorca are easy to pick up from either Dublin or Belfast. Prices are at their highest during August – reckon on around £230/IR£220 return – but drop a little in the months either side. If you're prepared to book at the last minute, you'll sometimes get a cheaper deal, though you won't necessarily get the departure date you want. As another option, you might find that taking a budget flight from Dublin (with *Aer Lingus* or *British Midland*) or Belfast (*British Airways* or *British Midland*) to London, and then a London–Palma charter flight will save you a few pounds. Buying a *Eurotrain* ticket (through *USIT*) from

Dublin to London may cut costs slightly again, but by this time you're starting to talk about a journey of days and not hours. Students – and anyone under 31 – should contact *USIT*, which generally have the best discounts on Balearic flights.

Iberia have **scheduled flights** from Dublin to Mallorca via Barcelona four times weekly, with the cheapest return fare in low season costing IR£220, rising to IR£250 in July and August. These cheapest, "Economy Class" fares have several restrictions – you can't change your departure date, you need to book at least fourteen days in advance, and you can't extend your visit beyond the maximum of a month. A "Club Class" ticket, without restrictions, from Dublin to Mallorca runs to about IR£690 return all year. For Menorca, you change at Barcelona; the fares are the same as for Dublin–Mallorca. *British Airways* have three flights a day from Belfast to Barcelona, from where *Iberia* operate onward services to Mallorca and Menorca (see below); the cheapest, high-season ticket from Belfast to Barcelona costs around £350 return. Watch out for special offers from the scheduled airlines, which can reduce fares by anything up to forty percent.

Finally, if you book a Balearic **package holiday**, you may well find you're routed via London, with an add-on fare for the connection from Ireland. A two-week package to Mallorca or Menorca (based on four people in a reasonably comfortable self-catering apartment) will cost about £240 per person in low season, rising to £440 high season, from Belfast; from about IR£280 (low) to IR£450 (high) from Dublin.

Airlines in Ireland

Aer Lingus, 42 Grafton St, Dublin (☎01/705 6705); 2 Academy St, Cork (☎021/327 155); 136 O'Connell St, Limerick (☎061/474 239); 46 Castle St, Belfast BT1 1AB (☎01232/245 151).

British Airways, c/o *Aer Lingus*, 42 Grafton St, Dublin (☎1-800/626 747); 9 Fountain Centre, College St, Belfast BT1 6HR (☎0345/222 111).

British Midland, Nutley, Merrion Rd, Dublin 2 (☎01/283 8833); Suite 2, Fountain Centre, College St, Belfast BT1 6ET (☎0345/554 554).

Iberia, 54 Dawson St, Dublin 2 (☎01/677 9846).

Travel agents in Ireland

Budget Travel, 134 Lower Baggot St, Dublin 2 (☎01/661 1866). *Self-catering apartments and studios; also sells flight-only charters.*

Joe Walsh Tours, 8–11 Lower Baggot St, Dublin 2 (☎01/676 3053). *General budget fares and packages agent.*

JWT Holidays, 34 Grafton St (☎01/671 8751) and 69 Upper O'Connell St (☎01/872 2555), Dublin. *Package tour specialists.*

Liffey Travel, Abbey Mall, 13 Lower Liffey St, Dublin 1 (☎01/873 4900). *Package tour specialists.*

Thomas Cook, 118 Grafton St, Dublin (☎01/677 1721); 11 Donegall Place, Belfast BT1 5AJ (☎01232/554 455). *Package holiday and flight agent, with occasional discount offers.*

USIT, O'Connell Bridge, 19–21 Aston Quay, Dublin 2 (☎01/679 8833); 10–11 Market Parade, Cork (☎021/270 900); Victoria Place, Eyre Square, Galway (☎091/565 177); Central Buildings, O'Connell St, Limerick (☎061/415 064); 36–37 Georges Street, Waterford (☎051/72601); Fountain Centre, College St, Belfast BT1 6ET (☎01232/242 562); 33 Ferryquay St, Derry (☎01504/371 888). *Student and youth specialist for flights and trains*

Getting there from the US and Canada

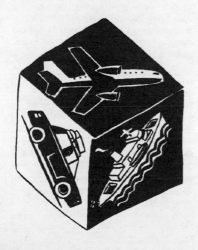

There are no direct flights from any part of North America to Mallorca or Menorca. The nearest you'll get are *Iberia* airline's one-stop flights from Los Angeles, Miami, New York, Montréal and Toronto, via Madrid, to Palma, Mallorca. *Iberia* offer competitive rates for their transatlantic flights, so they should be your first line of enquiry. The most obvious alternative is to search for the least expensive transatlantic fare offered by any airline to Madrid or Barcelona, from where an *Iberia* domestic flight will shuttle you across to the islands. Most major North American airports have direct flights to Madrid, some to Barcelona too.

Regardless of where you buy your tickets, the **fare** will depend on the season. It'll be highest from July to early September, with a drop during the "shoulder" seasons, May to June and late

September to October, and you'll get the best deal during the low season, from November to April.

From the US

Barring special offers, the cheapest of the airlines' published fares are usually **Apex** and **Super Apex** tickets, although these carry certain restrictions concerning the length of your stay (usually a maximum of one month), and the latest date for payment for your ticket (usually 14 or 21 days before departure); furthermore, you will be penalized if you change your schedule.

On *Iberia's* one-stop flights to Palma, Mallorca, the Apex fare (maximum stay one month, payment 21 days before departure) from Los Angeles (1 flight daily; 12hr) is $1108 high season, $858 low season; from Miami (1 daily; 8hr) $958 high, $708 low; and from New York (1 daily; 8hr) $868 high, $618 low. Travelling on any of these tickets, however, you can't break your journey in Madrid. If you want to stopover in mainland Spain, you'll need to purchase one ticket for the transatlantic leg and then a separate ticket for the onward flight to Mallorca or Menorca. The price of an *Iberia* Apex fare to Madrid from New York is $808 ($558 low), from Los Angeles $1048 ($798 low) and from Miami $898 ($648 low). The onward flight from Madrid to Palma costs $135 each way, the same price whether you book it in the States or when in Spain (see also "Getting there from the rest of Spain", p.14).

It's hard to beat these prices with any other airline unless they're running a special offer. If you want to try, the box below details leading airlines with services from the States to Madrid

and/or Barcelona. The advantage of Barcelona as an intermediate destination is its proximity to Mallorca and Menorca, with frequent onward *Iberia* flights costing $90 each way. To try to cut the costs, you could go through a **specialist flight agent** – either a consolidator, who buys up blocks of tickets from the airlines and sells them at a discount, or a discount agent, who wheels and deals in blocks of tickets offloaded by the airlines, and often offers special student and youth fares and a range of other travel-related services such as travel insurance, rail passes, car rentals, tours and the like. You may be able to get up to fifty percent off the Apex fares quoted by the airlines if you approach a flight agent, especially if you're under 26. Bear in mind, though, that penalties for changing your plans can be stiff. Remember too that these companies make their money by dealing in bulk – don't expect them to answer lots of questions.

From Canada

There's not much choice when it comes to flying direct from Canada to Spain, never mind the Balearics. *Iberia* operate the only services, twice-weekly flights from both **Montréal** and **Toronto** via Madrid to Palma, Mallorca. The *Iberia* Apex fare (maximum stay one month, payment 21 days before departure) to Mallorca from Toronto or Montréal is around CDN$1320 in low season, CDN$1555 in peak season. Travelling on these tickets, however, you can't break your journey in Madrid. If you want to stopover there, you'll need to purchase one ticket for the transatlantic leg and then a separate ticket for an onward flight to Mallorca or Menorca (see "Getting there from the rest of Spain", p.14). The price of an *Iberia* Apex fare to

---

Airlines in North America

American Airlines (☎1-800/433-7300). *Chicago, Dallas and Miami to Madrid.*

Continental Airlines (domestic ☎1-800/525-0280; international ☎1-800/231-0856). *Newark to Madrid.*

Delta Airlines (domestic ☎1-800/221-1212; international ☎1-800/241-4141; in Canada, call directory enquiries, ☎1-800/555-1212, for local toll-free number). *Atlanta to Madrid.*

Iberia (in US ☎1-800/772-4642; in Canada ☎1-800/423-7421). *Flights to Mallorca via*

Madrid from Toronto, Montréal, Miami, New York and Los Angeles, plus special deals such as fly-drive.

TWA (domestic ☎1-800/221-2000; international ☎1-800/892-4141). *New York to Barcelona and Madrid.*

United Airlines (domestic ☎1-800/241-6522; international ☎1-800/538-2929). *Washington DC to Madrid.*

Discount travel companies in North America

Air Brokers International, 323 Geary St, Suite 411, San Francisco, CA 94102 (☎1-800/883-3273). *Consolidator.*

Airhitch, 2472 Broadway, Suite 200, New York, NY 10025 (☎212/864-2000). *Standby-seat broker. For a set price, they guarantee to get you on a flight as close to your preferred destination as possible, within a week.*

Council Travel, 205 E 42nd St, New York, NY 10017 (☎1-800/226-8624 or 212/661-1450), and branches in many other US cities. *Student/ budget travel agency.*

Educational Travel Center, 438 N Frances St, Madison, WI 53703 (☎1-800/747-5551 or 608/256-5551). *Student/youth and consolidator fares.*

Interworld Travel, 800 Douglass Rd, Miami, FL 33134 (☎305/443-4929). *Consolidator.*

STA Travel, 48 East 11th St, New York, NY 10003 (☎1-800/777-0112 or 212/477-7166), and other branches in the Los Angeles, San Francisco and Boston areas. *Worldwide*

discount travel firm specializing in student/ youth fares.

TFI Tours International, 34 W 32nd St, New York, NY 10001 (☎1-800/745-8000). *Consolidator; other offices in Las Vegas, San Francisco, Los Angeles.*

Travac, 989 6th Ave, New York NY 10018 (☎1-800/872-8800). *Consolidator, with another branch in Orlando.*

Travel Avenue, 10 S Riverside, Suite 1404, Chicago, IL 60606 (☎1-800/333-3335). *Discount travel agent.*

Travel Cuts, 187 College St, Toronto, ON M5T 1P7 (☎416/979-2406). *Canadian student travel organization with branches all over the country.*

UniTravel, 1177 N Warson Rd, St Louis, MO 63132 (☎1-800/325-2222). *Consolidator.*

Worldtek Travel, 111 Water St, New Haven, CT 06511 (☎1-800/243-1723). *Discount travel agency.*

Madrid from Montréal or Toronto is CDN$1450 high season, CDN$1205 low. Within Canada, connecting flights to Toronto or Montréal will add about CDN$200–500 to the above fares. **Discount travel agents** deal mainly in flights via London (usually using a combination of airlines), though other European routings are possible. They may be able to knock up to fifty percent off the Apex fares quoted by the airlines, especially if you're under 26.

Getting there from Australia and New Zealand

There are no direct flights to any part of Spain from Australia or New Zealand. The best you can do – both in terms of flight time and prices – is to fly via London. The major airlines utilize a variety of routings to London, with the faster services taking about 21 hours from Sydney, 18 hours from Perth. From London, there are regular direct scheduled flights and charters to Mallorca and Menorca (see "Getting there from Britain"). This onward flight adds an extra two hours or so to the travelling time. You'll get the best deals by buying the tickets separately – bargain-basement flights to the islands are easy to pick up in London – but in Australasia some airlines will ticket you on through London (with a different airline) to Mallorca or Menorca, allowing a UK stopover too. Booking ahead as far as possible is the best way to secure the most reasonable prices, and it's almost invariably cheaper (by up to 50 percent) to buy tickets through discount and travel agents rather than the airlines.

Fares

Fares to Europe change according to the time of year you travel. Mid-May to the end of August, December and the first half of January are the high season; mid-January to the end of February, October and November the low season; and the rest of the year the shoulder season. The current lowest standard return fares to London (low/high season) are around A$1190/1860 from Australia, NZ$1500/2000 from New Zealand.

Though they charge heavily for cancellations or alterations, **discount agents** can usually provide far better prices than these – from A$930/NZ$1212 for a low-season fare. Full-time students, and those aged under 26 or over 60, can also make big savings through specialist agents. Some are listed in the box opposite, and others can be found in the travel sections of the major Saturday newspapers.

Airlines in Australia and New Zealand

Air New Zealand, 5 Elizabeth St, Sydney (☎02/9223 4666); Quay Street, Auckland (☎09/357 3000).

British Airways, 64 Castlereagh St, Sydney (☎02/9258 3300); Queen Street, Auckland (☎09/356 8690). *Daily to London from all major Australian airports except Cairns and Darwin.*

Iberia, 131 Elizabeth St, Brisbane (☎07/229 7155); 543 King St, Melbourne (☎03/321 6874); 43 Ventnor Ave, Perth (☎09/322 1355); 403 George St, Sydney (☎02/239 1722). *No flights to Europe from Australasia, but easily the widest range of flights into Mallorca and Menorca from London and other European destinations.*

Qantas, Chifley Square, Sydney (☎02/957 0111); Qantas House, 154 Queen St, Auckland (☎09/357 8900). *Twice-daily flights to London from all the mainland state capitals.*

Singapore Airlines, 17 Bridge St, Sydney (☎02/9236 0144); Lower Ground Floor, West Plaza Building, cnr Customs and Albert streets, Auckland (☎09/379 3209). *Twice-daily flights to London from major Australian airports via Singapore.*

Travel and discount agents in Australia and New Zealand

Accent on Travel, 545 Queen St, Brisbane (☎07/3832 1777).

Anywhere Travel, 345 Anzac Parade, Kingsford, Sydney (☎02/663 0411).

Brisbane Discount Travel, 360 Queen St, Brisbane (☎07/3229 9211).

Budget Travel, 16 Fort St, Auckland; other branches around the city (☎09/309 4313; toll-free 0800/808 040).

Destinations Unlimited, 3 Milford Rd, Milford, Auckland (☎09/486 1303).

Flight Centres Australia: Circular Quay, Sydney (☎02/9241 2422); Bourke St, Melbourne (☎03/650 2899); plus other branches nationwide. New Zealand: National Bank Towers, 205–225 Queen St, Auckland (☎09/309 6171); Shop 1M, National Mutual Arcade, 152 Hereford St, Christchurch (☎09/379 7145); 50–52 Willis St, Wellington (☎04/472 8101); other branches countrywide.

Northern Gateway, 22 Cavenagh St, Darwin (☎08/8941 1394).

Harvey World Travel, Princess Highway, Kogarah, Sydney (☎02/567 099); branches nationwide.

Passport Travel, 320b Glenferrie Rd, Malvern, Melbourne (☎03/9824 7183).

STA Travel, Australia: 732 Harris St, Ultimo, Sydney (☎02/9212 1255; toll-free 1800/637 444); 256 Flinders St, Melbourne (☎03/9347 4711); other offices in Townsville, state capitals and major universities. New Zealand: Travellers' Centre, 10 High St, Auckland (☎09/366 6673); 233 Cuba St, Wellington (☎04/385 0561); 223 High St, Christchurch (☎03/379 9098); other offices in Dunedin, Palmerston North, Hamilton and major universities.

Thomas Cook, 96 Anzac Ave, Auckland (☎09/379 3920); branches throughout New Zealand.

Topdeck Travel, 45 Glenfell St, Adelaide (☎08/8232 7222).

Tymtro Travel, 428 George St, Sydney (☎02/9223 2211).

UTAG Travel, 122 Walker St, North Sydney (☎02/956 8399); branches throughout Australia.

Getting there from the rest of Spain

Menorca and especially Mallorca are easily reached by plane and ferry from mainland Spain and from Ibiza. Obviously, the main advantage of a flight over a ferry journey is its speed: Barcelona to Palma, for example, takes just forty minutes compared to the ferry trip of eight hours. By plane, there's also the advantage of a wider range of jumping-off points: regular scheduled flights link many of Spain's major cities with Mallorca and several with Menorca too. By ferry, you're confined to five

departure ports – Ibiza, Tarragona, Valencia and Dénia for Mallorca, and Barcelona for both Mallorca and Menorca. Ticket prices also favour aircraft travel: it is less expensive by ferry, but not by much, and not enough to justify the extra time and trouble – unless, that is, you're in or near one of the departure ports anyway. However, if you're taking your own vehicle over to the islands, you will have to travel by boat. For details of ferries and flights between Mallorca and Menorca, see p.30.

By air from the mainland

The vast majority of **flights** from the mainland to Mallorca and Menorca are operated by Spain's national carrier, *Grupo Iberia*, a multi-headed conglomerate that incorporates, amongst its several subsidiaries, *Iberia* and *Aviaco*. These two companies combine to link a range of mainland cities with Mallorca and – to a far lesser degree – Menorca. The *Iberia* group has sales offices in every major Spanish city and most capital cities abroad. Seat availability isn't usually a problem and the fares are very reasonable, with flights into Mallorca from Valencia, for instance, costing 12,000ptas, from Madrid 16,000ptas and from

---

Iberia offices and flight frequencies

In addition to their many mainland offices, *Iberia* have a nationwide domestic flight reservation and information line on ☎901/333111. The route frequencies given below cover direct flights to Mallorca unless otherwise specified.

Alicante Avda Frederico Soto 9; ☎96/521 8613 (3 daily, 45min).

Barcelona Passeig de Gràcia 30; ☎93/412 7020 (Mallorca 9 daily, 40min; Menorca 3–6 daily, 35min).

Bilbao Ercilla 20; ☎94/424 1935 (1 daily, 1hr 10min).

Ibiza Passeig Vara de Rey 15; ☎971/300833 (5 daily, 30min).

Madrid Velázquez 130; ☎91/411 1011 (Mallorca 6–9 daily, 1hr 10min; Menorca 1–2 daily, 1hr 10min).

Málaga Molina Lario 13; ☎95/213 6146 (3–4 weekly, 1hr 10min).

Menorca Aeroport Menorca ☎971/369015.

Palma, Mallorca Passeig d'es Born 10; ☎971/262600.

Sevilla Almirante Lobo 2; ☎95/422 8901 (3 weekly, 1hr 15min).

Valencia Paz 14; ☎96/352 7552 (Mallorca 3 daily, 40min; Menorca June–Sept 4 weekly, 50min).

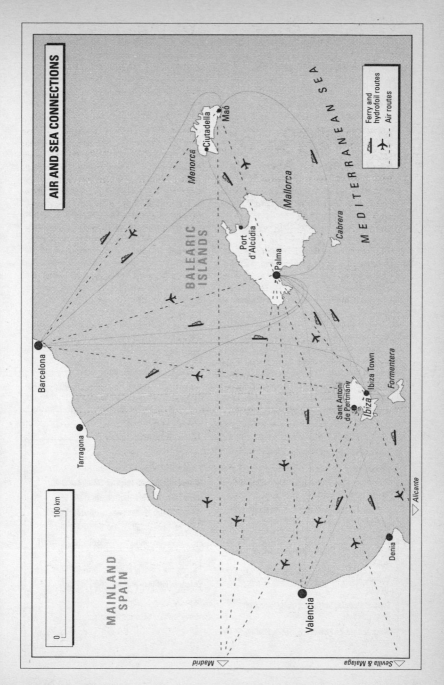

AIR AND SEA CONNECTIONS

Ferry and hydrofoil routes
Air routes

MEDITERRANEAN SEA

BALEARIC ISLANDS

Menorca
Ciutadella
Maó

Mallorca
Cabrera
Port d'Alcúdia
Palma

Barcelona

Tarragona

Ibiza Town
Sant Antoni de Portmany
Ibiza
Formentera

Alicante

Denia

MAINLAND SPAIN

100 km

0

Valencia

Madrid

Sevilla & Malaga

Barcelona 10,500ptas (return fares are double). It's sometimes possible to get a cheaper ticket on a charter flight (mostly from Madrid), but you'll have to plod around local travel agents once in Spain – they're listed under *viajes agencias* in the yellow pages.

By ferry from the mainland

Ferry fares vary a little according to the season and between the two shipping lines involved, but, surprisingly, hardly at all between routes – in other words, your fare on a *Trasmediterranea* boat will be much the same whether you travel from Barcelona to Maó or Valencia to Palma. On *Trasmediterranea* services, advance **reservations** are advised for ferry and more particularly hydrofoil travel from mid-June to mid-September, but they're not required. *Flebasa* only accept bookings on their Barcelona route.

The **Trasmediterranea** shipping company operates the majority of services between the mainland and the Balearic islands. Their main routes are from **Barcelona to Palma** (1–2 daily; 8hr), **Barcelona to Maó** (2–3 weekly; 9hr), **Valencia to Palma** (6 weekly; 9hr), and **Tarragona to Palma** by hydrofoil (June–Sept 5 weekly; 3hr 45min). Other *Trasmediterranea* hydrofoils sail from Valencia via Ibiza to Palma (June–Sept 2 weekly; 5hr 15min), and they have other ferries linking Barcelona and Ibiza (2–4 weekly; 10hr), Valencia and Ibiza (1 weekly; 9hr), and Valencia and Maó (1 weekly via Palma). **Tickets** can be purchased from the *Trasmediterranea* office at the port of embarkation either in advance or on arrival. The

company also has a sales office in Madrid and authorizes certain travel agents to sell its tickets both in other Spanish cities and, far more infrequently, elsewhere in Europe. Within Spain, ask at the local tourist office for the address; abroad, Spanish Tourist Offices will have the details (see the box on p.22). In the UK, the official agent is *Southern Ferries*, 179 Piccadilly, London W1V 9DB (☎0171/491 4968).

Prices vary according to season (high-season fares apply from July to mid-September), but the differences are marginal, as are the savings to be made from buying a return, rather than a single ticket. The single passenger fare on a **ferry** from either Barcelona or Valencia to Palma, Maó or Ibiza currently costs 6000ptas; children (2–11 years old) travel half-price, infants (under-2) go free. There are night-time sailings on most routes, when a **cabin** is extremely useful, especially if you're travelling with children. Double cabins cost 27,550ptas one way (15,960ptas for single occupancy), while a triple cabin are charged at 31,350ptas, a four-berth 39,900ptas. The tariffs for cars are mainly determined by length: for the trip from Barcelona or Valencia to any of the Balearic islands, cars of up to 2.5 are charged at 10,450ptas, standard-sized cars (2.5 to 4.5 metres) 16,720ptas, and those between 4.5 and 6 metres 20,900ptas. On the *Trasmediterranea* **hydrofoils** from Tarragona and Valencia (via Ibiza) to Palma, a single adult passenger fare is 6600ptas. Vehicles up to 6m long (the maximum permitted) and 1.8m high cost 16,800ptas each way.

Balearics ferry companies

FLEBASA

Barcelona Estació Marítim, Vilanova i la Geltrú; ☎93/815 9250.

Ciutadella, Menorca Moll Comercial; ☎971/480012.

Dénia Estación Marítima; ☎96/578 4011.

Ibiza town Estació Vieja Formentera; ☎971/314005.

Palma, Mallorca Estació Marítim No. 3; ☎971/405360.

Port d'Alcúdia, Mallorca Moll Comercial; ☎971/546454.

Sant Antoni de Portmany, Ibiza Edificació Far 1; ☎971/342871.

TRASMEDITERRANEA

Barcelona Estació Marítim; ☎93/443 2532.

Ibiza town Estació Marítim; ☎971/315050.

Madrid Pedro Muñoz Seca 2; ☎91/431 0700.

Maó, Menorca Moll Comercial; ☎971/366050.

Palma, Mallorca Estació Marítim No. 2; ☎971/405014.

Tarragona Passeig Marítim; ☎977/225506.

Valencia Estació Marítim; ☎96/367 6512.

The only seaborne alternative to the Trasmediterranea services is the smaller **Flebasa** ferry company, which links **Dénia**, on the Spanish mainland, with Sant Antoni de Portmany on Ibiza (1–3 daily; 3hr) and **Palma** (1 daily; 9hr). The single passenger fare from Dénia to Palma is around 5330ptas, with vehicle rates starting at about 14,500ptas one way. You can't, however, break your journey in Ibiza and continue by ferry to Palma without incurring a further charge: you would have to pay full fare for the Ibiza–Palma leg, 2950ptas per adult, from 6950ptas per car. *Flebasa* also run a ferry from Vilanova i la Geltrú, 8km south of **Barcelona**, to Mallorca's **Port d'Alcúdia** (1–2 daily; 7hr), on which the same rates apply as on the Dénia–Palma route. *Flebasa*'s main **hydrofoil** service – which does not carry vehicles – operates from mid-June to mid-September, linking Dénia with Ibiza town (1 daily; 2hr) and then Palma (1 daily; 4hr 30min). Tariffs are 5220ptas per person Dénia–Ibiza, 6220ptas Dénia–Palma, and 3950ptas Ibiza–Palma.

Flebasa **tickets** are only available at the dockside in the ports of embarkation. The company's office at Vilanova i la Geltrú, near Barcelona, is the only one to take advance reservations; at the other ports you should show up at least an hour before departure time.

From Ibiza and Formentera

Getting to Mallorca from **Ibiza** couldn't be simpler. *Iberia* operate four to five **flights** daily between the two islands. The journey takes thirty minutes and costs around 6300ptas one way (double for the return). There's usually no problem with seat availability, but you need to book ahead during the height of the season. There are, however, no direct flights from Ibiza to Menorca – you're routed via Mallorca at a one-way cost of 12,600ptas. For flights between Mallorca and Menorca see p.30.

By **ferry**, *Trasmediterranea* runs a twice-weekly, five-hour service from Ibiza town to Palma, with the one-way adult passenger fare costing around 4200ptas (8400ptas return). Plying the same route, the company's **hydrofoils** (June–Sept 2 weekly; 2hr 15min) charge similar passenger rates, but also offer day return fares at around thirty percent less. Both the ferries and the hydrofoils charge 6600ptas one way for standard-sized cars. Once daily, *Flebasa*'s Dénia ferry continues beyond Ibiza's Sant Antoni de Portmany to reach Palma, and its Dénia hydrofoil, which is routed via Ibiza town, sails to Palma (see "By ferry from the mainland" above, for full details).

There are no ferry or hydrofoil services from Ibiza to Menorca, but you can island-hop via Mallorca. For details of ferries between Mallorca and Menorca, see p.30.

Formentera has no airport and is linked by direct ferry only with Ibiza. *Flebasa* links the island with Ibiza town by both ferry (4 daily; 1hr) and hydrofoil (mid-July to Sept 10 daily; 20min; no vehicles). Single adult fares by ferry are 850ptas (cars from 3000ptas), while the hydrofoil costs 1600ptas one way.

Visas and red tape

Citizens of EC countries (and Norway and Iceland) need only a valid national identity card to enter Spain for up to ninety days. Since Britain has no identity card system, however, British citizens do have to take a passport. US and Canadian citizens require a passport but no visa and can stay for up to ninety days. Australians and New Zealanders need to obtain a sixty-day visa before departing for Spain. Visa requirements do change,

however, and it is always advisable to check the current situation.

To stay longer, EC nationals (and citizens of Norway and Iceland) can apply for a *permiso de residencia* (residence permit) once in Spain. You'll either have to produce proof that you have sufficient funds (officially 5000ptas a day) to be able to support yourself without working – easiest done by keeping bank exchange forms every time you change money – or a contract of employment (*contrato de trabajo*), or something to prove you are self-employed (for example as a teacher), which involves registering at the tax office. Other nationalities will either need to get a special visa from a Spanish consulate before departure (see below for addresses), or can apply for one ninety-day visa extension, showing proof of sufficient funds, once in Spain. In Mallorca, further advice can be obtained from the various consulates listed on p.81; nationalities not represented should contact their representative in Madrid.

Duty-free restrictions

All **EC citizens** are covered by the same **duty-free restrictions**, limiting purchases at duty-free shops to – amongst other regulations – a maximum of 200 cigarettes (or 250g of tobacco), two litres of wine, and one litre of strong spirits or two litres of fortified wine (sherry etc) per person. In addition, every EC citizen has a **traveller's allowance**, whereby items bought in one EC country and brought back directly to another are deemed for personal use and do not attract taxes. The maximum levels per adult are generous: 800 cigarettes (or 1kg of tobacco), 10 litres of strong spirit, 90 litres of wine and 110 litres of beer. If you keep within these limits and are travelling direct from one EC state to another, you don't need to make a declaration to customs at your place of entry.

Residents of the USA can take home up to $400 worth of goods purchased overseas duty-free, including a litre of alcohol or wine, 200 cigarettes and 100 cigars. **Canadians** are exempt from paying duty on up to $300 worth of goods after spending seven days out of the country

---

Spanish embassies and consulates abroad

Australia 15 Arkana St, Yarralumla, Canberra ACT 2600 (☎616/273 3555 or 273 3845).

Canada 350 Sparks St, Suite 802, Ottawa, Ontario KIR 7S8 (☎613/237 2193 or /237 2194).

Ireland 17A Merlyn Park, Ballsbridge, Dublin 4 (☎01/269 1640 or 269 2597).

UK 39 Chesham Place, London SW1X 8SB (☎0171/235 5555); Suite 1a, Brook House, 70 Spring Gardens, Manchester M22 2BQ (☎0161/236 1233).

USA 2700 15th St NW, Washington DC 20009 (☎202/265 0190); 150 East 58th St, New York, NY 10155 (☎212/355 4090); 6300 Wilshire Blvd, Los Angeles, CA 90048 (☎213/658 6500).

(those goods may include up to 40 ounces of spirits or wine, 24 twelve-ounce bottles of beer and 200 cigarettes). Travellers returning to **Australia** can bring in $400 worth of "gifts" duty-free, plus 250 cigarettes or 250g of tobacco and one bottle of alcohol (beer, wine or spirits). **New Zealand** permits $700 worth of gifts, plus 4.5 litres of wine or beer, 1125ml of spirits, and 200 cigarettes or 250g tobacco or 50 cigars, or a mixture of these not exceeding 250g.

Insurance

As an EC country, Spain has free reciprocal health agreements with other member states. To take advantage, British citizens will need form E111, available over the counter from most post offices. Treatment within this scheme is, however, only provided by practitioners within the Spanish health care system, the *Instituto Nacional de la Salud*, whereas most doctors on the islands are more accustomed to – or only deal with – private insurance work (see also "Health", below). Taking out your own medical insurance means you won't have to hunt around for a doctor who will treat you for free, and will also cover the cost of items not within the EC scheme's purview, such as dental treatment and repatriation on medical grounds. It will usually also cover your baggage and tickets in case of theft, as long as you get a report from the local police. Non-EC residents will need to insure themselves for all eventualities, including medical costs.

Note that some **bank** and **credit cards** have medical or other insurance included, and travel insurance is sometimes covered if you pay for your trip with a credit or charge card.

Insurance in Britain and Ireland

In **Britain** and **Ireland**, travel insurance schemes (around £15–22 per person for a fortnight, £21–29 for a month) are sold by almost every travel agent and bank, and direct by several specialist insurance firms. Please note that if you're engaging in high-risk outdoor activities (for example mountaineering), you'll probably have to pay an extra premium; ask your insurers for advice.

> **Travel insurance companies in the UK and Ireland**
>
> *Endsleigh Insurance*, 97–107 Southampton Row, London WC1B 4AG; ☎0171/436 4451.
>
> *Columbus Travel Insurance*, 17 Devonshire Square, London EC2M 4SQ; ☎0171/375 0011.
>
> *Frizzell Insurance*, Frizzell House, County Gates, Bournemouth, Dorset BH1 2NF; ☎01202/292 333.
>
> *Accidental and General Insurance Brokers*, 105 Royal Ave, Belfast; ☎01232/325 711.
>
> *Sun Alliance*, Sun Alliance House, 13–17 Dawson St, Dublin 2; ☎01/677 1851.

North American insurance

In the **US and Canada**, insurance tends to be much more expensive, and may cover medical costs only. As well as the perks of their bank and credit cards, travellers should check their **existing insurance schemes** before taking out specific travel insurance. Canadians are often insured by their provincial health plans, while holders of ISIC cards – and some other student/

Travel insurance companies in North America

Access America ☎ 1-800/284-8300

Carefree Travel Insurance ☎ 1-800/323-3149

Desjardins Travel Insurance – Canada only
☎ 1-800/463-7830

International Student Insurance Service (ISIS) – sold by STA Travel ☎ 1-800/777-0112

Travel Assistance International ☎ 1-800/821-2828

Travel Guard ☎ 1-800/826-1300

Travel Insurance Services ☎ 1-800/937-1387

teacher/youth cards – are entitled to accident coverage and hospital in-patient benefits for the period during which the card is valid. Furthermore, students will often find that their student health coverage extends during the vacations and for one term beyond the date of last enrolment. Homeowners' or renters' insurance often covers theft or loss of documents, money and valuables while overseas, though conditions and maximum amounts vary from company to company.

Only after exhausting the possibilities above might you want to contact a specialist **travel insurance** company. Policies are quite comprehensive, anticipating everything from charter companies going bankrupt to delayed or lost baggage, by way of sundry illnesses and accidents. **Premiums** vary widely, so shop around. The most reasonable ones are usually offered through student/youth agencies (*STA*'s policies range from about $50–70 for fifteen days to $500–700 for a year, depending on the amount of financial cover). Note also that very few insurers will arrange on-the-spot payments in the

event of a major expense or loss; you will usually be reimbursed only after going home. If you're planning on doing any **trekking** or **mountaineering**, you'll need to take out an additional rider to cover these activities, thereby adding an extra 20–50 percent to the premium.

None of these policies insures against theft overseas. North American travel policies apply only to items lost from, or damaged in, the custody of an identifiable, responsible third party – a hotel porter or an airline, for example. Even in these cases, however, you will have to contact the local police and have them file a report so that your insurer can process the claim.

Australasian insurance

In **Australia** and **New Zealand**, travel insurance is put together by the airlines and travel agent groups (see box below) in conjunction with insurance companies. They're all comparable in premium and coverage – a typical policy for Europe will cost A$180/NZ$210 for a month, A$260/NZ$300 for two months and A$330/NZ$380 for three months. Most adventure sports are covered, but check the policy first.

Travel insurance companies in Australia and New Zealand

UTAG, 347 Kent St, Sydney; ☎ 02/9819 6855 or 1800/809 462.

AFTA, 144 Pacific Hwy, North Sydney; ☎ 02/956 4800.

Cover More, Level 9, 32 Walker St, North Sydney; ☎ 02/9202 8000 or 1800/251 881.

Ready Plan, 141–147 Walker St, Dandenong, Victoria; ☎ 1800/337 462.

10th Floor, 63 Albert St, Auckland; ☎ 09/379 3208.

Travellers with disabilities

Despite their popularity as holiday destinations, Mallorca and Menorca pay scant regard to their disabled visitors, with facilities lagging way behind those of most other EC regions. That said, there are hotels on both islands with wheelchair access and other appropriate facilities, and attitudes are beginning to change – by law all new public buildings in Spain are required to be fully accessible.

Flying to the islands is the least of the difficulties, as all the scheduled airlines concerned, including the main carrier, *Iberia*, cater for (or will

---

Contacts for travellers with disabilities

GENERAL

Spanish National Tourist Office (see p.22 for addresses). *Publishes a fact sheet listing useful addresses and some accessible accommodation.*

Organización Nacional de Ciegos de Espana, Plaça Bisbe Berenguer de Palou, Palma, Mallorca (☎971/469311). *ONCE, the Spanish organization for the visually impaired, is active and influential, thanks in part to its huge lottery. It sells braille maps and can arrange trips: write for details.*

AUSTRALIA AND NEW ZEALAND

ACROD (Australian Council for Rehabilitation of the Disabled), PO Box 60, Curtin ACT 2605 (☎06/682 4333); 55 Charles St, Ryde (☎02/9809 4488). *General travel information.*

Disabled Persons Assembly, PO Box 10, 138 The Terrace, Wellington (☎04/472 2626). *Advice and general travel information.*

UK AND IRELAND

Holiday Care Service, 2nd floor, Imperial Building, Victoria Rd, Horley, Surrey RH6 9HW (☎01293/774 535). *Information on all aspects of travel. Issues factsheets on both Mallorca and Menorca which include detailed descriptions of wheelchair-accessible and other suitable hotels and apartments.*

Irish Wheelchair Association, Blackheath Drive, Clontarf House, Dublin 3 (☎01/833 8241). *General advice on holidays and accommodation.*

RADAR, 12 City Forum, 250 City Rd, London EC1V 8AS (☎0171/250 3222; Minicom ☎0171/ 250 4119). *A good source of advice on holidays and travel abroad.*

USA AND CANADA

Directions Unlimited, 720 N Bedford Rd, Bedford Hills, NY 10507 (☎1-800/533-5343). *Tour operator specializing in custom tours for people with disabilities.*

Jewish Rehabilitation Hospital, 3205 Place Alton Goldbloom, Montréal, PQ H7V 1R2 (☎514/688 9550). *Guidebooks and travel information.*

Mobility International USA, PO Box 10767, Eugene, OR 97440 (Voice and TDD: ☎503/343-1284). *Information and referral services, access guides, tours and exchange programs. Annual membership $20 (includes quarterly newsletter).*

Society for the Advancement of Travel for the Handicapped (SATH), 347 5th Ave, New York, NY 10016 (☎212/447-7284). *Non-profit travel-industry referral service that passes queries on to its members as appropriate; allow plenty of time for a response.*

Travel Information Service, Moss Rehabilitation Hospital, 1200 West Tabor Rd, Philadelphia, PA 19141 (☎215/456-9600). *Telephone information and referral service.*

Twin Peaks Press, Box 129, Vancouver, WA 98666 (☎206/694-2462 or 1-800/637-2256). *Publisher of the* Directory of Travel Agencies for the Disabled *($19.95), listing more than 370 agencies worldwide;* Travel for the Disabled *($14.95); the* Directory of Accessible Van Rentals *and* Wheelchair Vagabond *($9.95), loaded with personal tips.*

assist) disabled travellers to some degree. If you're driving down, the *Brittany Ferries* crossing from Plymouth to Santander offers good facilities, as do most of the cross-Channel ferries. On Mallorca and Menorca themselves, however, **transport** is a real problem, as buses and trains are not equipped for wheelchairs, and none of the islands' car rental firms have vehicles with hand controls – though at least the taxi drivers are usually helpful. Note also that the more remote roads along the coast and out in the countryside have very rough surfaces. Toilet facilities for disabled visitors are a rare sight anywhere.

Information and maps

The Spanish National Tourist Office (SNTO) produces and gives away a wide range of maps, pamphlets and special interest leaflets on Mallorca and Menorca. Contact, or better still visit, one of their offices before you leave and stock up. In particular, try to get hold of the booklet listing all the Balearic Islands' hotels, *hostals* and campsites, as this is printed in Madrid and can be difficult to obtain on the islands themselves.

Information offices in Mallorca and Menorca

In **Mallorca**, the main provincial and municipal **tourist offices** in Palma (see p.60) will provide free maps of the town and the island, and leaflets detailing all sorts of island-wide practicalities – from bus and train timetables to lists of car rental firms, ferry schedules and boat excursion organizers. Outside of Palma, many of the larger settlements and resorts have seasonal tourist offices (addresses are detailed in the guide). These vary enormously in quality, and while they are generally extremely useful for local information, they cannot be relied on to know anything about what goes on outside their patch. In **Menorca**, there are efficient year-round tourist offices in the two main towns, Maó and Ciutadella, but nowhere else. **Opening hours** vary considerably, but the larger tourist offices are all open at least from Monday to Friday, from 8am or 9am to 2pm or 3pm. The smaller concerns operate from April or May to September or October, usually from Monday to Friday in the mornings. We've given details of opening times throughout the guide, though you can't always rely on the officially posted hours in remoter spots.

SNTO offices abroad

Australia 203 Castlereagh St, Suite 21A, PO Box A-685, Sydney, NSW (☎02/9264 7966).

Canada 102 Bloor St West, 14th Floor, Toronto, Ontario (☎416/961 31 31).

Netherlands Laan Van Meerdervoort 8, 2517 AJ Den Haag (☎70/346 59 00).

UK 57–58 St James's St, London SW1A 1LD (☎0171/499 0901 or 499 1169; fax 0171/629 4257). *The phone is invariably engaged; write, visit or fax.*

US Water Tower Place, Suite 915 East, 845 North Michigan Ave, Chicago, IL 60611 (☎312/642-1992); 383 Wilshire Blvd, Suite 960, Beverly Hills, Los Angeles, CA 90211 (☎213/658-7188); 1221 Brickell Ave, Suite 1850, Miami, FL 33131 (☎305/358-1992); 665 Fifth Ave, New York, NY 10022 (☎212/759-8822).

Maps

For most visitors, the **maps** in this guide –
supplemented by the free road and town maps
issued by the tourist offices – will suffice, though
if you're planning to explore the islands' nooks
and crannies by bike or car, you'll need a more
detailed road map. Many alternatives are widely
available from island newsagents, filling stations,
souvenir shops and bookshops; you shouldn't
pay more than 900ptas for any of the road maps
detailed below. If you buy supplementary maps,
it's important to remember that all town and
street **signs** on the islands have recently been
translated into the local language, **Catalan**,

Map outlets

AUSTRALIA

The Map Shop, 16a Peel St, Adelaide (☎08/
8231 2033).

Bowyangs, 372 Little Burke St, Melbourne
(☎03/9670 4383).

Perth Map Centre, 891 Hay St, Perth (☎09/322
5733).

Travel Bookshop, 20 Bridge St, Sydney (☎02/
9241 3554).

CANADA

Open Air Books and Maps, 25 Toronto St,
Toronto, ON M5R 2C1 (☎416/363 0719).

Ulysses Travel Bookshop, 4176 St-Denis,
Montréal (☎514/289 0993).

World Wide Books and Maps, 1247 Granville
St, Vancouver, BC V6Z 1E4 (☎604/687 3320).

IRELAND

Easons Bookshop, 40 O'Connell St, Dublin
(☎01/873 3811).

Fred Hanna's Bookshop, 27–29 Nassau St,
Dublin (☎01/677 1255).

Hodges Figgis Bookshop, 56–58 Dawson St,
Dublin (☎01/677 4754).

NEW ZEALAND

Specialty Maps, 58 Albert St, Auckland (☎09/
307 2217).

UK

Daunt Books, 83 Marylebone High St, London
W1M 3DE (☎0171/224 2295).

National Map Centre, 22–24 Caxton St,
London SW1H 0QU (☎0171/222 4945).

Stanfords, 12–14 Long Acre, London WC2E
9LP (☎0171/836 1321); 52 Grosvenor Gardens,
London SW1W 0AG; and 156 Regent St, London
W1R 5TA.

The Travel Bookshop, 13–15 Blenheim
Crescent, London W11 2EE (☎0171/229 5260).

The Travellers Bookshop, 25 Cecil Court,
London WC2N 4EZ (☎0171/836 9132).

John Smith and Sons, 57–61 St Vincent St,
Glasgow G2 5TB (☎0141/221 7472).

Maps by **mail order** are available from
Stanfords (☎0171/836 1321).

USA

The Complete Traveler Bookstore, 199
Madison Ave, New York, NY 10016 (☎212/685-
9007); 3207 Fillmore St, San Francisco, CA
92123 (☎415/923-1511).

Elliot Bay Book Company, 101 S Main St,
Seattle, WA 98104 (☎206/624-6600).

Forsyth Travel Library, 9154 W 57th St,
Shawnee Mission, KS 66201 (☎1-800/367-7984).

Map Link Inc, 25 E Mason St, Santa Barbara,
CA 93101 (☎805/965-4402).

Phileas Fogg's Books & Maps, #87 Stanford
Shopping Center, Palo Alto, CA 94304 (☎1-800/
233-FOGG in California; ☎1-800/533-FOGG elsewhere in US).

Rand McNally,* 444 N Michigan Ave, Chicago,
IL 60611 (☎312/321-1751); 150 E 52nd St, New
York, NY 10022 (☎212/758-7488); 595 Market
St, San Francisco, CA 94105 (☎415/777-3131);
1201 Connecticut Ave NW, Washington, DC 2003
(☎202/223-6751).

Sierra Club Bookstore, 730 Polk St, San
Francisco, CA 94109 (☎415/923-5500).

Travel Books & Language Center, 4931
Cordell Ave, Bethesda, MD 20814 (☎1-800/220-
2665).

Traveler's Bookstore, 22 W 52nd St, New York,
NY 10019 (☎212/664-0995).

* For other locations, or for maps by mail order,
call ☎ 1-800/333-0136 (ext 2111).

---

making Castilian (ie Spanish) maps obsolete. To ensure you're buying a Catalan map, check out the spelling of Port de Pollença on Mallorca (Puerto de Pollença in Castilian), and, on Menorca, Maó (Mahón in Castilian). Just to confuse matters, however, some maps switch between the two languages.

The best Catalan map of Mallorca, entitled *Mallorca*, is published by the *Ministerio de Obras Públicas* (Ministry of Public Works). This accurately portrays the island's most important highways and principal byways, and provides topographical details too. It's not, however, as easy to get as most of its rivals – to buy a copy you'll need to consult a specialist map shop either before you go (see previous page) or in Mallorca. More widely available alternatives include the easy-to-follow Catalan *Mallorca and Palma* (1:175,000), a local government publication equipped with a large-scale, indexed plan of Palma and brief descriptions of the city's tourist attractions. Its only drawbacks are the absence of geographical features and some waywardness when it comes to depicting the island's byroads. There's also the *Firestone* map of *Mallorca* (1:125,000; no. T-26), which usefully indicates distances between settlements, marks salient geographical features and provides street plans of Palma and the

bigger resorts – but it's in Castilian and badly needs an update.

For **Menorca**, the most detailed and veracious Catalan maps are by *Eurotour*, though the English version is incongruously titled *Minorca* (1:75,000). These maps show all the island's major and minor roads, the only problem being that they don't effectively indicate which country lanes are easily driveable and which aren't. The same caution applies to the clear and accurate *Firestone* map of *Menorca* (1:75,000; no. E-54), which also has the drawback that the nomenclature is a baffling mix of Castilian and Catalan.

Serious **hikers** are poorly provided for: there are no really reliable maps with walking trails marked. The *IGN* (*Instituto Geográfico Nacional*) issues **topographical maps** of the Balearics at the 1:25,000 and 1:50,000 scales, based on an aerial survey of 1979, but many minor roads and footpaths simply don't appear and even crags and cliffs are not always shown. As a precaution, some hikers cross-check *IGN* maps with their rather out-of-date predecessors, the *Mapa Militar* (military maps), which are available at both 1:50,000 and 1:25,000 scales. These maps are available from bookshops in Palma, Maó and Ciutadella (see the relevant "Listings" in the guide for addresses), or from a few specialist suppliers overseas.

Health

No inoculations are required for the Balearics and the only likely blight to your holiday may be an upset stomach, or a ferocious hangover. To avoid the former, wash fruit and avoid *tapas* dishes that look like they were cooked last week. Many islanders also avoid consuming mayonnaise during the summer.

Pharmacies, doctors, emergencies and dentists

If you should fall ill, for minor complaints it's easiest to go to a **farmàcia** – there are plenty of them and they're listed in the Balearic islands' yellow pages (details of several in the main towns are given in the guide). Pharmacists are

highly trained, willing to give advice (often in English), and able to dispense many drugs which would be available only on prescription in many other countries. Most keep usual shop hours (ie 9am–1pm & 4–7pm); in Palma and Maó some open late and at weekends, and a rota system keeps at least one open 24 hours a day. In both towns, the rota is displayed in the window of every pharmacy, or you can check at reception in one of the better hotels. Outside the towns, you'll find a *farmàcia* in most of the larger villages, though there's not much chance of late-night opening or of an English-speaking pharmacist unless you're staying in a resort area.

In more serious cases you can get the address of an **English-speaking doctor** from your consulate, hotel, local *farmàcia* or tourist office. If you're seeking free treatment under the EC health scheme, double check that the doctor is working within the Spanish health care system (the *Instituto Nacional de la Salud*). Even within the EC agreement, you still have to pay forty percent of **prescription** charges (senior citizens are exempt). Neither do most private insurance policies help cover prescription charges – their "excesses" are usually greater than the cost of the medicines.

In medical **emergencies**, telephone the **Creu Roja** (Red Cross), which operates the islands' main ambulance service – in Mallorca ☎202222, in Menorca ☎361180. If you're reliant on free treatment within the EC health scheme, try to remember to make this clear to the ambulance staff and, if you're whisked off to hospital, to the medic you subsequently encounter. It's a good idea to hand over a photocopy of your E111 on arrival at hospital, or else you may be mistaken for a private insurance job and billed accordingly. Hospital charges are as much as 14,000ptas per visit (see also "Insurance" on p.19–20).

Dentists are all private – you'll pay around 5000ptas for having a cavity filled. A comprehensive list of *dentistas* can be found in the yellow pages, or ask at your hotel or *hostal* reception.

Contraceptives

Condoms no longer need to be smuggled into Spain as they did during the Franco years. They're available from most *farmàcias*, and from all sorts of outlets – like bars and vending machines – in the resorts.

Costs, money and banks

In terms of food, wine and transport, Mallorca and Menorca remain budget destinations for northern Europeans, North Americans and Australasians. However, Balearic hotel prices have increased considerably over the last few years, so independent travellers on any kind of budget will have to plan their accommodation carefully and, in summer, when vacant rooms are scarce, reserve well in advance. Another serious expense may be partying: nightclubs can rush you thousands of pesetas in the space of a few hours.

More precise costs for places to stay and eat are given in the guide, and you should consult the box on p.31 for general guidelines on accommodation prices. On average, if you're prepared to buy your own picnic lunch, stay in inexpensive *hostals* and hotels, and stick to the cheaper bars and restaurants, you could get by on around £20–25 (approximately US$30–40) a day per person. If you intend to stay in three-star hotels and eat at quality restaurants, then you'll need more like £50/$75 a day per person, with the main variable being the cost of your room – and bear in mind that room prices rise steeply as the season progresses. On £80/$120 a day and upwards, you'll be limited only by your energy reserves – though if you're planning to stay in a five-star hotel, this figure won't even cover your bed. On both islands, **eating out** is excellent value, and even in a top-notch restaurant in Palma a superb meal will only set you back around £15/US$23 – though, of course, you'll pay well over the odds for food and drink in the tourist resorts. As always, if you're travelling alone you'll spend much more than you would in a group of two or more – sharing rooms saves a lot of money.

One other cost is **IVA**, a 7 percent sales tax levied on most goods and services. Check in advance to see if IVA is included in the price of your bigger purchases; otherwise, especially in more expensive hotels and restaurants, you may be in for a bit of a shock.

Money and the exchange rate

The Spanish currency is the **peseta**, indicated in this book as "ptas". **Coins** come in denominations of 1, 5, 10, 25, 50, 100, 200 and 500 pesetas; **notes** as 1000, 2000, 5000 and 10,000 pesetas.

The **exchange rate** for the Spanish peseta is at the time of writing around 190 to the pound sterling, 180 to the Irish punt, 300 to the US dollar, 390 to the Canadian dollar, 395 to the Australian dollar and 440 to the NZ dollar. You can take in as much money as you want (in any form), although amounts over 1 million pesetas must be declared; you can take a maximum of 500,000 pesetas out unless, that is, you can prove that you brought more with you in the first place.

Travellers' cheques and credit cards

The safest way to carry your funds is in **travellers' cheques**; the usual fee for their purchase is one percent of face value. Make sure to keep the purchase agreement and a record of cheque serial numbers safe and separate from the cheques themselves. In the event that cheques are lost or stolen, the issuing company will expect you to report the loss forthwith. Consequently, when you buy your travellers' cheques, ensure you have details of the company's emergency contact numbers or the address of their local office. Most companies claim to replace lost or stolen cheques within 24 hours. *American Express* cheques are sold through most North American, Australasian and European banks, and they're the most widely accepted cheques in Spain. *American Express* also have offices in Palma and Port de Pollença in Mallorca, and Maó in Menorca – see the relevant chapters for addresses. When you cash your cheques in the Balearics, guard against outrageous **commissions** (usually they're 400–500ptas per transaction); if commission is waived, make sure that the exchange rate doesn't deteriorate drastically to compensate the bank.

If you have an ordinary British/EC bank account you can use **Eurocheques** with a Eurocheque card in many banks and can write out cheques in pesetas in shops and hotels. Most Eurocheque cards, many *Visa*, *Mastercard* (*Access*) and British bank/cash cards, as well as US cards in the Cirrus or Plus systems, can also be used for withdrawing cash from **ATMs** in Spain; check with your bank to find out about these reciprocal arrangements – the system is highly sophisticated and can often give instructions in a variety of languages. Make sure you have a personal identification number (PIN) that's designed to work overseas.

Credit cards are particularly useful for car rental, cash advances (though these attract a high rate of interest from the date of withdrawal) and hotel bills. *American Express*, *Visa* and *Mastercard* are all widely accepted.

Changing money

Spanish **banks** and **savings banks** have branches in all but the smallest of Balearic towns, and nearly all of them will change foreign currency and travellers' cheques (albeit with occasional reluctance for the more obscure brands). The *Banco de Bilbao*, *Banco March*, *Banco de Credito Balear* and *Banco de Santander* are four of the most widespread banks, while *Sa Nostra* and *La Caixa* are the biggest savings banks on the islands. All of them also handle Eurocheques, and most give cash advances on credit cards.

From October to May, **banking hours** are generally Monday to Thursday 8.30am–4.30pm, Friday 8.30am–2pm and Saturday 8.30am–1pm. From June to September, hours are usually Monday to Friday 8.30am–2pm. Outside these hours, most major hotels and many travel agents will change money at less generous rates and with variable commissions, as will the many **exchange kiosks** that are concentrated in the tourist areas. Legally, exchange rates must be on public display.

Wiring money

Having **money wired** from home is never convenient or cheap, and should be considered a last resort. One option is to have your own bank send the money through, and for that you need to nominate a receiving bank in the Balearics. Any local branch will do, but those in Maó, Palma and Ciutadella will probably be more familiar with the process. Naturally, you need to confirm the cooperation of the local bank before you set the wheels in motion back home. The sending bank's fees are geared to the amount being transferred and to the urgency of the service you require – the fastest transfers, taking two or three days, start at around £12 for the first £300–400. The receiving bank charges a commission too – expect a 2000ptas charge on amounts up to £300–400.

Money can also be wired via *American Express*, with the funds sent by one office and available for collection at the company's local offices, in Palma and Port de Pollença, Mallorca, and Maó, Menorca, within minutes – see the relevant chapters for addresses. All transactions are done in US dollars. Again, charges depend on the amount being sent, but as an example, wiring $400 from Britain to Spain will cost $20, $4000 will cost $150. The maximum that can be sent in one go is $7000.

Getting around

On both Mallorca and Menorca, you're spoiled for choice when it comes to transport. There's a reliable bus network between all the major settlements, a multitude of taxis, a plethora of car rental firms (which keeps prices down to a minimum, especially off-season), plenty of bicycles and mopeds to rent, as well as a couple of minor rail lines on Mallorca. Distances are small and consequently the costs of travel limited, whether in terms of petrol or the price of a ticket. Even on Mallorca, the larger of the two islands, it's only 120km from Andratx in the west to Cala Rajada in the northeast, and from Palma on the south coast to Alcúdia on the north shore is a mere 60km. Menorca has only one major road, which traverses the island from Ciutadella in the west to Maó in the east, a distance of just 45km.

Hopping from one island to the other is easy and economical too, as there are regular inter-island flights, hydrofoils and car ferries – though you're advised to book well in advance in July and August.

Buses

Both Mallorca and Menorca have an extensive network of **bus services** linking the main towns – Palma, Maó and Ciutadella – with most of the villages and resorts of the coast and interior. These main bus routes are supplemented by more intermittent local services between smaller towns and between neighbouring resorts. Ticket **prices** are reasonable: the one-way fare from Palma to Alcúdia is 370ptas, from Palma to Cala Rajada 840ptas, and from Maó to Ciutadella 425ptas. Only Palma is large enough to have its own public transit system, with a multiplicity of bus services linking the city centre with the suburbs and beach resorts that surround it – see p.60 & p.84 for more on this.

On all island bus services, destinations are marked on the front of the bus. Passengers enter the bus at the front and buy tickets from the driver, unless they have been bought in advance at a bus station. Bus stops are mostly indicated with the word *parada*. A confusing variety of bus companies operate the various routes on Mallorca, while all buses on Menorca are run by *Transportes Menorca* (☎360361); a synopsis of services is readily available from most tourist offices.

On the whole buses are reliable and comfortable enough, the only significant problem being that many country towns and villages do not have a bus station or even a clearly marked *parada*, which can be very confusing, as in some places buses leave from the most obscure parts of town. Remember also that bus services are drastically reduced on **Sundays** and **holidays**, and it's best not even to consider travelling out in the sticks on these days. The Catalan words to look out for on timetables are *diari* (daily), *feiners* (workdays, including Saturday), *diumenge* (Sunday) and *festius* (holidays).

Trains

Mallorca has its own toy-town electric **railways**, with 914mm-gauge trains travelling through the mountains from Palma to Sóller (28km), and across the flatland of the interior from Palma to Inca (29km). Each line has its own station, next door to each other on Palma's Plaça Espanya. Neither line is as fast as the bus, but the trip over to Sóller takes you through some of Mallorca's most magnificent scenery (the line to Inca passes through some of its most tedious). The standard return fare from Palma to Sóller is 760ptas and to Inca 500ptas.

Taxis

The excellence of the islands' bus services means it's rarely necessary to take a **taxi**, though it is a fast and easy way of reaching your resort from the airport and, perhaps more importantly, of getting back to your hotel after a day's hiking. In the latter case, you should arrange collection details before you set out – there's no point wandering round a tiny village hoping a taxi will show. Throughout the Balearics, the taxis of each town and resort area have their own livery – Palma taxis, for example, are black with a cream-coloured roof and bonnet. Local journeys are all metered, though there are supplementary charges for each piece of luggage and for night and Sunday travel. For longer journeys, there are official prices, which are displayed at the islands' airports, and at some taxi stands and tourist offices. Naturally, you're well advised to check the price with the driver *before* you set out. Fares are reasonable, but not cheap: from the airport to downtown Palma, a distance of around 11km, will cost you in the region of 1500ptas, while the fare from Palma airport to Port d'Andratx (37km) is 4800ptas, Maó to Ciutadella (45km) 4775ptas.

Driving and vehicle rental

Getting around on public transport is easy enough, but you'll obviously have a great deal more freedom if you have your own vehicle; on Menorca especially, the more attractive and secluded beaches are only accessible under your own steam. Major roads are generally good, though side roads are very variable – unpaved minor roads are particularly lethal after rain. Traffic is generally well behaved (even if Spain does have one of the highest incidences of traffic accidents in Europe), but noisy, especially in Palma, where the horn is used as a recreational tool as well as an instrument of warning. **Fuel** (*gasolina*) comes in four grades. Different companies use different brand names, but generally *Super Plus* is 98-octane fuel, selling at about 117ptas per litre; *Super* is 96-octane – equivalent to four-star in the UK – selling at about 110ptas per litre, and often without lead (*sense plom*); and *Mezcla*, or *Normal*, is 90-octane, available for about 100ptas per litre. Diesel (*gasoleo* or *gasoil*) costs about 90ptas per litre. Both Menorca and Mallorca are well supplied with filling stations, a few of which open 24 hours a day, seven days a week; most, however, close around 9pm or 10pm and on public holidays.

Most foreign **driving licences** are honoured in Spain – including all EC, US and Canadian ones – but an **International Driver's Licence** (available at minimal cost from your home motoring organization) is an easy way to set your mind at rest. If you're bringing your own car, you must have adequate insurance, a green card (available from your insurers or motoring organization), and a **bail bond** (a document to be shown to the police if you're involved in anything but the most trivial of accidents – without it, they'll almost certainly imprison you and impound your vehicle pending an investigation). Extra insurance coverage for unforeseen legal costs is also well worth having, as is an appropriate **breakdown** policy from a motoring organization. In Britain, for example, the *RAC* and *AA* charge members and non-members about £80 for a month's Europe-wide breakdown cover, with all the appropriate documentation, including green card and bail bond, provided.

Throughout the Balearics **speed limits** are posted – maximum on urban roads is 60kph, other roads 90kph, motorways 120kph – and on the main highways speed traps are fairly frequent. If you're stopped for any violation, the Spanish police can (and usually will) levy a stiff on-the-spot fine of up to 10,000ptas before letting you go on your way, their draconian instincts reinforced by the fact that few tourists are likely to appear in court to argue the case. Most **driving rules** and regulations are pretty standard (seat belts are compulsory and "Stop" signs mean exactly that), but remember that a single, unbroken white line in the middle of the road means no overtaking – even if the rule is frequently ignored. Note also that drivers often sound their horns when overtaking; you yield to traffic coming from the right at all junctions, whether or not there's a give way sign; and be prepared for road signs that give very little advance warning (if any at all) of the turning you might require. On major trunk roads, turnings that take vehicles across oncoming traffic are being phased out and replaced by traffic lights, with a minor exit and access to the lights on the near side of the major road. Finally, drivers do not have to stop (and usually don't) at zebra crossings, which merely indicate a suitable pedestrian crossing place. If you come to an abrupt stop at a crossing, as you might do in Britain, the pedestrians will be amazed and someone may well crash into your rear end. As ever, don't drink and drive.

Car rental

There are scores of companies on Mallorca and Menorca offering **car rental** (still rendered in Castilian, *coches de alquiler*), their offices throng-ing the islands' resorts, larger towns and airports: most of the major international players have outlets and dozens of small companies make up the remainder. The most useful addresses are given in the Palma, Maó and Ciutadella "Listings"; comprehensive lists are available from the islands' tourist offices. To rent a car, you'll have to be 21 or over (and have been driving for at least a year), and you'll need a credit card – though some places will accept a hefty deposit in cash. Bear in mind, too, that car rental firms do not allow you to transport their vehicles from one island to another; and that if you're planning to spend much time driving the islands' rougher tracks, you'll probably be better off with a moped, or even a four-wheel drive (about 30 percent more expensive than the average car). Rental **charges** vary enormously: out-of-season costs for a standard car can come down to as little as 2000ptas per day with unlimited mileage; in July and August, by comparison, the same basic vehicle could set you back 4500ptas a day (though weekly prices are slightly better value, and special rates operate at the weekend). The big companies all offer competitive rates, but you can often get a better deal through someone in contact with local vehicle rental firms, such as *Holiday Autos*. If you choose to deal directly with smaller, local companies, proceed with care. In particular, check the policy for the excess applied to claims, and ensure that it includes a bail bond (see above), collision damage waiver (applicable

---

Car rental agencies

AUSTRALIA		NORTH AMERICA	
Avis	☎ 1800/225 533	*Avis*	☎ 1-800/331-1084
Budget	☎ 13 2848	*Budget*	☎ 1-800/527-0700
Hertz	☎ 13 1918	*Hertz*	Canada ☎ 1-800/263-0600
			US ☎ 1-800/654-3001
		Holiday Autos	☎ 1-800/422-7737
IRELAND		*National*	☎ 1-800/CAR-RENT
Avis	☎ 02/128 1100		
Budget	☎ 01/844 5150		
Europcar/InterRent	☎ 01/668 1777	**UK**	
Hertz	☎ 01/660 2255	*Avis*	☎ 0181/848 8733
Holiday Autos	☎ 01/454 9090	*Budget*	☎ 0800/181 181
		Europcar/InterRent	☎ 0345/222 525
NEW ZEALAND		*Hertz*	☎ 0345/555 888
Avis	☎ 09/525 1982	*Holiday Autos*	☎ 0171/491 1111
Budget	☎ 09/275 2222		
Hertz	☎ 09/309 0989		

if an accident's your fault), and, in general, adequate levels of financial cover. **Fly-drive** deals are well worth investigating. In Britain, for example, *Viva Air*, an associate company of *Iberia*, offer *Avis* cars from just £111 a week in the low season, £136 in high season (including unlimited mileage, collision damage waiver, bail bond, insurance and VAT), as long as you book your flight to Mallorca or Menorca with *Iberia*.

Moped rental

Widely available on both islands, **mopeds** are a popular means of transport, especially for visiting remoter spots. Prices start at 1700ptas per day, including insurance and crash helmets, which must be worn. Be warned, however, that the insurance often excludes theft – always check with the company first. You will generally be asked to show some kind of driving licence, and to leave a deposit on your credit card, though most places will accept cash as an alternative. We've listed names and addresses of rental companies throughout the guide where most appropriate; tourist offices on the islands will provide comprehensive lists of suppliers.

Cycling

Cycling can be an inexpensive and flexible way of getting around both Menorca and far hillier Mallorca, and of seeing a great deal of the country that would otherwise pass you by. The Spanish are keen cycling fans, which means that you'll be well received and find reasonable facilities, while cars will normally hoot before they pass – though this can be alarming at first. Scenic Mallorca is especially popular with cyclists and its tourist office produces a free specialist leaflet, the "Guia del Ciclista", which details suggested itineraries and indicates distances and levels of difficulty. **Renting a bike** (about 1200ptas per day, 6000ptas per week) is easy enough as there are dozens of suppliers (there's usually one at every resort) and tourist offices will provide a list or advise you of the nearest outlet; we've also listed a few in the guide. If you've brought your own bike, **parts** can often be found at auto repair shops or garages – look for

Michelin signs – and there are bike shops in the larger towns.

Getting your own bike to the islands should present few problems. Most **airlines** are happy to take them as ordinary baggage provided they come within your allowance (though it's sensible to check first: crowded charter flights may be less obliging). Deflate the tyres to avoid explosions in the unpressurized holds. **Ferries** between the islands charge 1250ptas for transporting a bike one way, ferries from the mainland to the islands 2130ptas.

Flights and ferries between Mallorca and Menorca

Iberia airlines, who have a monopoly on **inter-island flights**, fly four times a day from Mallorca to Menorca and vice versa. Flying time is just thirty minutes and fares are cheap, with a one-way ticket costing 6300ptas (12,600ptas return) throughout the year. There's rarely a problem with availability, except in the peak season when it's a good idea to reserve a seat ahead of time by phoning any *Iberia* office (see p.14 for addresses of *Iberia* offices in Spain, the "Getting there" sections for offices abroad).

Trasmediterranea operate a once-weekly car and passenger **ferry** service between **Palma** and **Maó**; the sailing time is six hours and the one-way adult fare is 4300ptas, with a standard-size car (up to 4.5m) costing 11,300ptas. Reservations are not required, but are a good idea in summer. Alternatively – and far more economically – *Flebasa Lines* have a ferry service between Mallorca's **Port d'Alcúdia** and **Ciutadella** on Menorca (mid-April to Dec 2 daily; 3hr 30min). Adult passengers pay 2950ptas one way, and a standard-size car (up to 4.5m) costs 6950ptas. A *Flebasa* **hydrofoil** (no cars; mid-June to mid-Sept 3 daily; 1hr) also runs this route, charging 3950ptas per person one way. Advance reservations are not accepted by *Flebasa*, but you should turn up at their dockside office a good hour before sailing time – two hours at the height of the season. Addresses and phone numbers for *Trasmediterranea* and *Flebasa* are given on p.16.

Accommodation

Although package-tour operators have a stranglehold on thousands of hotel rooms, villas and apartments in both Menorca and Mallorca, reasonably priced rooms are still available to the independent traveller, even though the options are severely limited in the height of the season. Off season you should be able to get a simple, medium-sized double room with shower and sink for around 3000ptas, whereas in August the same double, if available, can set you back as much as 4500ptas – though this still compares reasonably well with much of the rest of Europe. You can, however, comfortably spend 8000ptas and upwards in hotels with three or more stars – some of them being very firmly in the super-luxury class.

Vacant rooms are at their scarcest from late June to early September, when advance **reservations** are strongly recommended. Most hoteliers speak at least a modicum of English, so visitors who don't speak Catalan or Spanish can usually book over the phone, but a confirming letter or fax is always a good idea. In Mallorca the easiest place to get a room is Palma, with Sóller lagging not far behind, but don't forget the five monasteries on the island that offer accommodation – they're a good bet for vacancies, even in high summer. In Menorca, accommodation is far thinner on the ground than in Mallorca – only Maó, Ciutadella and Fornells are likely bases for a visit.

It's often worth **bargaining** over room prices, especially outside of peak season and at fancier hotels, since the posted tariff doesn't necessarily mean much. Many hotels have rooms at different prices, and tend to offer the more expensive ones first. If there are more than two of you, most places have rooms with three or four beds at not a great deal more than the double-room price, which represents a real saving. On the other hand, people travelling alone invariably get the rough end of the stick. We've detailed where to find places to stay in most of the destinations listed in the guide, from the most basic of rooms to luxury hotels, and given a price range for each (see below). We've also indicated where an establishment closes over the winter – this is the case with a few hotels in Mallorca, while in Menorca almost all tourist facilities close down from November to March.

Fondas, casas de huéspedes, pensions, hostals and hotels

The one thing all travellers need to grasp is the elaborate diversity of types of places to stay – though in practice the various categories often overlap. The least expensive places are **fondas**,

---

Accommodation price codes

After each accommodation entry in this book you'll find a symbol that corresponds to one of nine price categories. These categories represent the minimum you can expect to pay for a double room in high season; for a single room, expect to pay around two-thirds the price of a double. The only ① options are youth hostels, where you'll get a dorm bed, and monasteries.

Note that in the more upmarket *hostals* and *pensions*, and in anything calling itself a hotel, you'll pay a **tax** (*IVA*) of 7 percent on top of the room price.

① Under 2000ptas	④ 4000–6000ptas	⑦ 10,000–14,000ptas
② 2000–3000ptas	⑤ 6000–8000ptas	⑧ 14,000–20,000ptas
③ 3000–4000ptas	⑥ 8000–10,000ptas	⑨ Over 20,000ptas

Accommodation signs

The various categories of accommodation in Spain are identifiable by square blue signs inscribed with the following letters in white.

F	CH	P	H^{S}	H^{S}R	H
fonda	casa de huéspedes	pensió	hostal	hostal-residencia	hotel

---

casas de huéspedes and **pensions** (*pensiones* in Castilian; further categorized with either one or two stars). Establishments in these categories are few and far between in the Balearics, and the distinctions between them blurred, but in general you'll find food served at *fondas* and *pensions* (some will only rent rooms on a meals-inclusive basis), while *casas de huéspedes* – literally "guest houses" – are often used as long-term lodgings. Confusingly, the name of many *pensions* does not follow their designation – lots of *pensions* call themselves *hostals* and vice versa. As a result, the name isn't always a reliable guide to the establishment's price, though the sign outside usually is (see above).

Slightly more expensive are **hostals** (*hostales* in Castilian) and **hostal-residencias**, categorized from one to three stars; a one-star *hostal* generally costs about the same as a *pensió*. Many *hostals* offer good, functional rooms, often with a private shower; the *residencia* designation means that no meals other than breakfast are served.

Moving up the scale, **hotels** are also star-graded by the authorities, from one to five stars. One-star hotels cost no more than three-star *hostals* (sometimes they're cheaper), but at three stars you pay a lot more, and at four or five you're in the luxury class with prices to match.

It's safe to assume that bedrooms in a hotel will be adequately clean and furnished, but in the lower categories you're well advised to ask to see the room before you part with any money. Standards vary greatly between places in the same category (even between rooms in the same *hostal*) and it does no harm to check that there's hot water if there's supposed to be, or that you're not being stuck at the back in an airless box. Note that bathrooms in many *pensions* and *hostals* (some hotels too) will not actually have baths, only showers.

A word about **complaints**: by law, each establishment must display its room rates and there should be a card on the room door show-ing the prices for the various seasons. If you think you're being overcharged, take it up first with the management; you can usually produce an immediate resolution by asking for one of the *hojas de reclamaciones* (complaints forms) that all places are obliged by law to keep. The threat of filling in a form is usually in itself enough to make the proprietor back down.

Monasteries

In recent times Mallorca's **monasteries** have become severely underpopulated and several now let out empty cells to visitors of both sexes. They're all in delightful settings in the mountains: the Santuari de Sant Salvador near Felanitx, the Ermita de Nostra Senyora de Bonany near Petra, the Ermita de Nostra Senyora del Puig outside Pollença, the Monastir de Nostra Senyora de Lluc, and the Santuari de Nostra Senyora de Cura on Puig Randa near Algaida (specific details of each are given in the guide). There's an increasing demand for this simple, cheap form of accommo-dation so, although it's possible just to turn up and ask for a room, you'd be well advised to either telephone ahead or, if your Spanish isn't good enough, get the local tourist office to make a reservation on your behalf. For a double room, you can expect to pay around 1500ptas at most of these monasteries, though it's twice that at Lluc, the most visited and commercialized of the five. Reasonably priced food is usually available, but check arrangements when you book.

Youth hostels

There are only two **youth hostels** (*albergues juveniles*) on Mallorca – one near Palma, the other outside Alcúdia – and none on Menorca. Both are open in the high season only and tend to be block-booked by school groups, so unless you reserve a bed well in advance you shouldn't rely on either as a viable source of cheap accom-modation. At both, the price of a bed is about 1300ptas (1700ptas if you're over 26) and you'll need a sheet sleeping bag. The hostels are operated by the *Hostelling International* (HI) and they expect you to have a membership card, available from your home hostelling organization, although it is possible to buy a card on the spot. Specific details of each hostel are given in the guide.

Fincas

Many of Mallorca's old stone **fincas** (farmhouses) have been snaffled up for use as second homes, and some are now leased by the owners to package-tour operators for the whole, or part of the season – *Individual Travellers Spain* (see p.5) has one of the best selections. Out of the tour operators' main season, these *fincas* often stand idle – ask around the villages of the northwest coast to see if someone's prepared to rent one out informally. At any time of the year, though preferably well in advance of your holiday, it's worth approaching the *Asociation de Agroturismo Balear*, c/Gremio Boters 24, Palma (☎971/430674), which issues a booklet detailing some of the finest *fincas* and takes bookings. Some are very luxurious and situated in remote, beautiful spots – though others form part of a working farm – and they're not cheap. Prices range from 6000ptas to 12000ptas per person per night, with a 3000ptas surcharge from April to September.

Camping

There are just two official **campsites** (*càmpings*) on Mallorca, the *Platja Blava*, beside the main road between Port d'Alcúdia and Ca'n Picafort, and the *Club San Pedro* (April–Sept), outside the village of Colònia de Sant Pere, at the east end of the Badia d'Alcúdia (Bay of Alcúdia). Both are Class 1C campsites, occupying attractive seaside locations. Each has about 500 pitches – taking tents, trailer caravans and motorcaravans – and a comprehensive range of facilities, including a grocery store, laundry room, swimming pool, bicycle and pedalo rental, bars and restaurants and all sorts of sports amenities. Needless to say, both sites heave with tourists in the summer, when it's best to make a reservation well ahead of time. The ad hoc campsite at the Monestir de Lluc provides a far cheaper alternative. Menorca's facilities are modest, the only authorized campsite being the *S'Atalaia*, a Class 3C affair that can accommodate 100 campers, just outside the resort of Cala Santa Galdana. Prices and specific details of each site are given in the relevant chapters.

Camping off-site is legal, but not encouraged, and has various restrictions attached. Spanish regulations state that you're not allowed to camp "in urban areas, areas prohibited for military or touristic reasons, or within 1km of an official campsite". What this means in effect is that you can't camp on resort beaches (though there is some latitude if you're discreet), but you can camp out almost anywhere in the countryside, providing you act sensitively and use some common sense: whenever possible ask locally first and/or get the permission of the landowner.

Eating and drinking

In the *Eating and drinking* section that follows we've generally given the **Catalan** names for food and drink items. Most restaurants, cafés and bars have **multilingual** menus (including English), but out in the sticks, in the cheaper cafés and restaurants, there may be no menu at all, and the waiter will rattle off the day's dishes in Catalan. The latter is, of course, the islands' first language, but Castilian (ie Spanish) is also used by restaurateurs – where useful, we've given the **Castilian** names alongside the Catalan names.

Traditional Balearic food, which has much in common with Catalan food, is far from delicate, but its hearty soups and stews, seafood dishes and spiced meats can be delicious. In common with other areas of Spain, this regional cuisine has, after many years of neglect, experienced something of a renaissance, and nowadays restaurants offering *Cuina Mallorquína* are comparatively commonplace and should not be missed. Neither should a visit to one of the islands' many pastry shops (*pastisserias*), where you'll find the sweetest of confections and the Balearics' gastronomic pride and joy, *ensaimadas* (spiralled flaky pastries).

On both islands, the distinction between **cafés** (or *cafeterias*) and **restaurants** is blurred. The bulk serve both light snacks and full meals, with the best deals often appearing as the *menú del día*

(menu of the day). At either end of the market, however, the differences become more pronounced: in the more expensive restaurants, there is usually a *menú del día*, but the emphasis is on à la carte; by contrast, the least expensive cafés only serve up simple snacks, and in their turn are often indistinguishable from the islands' **bars**, also known as *cellers* and *tavernas*. Before the tourist boom, these snacks always consisted of traditional dishes prepared as either *tapas* (small snacks) or *racions* (larger ones). Today, it's often chips, pizzas and sandwiches, but in Palma there's still a lively *tapas* scene, allowing you to move from place to place sampling a wide range of local specialities.

Opening hours vary wildly, but as a general rule cafés and *tapas* bars open from around 9am at least until early in the evening, many till late at night; restaurants are open from around noon until 2, 3 or sometimes 4pm, before reopening in the evening from around 6 or 7pm until 10 or 11pm. Those restaurants with their eye on the tourist trade often stay open all day and can be relied upon on Sundays, when many local spots close. There's rarely any need to **reserve** a restaurant table in Mallorca or Menorca – for the few places where it's advisable, we've given the phone numbers in the guide.

Breakfast, snacks and sandwiches

For **breakfast** you're best off in a bar or café. Some *hostals* and most hotels will serve the "Continental" basics, but it's generally cheaper and more enjoyable to go out to breakfast. A

Some common fillings for *bocadillos* are:

Catalan	Castilian	English
Tonyina	*Atún*	Tuna
Butifarra	*Butifarra*	Catalan sausage
Xoriç	*Chorizo*	Spicy sausage
Pernil salat	*Jamón serrano*	Cured ham
Cuixot dolç	*Jamón York*	Cooked ham
Llom	*Lomo*	Loin of pork
Formatge	*Queso*	Cheese
Salami	*Salami*	Salami
Salxitxó	*Salchichón*	Sausage
Truita	*Tortilla*	Omelette

traditional Balearic breakfast dish is *pa amb tomàquet* (*pan con tomate* in Castilian) – a massive slice of bread rubbed with tomato, olive oil and garlic, which you can also have topped with ham – washed down with a flagon of wine. If that sounds like gastric madness, other breakfast standbys are *torradas* (*tostadas*; toasted rolls) with oil or butter and jam, and *xocolata amb xurros* (*chocolate con churros*) – long, fried tubular doughnuts that you dip into thick drinking chocolate. Most places also serve *ou ferrat* (*huevo frito*; fried egg) and cold *truita* (*tortilla*; omelette), both of which make an excellent breakfast.

Coffee and **pastries** (*pastas*), particularly croissants and doughnuts, are available at some bars and cafés, though for a wider selection of cakes you should head for a *pastisseria* (pastry shop) or *forn* (bakery), which have an excellent reputation in the rest of Spain. These often sell a wide array of appetizing baked goods besides the obvious bread, croissants and *ensaimadas*. For ordering coffee see "Soft drinks and hot drinks", below.

Some bars specialize in **sandwiches** (*bocadillos*), both hot and cold, and as they're usually outsize affairs in French bread they'll do for breakfast or lunch. In a bar with *tapas* (see

---

Tapas and racions

Catalan	Castilian	English
Olives	*Aceitunas*	Olives
Pilotes	*Albóndigas*	Meatballs, usually in sauce
Anxoues	*Anchoas*	Anchovies
Cargols de mar	*Berberechos*	Cockles
Anxoua	*Boquerones*	Fresh anchovies
Calamars	*Calamares*	Squid, usually deep fried in rings
Calamars amb tinta	*Calamares en su tinta*	Squid in ink
Tripa	*Callos*	Tripe
Caragol	*Caracoles*	Snails, often served in a spicy/curry sauce
Carn amb salsa	*Carne en salsa*	Meat in tomato sauce
Xampinyons	*Champiñones*	Mushrooms, usually fried in garlic
Calamarins	*Chipirones*	Whole baby squid
Xoriç	*Chorizo*	Spicy sausage
Bollit	*Cocido*	Stew
Croqueta	*Croqueta*	Fish or chicken croquet
Empanada petita	*Empanadilla*	Fish/meat pasty
Ensalada Russa	*Ensaladilla*	Russian salad (diced vegetables in mayonnaise)
Escalibada	*Escalibada*	Aubergine and pepper salad
Gambes	*Gambas*	Prawns
Fabes	*Habas*	Broad beans
Fabes amb cuixot	*Habas con jamón*	Beans with ham
Fetge	*Hígado*	Liver
Ou bollit	*Huevo cocido*	Hard-boiled egg
Musclos	*Mejillones*	Mussels (either steamed, or served with diced tomatoes and onion)
Navallas	*Navajas*	Razor clams
Pa amb tomàquet	*Pan con tomate*	Bread, rubbed with tomato and oil
Patates amb all i oli	*Patatas alioli*	Potatoes in mayonnaise
Patates cohentes	*Patatas bravas*	Fried potato cubes with spicy sauce and mayonnaise
Prebes	*Pimientos*	Peppers
Pinxo	*Pincho moruno*	Kebab
Pop	*Pulpo*	Octopus
Ronyons amb Xeres	*Riñones al Jerez*	Kidneys in sherry
Sepia	*Sepia*	Cuttlefish
Sardines	*Sardinas*	Sardines
Truita Espanyola	*Tortilla Española*	Potato omelette
Truita Francesa	*Tortilla Francesca*	Plain omelette

---

below), you can have most of what's on offer put in a sandwich, and you can often get them prepared (or buy the materials to do so) at grocery shops as well. Menorcan **cheese** (*formatge*) is popular throughout Spain – the best is hard with a rind, similar to British cheddar.

Tapas

Tapas are small portions, three or four chunks of fish, meat or vegetables, or a dollop of salad, which traditionally used to be served up free with a drink. These days you have to pay for anything more than a few olives, but a single helping rarely costs more than 150–300ptas unless you're somewhere very flashy. **Racions** (*raciones* in Castilian) are simply bigger plates of the same, served with bread and costing around 400–600ptas, and are usually enough in themselves for a light meal. (Make it clear whether you want a *ració* or just a *tapa*.) The more people you're with, of course, the better, and half a dozen or so different dishes can make a varied and quite filling meal for three or four people.

One of the advantages of eating *tapas* in bars is that you are able to experiment. Most places have food laid out on the counter, so you can see what's available and order by pointing without necessarily knowing the names; others have blackboards (see the lists on previous page).

Balearic dishes and specialities

Many of the specialities that follow come from the Balearics' shared history with Catalunya. The more elaborate fish and meat dishes are generally only found in fancier restaurants.

Pastries (*Pastas*)

Cocaroll	Pastry containing vegetables and fish
Ensaimada	Flaky spiral pastry with fillings such as *cabello de ángel* (sweetened citron rind)
Panades	Pastry with peas, meat, *sobrasada* (see below) or fish

Soup (*Sopa*)

Carn d'olla	Mixed meat soup
Escudella	Mixed vegetable soup
Sopa d'all	Garlic soup
Sopas Mallorquínas or Menorquínas	Vegetable soup, sometimes with meat and chick peas

Salad (*Amanida*)

Amanida Catalana	Salad with sliced meat and cheese
Escalivada	Aubergine, pepper and onion salad
Esqueixada	*Bacallà* salad with peppers, tomatoes, onions and olives

Starters

Entremesos	Hors d'oeuvres of mixed meat and cheese

Espinacs a la Catalana	Spinach with raisins and pine nuts
Fideus a la cassola	Baked vermicelli with meat
Llenties guisades	Stewed lentils
Pa amb oli	Bread rubbed with olive oil, eaten with ham, cheese or fruit
Samfaina	Ratatouille-like stew of onions, peppers, aubergine and tomato
Truita (d'alls tendres, de xampinyons, de patates)	Omelette/tortilla (with garlic, mushrooms or potato); don't order trout by mistake

Rice dishes

Arròs negre	"Black rice", cooked with squid ink
Arròs a banda	Rice with seafood, the rice served separately
Arròs a la marinera	Paella: rice with seafood and saffron
Paella a la Catalana	Mixed meat and seafood paella; sometimes distinguished from a seafood paella by being called *Paella a Valencia*

Meat (*Carn*)

Albergínies en es forn	Stuffed aubergines filled with grilled meat
Botifarra amb mongetes	Spicy blood sausage with white beans
Conill (all i oli)	Rabbit (with garlic mayonnaise)

Escaldum	Chicken and potato stew in an almond sauce	*A la planxa/a la brasa*	Grilled
Estofat de vedella	Veal stew	Rostit	Roast
Fetge	Liver	Fregit/frit	Fried
Fricandó	Veal casserole	Farcit	Stuffed/rolled
Frito Mallorquín	Pigs' offal, potatoes and onions cooked with oil	Guisat	Casserole
Mandonguilles	Meatballs, usually in a sauce with peas		

Desserts (*Postres*)

Perdius a la vinagreta	Partridge in vinegar gravy
Pollastre (farcit, amb gambas, al cava)	Chicken (stuffed, with prawns, or cooked in *Cava*
Porc (rostit)	Pork (roast)
Sobrasada	Finely minced pork sausage, flavoured with paprika

Arròs amb llet	Rice pudding
Crema Catalana	Crème caramel, with caramelized sugar topping
Gelat	Ice cream
Mel i mató	Curd cheese and honey
Postres de músic	Cake of dried fruit and nuts
Turrón	Almond fudge
Xurros	Deep-fried doughnut sticks (served with hot chocolate)
Yogur	Yoghurt

Fish (*Peix*) and shellfish (*marisc*)

Bacallà (amb samfaina)	Dried cod (with ratatouille)
Caldereta de llagosta	Lobster stew
Cloïsses	Clams, often steamed
Espinagada de Sa Pobla	Turnover filled with spinach and eel
Greixonera de peix	Menorcan fish stew, cooked in a pottery casserole
Guisat de peix	Fish and shellfish stew
Llagosta (amb pollastre)	Lobster (with chicken in a rich sauce)
Lluç	Hake, a common dish either fried or grilled
Musclos al vapor	Steamed mussels
Pop	Octopus
Rap a l'all cremat	Monkfish with creamed garlic sauce
Sarsuela	Fish and shellfish stew
Suquet	Fish casserole
Tonyina	Tuna
Truita	Trout (sometimes stuffed with ham, *a la Navarre*)

Market shopping

Vegetables (*Verdures/Llegumes*)

Albergínies	Aubergines
Cebes	Onions
Concombre	Cucumber
Esparrecs	Asparagus
Mongetes	Beans
Pastanagues	Carrots
Patatos	Potatoes
Pèsols	Peas
Tomàquets	Tomatoes
Xampinyons (also *bolets, setes*)	Mushrooms

Fruit (*Fruita*)

Plàtan	Banana
Maduixes	Strawberries
Meló	Melon
Pera	Pear
Pinya	Pineapple
Poma	Apple
Pressec	Peach
Raïm	Grapes
Taronja	Orange

Sauces and terms

Salsa mahonesa	Mayonnaise
Allioli	Garlic mayonnaise
Salsa romesco	Spicy tomato and wine sauce to accompany fish (from Tarragona)

Some common Catalan and Castilian food terms

English	Catalan	Castilian	English	Catalan	Castilian
Basics			**Meals**		
Bread	Pa	Pan	to have breakfast	Esmorzar	Desayunar
Butter	Mantega	Mantequilla	to have lunch	Dinar	Comer
Cheese	Formatge	Queso	to have dinner	Sopar	Cenar
Eggs	Ous	Huevos			
Oil	Oli	Aceite			
Pepper	Pebre	Pimienta	**In the restaurant**		
Salt	Sal	Sal	Menu	Carta	Carta
Sugar	Sucre	Azucar	Bottle	Ampolla	Botella
Vinegar	Vinagre	Vinagre	Glass	Got	Vaso
Garlic	All	Ajo	Fork	Forquilla	Tenedor
Rice	Arròs	Arroz	Knife	Ganivet	Cuchillo
Fruit	Fruita	Fruta	Spoon	Cullera	Cuchara
Vegetables	Verdures/	Verduras/	Table	Taula	Mesa
	Llegumos	Legumbres	The bill	El compte	La cuenta

Meals and restaurants

Regular meals are usually eaten in a *cafeteria* or *restaurant*, but if your main criteria are simply price and quantity, seek out a **comedor** (dining room), usually found at the back of a bar or – out in the sticks – as the dining room of a *pensió*. These places are often virtually unmarked and discovered only if you pass an open door – though you won't find them in tourist resorts. Since they're essentially workers' cafés they tend to serve more substantial meals at lunchtime than in the evenings (when they may be closed altogether), and typically you'll pay 600–900ptas for a complete meal, including a drink. Another budget alternative is to eat in a bar or a **cafeteria** – many are mixtures of the two – where the food will often be something like egg, steak or chicken and chips, or *calamars* and salad, usually with bread and sometimes with a drink included. This will generally cost in the region of 500–900ptas, depending on how much you're eating.

Restaurants run from simple formica table and check-tablecloth affairs to expense-account palaces. They nearly all have a daily set menu – the **menú del día** – which is usually on offer alongside the à la carte menu, though some of the more basic places might *only* serve a *menú del día*. This consists of three or four courses, including bread, wine and service, and usually costs 800–1200ptas, occasionally quite a bit more in flash restaurants and at seaside resorts.

Most *restaurants* and *cafeterias* in Mallorca and Menorca, especially in the resort areas, are reliant on the tourist industry and ignore the strong flavours of traditional cuisine for the blandness of pizzas, hamburgers and pastas, or else dish up a hotch-potch of sanitized Spanish favourites such as omelettes, paella and grilled meats. However, there are still plenty of places – highlighted in the guide – where the food is more distinctive and flavoursome. Fresh **fish and seafood** can be excellent, though it's almost always expensive – much of it is imported, despite the local fishing industries around the Balearics and on the Catalan coast. Nevertheless, you're able to get hake, cod (often salted) and squid at very reasonable prices, while fish stews (*sarsuelas*) and rice-based *paellas* are often truly memorable. **Meat** can be outstanding too, usually either grilled and served with a few fried potatoes or salad, or – like ham – cured or dried and served as a starter or in sandwiches. Veal is common, served in great stews, while poultry is often mixed with seafood (chicken and prawns) or fruit (chicken/duck with prunes/pears).

Vegetables rarely amount to more than a few chips or boiled potatoes with the main dish, though there are some splendid vegetable concoctions to watch out for, such as *tumbet* (pepper, potato, pumpkin and aubergine stew with tomato purée). It's more usual to start your meal with a **salad**, either a standard green or mixed affair, or one of the islands' own salad mixtures, which come garnished with various vegetables, meats and cheeses. **Dessert** in the cheaper places is nearly always fresh **fruit** or *flam*, the local version of *crème caramel*; look out also for *crema Catalana*, with a caramelized sugar coating, the Catalan version of *crème brûlée*, and *músic*, dried fruit-and-nut cake.

In all but the most rock-bottom establishments it is customary to leave a small **tip**; the amount is up to you, though ten percent of the bill is sufficient. Service is normally included in a *menú del día*. The other thing to take account of is **IVA**, a seven percent tax which is either included in the given prices (in which case it should say so on the menu) or added to your bill at the end.

Vegetarians and special diets

If you eat fish but not meat you should relish your holiday – the range of seafood is magnificent. The *menú del día* nearly always features a fish dish, and there are plenty of vegetable and egg dishes, as well as fruit, to be going on with. Even out in the country, you'll often find trout on the menu. If you're a **vegetarian** your diet will be a little more limited, though in Palma there are a couple of vegetarian restaurants (see p.78), or you can alternate your diet by trying one of the ethnic restaurants. Outside Palma – and especially away from the coast – things get a little harder. But although the choice isn't so great, there are always large salads on offer, and nearly everywhere will cook you fried eggs and chips or an omelette if you ask.

If you're a **vegan**, you're either going to have to compromise or accept weight loss if you're away for any length of time. Some salads and vegetable dishes are strictly vegan – like *espinacs a la Catalana* (spinach, pine nuts and raisins) and *escalivada* (aubergine and peppers) – but they're few and far between. Fruit and nuts are widely available though, and most pizza restaurants will serve you a vegetarian pizza without cheese – ask for *vegetal sense fromatge* (in Castilian, *vegetal sin queso*).

For vegetarian and vegan **shopping**, use the markets – where you can buy ready cooked lentils and beans, and pasta – or look out for

shops marked *Aliments regim* (*dietetica* in Castilian), which sell soya milk and desserts, vegetarian biscuits, and so on.

Wine

Wine (*vi* in Catalan, *vino* in Castilian), either red (*negre, tinto*), white (*blanc, blanco*) or rosé (*rosado*), is the invariable accompaniment to every meal and is, as a rule, extremely cheap. In bars, cafés and budget restaurants, it may be whatever comes out of the barrel, or the house bottled special (ask for *vi/vino de la casa*). In a bar a small glass of wine will generally cost anything from 40 to 100ptas; in a restaurant prices start at around 250ptas a bottle, and even in the poshest of places you'll be able to get a bottle of house wine for under 1000ptas. If you're having the *menú del día*, house wine will be included in the price – you'll get a third- to a half-litre per person.

On both islands, all the more expensive restaurants, the supermarkets, and some of the cheaper cafés and restaurants carry a good selection of Spanish wines. The thing to check for is the appellation **Dénominación d'Origen (DO)**, which indicates the wine has been passed as of sufficiently high quality by the industry's watchdog, the *Instituto Nacional de Dénominaciónes d'Origen* (*INDO*). Forty regions of Spain currently carry *DO* status, including the north central region that produce's Spain's most famous and widely distributed **red wine**, **Rioja**. Even though there's now a profusion of reds being produced all over the country, it's hard to match *Rioja* for reliability and finesse. The wines are generally made of the *tempranillo* and *garnacha* grapes and are classified according to their age. At one end of the scale, *joven* indicates a young inexpensive, straightforward wine which has spent no time in wood. Wines labelled *con crianza* (with breeding) or *reserva* have received respectively moderate and generous ageing in oak casks and in the bottle. At the top of the scale, in both price and quality, are the *gran reserva* wines, which are only produced in the best years and which have to spend at least two years in the cask followed by three in the bottle before being offered for sale. The names to look for in red *Rioja* include **Martínez-Bujanda**, **Tondonia** and **Monte Real**.

The region of **Navarra** also produces excellent wine using similar techniques and grape varieties at a fraction of the price. The labels to watch for

---

Vegetarian phrases

In **Catalan**, try *Sóc vegetarià/ana. Es pot menjar alguna cosa sense carn?* (I'm a vegetarian. Is there anything without meat?); in **Castilian**, that's *Soy vegetariano/a. Hay algo sin carne?* Or you may be better understood if you simply say – in Catalan – *No puc menjar carn* (I can't eat meat).

---

here are **Chivite** and **Señorío de Sarría**. Around Barcelona, the region of **Penedès** was long renowned for its heavy and coarse red wines, responsible for countless hangovers. These days things have improved and the vinous produce of firms like **Torres** and **Masía Bach** have already established a solid reputation. Nevertheless, it is the reds of the **Ribera del Duero** region, 120km north of Madrid, which have attracted most recent attention, with wines such as **Protos**, **Viña Pedrosa** and **Pesquera** offering the smooth integration of fruit and oak that is the hallmark of good Spanish wine.

Spain's **white wines** have not enjoyed the same reputation as the reds. Traditionally, they tended to be highly alcoholic and over-oaked. Unusually, Spain's best white, the **Rioja Blanca** made by **Marquès de Murrieta**, descends from this tradition, though it offers a smooth-tasting marriage of oak and lemony fruit. However, the demands of the export market have recently led to new approaches to white wine-making, and the result has been clean, fruity and dry wines that tend to be competent rather than memorable. The best of this style has to be **Marquès de Riscal Blanco** from Rueda, just south of Valladolid.

Spain's growing reputation for **sparkling wine** has been built on the performance of two producers, *Freixenet* and *Codorníu*, which hail from a small area west of Barcelona. Local grape varieties are used and the best examples, known as *cava*, are made by the same double-fermentation process as is used in champagne production.

Other alcoholic drinks

Fortified wines and spirits in the Balearics are those you can find throughout Spain. The classic Andalucian wine, **sherry** – *Vino de Jerez* – is served chilled or at room temperature, a perfect drink to wash down *tapas*. The main distinctions are between *fino* or *Jerez seco* (dry sherry), *amontillado* (medium), and *oloroso* or *Jerez dulce*

Mallorcan wine

Wine production has flourished in the Balearics since classical times. In the nineteenth century, sweet Malvasia – wine similar to Madeira – was exported in great quantity, until the vineyards were devastated by the *phylloxera* louse whose activities changed the course of European wine history in the 1870s. Indeed, vine cultivation never re-established itself on Ibiza or Menorca, and, with the best will in the world, Mallorcan wines were not taken seriously until very recently.

In the last few years, however, a concerted attempt has been made to raise the standards of Mallorcan wine-making, driven on one side by the tourist industry and on the other by the realization amongst local producers that the way forward lay in exporting wine that matched international standards. This meant new methods and new equipment. Mallorca's leading wine is **Binissalem**, from around the eponymous village northeast of Palma. Following vigorous local campaigning, it was justifiably awarded its *Denominación d'Origen* (*DO*) credentials in 1991.

Red Binissalem is a robust and aromatic wine made predominantly of the local Mantonegro grape. It is not unlike *Rioja*, but it has a distinctly local character, suggesting cocoa and strawberries. The best producer of the wine is **Franja Roja**, who make the **José Ferrer** brand – well worth looking out for, with prices starting at around 250ptas per bottle, 1000ptas for the superior varieties. Red

Binissalem is widely available throughout Mallorca, and the *Franja Roja Bodega*, c/ Conquistador 103, Binissalem, welcomes visitors by prior appointment (☎511050).

White and rosé *Binissalem* struggle to reach the same standard as the red. However, the **Binissalem Blanco** made by **Herederos de Ribas** is a lively and fruity white that goes well with fish. Also around the island are various country wineries making inexpensive and unpretentious wine predominantly for local consumption, such as the **Muscat Miguel Oliver** or the **Celler Son Calo**. The best places to sample these local, coarser wines is in the *cellers* and bars of the country towns of the interior – we've recommended several in the guide.

If you're visiting the Balearics in late September, you can catch Binissalem's **Festival of the Grape Harvest** (*Festa d'es Verema*), which takes place during the week leading up to the last Sunday of the month. Saturday is the best day, with a procession of decorated floats and a good deal of free wine. On a more sedate level, Palma's **Food Week** (*Setmana de Cuina Mallorquína*) takes place in the middle of May all over the centre of town, with stalls featuring the cuisine and wine of the island. The best selection of wines available in Mallorca is at Palma's **El Centro del Vino y del Cava**, c/ Bartomeu Rossello-Porcel 19 (☎452990); in Menorca, try Maó's **Xoriguer**, Plaça Carme 16 (☎362611).

(sweet), and these are the terms you should use to order. In mid-afternoon – or even at breakfast – many islanders take a *copa* of **liqueur** with their coffee. The best – certainly to put in your coffee – is **coñac**, excellent Spanish brandy, mostly from the south and often deceptively smooth. If you want a brandy from Mallorca, try the mellow, hard-hitting *Suau*, and from Catalunya, look for *Torres*. Other good brands include *Magno*, *Veterano* and *Soberano*. Most other spirits are ordered by brand name, too, since there are generally cheaper Spanish equivalents for standard imports. *Larios* **gin** from Malaga, for instance, is about half the price of *Gordons*, but around two-thirds the strength and a good deal rougher. The Menorcans, who learnt the art of gin-making from the British, still produce their own versions of the liquor, in particular the waspish *Xoriguer*. Always specify *nacional* to avoid getting an expensive foreign brand.

Almost any **mixed drink** seems to be collectively known as a *Cuba Libre* or *Cubata*, though strictly speaking this is rum and Coke. For mixers, ask for orange juice (*suc de taronja* in Catalan) or lemon (*llimona*); tonic is *tònica*.

Cervesa, pilsner-type beer (more usually seen in Castilian, *cerveza*), is generally pretty good, though more expensive than wine. The two main brands you'll see everywhere are *San Miguel* and *Estrella*, though keep an eye out in Palma for draught *cerveza negra* – black fizzy beer with a bitter taste. Beer generally comes in 300ml bottles or, for a little bit more, on tap – a *cana* of draft beer is a small glass, a *cana gran* larger. Equally refreshing, though often deceptively strong, is **sangría**, a wine-and-fruit punch which you'll come across at *festas* and in tourist resorts.

Soft drinks and hot drinks

Soft drinks are much the same as anywhere in the world, but one local favourite to try is *orxata* – *horchata* in Castilian – a cold milky drink made from tiger nuts. Also, be sure to try a *granissat* (iced fruit-squash); popular flavours are *granissat de llimona* or *granissat de café*. You can get these drinks from **orxaterias** and from **gelaterias** (ice cream parlours; *heladerías* in Castilian).

Although you can drink the **water** almost everywhere, it usually tastes better out of the bottle – inexpensive *aigua mineral* comes either sparkling (*amb gas*) or still (*sense gas*).

Coffee – served in cafés, bars and some restaurants – is invariably espresso, slightly bitter

and, unless you specify otherwise, served black (*café sol*). A slightly weaker large black coffee is called a *café Americano*. If you want it white ask for *café cortado* (small cup with a drop of milk) or *café amb llet* (made with hot milk). For a large cup ask for a *gran*. Black coffee is also frequently mixed with brandy, cognac or whisky, all such concoctions being called *carajillo*; liqueur mixed with white coffee is a *trifásico*. **Decaffeinated** coffee (*descafeinat*) is increasingly available, though in fairly undistinguished sachet form. **Tea** (*te*) comes without milk unless you ask for it, and is often weak and insipid. If you do ask for milk, chances are it'll be hot and UHT, so your tea isn't going to taste much like the real thing. Better are the **infusions** that you can get in most bars, like mint (*menta*), camomile (*camamilla*) and lime (*tiller*).

Where to drink

You'll do most of your everyday drinking – from morning coffee to nightcap – in a **bar** or **café** (between which there's little difference). Very often, you'll eat in here too, or at least snack on some *tapas*. Bars situated in old wine cellars are sometimes called *cellers* or *tavernas*; bodegas traditionally specialize in wine. In Palma you

Drinks		
English	*Catalan*	*Castilian*
Alcohol		
Beer	*Cervesa*	*Cerveza*
Wine	*Vi*	*Vino*
Champagne	*Xampan/Cava*	*Champan/Cava*
Hot drinks		
Coffee	*Café*	*Café*
Espresso coffee	*Café sol*	*Café solo*
White coffee	*Café amb llet*	*Café con leche*
Decaff	*Descafeinat*	*Descafeinado*
Tea	*Te*	*Té*
Drinking chocolate	*Xocolata*	*Chocolata*
Soft drinks		
Water	*Aigua*	*Agua*
Mineral water	*Aigua mineral*	*Agua mineral*
(sparkling)	*(amb gas)*	*(con gas)*
(still)	*(sense gas)*	*(sin gas)*
Milk	*Llet*	*Leche*
Juice	*Suc*	*Zumo*
Tiger nut drink	*Orxata*	*Horchata*

also have the choice of drinking in rather more salubrious surroundings, in the the so-called *bars modernos* – designer bars, for want of a better description. Some of these are quite extraordinarily chic and stylish, sights in their own right, but their drinks are invariably very expensive – locals hang out for hours while imbibing very little.

Bar **opening hours** are difficult to pin down, but you should have little difficulty in getting a drink somewhere in Palma until 2am or perhaps 3am. Elsewhere you're OK until at least 11pm, sometimes midnight. The islands' nightclubs tend to close by 2 or 3am. Some bars close on Sundays and, in the resorts, don't expect much to be happening out of season.

Post, phones and the media

On Mallorca and Menorca there are **post offices** (*correus*) in every town and many villages, most of them handily located on or near the main square. Opening hours are usually Monday to Friday 9am–2pm, though the main post offices in Palma and Maó open through the afternoon and on Saturday mornings too. All post offices close on public holidays. You can send letters to any post office by addressing them **"Poste Restante"**, followed by the surname of the addressee (preferably underlined and in capitals), and then the name of the town and province. To collect, take along your passport or identity card and – if you're expecting post and your initial enquiry produces nothing – ask the clerk to check under all of your names as letters are often filed under first or middle names. Alternatively, *American Express*, which has agents in Maó, Port de Pollença and Palma (addresses in the guide), will hold incoming mail for a month on behalf of card and travellers' cheque holders.

Outbound post is reasonably reliable, with letters or cards taking around a week to ten days to reach Britain and Ireland, ten days to a fortnight for North America, and about three weeks to Australasia. You can buy **stamps** (*segells*) at tobacconists (look for the brown and yellow; *tabac* sign) and at scores of souvenir shops as well as at post offices. Post boxes are yellow; on those where there's a choice of posting slots, pick the flap marked *províncies i estranger* or *altres destinos*. Postal rates are inexpensive, with postcards and small letters costing around 60ptas to anywhere in Europe, 90ptas worldwide.

Telephones

You can make domestic and international phone calls with equal ease from Spanish public **telephones**, which generally work well. Alternatively, if you can't find one, many bars have pay phones you can use (plenty of hotel rooms have phones, but there's always an exorbitant surcharge for their use). Most public telephones display instructions in English (amongst several languages) and a list of Spanish provincial and some overseas dialling codes. They take 25- or 100-peseta pieces or phone cards of 1000ptas or 2000ptas, which can be purchased at tobacconists. Within Spain, the **ringing tone** is long, whereas **engaged** is shorter and rapid; the standard response to a call anywhere in Spain is to the point – *digáme* (speak to me). For international calls, you're best off shovelling in at least 200ptas to ensure a connection – and make sure you have a good stock of 100-peseta pieces on hand if you're intending to have a conversation of any length.

International and domestic **rates** are slightly cheaper after 10pm and before 8am, and after 2pm on Saturday and all day Sunday. Making a **collect** or **reverse-charge call** (*cobro revertido*) can be a bit of a hassle, especially if your Spanish, the language in which the phone company conducts its business, is poor: it's best to ring the international operator for advice.

Newspapers and magazines

British and other European newspapers, as well as *USA Today* and the *International Herald Tribune*, are all widely available in the resort areas and larger towns of Mallorca and Menorca. These are supplemented by a ragbag of locally produced English papers and journals, the most informative of them being the *Majorca Daily Bulletin*. Of the **Spanish newspapers**, the best two are *El País* – liberal, pro-government, and the only one with much serious analysis or foreign news coverage – and its rival, *El Mundo*, a left-of-centre broadsheet that has taken a far more critical line on the Socialist government. Other national papers include *ABC*, solidly elitist with a hard moral line against abortion and divorce, and the equally conservative *La Vanguardia*. Printed in Catalan, *Avui* is the chief nationalist paper, but its main competitor, the Catalan *El Diari de Barcelona*, is more liberal. On the Balearics, there are several rather modest local papers, of which *Ultima Hora* and *Diario de Mallorca* are the most substantial.

Amongst a plethora of glossy **magazines**, Spain's most interesting offering is *Ajo Blanco*, a monthly from Barcelona with an eclectic mix of politics, culture and style. The more arty and indulgent *El Europeo*, a massive quarterly publication from Madrid, can also be worth a browse. And of course, Spain is the home of *Holà* – the original of *Hello*.

TV and radio

On the Balearics you can pick up the two main national **TV channels**, *TV1* and *TV2*, a couple of Catalan channels, *TV3* and *Canal 33*, and the private *Antena 3* channel. You'll inadvertently catch more TV than you expect sitting in bars and restaurants, and on the whole it's a fairly entertaining mixture of kitsch game shows and foreign-language films and TV series dubbed into Spanish. Soaps are a particular speciality, either South American *telenovas*, which take up most of the daytime programming, or well-travelled British or Australian exports, like *EastEnders* (*Gent del Barri*) and *Neighbours* (*Veins*). Sports fans are well catered for, with regular live coverage of football and basketball matches – in the football season, you can watch one or two live matches a week in many bars.

If you have a **radio** that picks up short wave, you can tune in to the *BBC World Service*, broadcasting in English for most of the day on 3955, 6195, 7150, 9410, 12095 and 15070 KHz. The *Majorca Daily Bulletin* and other English papers printed in the Balearics detail broadcasting schedules.

Opening hours and public holidays

Although there's been some movement towards a North European working day in Mallorca and Menorca – especially in Palma and the major tourist resorts – most shops and offices still close for a siesta of at least two hours in the hottest part of the afternoon. There's a lot of variability, but basic working hours are generally 9am–1pm and 4–7pm; notable exceptions are the extended hours operated by the largest department stores, some important tourist attractions and most tourist/souvenir shops.

Museums and churches

Almost without exception, **museums** take a siesta, closing between 1pm and 3pm in the afternoon, while many close on Sundays and some on Saturdays and Mondays too. Don't be surprised if the official opening times of the less-visited museums are disregarded. Admission charges are usually in the region of 300ptas per person, irrespective of the size of the collection or the quality of the exhibits.

Palma cathedral, arguably the islands' key sight, attracts an entrance fee of 300ptas, but other **churches** are almost always free. They generally close for a two- or three-hour siesta, but the least significant churches are kept locked, opening (if at all) only for worship in the early morning and/or the evening (around 6–9pm). Consequently, you'll have to either try at these times, or find someone with a key – not as difficult as it sounds as a sacristan or custodian almost always lives nearby, and someone will know where to direct you; you're expected to give a small donation.

Public holidays

Public holidays – as well as scores of local festivals (see below) – may well disrupt your travel plans at some stage. There are fourteen Spanish national holidays per year, most of which are keenly observed in the Balearics. The resorts are generally oblivious to them, but elsewhere in the islands almost all businesses and shops close, and it can prove difficult to find a room. Similarly, vacant seats on planes and buses (which are in any case reduced to a skeleton service) are at a premium.

Spanish national holidays

January 1: New Year's Day (*Año Nuevo*).

January 6: Epiphany (*Reyes Magos*).

March 19: St Joseph's Day (*San José*).

Good Friday (*Viernes Santo*).

May 1: Labour Day (*Día del Trabajo*).

Corpus Christi (early or mid-June).

June 24: St John's Day (*San Juan*, the king's name-day).

June 29: St Peter and St Paul (*San Pedro y San Pablo*).

July 25: St James's Day (*Santiago*).

August 15: Assumption of the Virgin (*Asunción*).

October 12: Discovery of America Day (*Día de la Hispanidad*).

November 1: All Saints (*Todos los Santos*).

December 8: Immaculate Conception (*Inmaculada Concepción*).

December 25: Christmas Day (*Navidad*).

Festivals, the Bullfight and football

It's hard to beat the experience of arriving in a town to discover the streets decked out with flags and streamers, a band playing in the square and the entire population out celebrating the local **festa** (in Castilian, *fiesta*). Everywhere in Mallorca and Menorca takes at least one day off a year to devote to partying. Usually it's the local saint's day, but there are celebrations, too, of harvests, deliverance from the Moors, of safe return from the sea – any excuse will do.

Each festival is different, with a particular local emphasis, but there is always music, dancing, traditional costume and an immense spirit of enjoyment. The main event of most *festas* is a parade, either behind a revered holy image or a more celebratory affair with fancy costumes and *gigantones*, giant carnival figures that run down the streets to the delight, or terror, of children.

Although these *festas* take place throughout the year – and it's often the obscure and unexpected event which proves to be most fun – **Holy Week** (*Setmana Santa*) stands out, its passing celebrated in many places with magnificent processions.

The box overleaf gives the highlights of Mallorca and Menorca's festival year; for information about less prominent festivals, try local tourist offices. Remember that, although outsiders are nearly always welcome at a *festa*, you will have difficulty finding a room, and should try to book your accommodation well in advance.

The Bullfight

In recent years the popularity of the **Bullfight** (*Los Toros*) has declined across Spain, though it was never as big a deal in Catalunya and the Balearics as elsewhere. Yet Mallorca does have two main rings – one in Palma, the other in Muro – which still attract large crowds. The spectators turn up to see the *matadores* dispatch the bulls cleanly and with "artistic merit", which they greet with thunderous applause and the waving of handkerchiefs; a prolonged and messy kill will get the audience whistling. Some Spaniards do, of course, object to the whole spectacle, but opposition is not widespread and if Spaniards tell you that bullfighting is controversial, they are more likely to be referring to new refinements to the "sport", especially the widespread but illegal shaving down of bulls' horns. The horns are as sensitive as fingernails a few millimetres in, and the paring down deters the animals from charging and affects their balance, thereby reducing the danger to the *matador*.

Whether you attend a bullfight, obviously, is down to you. If you spend any time at all in Mallorca and Menorca during the season (which runs from March until October), you may well encounter *Los Toros* on a bar TV, and that will probably make up your mind. Many neutrals are particularly offended by the use of horses: padded up for protection, the horses are repeatedly charged by the bulls, which clearly terrifies them – though they can't make their feelings heard as their vocal chords have been cut out. If you want to know more about the **opposition to bullfighting**, Spain's Anti-Bullfight Committee (*Comité Antitaurino*) can be contacted by mail at Apartado 3098, 50080 Zaragoza.

Festival calendar for Mallorca and Menorca

January

16 The *Revetla de Sant Antoni Abat* (Eve of St Antony's Day) is celebrated by the lighting of bonfires (*foguerons*) in Palma and several of Mallorca's villages – especially Sa Pobla, where the inhabitants move from fire to fire, dancing round in fancy dress and eating traditional eel and vegetable patties, *espinagades*. Also observed in Maó.

17 The *Beneides de Sant Antoni* (Blessing of St Antony). St Antony's feast day is marked by processions in many of Mallorca's country towns, notably Sa Pobla and Artà, with farmyard animals herded through the streets to receive the saint's blessing and protection against disease.

17 *Processó d'els Tres Tocs* (Procession of the Three Knocks). Held in Ciutadella (Menorca), this procession commemorates the victory of Alfonso III over the Muslims here on January 17, 1287. There's a mass in the cathedral first and then three horsemen – dressed in black evening suits and riding boots – lead the way to the old city walls, where the eldest of the trio knocks three times with his flagstaff at the exact spot the Catalans first breached the walls.

19 The *Revetla de Sant Sebastià*. Palma has more bonfires, singing and dancing for St Sebastian.

20 The *Festa de Sant Sebastià*. This feast day is celebrated in Pollença (Mallorca) with a procession led by a holy banner (*estenard*) picturing the saint. It's accompanied by *Cavallets* (literally "merry-go-rounds"), two young dancers each wearing a cardboard horse and imitating the animal's walk. Of medieval origin, you'll see *Cavallets* at many of the islands' festivals.

February

Carnaval Towns and villages throughout the islands live it up during the week before Lent with marches and fancy dress parades. The biggest and liveliest are in Palma, where the shindig is known as *Sa Rua* (the Cavalcade).

March/April

Setmana Santa (Holy Week) is as widely observed as everywhere else in Spain. On Maunday Thursday in Palma, a much venerated icon of the crucified Christ, *La Sang*, is taken from the eponymous church on the Plaça del Hospital (off La Rambla) and taken in procession through the city streets. There are also solemn Good Friday (*Divendres Sant*) processions in many towns and villages, with the more important taking place in Palma, Sineu (Mallorca) and Maó. Most holy of all, however, is the Good Friday *Davallament* (The Lowering), the culmination of Holy Week in Pollença. Here, in total silence and by torchlight, the inhabitants lower a figure of Christ down from the hill-top Oratori to the church of Nostra Senyora dels Angels below. During Holy Week there are also many *Romerias* (pilgrimages) to the islands' holy places, with one of the most popular being the climb up to the Ermita Santa Magdalena, near Mallorca's Inca. The Monestir de Lluc, which possesses Mallorca's most venerated shrine, is another religious focus during this time, with the penitential trudging round its *Camí dels Misteris del Rosari* (The Way of the Mysteries of the Rosary).

Mid-May

The *Festa de Nostra Senyora de la Victòria* in Port de Sóller, Mallorca, features mock battles between Christians and infidels in commemoration of the thrashing of a band of Turkish pirates in 1561. Lots of booze and firing of antique rifles (in the air).

June

Corpus Christi At noon in the main square of Pollença an ancient and curious dance of uncertain provenance takes place – the *Ball de les Àguiles* (Dance of the Eagles) – followed by a religious procession.

23–25 In Ciutadella, the midsummer *Festa de Sant Joan* has been celebrated since the fourteenth century. There are jousting competitions, folk music, dancing, processions and pilgrimages. A particular highlight is on the Sunday before the 24th, when the *S'Homo d'es Bé* (the Man of the Sheep) leads a party of horsemen through the town. Clad in animal skins and carrying a lamb in honour of St John, he invites everyone to the forthcoming knees-up.

July

15–16 *Día de Virgen de Carmen*. The day of the patron saint of seafarers and fishermen is celebrated in many coastal settlements – principally Palma, Port de Sóller, Colònia de Sant Pere, Porto Colom, Cala Rajada and Maó – with parades and the blessing of boats.

Third week The Reconquest of Menorca is celebrated in a festival in Mercadal.

25 The *Festa de Sant Jaume* in Alcúdia (Mallorca) celebrates the feast day of St James with a popular religious procession followed by all sorts of fun and games – folk dances, fireworks and the like. Similar festivities in Es Castell, Menorca, too.

August

2 *Mare de Déu dels Àngels*. Moors and Christians battle it out again, this time in Pollença.

Second weekend High jinks on horseback through the streets of the town, in the *Festa de Sant Llorenç* in Alaior (Menorca).

20 *Cavallet* (see above) dances in Felanitx, Mallorca.

Throughout August International Festival at Pollença, including art and sculpture exhibitions and chamber music.

September

Second week In Alaró (Mallorca), the *Nativitat de Nostra Senyora* (Nativity of the Virgin) is honoured by a pilgrimage to a hilltop shrine near the Castell d'Alaró.

October

Third Sunday *Festa d'es Butifarra*. Of recent origins, this festival follows on from tractor and automobile contests held in the Mallorcan village of Sant Joan. It features folk dancing and traditional music as well as the eating of specially prepared vegetable pies (*coca amb trampó*) and sausages (*berenada de butifarra*).

December

Christmas (*Nadal*) is especially picturesque in Palma, where there are Nativity plays in the days leading up to the 25th.

The corrida

Highly stylized, each bullfighting programme (*corrida*) begins with a **procession**, to the accompaniment of a *paso doble* by the band. Leading the procession are two *algauziles* or "constables", on horseback and in traditional costume, followed by the three *matadores*, who will each fight two bulls, and their personal teams, each comprising two mounted assistants – *picadores* – and three *banderillas*. At the back are the mule teams who will drag off the dead bulls. The beast is softened up by the *picadores*, who stab pikes into its withers, and then by the *banderillas*, who stick beribboned and sharpened sticks into the bull in preparation for the *matador*, who kills the animal off.

Tickets for *corridas* cost 2000ptas and up – much more for the prime seats and prestigious fights. The cheapest seats are *gradas*, the highest rows at the back, from where you can see everything that happens without too much of the detail; the front rows are known as the *barreras*. Seats are also divided into *sol* (sun), *sombra* (shade) and *sol y sombra* (shaded after a while), though these distinctions have become less relevant as more and more bullfights start later in the day, at 6pm or 7pm, rather than the traditional 5pm. The *sombra* seats are more expensive not so much for the spectators' personal comfort as for the fact that most of the action takes place in the shade. On the way in, you can rent **cushions** – two hours sitting on concrete is not much fun. Beer and soft drinks are sold inside.

Football

To foreigners, the bullfight is easily the most celebrated of Spain's spectacles. In terms of popular support in modern Spain, however, it ranks far below **futbol** (football or soccer). For many years, the country's two dominant teams have been *Real Madrid* and *FC Barcelona*, and these have shared the League title and Cup honours with repetitive regularity. Both teams are in Division 1 of Spain's four-division League (Divisions 1, 2A, 2B and 3), but you'll find the Balearics' two main teams, both Palma-based, in the lower echelons. *FC Mallorca* are struggling to survive in Division 2, whilst *Atletico Baleares* are up-and-coming and likely to be promoted from Division 3 next year. A visit to a match is good fun, the crowd noisy, enthusiastic and usually good-humoured. *FC Mallorca* play in the *Estadi Lluis Sitjar*, just to the north of Palma city centre on Avgda Argentina, near Plaça Madrid. *Atletico Baleares* play in the *Estadi Atletico*, beside the Via Cintura a couple of kilometres northwest of the city centre (EMT bus #7). The football season runs from September to March, matches are on Sunday afternoons every fortnight and tickets, which are available at the turnstiles, cost between 750ptas and 1200ptas.

Trouble, the police and sexual harassment

Many North European expatriates love Mallorca and Menorca for their lack of crime – and with good reason. In the islands' villages and small towns petty crime is unusual, and serious offences, from burglary to assault and beyond, extremely rare. Of the three larger towns, only Palma presents any problems, mostly low-key stuff such as the occasional fight and minor theft – commonsense precautions are normally enough to keep you out of any trouble. However, you should also be aware that some of the late-night bars of the seedier resorts are commonly colonized by noisy and aggressive male tourists. In this regard, S'Arenal and especially Magaluf have the worst reputations, but it's more a question of which bar you're in, rather than the resort you're staying at. If you've accidentally dropped into a rough house, get out while the going is good.

Emergency telephone numbers

Police (*Policía Municipal*) ☎ 092.

Firefighters (*Bombers*) ☎ 080 in Mallorca, ☎ 351011 in Menorca.

Ambulance (*Ambulància*): call the Creu Roja (Red Cross; in Castilian, *Cruz Roja*), ☎ 202222 in Mallorca, ☎ 361180 in Menorca.

If for some reason you do have dealings with the Spanish police, remember that, although they are polite enough in the normal course of events, they can be extremely unpleasant if you get on the wrong side of them. At all times, keep your cool.

Avoiding trouble

Almost all the problems tourists encounter in the Balearics are to do with **petty crime** – pickpocketing and bag-snatching – rather than more serious physical confrontations, so it's as well to be on your guard and know where your possessions are at all times. Sensible **precautions** include: carrying bags slung across your neck and not over your shoulder; not carrying anything in pockets that are easy to dip into; having photocopies of your passport, airline ticket and driving licence; leaving passports and tickets in the hotel safe; and noting down travellers' cheque and credit card numbers. When you're **looking for a hotel room**, never leave your bags unattended. If you have a **car**, don't leave anything in view when you park. Vehicles are rarely stolen, but luggage and valuables left in cars do make a tempting target. At **night** in Palma, avoid unlit streets, don't go out brimming with valuables, and try not to appear hopelessly lost.

Thieves often work in pairs and, although theft is far from rife on the Balearics, you should be aware of certain **ploys**, such as: the "helpful" person pointing out "birdshit" (shaving cream or something similar) on your jacket, while someone else relieves you of your money; the card or paper you're invited to read on the street to distract your attention; the move by someone in a café for your drink with one hand (the other hand is in your bag as you react to save your drink); and if you're studying postcards or papers at stalls, watch out for people standing unusually close.

What to do if you're robbed

If you're robbed, you need to **go to the police** to report it, not least because your insurance company will require a police report. Don't expect a great deal of concern if your loss is relatively small – and expect the process of completing forms and formalities to take ages. In the unlikely event that you're **mugged** or otherwise threatened, *never* resist, and try to reduce your contact with the robber to a minimum. Either just hand over what's wanted, or throw money in one direction and take off in the other. Afterwards, go straight to the police, who will be more sympathetic and helpful on these occasions – tourism is, after all, the islands' economic lifeblood, and many officers on the Balearics speak English.

The police

There are three basic types of **police**: the *Guardia Civil*, the *Policía Nacional* and the *Policía Municipal*, all of them armed.

The **Guardia Civil**, in green uniforms, are the most officious and the ones to avoid if possible. Though their role has been cut back since they operated as Franco's right hand, they remain a reactionary force (it was a *Guardia Civil* colonel, Tejero, who held the Cortes hostage in the unsuccessful coup attempt of February 1981). The brown-uniformed **Policía Nacional** are mainly seen in the cities, armed with submachine guns and guarding key installations. They are also the force used to control crowds and demonstrations, and are not known for their sensitivity.

If you do need the police – and above all if you're reporting a serious crime – you should always go to the more sympathetic **Policía Municipal**, who wear blue and white uniforms. In the **countryside**, however, there may only be the *Guardia Civil* and, although these rural officers are usually more helpful than their urban colleagues, they are inclined to resent the suggestion that any crime exists on their turf. Indeed, you may end up feeling as if you are the one who stands accused.

Offences

You ought to be aware of a few **offences** that you might commit unwittingly.

• In theory you're supposed to carry some kind of **identification** at all times, and the police can stop you in the streets and demand it. In practice they're rarely bothered if you're clearly a foreigner.

• **Nude bathing** or **unauthorized camping** (see p.33) are activities more likely to bring you into contact with officialdom, though a warning to cover up or move on is more likely than any real

confrontation. **Topless** tanning is commonplace at all the resorts, but in country areas, where attitudes are more traditional, you should take care not to upset local sensibilities.

• Spanish **drug laws** are in a somewhat bizarre state at present. After the Socialists came to power in 1983, cannabis use (possession of up to 8g of what the Spanish call *chocolate*) was decriminalized. Subsequent pressures, and an influx of harder drugs, have changed that policy and – in theory at least – any drug use is now forbidden. However, the police are, as a general rule, little worried about personal use of cannabis, though larger quantities (and any other drugs) are a very different matter.

Should you be **arrested** on any charge, you have the right to contact your **consulate** (see p.81 for the addresses on Mallorca). Unfortunately, many consulates are notoriously reluctant to get involved, though most are required to assist you to some degree if you have your passport stolen or lose all your money. If you've been detained for a drugs offence, don't expect any sympathy or help.

Sexual harassment

Spain's macho image has faded in the post-Franco years and these days there are few parts of the Balearics where foreign women, travelling alone, are likely to feel threatened, intimidated, or attract unwanted attention. The tendency of Spaniards to move around in mixed crowds, filling central bars, clubs and streets late into the night, also helps to make you feel less exposed. If you are in any doubt as to your safety, there are always taxis – plentiful and reasonably priced.

The major tourist **resorts** have their own artificial holiday culture, which has much to do with sex. The men (of all nationalities) who hang around in nightclubs and bars here pose no greater or lesser threat than similar operators at home, though the language barrier makes it harder to know who to trust. Amongst Spaniards, "dejame en paz" (leave me in peace) is a fairly standard rebuff. The **remoter parts of the interior** can pose problems for women too. In some areas you can walk for hours without seeing a soul or coming across an inhabited farm or house. It's rare that this poses a threat – help and hospitality are much more the norm – but you are certainly more vulnerable, and local men less accustomed to women being on their own.

Finding work

Unless you've some particular skill and have applied for a job advertised in your home country, the only real chance of long-term work in the Balearics is in language schools. However, there is much less work about than in the boom years of the early 1980s – schools are contracting rather than expanding – and you'll need to persevere if you're to come up with a rewarding position. To give yourself any kind of chance, you'll need some sort of recognized qualification, like a TEFL (Teaching English as a Foreign Language) or ESL (English as a Second Language) certificate.

Teaching and language work

Finding a **teaching** job is mainly a question of pacing the streets, stopping in at every language school around and asking about vacancies. For the addresses of schools look in the yellow pages under *Academias*. The best time to try is from the middle to the end of September when the schools know how many replacement teachers they need. Reputable schools will require you to have undergone at least a one-month intensive teacher training course and to give a demonstration lesson. If you intend to stay in the Balearics for any length of time, you'll need a *permiso de residencia* – see "Visas and red tape" p.18.

Other options are to try advertising **private lessons** (better paid, but harder to make a living at) in the local press; or, if you speak good Spanish, **translation work**, most of which will be business correspondence – look in the yellow pages under *Traducciones*. If you intend doing translation work, you'll usually need access to a fax and a PC.

Temporary work

If you're looking for **temporary work**, the best chances are in the **bars and restaurants** of the larger resorts. This may help you have a good time but it's unlikely to bring in very much money; pay (often from British bar owners) will reflect your lack of official status. If you turn up in spring and are willing to stay through the season you might get a better deal – also true if you're offering some special skill like windsurfing. Occasionally there are jobs on offer at **yacht marinas**, scrubbing down and servicing the boats of the well-heeled; just turn up and ask around, but don't be too hopeful.

Directory

ADDRESSES These are usually abbreviated to a standard format – c/Bellver 7 translates as Bellver street (*carrer*) no. 7, and Pl. Major 9 as Major square (*plaça*) no. 9. Plaça Rosari 5, 2è means second floor at no. 5 Plaça Rosari; Passeig d'es Born 15, 1–C means suite C, first floor, at no. 15 Passeig d'es Born. S/N (*sense número*) means without a number. In Franco's day, most avenues and boulevards were named after Fascist heroes and, although the vast majority were redesignated years ago, there's still some confusion in remoter spots. Another source of bafflement can be house numbers: some houses carry more than one number (the by-product of half-hearted reorganizations), and on many streets the sequence is impossible to fathom.

AIRPORT TAX There's no departure tax.

CHILDREN Most *hostals, pensions* and hotels welcome children and many offer rooms with three or four beds; restaurants and cafés almost always encourage families too. Many package holidays have child-minding facilities as part of the deal. For babies, food seems to work out quite well (some places will prepare food specially) though you might want to bring powdered milk – babies, like most Spaniards, are pretty contemptuous of the UHT stuff generally available. Disposable nappies and other basic supplies are widely available.

ELECTRICITY The current is 220 volts AC, with standard European-style two-pin plugs. Brits will need an adaptor to connect their appliances, North Americans both an adaptor and a transformer.

LAUNDRIES Although there's the occasional self-service launderette (usually rendered in Castilian, *lavandería automática*), mostly you'll have to leave your clothes for a full (and somewhat expensive) laundry service. A dry cleaner is a *tintorería* (also Castilian).

TIME Spain is one hour ahead of the UK, six hours ahead of Eastern Standard Time, nine hours ahead of Pacific Standard Time, and seven hours behind Perth, Australia – except for brief periods during the changeovers to and from daylight saving. In Spain the clocks go back in the last week in March and forward again in the last week in September.

TOILETS Public toilets, which remain rare, are averagely clean but almost never have any paper (best to carry your own). They're commonly referred to as *los servicios* or *el lavabo. Dones* or the Castilian *Damas* (Ladies) and *Homes* or the Castilian *Caballeros* (Gentlemen) are the usual signs, though you may also see *Señoras* (Women) and *Señores* (Men).

The Guide

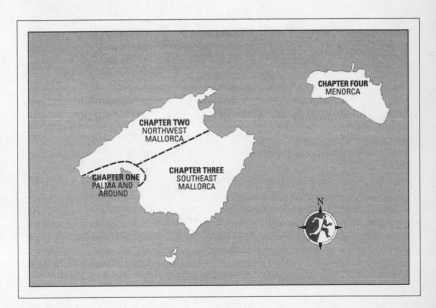

Chapter 1

Palma and around

P ALMA is an ambitious city. In 1983 it became the capital of
one of Spain's newly established autonomous regions, the
Balearic Islands, and since then it's shed the dusty provin-
cialism of yesteryear, developing into a go-ahead and cosmopolitan
commercial hub of 300,000 people. The new self-confidence is plain
to see in the city centre, a vibrant and urbane place of careful coif-
fures and well-cut suits, which is akin to the big cities of the Spanish
mainland – and a world away from the heaving tourist enclaves of
the surrounding bay. There's still a long way to go – much of suburban Palma remains obdurately dull and somewhat dilapidated – but
the centre now presents a splendid ensemble of lively shopping
areas, mazy lanes and refurbished old buildings, all enclosed by
what remains of the old city walls and their replacement boulevards.
This geography encourages downtown Palma to look into itself and
away from the sea, even though its **harbour** – now quarantined by
the main highway – has always been the city's economic lifeline.

The Romans were the first to recognize the site's strategic value,
establishing a military post here, but real development came with
the Moors who made their **Medina Mayurka** a major seaport
protected by no fewer than three concentric walls. Jaume I of
Aragón captured the Moorish stronghold in 1229 and promptly
started work on the **cathedral**, whose mellow sandstone still towers
above the waterfront, presenting from its seaward side – in the sheer
beauty of its massive proportions – one of Spain's most stunning
sights.

As a major port of call between Europe and North Africa, Palma
boomed under both Moorish and medieval Christian control, but its
wealth and prominence came to a sudden end with the Spanish
exploitation of the New World: from the early sixteenth century,
Madrid looked west across the Atlantic and Palma slipped into
Mediterranean obscurity. One result of its abrupt decline has been
the preservation of much of the **old town**, whose narrow, labyrinthine streets and high-storeyed houses are at their most beguiling
behind the cathedral. This district possesses few specific sights, but

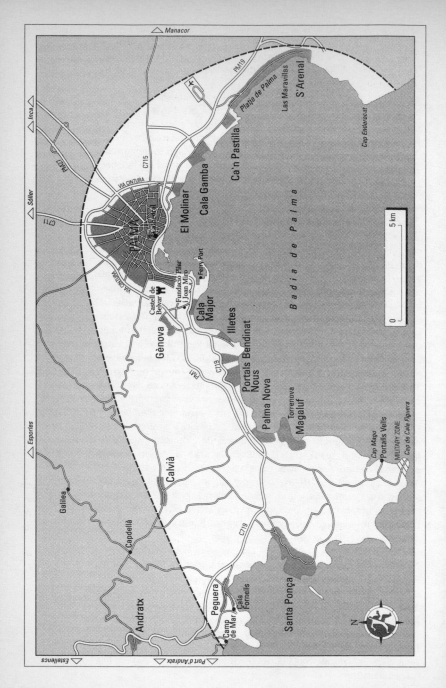

△ Manacor

PM19

Platja de Palma

Las Maravillas

S'Arenal

Cap Enderocat

Ca'n Pastilla

Cala Gamba

El Molinar

B a d i a   d e   P a l m a

C715

VIA CINTURA

PMA7 △

△ Inca

△ Sóller

PALMA
Catedral

C711

Ferry Port

5 km

0

△ Esporles

Fundació Pilar
i Joan Miró

Castell de
Bellver

Cala
Major

Illetes

Portals
Nous

Bendinat

Palma Nova

Torrenova

Magaluf

Cap Mago

Portals Vells

MILITARY ZONE

Cap de Cala Figuera

Gènova

PM1

C719

Calvià

Galilea

Capdellà

C719

Santa Ponça

Andratx

Peguera

Cala
Fornells

Camp
de Mar

Port d'Andratx △

△ Estellencs

N

THE GUIDE: CHAPTER 1

it's a delightful place to wander, especially as an ambitious renovation programme is rapidly returning the area to its old elegance. The pick of Palma's other historic attractions are the fourteenth-century **Castell de Bellver** and the heavyweight Baroque of the **Basílica de Sant Francesc**.

Yet for most visitors, Palma's main appeal is its sheer vitality: at night scores of excellent **restaurants** offer the best of Spanish, Catalan and Mallorcan cuisine, while the city's **cafés** buzz with purposeful chatter. Palma also boasts **accommodation** to match most budgets, making it a splendid base from which to explore the island. In this respect, the city is far preferable, at least for independent travellers, to the string of resorts along the **Badia de Palma** (Bay of Palma), where nearly all the accommodation is block-booked by tour operators. If you are tempted by a cheap package, it's as well to bear in mind that the more agreeable of the resorts lie to the west of the city, where a hilly coastline of rocky cliffs and tiny coves is punctuated by mostly small, sandy beaches. Development is ubiquitous, but well-to-do **Illetes** has several excellent hotels and a couple of lovely cove beaches; pint-sized **Cala Fornells** has a fine seashore setting and a pair of good hotels, with the spacious sandy shoreline of family-oriented **Peguera** in easy reach; and then there's **Camp de Mar**, set in an attractive wooded bay fringed by another good beach. Places to avoid include the massive villa complex of **Santa Ponça**, lager-swilling **Magaluf** and all the resorts to the east of Palma. Here the pancake-flat shoreline is burdened by a seamless band of skyscrapers stretching from **Ca'n Pastilla** to **S'Arenal** – behind what is, admittedly, one of the island's longest and most impressive beaches, the **Platja de Palma**.

Arrival, orientation and information

Mallorca's international **airport** is 11km east of Palma, immediately behind the resort of Ca'n Pastilla. It has two terminals, the main Terminal A and Terminal B, which handles charter flights and is only open in high season (a third terminal is scheduled for completion in 1996). The airport's **tourist office**, with lists of car rental outlets, hotels and *hostals*, and general island information (Mon–Sat 9am–2pm & 3–8pm, Sun 9am–2pm; ☎260803), is in Terminal A, as is the useful **hotel reservation desk** operated by the *Ultramar Express* travel agency (daily 9am–8.30pm; ☎262649). Terminal A also has 24-hour **cash card and credit card machines**, and both terminals have **car rental** and **currency exchange** facilities. If you're collecting someone from the airport by car, there's a free five-minute stop zone, as well as a rather confusing **car park**: when you arrive, grab a ticket from the machine at the car park entrance;

For full details of ferries and flights between the islands and from the mainland, see Basics.

before departure, take the ticket to one of the separate pay machines (125ptas for short stays), which allow you twenty minutes' grace to find your vehicle and leave.

The airport is linked to the city and the Bay of Palma resorts by a frenetic highway (*autopista*), which shadows the shoreline from S'Arenal in the east to Magaluf in the west. The least expensive way to reach Palma from the airport is by **bus #17** (daily, every 20min from 8am to midnight, plus 1am, 6am and 7am; 230–275ptas one way) to the Plaça Espanya, on the north side of the centre; **taxis** will set you back about 2000ptas.

The Palma **ferry terminal** is about 4km west of the city centre, linked to town by bus #1; to catch it, walk 200m out of the terminal to the main road, cross the bridge, then turn right and proceed another 200m as far as the marked bus stops – you want the far

PALMA

ACCOMMODATION
1 Almudaina
2 Araxa
3 Bonany
4 Borne
5 Brondo
6 Cannes
7 Costa Azul
8 Cuba
9 Liceo
10 Mirador
11 Monleón
12 Palladium
13 Pons
14 Regina
15 Ritzi
16 San Lorenzo
17 Saratoga
18 Sol Bellver
19 Sol Jaime III
20 Sol Palas Atenea
21 Terminus
22 Valencia

- - - ORA (Restricted Parking Area)

0   400m

(harbour) side of the road for Palma. Buses usually run every hour
to the Plaça de la Reina, at the foot of the Passeig d'es Born, and
the Plaça Espanya, but beware of reduced services on Sundays and
holidays (daily 8am–9pm; 140–185ptas).

Orientation

Almost everything of interest in Palma is located in the city centre, a
roughly circular affair whose southwestern perimeter is defined by
the cathedral and the remains of the old city walls, which in turn
abut the coastal motorway and the harbour. The city centre's landward limits are determined by a zigzag of wide boulevards built
beside or in place of the old town walls – **Avinguda Argentina** and
Avinguda Gabriel Alomar i Villalonga connect with the motorway,
thereby completing the circle. The **Via Cintura**, the ring road

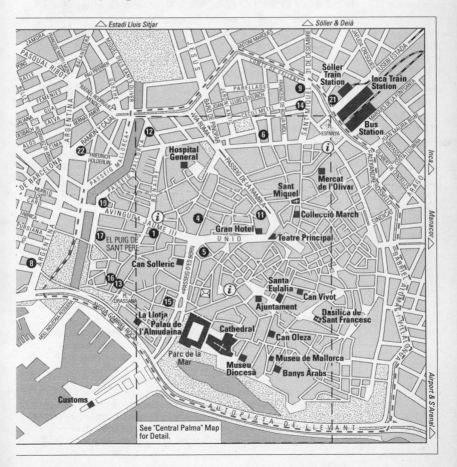

around the suburbs, creates a much larger, outer circle. The city centre itself is crossed by four interconnected avenues, **Passeig d'es Born, Avinguda Jaume III**, c/de la Unio (which becomes c/de la Riera at its eastern end) and **Passeig de la Rambla**. Your best bet is to use these four thoroughfares to guide yourself round the centre – Palma's jigsaw-like side streets and squares can be very confusing. Central Palma is about 2km in diameter, roughly forty minutes' walk from one side to the other. If you're in a hurry, take a **taxi**: fares are reasonable and there are ranks outside all the major hotels.

To reach the city's outskirts, take the **bus**. Almost all *EMT* services pass through Plaça Espanya, linking the centre with the suburbs and the nearer tourist resorts. Each *EMT* bus stop sports a large route map with timetable details. Tickets, available from the driver, cost 140ptas per journey within the city, 170ptas for a trip to the outskirts. Under the *Bono-Bus* scheme, a book of ten tickets costs 630ptas for the inner and 875ptas for the outer zone; books are available from most tobacconists (look for the brown and yellow *tabac* signs). **Island-wide buses** are operated by several other companies. Most use the bus station on the east side of the Plaça Espanya, though a few leave from the surrounding side streets: the most significant of these are the services run by *Bus Nord Balear* (☎427187) to Valldemossa, Deià, Sóller and Port de Sóller, which stop outside the *Bar La Granja* (where you can buy tickets), c/ Arxiduc Lluis Salvador 1; and the *Autocares Grimalt* services (☎463527) to southeast Mallorca – principally Colònia de Sant Jordi, Cala Figuera and Porto Petro – which stop outside the *Bar Alcala* (where you can buy tickets), Avgda Alexandre Rossello 32. The island's two tiny **train stations** are by the bus station on the east side of the Plaça Espanya – one line to Inca, the other to Sóller.

For details of the frequencies and journey times of buses and trains from Palma, see p.91. For further information on the delightful train journey from Palma to Sóller, see p.95.

Information

The provincial **tourist office** may be moving soon, but for the time being you'll find it at Avgda Jaume III, 10 (daily 9am–2.30pm & 3–8pm; ☎712216), while the main municipal office is at c/Sant Domingo 11, in the subway at the end of c/Conquistador (Mon–Fri 9am–8pm, Sat 9am–1.30pm; ☎724090). Both provide city and island-wide infor-

---

Parking in Palma

Trying to find a **car parking** space in downtown Palma can be a nightmare – you're well advised to leave your vehicle on the city's outskirts for visits of more than an hour or two. If you're staying downtown, choose a hotel with a car park. Parking in the city centre requires an ORA ticket on weekdays 9.30am–1.30pm and 5–8pm, and on Saturdays 9.30am–1.30pm. These are readily available from *ORA* parking meters but, although the cost is minimal (35ptas for 30min, 100ptas for 90min), the longest-lasting ticket only provides ninety minutes' parking, and fines are immediate and steep. Note also that if the time allowed overlaps into a free period, your *ORA* ticket is still valid when restricted time begins again.

mation, dispensing free maps, accommodation lists, bus schedules, ferry timetables, lists of car rental firms, boat trip details and all sorts of special interest leaflets, including the useful "Artesanía", which lists specialist suppliers of everything from pottery and pearls to books and handicrafts. The smaller municipal tourist office on Plaça Espanya (Mon–Fri 9am–8pm, Sat 9am–1pm) just provides the basics.

Arrival, orientation and information

Accommodation

There are around thirty *hostals* and twenty hotels dotted around Palma, and if you haven't got a reservation, your first move in the summer should be to pick up the official list from the tourist office. They won't, however, arrange accommodation for you, leaving that to the telephone booking facility of the **Mallorca Hotel Federation** (daily 9am–2pm & 4.30–7.30pm; ☎ 430674).

The bulk of Palma's **budget accommodation** is in the city centre and, fortunately enough, this is by far the most diverting area to stay in – the immediate suburbs are quite unprepossessing. The best areas to look are along the side streets off the Passeig d'es Born and around the Plaça Espanya. There are clusters of **fancier hotels** on the Passeig Mallorca and to the west of the centre along Avinguda Gabriel Roca, overlooking the waterfront. In all price brackets, it's best to book well in advance in high summer; at other times the establishments listed below are likely to have vacancies.

The nearest youth hostel to Palma is in the resort of Sometimes, a twenty-minute bus ride from town – see p.85.

Accommodation price symbols

The symbols used in our accommodation listings denote the following price ranges:

① Under 2000ptas   ④ 4000–6000ptas   ⑦ 10,000–14,000ptas
② 2000–3000ptas   ⑤ 6000–8000ptas   ⑧ 14,000–20,000ptas
③ 3000–4000ptas   ⑥ 8000–10,000ptas   ⑨ Over 20,000ptas

For more details see p.31.

Inexpensive

Hostal Bonany, c/Almirall Cervera 5; ☎ 737924. Faded one-star *hostal* on a quiet residential street, about 3km west of the city centre, close to Castell de Bellver. ③.

Hostal-residencia Brondo, c/Can Brondo; ☎ 719043. Down a narrow alley off Plaça Rei Joan Carles I, no-frills accommodation in an old, high-storeyed house. ③.

Hostal-residencia Cuba, c/Sant Magí 1; ☎ 738159. Seedy, dilapidated cheapie in a big old building near the bottom of Avgda Argentina; for emergencies only. ②.

Hostal Liceo, Avgda Comte de Sallent 5; ☎ 217619. Unattractive, noisy last resort, beside a busy boulevard in an ugly part of town. ②.

Hostal-residencia Monleón, Passeig de la Rambla 3; ☎ 715317. Gloomy and slightly down-at-heel *hostal* in an old-fashioned 1950s building at the foot of La Rambla; usually has vacancies. ③.

Accommodation	Hostal-residencia Pons, c/Vi 8; ☎722658. Simple rooms in a lovely old house with a courtyard and house plants. In the old part of town, near the Passeig d'es Born. ③.

Hostal-residencia Regina, c/Sant Miquel 77; ☎713703. Dreary two-storey modern building bordering a busy shopping street to the north of the old part of town. ③.

Hostal Ritzi, c/Apuntadors 6; ☎714610. Basic one-star rooms in an ancient five-storey house off the Passeig d'es Born. ③.

Hostal-residencia Terminus, c/Eusebi Estada 2; ☎250014. Two-star establishment beside the train station, with a quirkily old-fashioned foyer and fairly large bedrooms. ③.

Hostal-residencia Valencia, c/Ramon y Cajal 21; ☎733147. Modern, 30-room *hostal* on the northern edge of the city centre. Spruce, almost antiseptic rooms, some with balconies overlooking the boulevard. ③.

Moderate

Hostal Borne, c/Sant Jaume 3; ☎712942. Comfortable and justifiably popular mid-price choice in an excellent downtown location. Set in an old, refurbished mansion with its own courtyard café. ⑤.

Hotel Cannes, c/Cardenal Pou 8; ☎726943. Unprepossessing 50-room hotel in a grittily modern part of town by the Plaça Espanya, but close to the principal shopping areas. ④.

Hotel Costa Azul, Avgda Gabriel Roca 7; ☎731940. Standard high-rise, popular with package tours, with balconied rooms overlooking the bay. ⑥.

Hotel Mirador, Avgda Gabriel Roca 10; ☎732046. Slightly old-fashioned high-rise hotel overlooking the bay, popular with Spanish business folk. Considering its bayside location, room rates are very reasonable. ⑥.

Expensive

Hotel Almudaina, Avgda Jaume III, 9; ☎727340. Smart modern rooms above a noisy street right in the centre, opposite the tourist office. ⑦.

Hotel Araxa, c/Alférez Cerdá 22; ☎731640. Attractive, three-storey modern hotel with pleasant gardens and an outdoor swimming pool. Most rooms have balconies. In a quiet residential area about 2km west of the centre, not far from the Castell de Bellver. ⑦.

Hotel-residencia Palladium, Passeig Mallorca 40; ☎713945. Clean, trim and tidy three-star accommodation in a modern tower. No dining room. ⑦.

Hotel San Lorenzo, c/Sant Llorenç 14; ☎728200. Delightful four-star hotel set in a luxuriously modernized seventeenth-century mansion, with a rooftop swimming pool. Located among the ancient side streets west of the Passeig d'es Born. Six rooms only, so reservations are essential. ⑧.

Hotel Saratoga, Passeig Mallorca 6; ☎727240. Excellent, newly refurbished hotel with rooftop swimming pool. Most rooms have balconies overlooking the boulevard. ⑦.

Hotel Sol Bellver, Avgda Gabriel Roca 11; ☎736744. Well-maintained chain hotel with balconies overlooking the harbour, a 10-min walk west of the city centre. Standard high-rise, but the rooms are comfortable. ⑧.

Hotel Sol Jaime III, Passeig Mallorca 14; ☎725943. Agreeable three-star with tidy modern rooms, mostly with balconies. Very reasonable prices. ⑦.

Hotel Sol Palas Atenea, Avgda Gabriel Roca 29; ☎281400. Classy and classic 1960s-style foyer leads to attractively furnished, comfortable rooms with balconies overlooking the bay. ⑨.

Hotel Son Vida, c/Son Vida; ☎790000. Sumptuous five-star hotel, with its own golf course, in a refurbished eighteenth-century mansion, 5km northwest of Palma. ⑨.

The City

There's not much argument as to where to start a tour of Palma –
it's got to be the **cathedral**, which dominates the waterfront from
the crest of a hill. Next door, Palma's other landmark is the **Palau
de l'Almudaina**, an important royal residence from Moorish times,
though successive modifications have destroyed most of its character and nowadays it's only worth a visit on a rainy day. Spreading
northeast behind the cathedral are the narrow lanes and ageing
mansions of the most intriguing part of the **old town**. A stroll here
is a pleasure in itself and, tucked away among the side streets, there
are two good diversions, the **Museu de Mallorca**, the island's most
extensive museum, and the Baroque **Basílica de Sant Francesc**.
North of the old town lies the heart of the early twentieth-century
city, where the high-sided tenements are graced by a sequence of
grand buildings in the **Modernista** style (the Spanish, and especially
Catalan, form of Art Nouveau), particularly on and around the
prestigious **Plaça Weyler**.

West of the city centre, you should consider a visit to the
Castell de Bellver, an impressive hilltop castle, and, perhaps, to the
far less imposing **Poble Espanyol**, which comprises detailed reproductions of important and typical buildings from every region of
Spain.

The cathedral

Legend has it that when Jaume I of Aragón and Catalunya and his
invasion force were off Mallorca in 1229, a fierce gale threatened to
sink the fleet. The desperate king promised to build a church dedicated to the Virgin Mary if the expedition against the Moors was
successful; it was, and Jaume fulfilled his promise, starting
construction work the next year. The king had a political point to
make too – he built his cathedral, a gigantic affair of golden sandstone, bang on top of the Great Mosque, inside the Almudaina, the
old Moorish citadel. The Reconquest was to be no temporary
matter.

*The cathedral is
open April–Oct
Mon–Fri
10am–6pm,
Sat
10am–2.30pm;
Nov–March
Mon–Fri
10am–3pm,
Sat 10am–2pm;
300ptas. For
the background
to Jaume I's
invasion, see
p.224.*

As it turned out, the **cathedral** (*La Seu* in Catalan) was five
hundred years in the making. Nonetheless, although there are architectural bits and bobs from several different eras, the church
remains essentially Gothic, with massive exterior buttresses – its
most distinctive feature – taking the weight off the pillars within.
The whole structure derives its effect from sheer height, impressive
from any angle but startling when viewed from the waterside
esplanade.

The doors and bell tower

The finest of the cathedral's three doors is the **Portal del Mirador**
(Lookout Door), which overlooks the Bay of Palma from the south

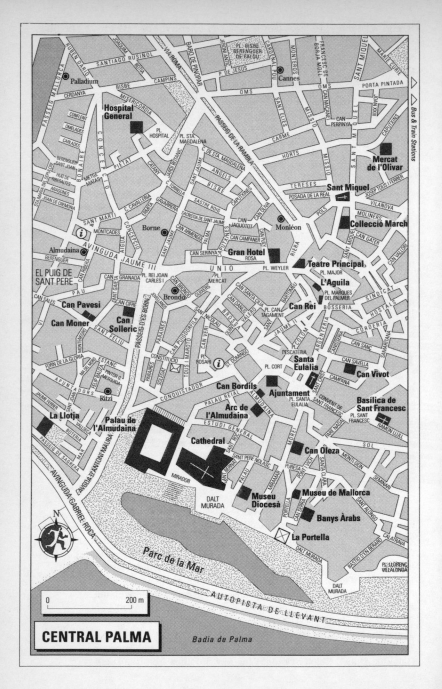

CENTRAL PALMA

0   200 m

Parc de la Mar

Badia de Palma

AUTOPISTA DE LLEVANT

facade. Dating from the late fourteenth century, the Mirador
features a host of Flemish-style, ecclesiastical figurines set around a
tympanum where heavily bearded disciples sit at a Last Supper. In
contrast, the west-facing **Portal Major** (Great Door), across from
the Almudaina, is a neo-Gothic disaster, an ugly reworking – along
with the sixty-metre-high flanking turrets – of a far simpler prede-
cessor that was badly damaged in an earthquake of 1851. On the
north side is a third door, the **Portal de l'Almoina**, decorated in a
simple Gothic design of 1498. Up above rises the solid squareness
of the **bell tower** (closed to the public), an incongruous, fortress-
like structure that clearly did not form part of the original design.
When the largest of the bells, the 5700-kilo N'Eloi, was tolled in
1857 it shattered most of the cathedral's windows.

The interior

Although the cathedral is entered through the museum on the north
side, the majestic proportions of its interior are seen to best advantage from the western end, by the Portal Major. In the central nave,
fourteen beautifully aligned, pencil-thin pillars rise to 21 metres
before their ribs branch out – rather like fronded palm trees – to
support the single-span, vaulted roof. The nave, at 44 metres high, is
one of the tallest Gothic structures in Europe and its length – 121
metres – is of matching grandeur. This open, hangar-like construction, typical of Catalan Gothic architecture, was designed to make
the high altar visible to the entire congregation, and to express the
mystery of the Christian faith, with kaleidoscopic floods of light that
filtered in through the **stained-glass windows**. Most of the original
glass was lost long ago, but recent refurbishment has returned many
windows to their former glory. There are seven rose windows, the
largest of which crowns the triumphal arch of the apse and boasts
over 1200 individual pieces of glass. The cathedral's designers also
incorporated a specific, carefully orchestrated artifice: twice a year,
at 6.30am on Candlemas and St Martin's Day, the sun shines through
the stained glass of the eastern window onto the wall immediately
below the rose window on the main, western facade.

The restoration work continues today, and as the medieval
windows are un-bricked and cleaned, so the cathedral re-emerges
from the gloom imposed by Renaissance, Baroque and neo-Gothic
architects. The first attempt to restore the church to its original
form was made at the beginning of the twentieth century when an
inspired local bishop commissioned the *Modernista* Catalan architect **Antoni Gaudí** to direct a full-blown restitution. At the time,
Gaudí was renowned for his fancifully embellished metalwork, and
his functionalist extrapolation of Gothic design was still evolving.
This experimentation led ultimately to his most famous and extravagant opus, the church of the Sagrada Família in Barcelona, but here
in Palma his work was relatively restrained. Flattened by a
Barcelona tram, Gaudí died in 1926; it was only in the 1960s that

his techniques were championed and copied across western Europe, and he was acknowledged as crucial to the development of modernism.

Gaudí worked on Palma's cathedral intermittently from 1904 to 1914, during which time he removed the High Baroque altar and shifted the ornate choir stalls from the centre of the cathedral, placing them flat against the walls of the presbytery. The new high altar, a medieval alabaster table of plain design, was then located beneath a phantasmagorical giant **baldachin**, suspended from the roof. This wrought-iron canopy, whose flowing lines are enhanced by hanging lanterns and a strangely angled Flemish tapestry, is supposed to symbolize the Crown of Thorns – it's not a great success, though to be fair, Gaudí never had time to complete it so it's impossible to say what the final version would have looked like.

Other examples of Gaudí's distinctive workmanship are dotted around the cathedral. The railings in front of the high altar are twisted into shapes inspired by Mallorcan window grilles, while the wall on either side of the Bishop's Throne, at the east end of the church, sports ceramic inlays with brightly painted floral designs. Yet Gaudí's main concern was to revive the Gothic tradition by giving light to the cathedral. To this end he introduced electric lighting, bathing the apse in bright artificial light and placing lamps and candelabra throughout the church. At the time, Gaudí's measures were deeply controversial; no choir had ever before been removed in Spain and electric lighting was a real novelty. The artistic success of the whole project, though, was undeniable, and it was immediately popular.

The aisles on either side of the central nave are flanked by a long sequence of chapels, dull affairs for the most part, dominated by dusty Baroque altars of gargantuan proportions and little artistic merit. The exception, and the cathedral's one outstanding example of the Baroque, is the **Capella de Corpus Christi**, at the head of the central nave to the left of the high altar. Begun in the sixteenth century, the chapel's tiered and columned altarpiece features three religious scenes, cramped and intense sculptural tableaux of – from top to bottom – *The Temptations of St Anthony*, *The Presentation of Jesus in the Temple* and *The Last Supper*. The massive stone pulpit next to the chapel was moved here by Gaudí, a makeshift location for this excellent illustration of the Plateresque style. Dated to 1531, the pulpit's intricate floral patterns and bustling Biblical scenes cover a clumsy structure whose upper portion is carried by telamons, male counterparts of the more usual caryatids.

Also of interest is the **Capella de la Trinidad** (Trinity Chapel) at the east end of the apse. Completed in 1329, this tiny chapel accommodates the remains of Jaume II and III, which were first stored in a tomb that operated rather like a filing cabinet, allowing the corpses to be venerated by the devout. This gruesome practice has been discontinued and the alabaster sarcophagi now enclosing the royal bones are modern additions.

The Museu de la Catedral

The ground floor of the bell tower and two adjoining chapterhouses have been turned into the **Museu de la Catedral** to accommodate an eclectic mixture of ecclesiastical treasures. The first room's most valuable exhibit, in the glass case in the middle, is a gilded silver monstrance of extraordinary delicacy, its fairy-tale decoration dating from the late sixteenth century. On display around the walls are assorted chalices and reliquaries and a real curiosity, the portable altar of Jaume I, a wood and silver chess board with each square containing a bag of relics.

The second room is mainly devoted to the Gothic works of the **Mallorcan Primitives**, a school of painters who flourished on the island in the fourteenth and fifteenth centuries, producing strikingly naive devotional works of bold colours and cartoon-like detail. The work of two of the school's leading fourteenth-century practitioners is displayed here, the so-called **Master of the Privileges**, whose love of minute detail and warm colours reveals an Italian influence, and the **Master of Bishop Galiana**, who looked to his Catalan contemporaries for his sense of movement and tight draughtsmanship. Later, the work of the Mallorcan Primitives shaded into the new realism of the Flemish style, which was to dominate Mallorcan painting throughout the sixteenth century – Joan Desi's *Panel of La Almoina* (c. 1500) illustrates the transition. In terms of content, look out for the tribulations of **Santa Eulalia**, whose martyrdom fascinated and excited scores of medieval Mallorcan artists. A Catalan girl-saint, Eulalia defied the Roman Emperor Diocletian by sticking to her Christian faith despite all sorts of ferocious tortures, which are depicted in ecstatic detail in several of the paintings here. Ultimately she was burnt at the stake and, at the moment of her death, white doves flew from her mouth.

Further works by the Mallorcan Primitives are displayed at the Museu de Mallorca – see p.69–70.

The third and final room, the **Baroque chapterhouse**, is entered through a playful Churrigueresque doorway, above which a delicate Madonna is overwhelmed by lively cherubic angels. Inside, pride of place goes to the High Baroque altar, a gaudy, gilded whopper surmounted by the Sacred Heart, a gory representation of the heart of Jesus that was very much in vogue during the eighteenth century. Some imagination went into the designation of the reliquaries displayed round the room – there's a piece of the flogging post, three thorns from Christ's crown and even a piece of the gall and vinegared sponge that was offered to the crucified Jesus. Of more appeal are a pair of finely carved, Baroque crucifixes, each Christ a study in perfect muscularity swathed in the flowing folds of a loincloth.

The Palau de l'Almudaina and around

Opposite the cathedral entrance stands the **Palau de l'Almudaina**, originally the palace of the Moorish *walis* (governors) and later of the Mallorcan kings. The present structure, built around a compact courtyard, owes much of its appearance to Jaume II (1276–1311), who spent the last twelve years of his life in residence here. Jaume converted the old fortress into a lavish palace that incorporated both Gothic and Moorish features, an uneasy mixture of styles conceived by the Mallorcan Pedro Selva, the king's favourite architect. The two most prominent "Moorish" attributes are the fragile-looking outside walls, with their square turrets and dainty crenellations, and the delicate arcades of the loggia, which is best viewed from the waterside esplanade.

The Palau de l'Almudaina is open April–Sept Mon–Fri 10am–7pm, Sat 10.30am–2pm; Oct–March Mon–Fri 10am–2pm & 4–6pm; 400ptas, free to EC citizens on Wed.

Once Mallorca was incorporated within the Aragonese kingdom, the Palau de l'Almudaina became surplus to requirements, though it did achieve local notoriety when the eccentric Aragonese king Juan I (1387–1395) installed an alchemist in the royal apartments, hoping he would replenish the treasury by turning base metal into gold.

Today, the palace serves a variety of official functions, housing the island's legislature, its military – whose camera-shy guards stand outside one of the entrances – and a series of state apartments kept in readiness for visiting dignitaries. Sometimes you're allowed to walk round the palace unescorted, but usually you'll get roped into one of the regular guided tours, whose energetic commentaries are repeated in three languages. Most of what you see – and there are considerable parts cordoned off – is tedious in the extreme, with the medieval rooms almost entirely devoid of ornamentation and the state apartments spruce and sterile. Saving graces are few and far between, but there are several admirable Flemish **tapestries**, fifteenth- and sixteenth-century imports devoted to classical themes such as Cleopatra's suicide. The palace also possesses a handful of **Flemish genre paintings**, fine still-life studies including one by the seventeenth-century Antwerp-based artist Frans Snyders, a contemporary of Rubens – in whose pictures he often painted the flowers and fruit. The guided tour finishes with a quick gallop round the Gothic **Capella de Santa Aina**, which is still used for army officers' Masses and weddings.

The Parc de la Mar, La Llotja and the harbour

A steep flight of steps leads down between the cathedral and the Palau de l'Almudaina to a handsomely restored section of the old city walls. Once these mighty fortifications edged the Mediterranean, but today they overlook the planted palm trees, concrete terraces and ornamental lagoon of the newly constructed **Parc de la Mar**. A wide and pleasant walkway travels along the top of the wall, cutting east to round the southern perimeter of old Palma. Also below the Almudaina are the tiered gardens of a small Moorish-style park, through which you can reach the foot of Avinguda d'Antoni Maura, an extension of the tree-lined Passeig d'es Born.

The Passeig d'es Born is covered on p.73.

Continuing west along the seafront, it's a couple of minutes' walk to the fifteenth-century **Llotja**, the city's former stock exchange. This carefully composed building, with its four octagonal turrets and tall windows, now hosts frequent and occasionally excellent exhibitions. The distinguished building next door – once the Admiralty Court – is closed to the public, but the outside is worth a second look for its elegant Renaissance gallery. Opposite La Llotja, a wide breakwater housing the customs building marks the start of Palma **harbour**, whose various marinas, shipyards, fish docks and ferry terminal extend west as far as Cala Major. The harbour is at its prettiest at this eastern end, in between La Llotja and the **Parc Cuarentena**, an attractive terraced garden situated a fifteen-minute walk away along the palm-lined esplanade.

The City

La Llotja is open Tues–Sat 11am–2pm & 5–9pm. The best views of the harbour are from the Castell del Bellver – see p.276.

The old town

The medina-like maze of streets at the back of the cathedral constitutes the heart of the **old town**, which extends north to Plaça Cort and east to Avinguda Gabriel Alomar i Villalonga. Long a neglected corner of the city, the district is now being refurbished, an ambitious and massively expensive project that's slowly restoring its antique charms. The area's general appearance is its main appeal, and you can spend hours wandering down narrow lanes and alleys, loitering in the squares, gawping at Renaissance mansions and peering up at imposing Baroque and Gothic churches.

The Museu Diocesà and Banys Àrabs

The closest specific sight to the cathedral, the **Museu Diocesà** (in Castilian, *Museo Diocesano*), is a short, signposted walk away on c/Mirador, but barely merits a visit. Situated within the seventeenth-century Bishop's Palace, the museum has an interesting assortment of tenth-century Moorish tiles, but it's mostly stuffed with dull religious artefacts, including some spectacularly unsuccessful sculptures.

A short stroll east from the museum along the city walls brings you to one of the town's medieval gates at the foot of c/Portella. North of the gate, take the first turning right for the **Banys Àrabs**, at c/Can Serra 7. One of the few genuine reminders of the Moorish presence, this tenth-century brick *hammam* consists of a small horseshoe-arched and domed chamber which was once heated through the floor. The remains are reasonably well preserved, but if you've been to the baths in Girona or Granada, these are anticlimactic; the garden outside, with tables where you can picnic, is perhaps nicer.

The Museu Diocesà is open April–Oct Mon–Fri 10am–1.30pm & 3–7pm, Sat 10am–1pm; Nov–March Mon–Fri 10am–1pm & 3–5pm; 200ptas.

The Banys Àrabs is open daily 9.30am–8pm; 125ptas. Bar Sa Murada is a good spot for a drinks break on c/Portella – see p.77.

The Museu de Mallorca

Close by, back on c/Portella, the **Museu de Mallorca** occupies Can Aiamans, a Renaissance mansion whose rambling rooms are a delightful setting for an enjoyable motley of Mallorcan artefacts, the earliest dating from prehistoric times, including a superb assortment of Gothic paintings.

The City

The Museu de Mallorca is open Tues–Sat 10am–2pm & 4–7pm, Sun 10am–2pm; 200ptas.

For more on the Master of the Privileges and the Mallorcan Primitives, see p.67.

Mansions in Palma

Most of medieval Palma was destroyed by fire, so the patrician **mansions** that characterize the old town today generally date from the reconstruction programme of the late seventeenth and early eighteenth centuries. Consequently they were built in the fashionable Renaissance style, with columns and capitals, loggias and arcades tucked away behind outside walls of plain stone, three or four storeys high. Surprisingly uniform in layout, entry to almost all of these mansions was through a great arched gateway that gave onto a rectangular **courtyard** around which the house was built. Originally, the courtyard would have been cheered by exotic trees and flowering shrubs, and equipped with a fancy stone and ironwork well-head, where visitors could water their horses. From the courtyard, a stone outside staircase led up to the main public rooms of the first floor – with the servants' quarters below and the family's private apartments up above.

Very few of these mansions are open to the public, and all you'll see for the most part is the view from the gateway – the municipality have actually started to pay people to leave their big wooden gates open. Several have, however, passed into the public domain, the **Can Aiamans**, now the home of the Museu de Mallorca, being the prime example; others worth making a detour to see are Can Oleza (see p.71), Can Vivot (p.71) and Can Solleric (p.73).

The collection begins on the ground floor, to the right of the entrance, with a few chunks of early Moorish masonry (Room 1) and some beautiful, highly decorated wooden panelling that's representative of Mudéjar artistry (Room 3). Retracing your steps, you'll come across a hotchpotch of prehistoric archeological finds in the room above the entrance desk and, carrying on up the stairs, the first of a couple of rooms devoted to the **Mallorcan Primitive** painters. On display in this first room are works by the Masters of Montesion and Castellitx and, best of the lot, a painting entitled *Santa Quiteria*, whose precisely executed, lifelike figures – down to the wispy beard of the king – are typical of the gifted Master of the Privileges. In the same room, there's also a curious thirteenth-century work of unknown authorship dedicated to St Bernard, with the saint on his knees devotedly drinking the milk of the Virgin Mary.

Beyond a room of religious statues, the second room of Gothic paintings is distinguished by a sequence of works by **Francesch Comes** (1379–1415), whose skill in catching the subtle texture of skin echoes his Flemish contemporaries and represents a softening of the early Mallorcan Primitives' crudeness. In his striking *St George*, the saint – girl-like, with typically full lips – impales a bright green dragon with more horns than could possibly be useful. One of the last talented exponents of the Mallorcan Gothic, the **Master of the Predellas**, is represented by his Bosch-like *Santa Margarita*, each crowd of onlookers a sea of ugly, deformed faces and merciless eyes. Like a cartoon strip, the work outlines the life of

Margaret of Antioch, one of the most venerated saints in medieval Christendom. During the reign of the Roman Emperor Diocletian (284–305 AD), she refused to marry a pagan prefect and was consequently executed after being tortured with extravagant gusto. As if this wasn't enough, she also had to resist more metaphysical trials: Satan, disguised as a dragon, swallowed her, but couldn't digest her holiness, so his stomach opened up and out she popped unharmed. This particular tribulation made Margaret the patron saint of pregnant women.

The Església de Santa Eulalia

Continuing on up the hill from the museum, c/Portella leads to c/Morei where, at no. 9, you'll find the **Can Oleza**, a sixteenth-century mansion with an expansive courtyard embellished by a handsome balustrade and a trio of Ionic columns. Just up the street, it's worth detouring left along c/Almudaina for a peek at the chunky remains of the old east gate, a remnant of the Moorish fortifications, and to see if the renovation of **Can Bordils**, one of the city's oldest mansions, at no. 9, has been completed.

The Can Oleza is not open to the public.

Built on the site of a mosque in the mid-thirteenth century, the **Església de Santa Eulalia** took just 25 years to complete and consequently possesses an architectural homogeneity that's unusual for Palma – though there was some later medieval tinkering, and nineteenth-century renovators added the belfry and remodelled the main (west) facade. The church is typically Gothic in construction, with a yawning nave originally designed – as in the cathedral – to give the entire congregation a view of the high altar. Today, however, the bricked-up windows keep out most of the light and ruin the effect. Framing the nave, the aisles accommodate twelve chapels, several of which – notably the first chapel on the right – sport fine Gothic paintings; in kitsch contrast, the hourglass-shaped high altarpiece is a Baroque extravagance of colossal proportions. This holy ground witnessed one of the more disgraceful episodes of Mallorcan history. During Easter week of 1435, a rumour went round that Jewish townsfolk had enacted a blasphemous mock-up of the Crucifixion. There was no proof, but the Jews were promptly robbed of their possessions and condemned to be burnt at the stake unless they adopted Christianity – the ensuing mass baptism was held at Santa Eulalia.

The Església de Santa Eulalia is open Mon–Fri 7am–1pm & 5–8pm, Sat & Sun 8am–1pm & 6–10pm. See p.67 for more on the saint's life.

Around the corner from the church, at c/Can Savella 2, is the eighteenth-century **Can Vivot**, another opulent mansion, with a main courtyard of red marble columns, graceful arches and a slender staircase.

The Can Vivot is not open to the public.

The Basílica de Sant Francesc

A brief walk away from the Plaça Santa Eulalia along c/Convent de Sant Francesc is the **Basílica de Sant Francesc**, a domineering pile that occupies the site of the old Moorish soap factory. Built for the

The City

The Basílica de Sant Francesc is open daily 9.30am–noon & 3–6pm; 75ptas.

Franciscans towards the end of the thirteenth century, the original church was a vast Gothic edifice which benefited from royal patronage after Jaume II's son, also named Jaume, became a member of the order in 1300. Subsequent Gothic remodellings replaced the initial wooden ceiling with a single-span, vaulted stone roof of imposing dimensions and added stately chapels to the nave and apse. The Basílica became the most fashionable church in medieval Palma and its friars received handsome kickbacks for entombing the local nobility inside its precincts. Increasingly eager to enrich themselves, the priests came to compete for possession of the corpses, while the various aristocratic clans vied with each other in the magnificence of their sarcophagi. These tensions exploded when a clansman, Jaume Armadams, had a jug of water emptied over his head on All Saints' Day, 1490. The congregation, gathered to pray before the tombs of the dead, went berserk and over 300 noblemen fought it out in the nave before the priests finally restored order. The ensuing scandal caused the Basílica to be closed for several years.

In the seventeenth century the church was badly damaged by lightning, prompting a thoroughgoing reconstruction which accounts for most of its present-day appearance. Dating from this period, the main **facade** displays a stunning severity of style, with its great rectangular sheet of dressed sandstone stretching up to an arcaded and balustraded balcony. The facade is pierced by a gigantic rose window of Plateresque intricacy and embellished by a **Baroque doorway**, whose tympanum features a triumphant Virgin Mary engulfed by a wriggling mass of sculptured decoration. Up above the Madonna is the figure of St George and on either side are

---

Ramon Llull

Nothing remains of Llull's foundation, but it's been replaced by the Santuari de Nostra Senyora de Cura – see p.151.

Beloved of Catholic propagandists, the life of **Ramon Llull** (1235–1315) was an exercise in redemption through carnal excess. As a young man, Llull was an ebullient rake in the retinue of the future Jaume II. His sexual adventures were not in the least impeded by his marriage, but they ground to a dramatic halt when, having pursued Ambrosia de Castillo, the woman of his immediate desire, into the church of Santa Eulalia on horseback, she revealed to him her diseased breasts. A deeply shocked Llull devoted the rest of his life to the Catholic faith, becoming a fearless missionary and dedicated scholar of theology, philosophy and alchemy. Exemplifying the cosmopolitan outlook of thirteenth-century Mallorca, Llull learnt to read, write and speak several languages, including Arabic, and travelled to France, much of Spain and North Africa. He also founded a monastery and missionary school on Puig Randa, 35km east of Palma, where he spent ten years in seclusion and wrote no fewer than 250 books and treatises. It was Llull's scholarship that attracted the attention of his old friend Jaume II, who summoned him to court in 1282. With royal patronage, Llull then established a monastic school of Oriental languages near Valldemossa, where he trained his future missionary companions. Llull was killed on his third evangelical excursion to Algeria in 1315, his martyrdom ensuring his subsequent beatification.

---

assorted saints – look out for the scholar and missionary Ramon Llull, who is shown holding a book. The strange statue in front of the doorway – of a Franciscan monk and an American Indian – celebrates the missionary work of **Junipero Serra**, a Mallorcan priest despatched to California in 1768, who subsequently founded San Diego, Los Angeles and San Francisco.

The City

For further details on the life and times of Junipero Serra, see p.153.

The church's interior, approached through a trim Gothic cloister, is disappointingly gloomy – too dark, in fact, to pick out all but the most obvious of its features. You can't, however, miss the monumental high **altar**, a gaudy affair of balustrades, lattice-work and clichéd figurines illustrative of the High Baroque. Less overblown are the rolling scrolls and trumpeteer-angel of the eighteenth-century **pulpit**, on the wall of the nave, and the ornate Gothic-Baroque frontispiece of the nearby organ. The second chapel on the left of the ambulatory shelters the **tomb of Ramon Llull**, whose bones were brought back to Palma after his martyrdom in Algeria in 1315. Considering the sanctity of the man's remains, it's an odd and insignificant-looking affair, with Llull's alabaster effigy set in the wall to the right of the chapel altarpiece at a disconcertingly precarious angle.

Around Passeig d'es Born

Leaving the basilica, you can either wander the labyrinth of ancient side streets that stretches southeast as far as Avinguda Gabriel Alomar i Villalonga; or retrace your steps west to the Plaça Santa Eulalia, from where it's a brief walk along c/Cadena to the elegant nineteenth-century facades of the bustling **Plaça Cort**. One side of the square is dominated by the **Ajuntament** (Town Hall), a debonair example of the late Renaissance style. Pop in for a look at the grand and self-assured foyer, which mostly dates from the nineteenth century, and the folkloric *gigantones* (giant carnival figures) tucked in against the staircase.

It's a five-minute walk from Plaça Cort to the stone sphinxes at the foot of the **Passeig d'es Born**, the city's principal promenade since the early fifteenth century, when the stream that ran here was diverted following a disastrous flash flood. Nowadays, this leafy avenue is too traffic-congested to be endearing, but it's still at the heart of the city, and in the immediate vicinity are some of Palma's most fashionable bars and restaurants. At no. 10, overlooking the *passeig*, is the fine Italianate loggia of **Can Solleric**, a lavish mansion of heavy wooden doors, marble columns and vaulted ceilings built for a family of cattle and olive oil merchants in 1763. Recently restored, the house now displays temporary exhibitions of modern art.

The Can Solleric is open Tues–Sat 11am–1.30pm & 5–8.30pm; free.

El Puig de Sant Pere

West of the Passeig d'es Born, in between Avinguda Jaume III and La Llotja, lies the ancient neighbourhood of **El Puig de Sant Pere** (Saint Peter's Mount), whose narrow lanes and alleys shelter a further group of patrician mansions – though most of the old houses were divided up into apartments years ago to cater for the district's sailors, dockers and fishermen. Specific sights include the late Renaissance facades of **Can Moner** and **Can Pavesi**, at c/Sant Feliu 8 and 10 respectively. There's a gruesome story behind the name of a tiny cul-de-sac off c/Estanc: **La Mà del Moro**, "the hand of the Moor", harks back to Ahmed, an eighteenth-century slave who murdered his master. After the subsequent execution, Ahmed's hand was chopped off and stuck above the doorway of the house down this tiny alley where the murder was committed.

Along Carrer de la Unio

At the top of Passeig d'es Born, the ponderous shopping and office buildings of **Avinguda Jaume III**, dating to the 1940s, march up towards the wide, walled water-channel that bisects the Passeig Mallorca. In the opposite direction, **c/de la Unio** leads to tiny **Plaça Mercat**, the site of two identical *Modernista* buildings, commissioned by a wealthy baker, Josep Casasayas, in 1908. Each is a masterpiece of flowing, organic lines tempered by graceful balconies and decorated with fern leaf and butterfly motifs. Just down the street, on **Plaça Weyler**, stands a further *Modernista* extravagance, the magnificent **Gran Hotel**. Its playful arches and balconies, columns and bay windows are awash with intricate floral trimmings and enlivened by brilliant polychrome ceramics inspired by Hispano-Arabic designs. As well as the offices of *Fundació La Caixa*, the cultural arm of the savings bank, the mundane interior accommodates a flash café-bar and a good art bookshop.

There's another excellent example of *Modernisme* across the street from the Gran Hotel in the floral motifs and gaily painted wooden panels of the **Forn des Teatre** (theatre bakery) at Plaça Weyler 9. Next door looms the Neoclassical frontage of the **Teatre Principal**, the city's main auditorium for classical music, ballet and opera, bearing a fanciful relief dedicated to the nine Muses of Greek mythology.

Beyond the theatre, the main street – now c/de la Riera – does a quick about-face to join the **Passeig de la Rambla**, whose plane trees shelter Palma's main flower market. The two statues at the foot of the boulevard, representing Roman emperors, were placed here in 1937 in honour of Mussolini's Italy – one set of Fascists tipping their municipal hats to another.

Around Plaça Major

From the theatre, a steep flight of steps leads up to **Plaça Major**, a large pedestrianized square built on the site of the headquarters of the Inquisition after their demolition in 1823. The square, a rather plain affair with a symmetrical portico running around its perimeter, once housed the fish and vegetable market, but nowadays it's popular for its pavement cafés.

The busy shopping street of c/Sant Miquel runs north from Plaça Major. Here, at no. 11, the **Banca March** occupies a fine Renaissance mansion whose *Modernista* flourishes date from a tasteful refurbishment of 1917. The building has two entrances, one to the bank, the other to the first-floor gallery of the **Collecció March**, which features part of the contemporary art collection of the March family. Thirty-six works are displayed, each by a different Spanish artist of the twentieth century, the intention being to survey the Spanish contribution to modern art. The earliest piece, *Tête de Femme* (1907), by Picasso, is of particular interest as it's one of the first of the artist's works to be influenced by the primitive forms that were to propel him, over the following decade, from the recreation of natural appearances into abstract art. Miró and Dalí are also represented, but the range of the whole collection, especially in terms of form and material, is quite extraordinary.

If you're in the vicinity, it's worth continuing up c/Sant Miquel to the **Església Sant Miquel**, whose sturdy exterior, the result of all sorts of architectural meddlings, hides a gloomy barrel-vaulted nave and rib-vaulted side chapels. The poorly lit high altarpiece, a Baroque classic with a central image celebrating St Michael, showcases the work of Francesc Herrara, a much-travelled Spanish painter of religious and genre subjects known for his vigorous compositions and tangy realism.

On the south side of Plaça Major lies the much smaller **Plaça Marquès del Palmer**, a cramped setting for two fascinating *Modernista* edifices. At no. 2, **Can Rei** comprises a five-storey apartment building splattered with polychrome ceramics and floral decoration, its centrepiece a gargoyle-like face set between a pair of dragons. The facade of the neighbouring **L'Àguila** building is of similar ilk, though there's greater emphasis on window space, reflecting its original function as a department store.

Continuing south, the shopping area in between Plaça Major and Plaça Cort remains one of the more agreeable parts of Palma. Its old-fashioned air is distilled from the three- and four-storey buildings that flank its main streets – principally **c/Colom** and **c/Jaume II** – embellished with an abundance of fancy iron-grilled balconies.

The Poble Espanyol

A couple of kilometres west of the old town, and reachable by bus #5 – the nearest stop is on c/Andrea Doria – the **Poble Espanyol** (Spanish Village) was built between 1965 and 1967, a kitsch, purpose-made tourist attraction, with Francoist intentions apparent in its celebration of everything Spanish. Walled like a medieval city, the village contains accurate reproductions of about twenty old and important buildings, such as Barcelona's Palau de la Generalitat, Seville's Torre del Oro, a segment of Granada's Alhambra, El Greco's house in Toledo, and the Ermita de San Antonio in Madrid.

The City

The Collecció March is open Mon–Fri 10am–6pm, Sat 10am–1.30pm; 300ptas. Other works from the March family's contemporary collection are displayed at the Parc Casa March in Cala Rajada – see p.160.

The Església Sant Miquel is open daily 8am–1pm & 6–8pm.

The Poble Espanyol is open April–Sept Mon–Sat 9am–8pm; Oct–March Mon–Sat 9am–6pm; 400ptas.

These are woven round the village's streets and squares, where you'll also find craft workshops, souvenir shops, restaurants and bars. It's all a bit daft – and school parties swamp the place – but it's an easy way of introducing yourself to Spanish architecture.

Next door to the village stands the **Palacio de Congresos** (Congressional Hall), a substantial modern complex built in the style of a Roman forum; it's used for official functions and is rarely open to the public.

The Castell de Bellver

The Castell de Bellver is open April–Sept daily 8am–7.30pm; Oct–March daily 8am–5.30pm; 240ptas, but free on Sun, when the castle museum is closed.

Boasting superb views of Palma and its harbour from a wooded hilltop some 3km west of the city centre, the **Castell de Bellver** is a handsome, strikingly well-preserved fortress built for Jaume II at the beginning of the fourteenth century. Of canny circular design, the castle's thick walls accommodate three imposing towers, while an overhead, single-span stone arch connects the main structure to a massive, freestanding keep. Dry moats and embankments add further lines of defence, crossed by footbridges set at oblique angles to each other. The castle was also intended to serve as a royal retreat from the summer heat, and so the austere outside walls hide a commodious circular courtyard, surrounded by two tiers of inward-facing arcades that originally belonged to the residential suites. The whole construction is ingenious, incorporating many skilful touches: the flat roof, for example, was designed to channel every drop of rainwater into a huge underground cistern. Improvements in artillery, however, soon rendered the fortress obsolete, and it didn't last long as a royal residence either. As early as the 1350s the keep was in use as a prison, a function it performed until 1915. More recently, part of the castle has been turned into a modest **museum** featuring a rag-bag of archeological finds and a miscellany of Roman sculpture, originally the collection of the eighteenth-century antiquarian Cardinal Antonio Despuig.

The Castell de Bellver is about 1km south of the Poble Espanyol, though not connected to it by bus. From the city centre, take **bus #3, #4 or #21** to Plaça Gomila, which leaves a steep one-kilometre walk up the hill. If you're driving, turn off Avgda Joan Miró onto the circuitous c/Camilo Jose Cela to reach the castle.

Eating and drinking

Eating in Palma is less pricey – or can be – than anywhere else in the Balearics. Inexpensive **cafés** and **tapas bars** are liberally distributed around the city centre, with a particular concentration in the side streets off the Passeig d'es Born and c/de la Unio. Most visitors eat breakfast in their hotel, so there's not the demand for specialist places you might expect in a big city – though most downtown cafés will be up and running by 9am if not earlier. On the other hand, for light lunches and snacks (*tapas*) you're spoiled for choice. You can chomp away in chic modernist surroundings, or join the crowds in simple formica and glass joints where the food more than compensates for the decor – and then there's everything in between.

The distinction between *tapas* bars and **restaurants** is blurred as many of the latter serve light snacks as well as full meals. Some of Palma's restaurants are geared up for the tourist trade, especially those along the seafront and Avgda d'Antoni Maura; it is, however, unfair to be snooty about them, as some serve delicious food and are popular with Spaniards also. If you venture a little further into the city centre, you'll discover more exclusively local haunts, some offering the finest of Catalan and Spanish cuisine. A smattering of restaurants specialize in ethnic foods such as Swedish and Italian, and there's a couple of vegetarian café-restaurants too. At all but the most expensive of places, 2500ptas will cover the cost of a starter and main course, as well as a bottle of wine – though you can expect prices to be jacked up in the summer.

Cafés and tapas bars

L'Angel Blau, c/Capiscolat. Chic, pint-sized *tapas* bar with classical music and smooth-tasting snacks. You'll walk past the place en route from the cathedral to the Museu Diocesà.

Bar Bosch, Plaça Rei Joan Carles I. One of the most popular and inexpensive *tapas* bars in town, the traditional haunt of intellectuals and usually humming with conversation. At peak times you'll need to be assertive to get served.

Bar Sa Murada, at the foot of c/Portella. Dreary snacks but, if you've been walking the old town, this is a good spot to soak up the sun from the relative quiet of a pedestrianized mini-plaza.

Bon Lloc, c/Sant Feliu 7. One of the few vegetarian café-restaurants on the island, centrally situated off the Passeig d'es Born. Informal atmosphere and good food at low prices. Open Tues–Sat 1 4pm and the odd evening, usually Fri and Sat 9–11pm.

Café Brondo, c/Can Brondo 7. Lively, fashionable *tapas* bar off Plaça Rei Joan Carles I, with the excellent *Restaurante Brondo* downstairs (see below).

Cafeteria Necar, Avgda Jaume III, 21. Popular with office workers and shoppers alike, this unassuming café serves filling snacks and lunches. Open from 8am Mon–Sat.

Ca'n Joan de S'Aigo, c/Can Sanç 10. A long-established coffee house with wonderful, freshly baked *ensaimadas* (spiral pastry buns) for just 85ptas and fruit-flavoured mousses to die for. Charming decor too, from the stylish water fountain to the traditional Mallorcan green-tinted chandeliers. C/Can Sanç is a tiny alley near Plaça Santa Eulalia; take c/Sant Crist and its continuation c/Canisseria, and turn right. Closed Tues.

Click Café-Restaurant, Passeig Mallorca 8, near the junction with Avgda Jaume III. Garishly painted modern café serving mundane food at bargain-basement prices. Open till late at night and on Sun.

Mayurqa, c/Sant Roc, northeast of the cathedral. Newly opened *tapas* bar, with old stone walls and squeaky modern furniture, which looks set to become a real humdinger.

Mesón Carlos I, c/Apuntadors 16. Traditional Spanish *tapas*, and good steaks, in timber-vaulted old house off the Passeig d'es Born.

Eating and drinking

Mesón Salamanca, c/Sant Jaume 3. Mostly Castilian cuisine in a tastefully refurbished, warren-like mansion off Avgda Jaume III. Delicious *tapas* on the ground floor (avoid the overpriced, stuffy restaurant upstairs).

Orient Express, c/Llotja de Mar 6, behind La Llotja. Idiosyncratic café-restaurant with an interior like the inside of a railway carriage. Salads, slightly overpriced, are its speciality; you'll have to wait for a seat at lunchtime.

El Pilon, c/Cifre 4. Vibrant, crowded *tapas* bar with the emphasis on Mallorcan dishes, on a side street off the north end of Passeig d'es Born.

Raixa, c/Can Savella 8. Wholesome, good-value vegetarian food, near the Basílica de Sant Francesc. Mon–Sat 1.30–4pm.

El Rey, Avgda Jaume III, opposite the tourist office. The best take-away pizza slices in town, a snip at 200ptas; or eat at the cramped café inside, where a whole pizza will set you back around 800ptas.

Verd de Llimona, c/Montenegro 7. Laid-back *tapas* bar open till late at night, but a little difficult to find: c/Montenegro is off c/Sant Feliu, a side street off the Passeig d'es Born.

La Zamorana, c/Apuntadors 14. Inexpensive *tapas* bar, one of several on this stretch, in a stucco cellar with hocks of meat hanging from the ceiling.

Restaurants

Asador Tierra Aranda, c/Concepció 4, off Avgda Jaume III; ☎714256. A high-class, carnivore's paradise in an old mansion: meats either grilled over open fires or roasted in wood-fired ovens, with suckling pig a speciality. Closed at lunchtime; dinner from 8pm.

La Bodega Santurce, c/Concepció 34; ☎710801. Unpretentious restaurant, with no menu, serving filling platters of Basque food at reasonable rates. Be prepared to share your table with other diners. Opening times are hard to fathom, but it's centrally situated, just off Avgda Jaume III.

Caballito del Mar, opposite La Llotja at Passeig Sagrera 5. Superb selection of seafood in trim, no-nonsense surroundings, with excellent, friendly service. Main courses around 2000ptas, but not to be missed.

Ca'n Eduardo, Moll Industria Pesquera 4; ☎721182. No-frills restaurant beside the fish market, with an enjoyable view of the harbour – it's across Avgda Gabriel Roca from the bottom of the gardens adjoining Avgda Argentina. Wonderful range of fresh fish, all simply prepared; tasty *menú del día* at around 2500ptas. Closed Sun and Mon.

Casa Gallega, c/Can Pueyo 6, north off Plaça Weyler. Quality Galician cuisine, particularly the seafood, in a downstairs *tapas* bar and upstairs restaurant.

Celler Sa Premsa, Plaça Bisbe Berenguer de Palou 8. Justly popular restaurant with delicious seafood, a 5-min walk west of the Plaça Espanya. Old bull-fighting photos and posters adorn the walls amidst a pot-pourri of dusty bygones; you'll probably share a table with other diners. Prices are surprisingly low – as little as 1600ptas per person for a three-course meal.

Celler Pagès, off c/Apuntadors at c/Felip Bauza 2. Traditional Mallorcan food in a tiny, inexpensive restaurant near Passeig d'es Born. Easy-going atmosphere, though stifling hot in the summer. Closed Sun.

Chez Sophie, c/Apuntadors 24. A wide variety of crepes, from just 400ptas, is this restaurant's speciality.

Forn de Sant Joan, c/Sant Joan 4. Extremely popular Catalan restaurant near La Llotja, one of several busy spots on this narrow alley. Fine fish dishes for around 1900ptas, *tapas* from 850ptas.

Los Gauchos, c/Sant Magí 78. At least once during your stay in Palma, it's worth trying out South American (ie Spanish colonial) cuisine. This unassuming Argentine restaurant is one of the best, though it's very meaty – steaks and brochettes of lamb are the specialities. It's in the slightly dilapidated district of Es Jonquet, the old fishermen's quarter just west of Avgda Argentina.

Es Parlament, c/Conquistador 11. All gilt-wood mirrors and chandeliers, this old and polished restaurant specializes in paella. The tasty and reasonably priced *menú del día* is recommended too. A favourite hangout of local politicians and lawyers.

Porto Pi, Avgda Joan Miró 174; ☎400087. Many swear this is the best restaurant in Palma – the prices certainly match the billing (reckon on 6000ptas per person and up) and you should dress fairly smartly. But the food is excellent, international nouvelle cuisine at its most imaginative. Located a couple of kilometres west of the city centre along the waterfront.

Restaurante Brondo, c/Can Brondo 7. Beneath the *tapas* bar of the same name, this restaurant is a real treat: the menu is imaginative, but broadly Catalan in style, and every dish is carefully prepared and presented.

Svarta Pannan, c/Can Brondo 5. Comfortable Swedish restaurant conveniently close to Plaça Rei Joan Carles I. The food isn't remarkable, but makes a refreshing change.

Nightlife and entertainment

Most of the cafés and all the *tapas* bars detailed above are quite happy just to ply you with drink, making the distinction between these establishments and the bars we've listed separately below somewhat artificial. Nonetheless, there's a cluster of lively **late-night bars** – mostly with music as the backdrop rather than the main event – amongst the narrow and ancient side streets backing onto Plaça Llotja. A second concentration of slightly more upmarket bars embellishes the bayside modernity of Avgda Gabriel Roca, between the *Club de Mar* marina and tiny Parc Cuarentena, about 3km west of the city centre. The grimy suburb of El Terreno, also west of the centre, below the Castell de Bellver, once accommodated Palma's best late-night bars. The district has gone downhill, and now features topless "entertainment" and porn shops, but it still possesses the occasional offbeat, hippy-flavour bar.

Nightclubs (*discotecas*) are not Palma's forte, but there are one or two of some merit in El Terreno and on Avgda Gabriel Roca. They're rarely worth investigating until around 1am and entry charges will rush you anything between 500ptas and 1000ptas, depending on the night and what's happening. The doormen often operate an informal dress code of one sort or another – if you want to get in, avoid beach gear.

Traditionally, Palma has had little to offer in terms of **performing arts**, but matters are on the mend with the resuscitation of the grand nineteenth-century *Teatre Principal*, Plaça Weyler 16 (booking office ☎725548; tickets 2500–7000ptas), which features classical concerts and opera, and the revamping of the *Teatre Municipal*, Passeig Mallorca 9B (☎739148), which has a more varied programme of contemporary drama, classic films, dance and ballet.

Late-night bars

Abacanto, Camí Son Nicolau, Indioteria. All flowers, fruit and subdued lighting, this long-established bar is in the same vein as *Ábaco*, below. Tucked away near an industrial estate in the suburb of Indioteria, off the Inca road, it's well-nigh impossible to find – take a taxi. Drinks about 1600ptas each.

Ábaco, just off c/Apuntadors at c/Sant Joan 1. Easily Palma's most unusual bar, with an interior straight out of a Busby Berkeley musical: fruits cascading down its stairway, caged birds hidden amid patio foliage, elegant music and a daily flower bill you could live on for a month. Drinks, as you might imagine, are extremely expensive but you're never hurried into buying one.

La Boveda, c/La Boteria, off Plaça Llotja. Classy, bustling bar, one of several on this short alley, with long, wide windows and wine stacked high along the back wall.

Es Cantó, Plaça Llotja. Candle-lit patio/pavement tables add a touch of romance to this pleasant bar.

El Gallo, Avgda Gabriel Roca. Café-bar, sometimes hectic, with strikingly bright and avant-garde furnishings and fittings, a couple of hundred metres east of Parc Cuarentena.

El Globo, at the junction of c/Apuntadors and c/Felip Bauza. Cramped and bustling with modern jazz as the soundtrack.

Latitude 39, c/Felip Bauza off c/Apuntadors. Tiny, upbeat bar, playing jazz, blues and sometimes classical music.

La Lonja, opposite La Llotja. A popular, well-established haunt, with revolving doors and pleasantly old-fashioned decor; the background music caters for (almost) all tastes.

Rustic, Plaça Mediterraneo, El Terreno. Pint-sized neighbourhood bar with lively atmosphere and reasonably priced drinks.

Ses Voltes, Parc de la Mar. Open-air spot which often has live acts – pop, jazz and rock to varying standards.

Twins, c/Sant Joan 7. Fashionable place with an upbeat tempo and boisterous crowd.

XL, Avgda Gabriel Roca, next door to Parc Cuarentena. Classy hangout with highly conspicuous, abstract decor featuring a series of geometrically arranged poles. Quality cocktails and an upmarket clientele.

Nightclubs

Club de Mar, at *Club de Mar* marina on Avgda Gabriel Roca. Smart, polished nightclub, sometime haunt of the rich and famous – dress up.

Discoteca Luna, Avgda Gabriel Roca 42. Loud and raucous disco with two bars inside and another couple outside in the garden.

Tito's Palace, Plaça Gomila 3, El Terreno, with a side entrance (via outdoor lifts) on Avgda Gabriel Roca. Long-established dance hall drawing huge crowds from many countries. The music lacks conviction, but it's certainly loud.

Waikiki, Plaça Mediterraneo, El Terreno. A laid-back nightclub behind a bizarre Polynesian-style facade. Live and soundtrack soul, jazz and R&B.

Listings

Airlines *Air France*, Avgda Jaume III, 16 (☎713500); *British Midland*, Avgda Joan Miró 16 (☎453122; airport ☎452764); *Iberia*, Passeig d'es Born 10 (☎262600); *Lufthansa*, Plaça Rosari 5, 3è (☎722840); *Sabena*, same office as *Air France*; *SAS*, Avgda Joan Miró 16 (☎452764).

Airport information Central switchboard ☎264666.

American Express At *Viajes Iberia*, Passeig d'es Born 14 (☎726743).

Banks There are plenty of banks on and around the Passeig d'es Born and Avgda Jaume III. *Banco de Credito Balear* has branches at Avgda Jaume III, 27, and Plaça Espanya 4; *Banca March* at Plaça Rei Joan Carles I, 5, and c/Sant Miquel 11; *Banco de Santander* at c/Jaume II, 18, and c/Bonaire 2. There are also British banks, with *Lloyds* at Passeig Mallorca 4 and *Barclays* sharing the premises of the *Banco de Credito Balear* at Avgda Jaume III, 27. The two biggest savings banks, which also handle currency exchange, have branches all over the city. *La Caixa* has a handy downtown branch at Passeig d'es Born 23; for *Sa Nostra* go to Avgda Jaume III, 18. There are 24-hour cash card and credit card machines dotted round the city too.

Beaches The closest beach to the city centre is the narrow strip of sand next to the *autopista* just beyond Avgda Gabriel Alomar i Villalonga. Swimming is not, however, recommended here as the water is too polluted. Instead most locals make the 20-min trip on bus #15 to the Platja de Palma (see p.84).

Bicycles Rent them at *Ciclos Bimont*, Plaça Progrés 19 (☎450505), for around 3000ptas a day, 12,000ptas a week. About a dozen shops sell bicycles, one of the biggest being *Ciclos Mallorca*, at c/Victor Pradera 22 (☎771713), and c/Joan Alcover 23 (☎467616). Go to *Maimó*, off Avgda Argentina at c/Pursiana 9 (☎730294), for repairs.

Bullfights Palma's bullfighting ring, Plaça Toros (☎751639), is a few blocks northeast of the Plaça Espanya along c/Reina Maria Cristina. Tickets and details from travel agents and hotel receptions.

Buses Details of all major Mallorcan bus services are available from the main tourist offices. City transit (*EMT*) enquiries on ☎295700; island-wide bus service information on ☎752224.

Car rental Mallorca's four biggest car rental companies have offices at the airport: *Atesa* (☎266100); *Avis* (☎260910); *Betacar* (☎743637); and *Hertz* (☎260809). In the city, there's a concentration – including many small concerns – along Avgda Gabriel Roca: *Hertz* are at no. 13 (☎732374); *Avis* at no. 16 (☎730720); and *Betacar* at no. 20 (☎737594). *Budget* are at c/de Manacor 40 (☎770700). The tourist office will supply a complete list of rental companies.

Cinema *ABC*, Avgda Alexandre Rossello 38 (☎464527), presents mainstream Spanish films, plus international blockbusters, usually dubbed.

Consulates *Belgium*, Passeig d'es Born 15, 1–C (☎7244786); *Germany*, Passeig d'es Born 15, 6è (☎722371); *Ireland*, c/Sant Miquel 68A (☎722504); *Netherlands*, Plaça Rosari 5, 2 (☎716493); *United Kingdom*, Plaça Major 3D (☎712445); *USA*, Avgda Jaume III, 26 (☎722660).

Dentists A comprehensive list of dentists (*dentistas*) is printed in the local yellow pages. A 24-hr referral service is provided by *Urgencias Dentales*, Avgda Joan Miró 294 (☎701558).

Doctors For a complete list look under *medicos* in the yellow pages. In the resort areas, most hotel receptions will be able to find an English-speaking doctor.

Emergencies *Creu Roja* (Red Cross) ☎202222 for an ambulance; **firefighters** ☎080; **police** (*Policia Municipal*) ☎092.

Ferries The main tourist offices have ferry schedules and tariffs. Tickets can usually be purchased at travel agents or direct from the ferry lines, which both have offices at the ferry port, about 4km west of the city centre. From Terminal 2, *Trasmediterranea* (Mon–Fri 8am–8pm, Sat 8am–1pm; ☎405014) operate ferries to Menorca, Ibiza, Tarragona, Barcelona and Valencia. From the adjacent Terminal 3, *Flebasa* (Mon–Fri 7.30am–1.30pm & 4.30–8pm, Sat & Sun 7.30am–1pm; ☎405360) sail to Ibiza and Dénia.

Hospital *Hospital General*, Plaça Hospital 3 (☎723806).

Listings

Laundry The most convenient self-service laundry is *Self-Press* at c/Annibal 14, off Avgda Argentina.

Library There's a library inside the Ajuntament (Town Hall) on Plaça Cort (Mon–Fri 8.30am–8.30pm, Sat 9am–1pm). Mallorca's main library, the Biblioteca Publica de Mallorca, is near the Basílica of Sant Francesc at c/Ramón Llull 3 (same times).

Maps and books *Librería Fondevila*, Costa de Sa Pols 18 (Mon–Fri 9.30am–1.30pm & 4.30–8pm, Sat 10am–1.30pm; ☎725616), has a wide selection of guidebooks and general maps of Mallorca, as well as a fairly good assortment of walking maps.

Markets Palma's big Rastrillo (flea market) is held every Sat morning, 8am–2pm, on Avgda Gabriel Alomar i Villalonga, between Plaça Porta d'es Camp and c/Manacor. There's a fresh fruit and vegetable market on Plaça Navegació, just west of Avgda Argentina, Mon–Sat 7am–2pm; a daily flower market on Passeig de la Rambla; and local farmers bring their produce (including animals for slaughter) to Plaça Pere Garau, a 15-min walk southeast of Plaça Espanya, on Tues, Thurs and Sat 7am–2pm.

Mopeds *RTR Rental*, Avgda Joan Miró 338 (☎402585).

Pharmacies *Farmacia Castañer*, Plaça Rei Joan Carles I, 3; *Farmacia Llobera*, Plaça Santa Eulalia 1; and *Farmacia Muret Mayoral*, Plaça Weyler 10. There's a *farmacia homeopatica* (homeopathic pharmacy) north of the city centre along Avgda Argentina, at c/Balanguera 3.

Post office The central *correu* is at c/La Constitució 5 (Mon–Fri 9am–9pm, Sat 9am–1pm).

Shopping Palma isn't big enough to sustain a wide range of special-interest shops, but the tourist office's island-wide leaflet "Artesanía" usefully lists shops by category – everything from fancy dress suppliers to crafts and record stores. In the city centre, porcelain and chinaware are sold at *Nacar*, Avgda Jaume III, 5; imitation pearls manufactured in Manacor (see p.154) at *Majorica*, Avgda Jaume III, 11; and the handiest record shop is *Palma Rock*, Avgda Argentina 18. There's a good toy shop, *Arlequin*, at c/de la Unio 5, and you can buy a camera and get your films developed at, amongst many places, *Casa Vila*, Avgda Jaume III, 10. The biggest department store in town is *Galerias Preciados*, Avgda Jaume III, 15 (Mon–Sat 10am–9pm).

Taxis Taxi ranks can be found outside major hotels. Alternatively, telephone *Taxis Palma* (☎401414) or *Radio Taxi* (☎755440).

Trains The tourist office has train timetable details or you can phone direct: Palma to Inca ☎752245; Palma to Sóller ☎752051.

Travel agencies There are scores of travel agents in Palma, listed in full in the yellow pages under *viajes agencias*. Two helpful downtown choices are *Wagons-Lits Cook*, Avgda d'Antoni Maura 16 (☎721842), and *Viajes Iberia*, Passeig d'es Born 14 (☎780448).

Weather Regional weather forecast on ☎094.

Wine Many shops and most supermarkets carry a reasonable range of Spanish wines. For a wider selection, the best place in town is *El Centro del Vino y del Cava*, c/Bartomeu Rossello-Porcel 19 (Mon–Fri 9am–1.30pm & 4.30–8pm, Sat 9am–1.30pm; ☎452990).

Around Palma

Arched around the sheltered waters of the **Badia de Palma** are the package tourist resorts that have made Mallorca synonymous with the cheap and tacky. In recent years the Balearic government have done their best to improve matters – greening resorts, restricting

high-rise construction, and redirecting traffic away from the coast –
but their inherited problems remain. In the 1960s and 1970s, the
bay experienced a building boom of almost unimaginable proportions as miles of pristine shoreline mushroomed concrete and glass
hotel towers, overwhelming the area's farms and fishing villages.
There were few (if any) planning controls and the legacy is the
mammoth sprawl of development that now extends, almost without
interruption, from S'Arenal in the east to Magaluf in the west – with
Palma roughly in the middle.

This thirty-kilometre-long stretch of coast is divided into a score
or more resorts, though it's often impossible to pick out where one
begins and the other ends. Nevertheless, most of the resorts have
evolved their own identities, either in terms of the nationalities they
attract, the income group they appeal to, or the age range they cater
for. **S'Arenal**, to the **east of Palma**, is mainly German, and concentrates on the bargain-basement youth scene with dozens of pound-
ing bars and discos open right through the night. One of Mallorca's
best **beaches**, the **Platja de Palma**, stretches west from S'Arenal as
far as **Ca'n Pastilla**. Yet, although the beach is superb, the flat
shoreline behind accommodates an ugly, seemingly endless strip of
restaurants, bars and souvenir shops.

West of Palma, the coast bubbles up into the low, rocky hills
and sharp coves that prefigure the mountains further west. The
sandy beaches here are far smaller – and some are actually artificial – but the terrain makes the tourist development seem less
oppressive. **Cala Major**, the first stop, was once the playground of
the jet set. It's hit hard times, and some of the grand old buildings
are in a sorry state of repair, but the **Fundació Pilar i Joan Miró**,
originally the home of Joan Miró and now an exhibition area for his
work, makes a fascinating detour. The neighbouring resort of
Illetes sports comfortable hotels and attractive cove beaches while,
moving west again, **Portals Nous** has an affluent and exclusive air
born of its flash marina. Next comes British-dominated **Palma
Nova**, a major package holiday destination popular with all ages,
and then youthful, very British and seedy **Magaluf**, where modern
high-rise hotels and thumping nightlife back a substantial sandy
beach. South of Magaluf there's a real surprise, for here at last is a
small portion of the coast that's not been developed – a pine-
studded peninsula sheltering the charming cove beach of **Portals
Vells**.

West of Magaluf, the coastal highway leaves the Bay of Palma
for the dreary villa-land of **Santa Ponça**, and **Peguera** beyond, a
large resort with attractive sandy beaches and a relaxed family
atmosphere. Next door, tiny **Cala Fornells** occupies a handsome
wooded cove, while just 3km along the highway lies **Camp de Mar**,
a pleasantly small-scale resort in an impressively large bay.

Although these resorts boast hundreds of **hotels**, *hostals* and
apartment buildings, nearly all are block-booked by the package

*Camp de Mar is
the last
significant
development
within Palma's
orbit – further
west the
scenery
assumes a
hillier, prettier
aspect as you
approach
Andratx or
Port d'Andratx
(covered in the
"Northwest
Mallorca"
chapter).*

tourist industry from June – sometimes May – to September or October, with frugal pickings for the independent traveller. Out of season, many places simply close down, but at those which remain open, it's well worth haggling over the price. In the account that follows we've selected some of the more interesting and enjoyable package hotels, as well as picking out several relatively inexpensive places where there's a reasonable chance of finding a vacancy independently in high season. We've concentrated on three smallish resorts where the tourist development is not too oppressive, Illetes, Cala Fornells and Camp de Mar, each with – or within easy striking distance of – a good sandy beach with safe bathing. Nightlife hasn't been a prime concern in this selection as the liveliest discos and clubs are, as a general rule, concentrated in the tackier spots.

There are hundreds of **restaurants** and cafés too, though the choice is not as diverse as you might expect. The vast majority serve either low-price pizzas and pastas or a sort of pan-European tourist menu. For the most part, standards are not very high, the dishes uninspired.

With Palma's Plaça Espanya as the hub, public **transport** along the coast is fast and efficient. *EMT* bus #15 travels the old coastal road through Ca'n Pastilla to S'Arenal, #21 heads west as far as Palma Nova, and #3 runs through Cala Major to Illetes. Another company, *Catalina Marques* (☎296417), operates the so-called "Playa Sol" routes, with frequent services to Magaluf, Santa Ponça, Peguera and Camp de Mar. **Driving** is straightforward too: the *autopista* shoots along the coast from S'Arenal to Palma Nova; or you can take the old coastal road (the C719 west of Palma), which meanders through most of the resorts at a snail's pace.

East to S'Arenal

The *autopista* heads east out of Palma between tourist resorts and the airport, with hundreds of mostly ruined windmills, built to pump water out of the marshy topsoil, being the only reminders of more pastoral days. The old coastal road – take the signposted turning off the *autopista* just beyond the city walls – sticks to the shore, tracking through the gritty suburbs of Portixol and El Molinar en route to CALA GAMBA, an unassuming township with a pleasant hoop-shaped harbour. Close by, CA'N PASTILLA is the first substantial tourist resort on this part of the coast. Its fifty-odd hotels and apartment buildings occupy a rough rectangle of land pushed tight against the seashore. The place is short on charm – and certainly too close to the airport for sonic comfort – but it does herald the start of the fine Platja de Palma.

S'Arenal

The **Platja de Palma**, the four-kilometre stretch of sandy beach that defines the three coterminous (and indistinguishable) resorts of SOMETIMES, LAS MARAVILLAS and S'ARENAL, is crowded with

serious sun-seekers, a sweating throng of bronzed and oiled bodies
slowly roasting in the heat. The beach is also a busy pick-up point,
the spot for a touch of verbal foreplay before the night-time binge-
ing begins. It is, as they say, fine if you like that sort of thing –
though older visitors look rather marooned. Running behind the
beach is a long main drag of bars, restaurants and souvenir shops,
so devoid of character that it's easy to become disoriented. To maintain your bearings, keep an eye out for the series of beach bars,
each numbered and labelled, in Castilian, *"balneario"*, strung along
the shore: Balneario no. 1 is by the Ca'n Pastilla marina, no. 9
beside S'Arenal harbour.

Singling out any part of this massive complex is a pretty pointless exercise, but the area around S'Arenal harbour does at least
have a concentration of **facilities**. There's car rental, currency
exchange, boat trips and nightclubs, and you can eat well at the
lively terrace bar of the harbourside *Club Nautico*, where the paella
is mouthwatering. The nearby *Pizzeria Italia II*, off the esplanade
at c/Berlin 6, is reliable and much less expensive, but for something
rather more distinctive, you'll have to head west to Ca'n Pastilla,
where the *O'Polpo*, off the resort's main drag at c/Singladura 21, is
an excellent Galician restaurant serving the finest seafood. S'Arenal
also boasts **Aquacity**, a huge leisure complex of swimming pools,
water flumes and kiddies' playgrounds, beside *autopista* exit 13.

*Aquacity is
open May daily
10am–5pm;
June–Sept
daily
10am–6pm;
1600ptas.*

All three resorts extend a few blocks inland to encompass dozens
of **places to stay**. The cheapest accommodation is provided by the
youth hostel, the *Playa de Palma*, at c/Costa Brava 13, Sometimes
(June–Sept; ☎260892; ①). To get there, take *EMT* bus #15 from
Plaça Espanya for the twenty-minute trip to the resort, and get off at
the nearby *Hotel Royal Cristina*; on foot, it's off the main road –
here c/Marbella – and a couple of minutes' walk from the beach
between Balneario no. 4 and no. 5. The hostel is fairly spick and
span, but it only has 65 beds so advance reservations are strongly
recommended. At the other end of the market, the four-star *Royal
Cristina*, on Arenas de Bilbao (☎492550; ⑧), offers luxury apartments and hotel rooms. Mid-range options include the comfortable,
two-star *Hotel Bahamas*, a ten-minute walk inland from the harbour
on Avgda d'Europa (mid-Jan to Sept; ☎263200; ⑤); the no-frills
Hotel Residencia Magallanes, c/Cannas 2 (May–Oct; ☎261468;
④), in the gritty side streets about 300m behind Balneario no. 8; and
the three-star *Hotel Torre Azul*, c/Sant Bartoloméu 24 (April–Oct;
☎269085; ⑥), a commodious establishment with its own pool about
350m behind S'Arenal harbour.

West to Cala Major and Gènova

Grimy **CALA MAJOR** snakes along a hilly stretch of coastline a kilometre or two beyond Palma's ferry port. Overlooking the main
street (a section of the C719 coast road), occasional *Modernista*
mansions and the Palau Marivent, still owned by the king of Spain,

Around Palma

The Fundació Pilar i Joan Miró, c/Juan de Saridakis 29, is open from mid-May to mid-Sept Tues–Sat 10am–7pm, Sun 10am–3pm; mid-Sept to mid-May Tues–Sat 11am–6pm, Sun 11am–2pm; 600ptas. EMT bus #20 passes the entrance 4 times daily.

are reminders of halycon days, but the present is more accurately represented by the fate of the *Hotel Nixe Palace*: once a byword for elegance, it lies abandoned and falling to bits.

At the east end of Cala Major, close to the *autopista*, a sign-posted turning leads up the hill the half-kilometre to the **Fundació Pilar i Joan Miró**, where Miró lived and worked for much of the 1960s and 1970s. Initially – from 1920 – the young Miró was involved with the Surrealists in Paris and contributed to all their major exhibitions: his wild calligraphy, supercharged with bright colours, prompted André Breton, the leading theorist of the movement, to describe Miró as "the most Surrealist of us all". In the 1930s he adopted a simpler style, abandoning the decorative complexity of his earlier work for a more minimalist use of symbols, though the highly coloured forms remained. Miró returned to Barcelona, the city of his birth, in 1940, where he continued to work in the Surrealistic tradition. Even from the relative isolation of Franco's Spain, he remained an influential figure, prepared to experiment with all kinds of media, right up until his death in Cala Major in 1983.

With views over the bay, the expansive hillside premises of the Fundació include Miró's old **studio**, an unassuming affair that has been left pretty much as it was at the time of his death. It's worth a quick gander for a flavour of how the man worked – tackling a dozen or so canvases at the same time – but unfortunately you're only allowed to peer through the windows. Opposite are the angular lines of the bright-white art gallery, the **Edificio Estrella**, which displays a rotating and representative sample of the artist's work drawn from a prodigious supply – Miró was nothing if not productive.

The Fundació holds 134 paintings, 300 engravings and 105 drawings, as well as sculptures, gouaches and preliminary sketches, more than 6000 works in all. There are no guarantees as to what will be on display, but you're likely to see a decent selection of his paintings, the familiar dream-like squiggles and half-recognizable shapes that are intended to conjure up the unconscious, with free play often given to erotic associations. The gallery also stores a comprehensive collection of Miró documents and hosts prestigious exhibitions.

Carrying on up the hill past the Fundació Miró, it's just over a kilometre to the village of **GÈNOVA**, a scrawny sort of place offering views of Palma down below and, rather surprisingly, several good **restaurants**. The pick of the bunch are the two *Ca'n Pedros*: the original, with its hanging smoked meats and old bullfighting posters, in the centre of the village, and a newer branch, at the top of the hill, which boasts an open-air terrace. At both, the speciality is snails, but the grilled meats are delicious too, and the *menú del día* will only set you back about 1000ptas.

Illetes

At **ILLETES**, just along the coast from Cala Major and 7km from Palma, a ribbon of restaurants, hotels and apartment buildings bestrides the steep hills that rise high above the rocky shoreline. There's precious little space left, but at least the generally low-rise buildings here are of manageable proportions. A string of tiny cove beaches punctuates the coast, the most attractive being the pine-shaded **Platja Cala Comtesa**, at the southern end of the resort, next door to a restricted military zone. The long main street, Passeig d'Illetes, runs past several good hotels. The most enjoyable is the *Bon Sol* (☎402111; ⑧), about halfway along, which tumbles down the cliffs to the seashore and its own artificial beach. A family-run concern, the hotel has all the conveniences you could want and the better rooms have fine views out over the bay. The clientele is staid and steady, befitting the antique-crammed interior. Another good choice is the *Hotel Albatros* (☎402211; ⑧), located near the north end of Passeig d'Illetes, where the rooms have balconies and air conditioning, there's a swimming pool and private access to the sea. There are similar facilities at the luxurious, four-star *Hotel Bonanza Playa* (☎401112; ⑨), overlooking the seashore close to the *Bon Sol*, while equally spacious lodgings are to be found a couple of minutes' walk south along the coast at the attractive *Hotel-residencia Illetes* (April–Oct; ☎402350; ⑧). For something less expensive, try the mundanely modern *Hotel Sol Playa Marina* (☎402700; ⑥), near the *Bon Sol*. Most visitors eat where they sleep, but there's a smattering of smart cafés on the main drag, including *Es Parral*, which serves Mallorcan cuisine from premises towards the south end of the resort. Far more expensive is the splendid *Restaurant Bonaire d'Illetes*, about halfway along the main street, whose speciality is oven-baked meat dishes.

Bendinat and Portals Nous

The C719 skirts Illetes but cuts through the peripheries of **BENDINAT**, a couple of kilometres further along the coast. On the south side of the road, the resort's leafy streets meander down to the seashore, lined by the villas of the well-to-do. It's a pretty spot and tucked away on a quiet, rocky cove is the charming *Hotel Bendinat*, c/Rossegada (May–Oct; ☎675725; ⑦), dating from the 1950s and built in the traditional hacienda style, with a beautiful arcaded terrace overlooking the sea. You can stay either in the main building, where most of the bedrooms have balconies, or in one of the trim, whitewashed bungalows that dot the gardens.

On its west side, Bendinat merges with the larger **PORTALS NOUS**, another ritzy settlement where polished mansions fill out the green and hilly terrain abutting the coast. There's a tiny beach too, set beneath the cliffs and reached via a flight of steps at the foot of c/Passatge del Mar. In contrast to the studied elegance of the side streets, the resort's main drag (also the C719) is disappointingly drab, though it does lead to the glitzy marina, one of Mallorca's most exclusive, where the boats look more like ocean liners than pleasure yachts. Close by, **Marineland** is one of the tackiest but

Marineland is open June–Aug daily 9.30am–6.45pm; Sept–Nov & Jan–May daily 9.30am–6pm; 1500ptas.

most popular attractions on the island, with shark tanks, crocodile pounds and an aquarium, as well as exploitative dolphin, sealion and parrot shows. Kids love the place; adults mostly suffer in silence.

Portals Nous has a number of three-star **hotels**, but, with much of the shoreline occupied by affluent private villas and apartments, they're restricted to the side streets, well away from the sea. Pick of the bunch is the comfortable *Fabiola*, c/Flores (☎675825; ⑤), set in the middle of the wealthiest part of town. The three-star *Hostal Portals*, inland from the main square, Plaça Espanya, at Avgda de América 15 (May–Oct; ☎676252; ④), is a good choice further down the price scale. For **food**, try the rows of restaurants and bars down at the marina. Some are exorbitantly overpriced, but *Esdi's*, Local no. 29, serves great seafood dishes from around 1800ptas.

Palma Nova and Calvià

Old Mallorca hands claim that **PALMA NOVA**, 4km from Portals Nous, was once a beauty spot, and certainly its wide and shallow bay, with good beaches among a string of bumpy headlands, still has its moments. But for the most part, the bay has been engulfed by a broad, congested sweep of hotels and tourist facilities. With the development comes a vigorous nightlife and a plethora of accommodation on or near the seashore – though, as elsewhere, most places are block-booked by tour operators throughout the season. The summertime **tourist office** (Mon–Fri 9am–1pm & 2.30–5pm; ☎682365), beside the beach on Passeig de la Mar, has supplies of "Wot's On", a monthly freebie detailing local events and entertainments, and issues free maps marking all the **hotels**. The nearby *Sol Trópico*, also on Passeig de la Mar though just off the seafront (☎680512; ⑥), is a well-maintained and good-looking modern hotel. Other options include the four-star *Hotel Sol Comodoro*, Passeig Cala Blanca (April–Oct; ☎680200; ⑦), a standard-issue tower with balconied double rooms looking out over the bay, and the comparable three-star *Hotel Aquarium*, Passeig de la Mar (April–Oct; ☎680308; ⑦), which faces the beach at the centre of the resort. As you might expect, prices drop as soon as you leave the seashore, at places such as the giant *Hotel Sol Mirlos* on c/Pinzones, a five-minute walk from the beach (☎681900; ⑥), and its identical neighbour *Hotel Sol Tordos* (April–Oct; ☎680250; ⑥).

Among scores of **restaurants**, *Tabú*, Passeig de la Mar 28, is one of the best, serving well-prepared standards at reasonable prices. Another good option is *Ciro's*, across the street at no. 3, a rather more formal – and expensive – restaurant, where the seafood can be relied upon and the terrace overlooks the sea.

Just 6km north of Palma Nova, tucked away in the hills behind the coast, is the tiny town of **CALVIÀ**, the region's administrative centre – hence the oversized town hall, paid for by the profits of the tourist industry. The parish church of **Sant Joan** dominates the town, its greying stone dating from 1245, though the Gothic subtleties mostly disappeared during a nineteenth-century refurbishment. Opposite the church, *Bar Rosita* serves coffee and cakes, and just down the hill, the excellent *Méson Ca'n Torrat* (closed Tues) specializes in roast legs of lamb. *EMT* bus #20 links Calvià with Palma via Palma Nova four times daily.

Magaluf and Portals Vells

Torrenova, on the chunky headland at the far end of Palma Nova, is a cramped and untidy development that slides into MAGALUF, whose high-rise towers march across the next bay down the coast. The local administration have recently tried their best to improve Magaluf's appearance, but there's not much they can do with the grim, flat, sprawling modern centre and a beach suffering from an acute excess of concrete. It doesn't help either that the resort's British visitors appear determined to create – or at least patronize – a bizarre caricature of their homeland: it's all here, from beans on toast with Marmite to pubs like *Tom Brown's* and *Benny Hill's*. Stuck on the western edge of Magaluf are a couple of giant-sized, purpose-built tourist attractions: **Aquapark**, with its swimming pools, water chutes, flumes and strange-looking water castle makes an enjoyable day out if you're travelling with children, but **El Dorado**, just opposite, is absolutely dreadful, a Wild West show town-cum-theme park that must be one of the most incongruous sights in Spain. In the unlikely event that you want to find a room in Magaluf, you can get a free map giving the location of all the resort's hotels at the seasonal **tourist office** (Mon–Fri 9am–1pm & 2.30–5pm; ☎131126), one block back from the beach on Plaça Magaluf.

Portals Vells

Things pick up beyond Magaluf, and indeed the pine-clad peninsula to the south of the resort has barely been touched by the developers. In consequence, however, there aren't any public buses down the peninsula – the nearest you'll get is Magaluf – so you'll have to drive, walk or hitch: an old country road begins at the C719 and proceeds across the harsh scrubland behind Magaluf, skirting the Aquapark before heading into the woods. After about 6km, a steep and dusty turning leads down to the tiny nudist beach of **Cala Mago** (still signposted in Castilian, "Playa El Mago"), where there's a beach bar, sunbeds and showers. Continuing down the peninsula a further 500m, a second turning twists down to the cove beach of **PORTALS VELLS**. Despite a bar-restaurant and a handful of discreet villas, it remains a delightful, pine-scented spot of glistening sand, rocky cliffs and clear blue water, especially appealing early in the morning before it gets crowded. Clearly visible from the beach are the **caves** of the headland on the south side of the cove. A footpath leads to the most interesting, an old cave church where the

Beyond Calvià, steep and narrow minor roads twist into the mountains of northwest Mallorca (covered in the next chapter), or you can cut back down to the coast at Santa Ponça (see p.90).

Aquapark is open June–Sept daily 10am–6pm; May & Oct daily 10am–5pm; 1600ptas.

holy-water stoup and altar have been cut out of the solid rock – the work of shipwrecked Genoese seamen, according to local legend.

Beyond the Portals Vells turning, the road continues for 1.5km as far as a broken-down barbed wire fence at the start of a military zone. You can't drive any further, but if the road isn't closed and guarded, it's OK to brave the no-entry signs and walk down the peninsula, rambling through the pine woods to reach the solitary Cap de Cala Figuera lighthouse after 1.5km.

From Santa Ponça to Camp de Mar

West of Palma Nova, the C719 trims the outskirts of SANTA PONÇA, perhaps the least endearing of all the resorts on this stretch of coast. Mostly a product of the 1980s, this sprawling, still-expanding conurbation has abandoned the concrete high-rises of yesteryear for a pseudo-vernacular architecture that's littered the hills with scores of tedious villas. That said, the aesthetic gloom is at least partly lifted by the setting – with rolling hills flanking a broad bay – and the substantial sandy beach offers safe bathing. The resort has some history too. The slender marina, situated about 2km west of the beach, abuts a bumpy promontory where a large stone cross commemorates the landing of Jaume I's Catalan army here in 1229. The small park at the foot of the cross is a quiet spot with pleasant sea views.

Peguera and Cala Fornells

PEGUERA, 6km from Santa Ponça, strings out along its lengthy main street – the Avinguda de Peguera – immediately behind several generous sandy beaches. There's nothing remarkable about the place, but it does have an easy-going air and is a favourite with families and older visitors alike. Towards the west end of the resort, a left turn off the high street, beside the *Gigante* supermarket, takes you the 1km up to CALA FORNELLS, whose chic, pueblo-style houses perch on the cliffs above a minuscule beach and concreted sunbathing slabs. Although Cala Fornells tends to be overcrowded during the daytime, at night the tranquillity returns, and it makes a good base for a holiday. You can also stroll out into the surrounding woods, where a clear and easy track leads west over the pine-scented hills for 1.5km to the stony cove beach of Caló d'es Monjo.

Cala Fornells has two fetching hotels, both behind the beach at the end of the access road: the sprucely modern, four-star *Coronado* (April–Sept; ☎686800; ⑨), where all 150 bedrooms have sea views and balconies, and the more sympathetic, green-shuttered and white-painted *Cala Fornells* (April–Dec; ☎686950; ⑥). If your wallet won't stretch as far as either of these two, consider staying in Peguera, where there are plenty of bargain-basement *hostals* in the characterless side streets behind the town centre. Try along c/Palmira – a turning off Avgda de Peguera about

700m east of the *Gigante* supermarket – where you'll find the no-frills *Hostal-residencia Sutimar* at no. 9 (April–Oct; ☎686952; ①); the marginally larger and more agreeable *Hostal-residencia Diamante* at no. 4 (☎686629; ③); and the much more comfortable *Hotel Maria Dolores*, with its own heated swimming pool, at Plaça Palmira 29 (☎686598; ④).

For **food**, *Pizza Valentino*, Avgda de Peguera 57, is cheap and cheerful, while the *Hotel Cala Fornells* (see above) has a good restaurant. At the top of the range, *La Gran Tortuga* (closed Mon), overlooking the seashore on the road to *Cala Fornells*, serves superb seafood, and has a terrace bar and even its own swimming pool; a three-course dinner will set you back about 4500ptas, but lunches are good too, and far less expensive.

Camp de Mar

Tucked away among the hills just 3km west of Peguera, **CAMP DE MAR** has an expansive beach and fine bathing, but is marred by the presence of a thumping great hotel, the *Playa*, dropped right on the seashore. All the same, this low-key resort is an amiable spot to soak up the sun and to use as a base for further explorations. There's a choice of two **hotels**, both modern high-rises where most of the spacious, balconied bedrooms look out to sea: the aforementioned *Hotel Playa* (April–Oct; ☎105025; ⑤), a British favourite, and the nearby German-geared *Hotel Lido* (May–Oct; ☎105100; ⑥). As far as **eating** is concerned, it's hard to resist the eccentric café stuck out in the bay and approached via a rickety walkway on stilts. Or try the *Bar La Siesta*, for romantic sunsets and wonderful paellas.

Heading west from Camp de Mar, a minor road twists over wooded hills to Port d'Andratx – see p.122.

Travel details

Local buses

EMT services from **Palma** to: the airport (#17; every 20min; 25min); Cala Major (#3; every 10min; 15min); Calvià (#20; 4 daily; 25min); Capdella (#20; 3 daily; 50min); Gènova (#4; every 30min; 25min); Illetes (#3; every 10min; 20min); Palma Nova (#21; every 20min; 30min); Portals Nous (#21; every 90min; 25min); S'Arenal (#15; every 10min; 30min).

Catalina Marques services (the "Playa Sol" routes) from **Palma** to: Camp de Mar (May–Oct every 15min, Nov–April every hour; 40min); Magaluf (11 daily; 25min); Palma Nova (11 daily; 20min); Peguera (May–Oct every 15min, Nov–April every hour; 35min); Portals Nous (11 daily; 15min); Port d'Andratx (May–Oct every 15min, Nov–April every hour; 45min).

Island-wide buses

From **Palma** to: Alaró (Mon–Sat 3 daily, 2 on Sun; 25min); Alcúdia (May–Oct Mon–Sat 10 daily, 5 on Sun; Nov–April 3 daily; 1hr); Andratx (Mon–Sat every 30min; 11 on Sun; 35min); Artà (Mon–Sat 4 daily, 1 on Sun; 1hr 25min); Banyalbufar (Mon–Sat 3 daily, 1 on Sun; 35min); Cala d'Or (2–4 daily; 1hr 10min); Cala Figuera (Mon–Sat 1–2 daily; 1hr 20min); Cala Millor (Mon–Sat 5–7 daily, 1–2 on Sun; 1hr 15min); Cala Rajada (Mon–Sat 4 daily, 1–2 on Sun;

1hr 30min); Ca'n Picafort (2–3 daily; 1hr); Colònia de Sant Jordi (2–4 daily; 1hr); Coves del Drac (Mon–Sat 2–4 daily, 1 on Sun; 1hr); Covetes (for Es Trenc beach; May–Oct 1 daily; 1hr); Deià (5 daily, except Oct–March Sun 3 daily; 45min); Esporles (Mon–Sat 4 daily, 2 on Sun; 20min); Estellencs (Mon–Sat 3 daily, 1 on Sun; 45min); Felanitx (3–4 daily; 50min); Inca (Mon–Sat 8 daily, 4 on Sun; 30min); Lluc (Mon–Sat 2 daily, 1 on Sun; 1hr); Manacor (Mon–Sat 7 daily, 2 on Sun; 55min); Petra (2–3 daily; 45min); Platja de Formentor (May–Oct Mon–Sat 1 daily; 1hr 15min); Pollença (3–5 daily; 1hr); Port d'Alcúdia (May–Oct Mon–Sat 10 daily, 5 on Sun; Nov–April 3 daily; 1hr 10min); Port de Pollença (3–5 daily; 1hr 10min); Port de Sóller (5 daily, except Oct–March 3 on Sun; 1hr 15min); Porto Colom (1–3 daily; 1hr 10min); Porto Cristo (Mon–Sat 7 daily, 2 on Sun; 1hr 10min); Porto Petro (2 daily; 1hr 10min); Santanyí (2–4 daily; 1hr); Sóller (5 daily, except Oct–March Sun 3 daily; 1hr 10min); Valldemossa (5 daily, except Oct–March Sun 3 daily; 30min).

From **Peguera** to: Andratx (May–Oct Mon–Sat 15 daily, 3 on Sun; Nov–April 2 daily; 10min); Port d'Andratx (May–Oct Mon–Sat 8 daily, 1 on Sun; 15min); Sant Elm (May–Oct Mon–Sat 7 daily, 1 on Sun; Nov–April 1 daily; 15min); Valldemossa (1 daily; 1hr 5min).

Trains

From **Palma** to: Binissalem (hourly; 30min); Inca (hourly; 40min); Sóller (5 daily; 1hr 15min).

Chapter 2

Northwest Mallorca

Mallorca is at its scenic best in the gnarled ridge of the **Serra de Tramuntana**, the imposing mountain range which stretches the length of the island's northwest shore, its rearing peaks and plunging seacliffs intermittently intercepted by valleys of olive and citrus groves. Midway along and cramped by the mountains is **Sóller**, an antiquated merchants' town that serves as a charming introduction to the region, especially when it's reached on the dinky rail line from Palma. From here, it's a short hop down to the coast at Port de Sóller, a popular resort on a deep and expansive bay. This geographical arrangement – the town located a few kilometres inland from the eponymous port – is repeated across Mallorca, a reminder of more troubled days when marauding corsairs obliged the islanders to live away from the coast. The mountain valleys in the vicinity of Sóller shelter the bucolic stone-built villages of **Fornalutx** and **Orient**, as well as the splendid oasis-like gardens of **Alfabia**, set beside the main Sóller–Palma road, the C711.

Southwest of Sóller, the main coastal road, the C710, threads up through the mountains to reach the beguiling village of **Deià**, tucked at the base of formidable cliffs and famous as the former home of Robert Graves. Beyond lies the magnificent Carthusian monastery of **Valldemossa**, whose echoing cloisters temporarily accommodated George Sand and Frédéric Chopin, and the gracious hacienda of **La Granja**, another compelling stop. Continuing southwest, the C710 wriggles high above the shoreline, slipping through a sequence of mountain hamlets, of which **Estellencs** is the most picturesque, its tightly terraced fields tumbling down the coastal cliffs. By the time the main road reaches its conclusion at **Andratx**, however, it's almost left the mountains; beyond, on Mallorca's southwestern tip, lie the safe waters of **Port d'Andratx**, a medium-sized resort draped around a handsome inlet.

The mountains **northeast of Sóller** are the highest portion of the Serra de Tramuntana – too severe, in fact, to allow for all but the most occasional access to the sea, with the C710 being forced

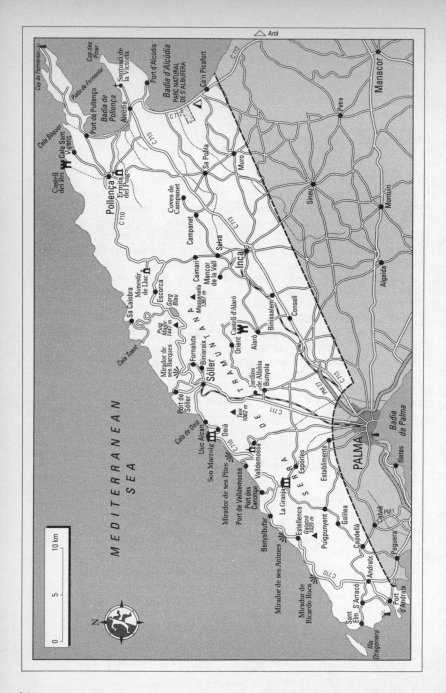

inland to weave its way amongst the craggy peaks. A rare exception is the extraordinary side road that snakes down to the overcrowded mini-resort of **Sa Calobra** and the far more appealing beach at **Cala Tuent**. But it's the expansive, well-appointed monastery of **Lluc** that remains the big draw around here – for religious islanders, who venerate an effigy of the Virgin known as La Moreneta, and tourists alike. Further along the coast, the outstanding attractions are the ancient town of **Pollença**, complete with its fine, cypress-lined Way of the Cross, and the **Península de Formentor**, a rocky finger of land noted for its sea vistas. The peninsula boasts the superb *Hotel Formentor*, but thinner wallets are usually confined to the low-key resort of **Port de Pollença** or the more upbeat and flashy **Port d'Alcúdia**, which doubles as a ferry port with services to Menorca and Barcelona.

The Serra de Tramuntana provides the best walking on Mallorca, with scores of **hiking trails** latticing the mountains. Generally speaking, paths are well marked, though apt to be clogged with thornbushes. There are trails to suit all aptitudes and all levels of enthusiasm, from the easiest of strolls to the most gruelling of long-distance treks. Details of several of the less strenuous walks are given within the text, and three potential hikes beginning in Valldemossa, Deià and Lluc, are selected for special treatment. Spring and autumn are the best times to embark on the longer trails; in mid summer the heat can be enervating and water is scarce. Bear in mind also that the mountains are prone to mists,

---

The train to Sóller

The 28-kilometre **train** journey from **Palma to Sóller** is a delight, dipping and cutting through the mountains and fertile valleys of the **Serra de Tramuntana**. Completed in 1911, the rail line was constructed on the profits of the orange and lemon trade, whose produce the railway was built to transport to Palma – at a time when it took a full day to make the trip by road. First the train has to clear the scratchy suburbs of Palma, but within about fifteen minutes it's running across pancake-flat farmland with an impenetrable-looking line of steep peaks dead ahead. After clunking through the outskirts of Bunyola, the train threads upwards to spend five minutes tunnelling through the mountains, where the noisy engine and dimly lit carriages give the feel of a rollercoaster ride. Beyond, out in the bright mountain air, are the steep valleys and craggy thousand-metre peaks at the heart of the Serra de Tramuntana, and everywhere there are almond groves, which are vivid with pinky-white blossom in January and February. The rolling stock, too, is tremendous, narrow carriages – the gauge is only 914mm – which seem straight out of Agatha Christie novels. There are five departures daily from Palma station throughout the year (sometimes six from Sóller), the whole ride taking just under an hour and a quarter. A return costs 760ptas (380ptas one way), though the mid-morning *Turist* train – whose only distinction is a brief photo-stop in the mountains at the Mirador Pujol D'en Banja – will set you back 1115ptas return (560ptas one way).

---

though they usually lift at some point in the day. For obvious safety reasons, lone mountain walking is not recommended.

As far as **beaches** are concerned, most of the region's coastal villages have a tiny, shingly strip, and only around the bays of Pollença and Alcúdia are there significantly more substantial offerings. The resorts edging these bays have the greatest number of hotel and *hostal* rooms, but from June to early September, and sometimes beyond, vacancies are extremely thin on the ground. Indeed, **accommodation** – especially if you have a tight itinerary and are travelling in the summertime – requires some forethought, though there's a reasonable chance of getting a room on spec in Sóller, and in the monasteries at Lluc and just outside Pollença. To compensate, distances are small – from Andratx to Port de Pollença via the C710 is only about 135km – the roads are good and the **bus** network is perfectly adequate for most destinations. **Taxis** can work out a reasonable deal too, if you're travelling in a group: for instance, the fare for the forty-kilometre trip from Palma to Sóller is 3800ptas.

Sóller and around

At **Sóller**, the terminus of the rail line from Palma the obvious option is to continue by tram down to the seashore, a rumbling, five-kilometre journey ending at Port de Sóller. If you pass straight through however, you'll miss one of the most laid-back and enjoyable towns on Mallorca, an ideal, and fairly inexpensive, base for exploring the surrounding mountains. To the northeast, Sóller's mellow mansions fade seamlessly into the orchards and farmland that precede the charming hamlets of **Biniaraix** and **Fornalutx**, both within easy walking distance. Further afield, on the landward side of the Serra de Tramuntana, the rustic delights continue amongst the verdant gardens of the **Jardins de Alfabia**, and at the hamlet of **Orient**, on the road to the remote ruins of the **Castell d'Alaró**. However, most visitors ignore these inland attractions and stick religiously to the coast, the focus of their attention being the popular but mundane resort of **Port de Sóller**. If the seashore is what you're after, there are much nicer bathing spots not far away – especially Cala Deià (see p.107) – but the port does offer good restaurants and a cluster of low-price hotels.

There are fast and frequent **buses** from Palma to Port de Sóller via Valldemossa, and more intermittent services along the main coastal road, the C710, from Andratx to Valldemossa, and on from Sóller and Port de Sóller to Port de Pollença and Port d'Alcúdia (summertime only). **Trains** from Palma to Sóller (see previous page), link with the ramshackle old **trams** to Port de Sóller, ex-San Francisco rolling stock from the 1930s which depart every hour for the fifteen-minute journey.

Sóller town

Rather than any specific sight, it's the general flavour of SÓLLER that appeals, its narrow, sloping lanes cramped by eighteenth- and nineteenth-century stone houses, whose fancy grilles and big wooden doors once hid the region's fruit-rich merchants. All streets lead to the main square, Plaça Constitució, an informal, pint-sized affair of crowded cafés and grouchy mopeds just down the hill from the train station. The square is dominated by the hulking mass of the church of **Sant Bartomeu**, a crude neo-Gothic remodelling of the medieval original, its only saving grace the enormous and precisely carved rose window stuck high in the main façade. Inside, the cavernous nave is suitably dark and gloomy, the penitential home of a string of gaudy Baroque altarpieces. A five-minute walk away at c/Sa Mar 9, the **Museu Municipal** comprises a rather half-hearted sequence of period rooms in a renovated merchant's mansion. It's hardly unmissable, but the antique kitchen, with its majolica plates and old pots and pans, is mildly diverting, and the chapel-shrine showcases some interesting votive offerings.

The Museu Municipal is open Mon–Sat 11am–1pm & 4–7pm; 100ptas.

Retracing your steps to the top of c/Mar, turn left along c/Bauza and keep going straight for the three-kilometre stroll to the pretty

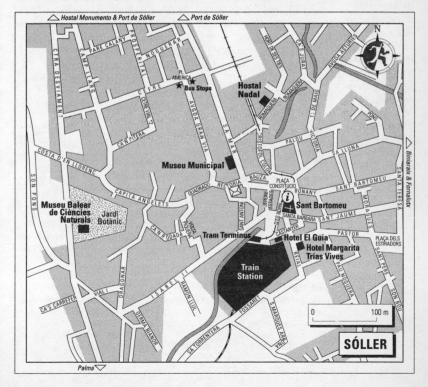

Sóller and around

The Museu Balear de Ciències Naturals and Jardí Botànic are open Tues–Sat 10.30am– 1.30pm & 5–8pm, Sun 10.30am– 1.30pm; free.

village of Biniaraix (see opposite); or turn right down c/Rectoria for the five-minute walk west to the brand new **Museu Balear de Ciències Naturals** (Balearic Museum of Natural Sciences), stuck beside the main Sóller–Port de Sóller road. This museum also occupies an old merchant's dwelling, but here the interior has been stripped out to accommodate the displays, which include a good assortment of fossils. There's also a section devoted to the leading botanists of yesteryear – including Archduke Ludwig Salvator (see p.110) – and another identifying and illustrating many species of local flora, a necessary introduction to the **Jardí Botànic** (Botanical Garden), which tumbles down the surrounding hillside. The gardens are in their infancy, so there's not much horticultural excitement at present, but when there is, you can expect an admission fee to match; the labelling is in Catalan, but English leaflets are available at reception.

Sóller practicalities

Sóller's antique trams trundle down to Port de Sóller and back every hour, every day of the week from 7am to 9pm; the trip takes 15min and costs 125ptas one way (buy tickets from the conductor on board).

Buses to Sóller arrive beside Plaça Amèrica, about five minutes' walk from Plaça Constitució, where the **Oficina d'Informació Turística** (Mon–Fri 9.30am–1.30pm; ☎630332) has its home in the town hall next to the church. **Guided walks** – graded from "easy" (8km) to "tiresome and difficult" (18km) – sometimes depart from here; ask for details, though mostly you'll need to sign up two days in advance. The newsagent directly across the square sells a reasonable range of local **hiking maps** (*IGN* and *Mapa Militar*).

Accommodation

In high season, there's far more chance of a **room** in Sóller's handful of hotels and *hostals* than down at the port.

Hotel El Guía, c/Castanyer 2; ☎630227. Easily the best place in town, this lovely, old-fashioned, one-star hotel is approached across a pretty little courtyard. Bygones litter the foyer, which leads to frugal but pleasant rooms. To get there, walk down the steps from the train station and turn right. April–Oct. ④.

Casa de Huéspedes Margarita Trías Vives, c/Reial 3; ☎634214. Basic rooms in an old terraced house close to the train station. April–Oct. ②.

Hostal-residencia Monumento, Carretera Port; ☎630118. Less convenient than its rivals – it's situated about 1km north of the centre beside the main road to the port – this two-star *hostal* has 20 reasonably comfortable rooms. May–Oct. ④.

Hostal-residencia Nadal, c/Romaguera 27; ☎631180. Simple, central two-star, in an old, neatly decorated house about five minutes' walk south of Plaça Constitució. ③.

Accommodation price symbols

The symbols used in our accommodation listings denote the following price ranges:

① Under 2000ptas	④ 4000–6000ptas	⑦ 10,000–14,000ptas
② 2000–3000ptas	⑤ 6000–8000ptas	⑧ 14,000–20,000ptas
③ 3000–4000ptas	⑥ 8000–10,000ptas	⑨ Over 20,000ptas.

For more details see p.31.

Eating and drinking

Sóller's **restaurant** scene, though not particularly diverse, is perfectly adequate for a short stay, while the town's **café-bars** provide an abundance of low-cost snacks and light meals during the day and early evening.

Bar Turismo, by the tram lines on Avgda d'es Born. Cosy bar with interesting English lending library, redolent of earlier expatriate days.

Café Es Firo, Plaça Constitució. Deep, dark café selling low-price snacks and coffee with a kick like a mule.

Café Madrid, just off Plaça Constitució on c/Bauza. Popular, no-frills café-bar, in traditional style, with hocks of ham hanging from the ceiling. Sandwiches start at 375ptas and the substantial *menú del día* costs 1100ptas.

Cafeteria Soller, Plaça Constitució. Tasty snacks and fresh *ensaimadas* in unpretentious surroundings; a good bet for breakfast.

Restaurant-bar Oasis, c/Cristófol Colom 5. Situated below Plaça Constitució by the Port de Sóller tram tracks, this enjoyable restaurant has the added benefit of a shaded terrace. Prices are cheap, too: paella, for instance, costs just 700ptas.

Restaurant El Guía, c/Castanyer 2. Not only a great place to stay, but also with a real treat of a restaurant. A little formal for some, but the prices are very reasonable, with a delicious *menú del día* for around 2000ptas. Closed Mon.

Biniaraix and Fornalutx

Following c/Sa Lluna from Sóller's main square, it takes about half an hour to stroll, or five minutes to drive east to **BINIARAIX**, passing orchards and farmland latticed with ancient dry-stone walls. The village, nestled in the foothills of the Serra de Tramuntana, is tiny, but boasts a small central square of trim stone buildings enlivened by a few cafés. Biniaraix is famous as the starting point for one of Mallorca's busiest hiking routes, commonly called the **Cornadors Circuit**. To get to the trailhead, walk east for a few metres from the square and turn right along Camí d'es Barranc. The thirteen-kilometre trail, which takes about six hours to negotiate, weaves a circuitous course through the mountains, ending up in Sóller. The first bit is the most diverting, following an old cobbled track – originally built for pilgrims on their way to Lluc – which ascends the **Barranc de Biniaraix**, a beautiful gorge of terraced citrus groves set in the shadow of the mountains.

After about ninety minutes you'll reach the head of the ravine, where a large barn sporting painted signs on its walls is the obvious landmark. Beyond this point the going gets appreciably tougher and the route more difficult to work out, so you'll need to have a hiking map with you. If you don't fancy taking on the whole circuit, you could make do with the climb to **L'Ofre Mirador**, a thousand-metre-high viewpoint about forty minutes' hike further west, which overlooks the *barranc* from one of the twin peaks of Es Cornadors mountain.

Fornalutx

FORNALUTX, a couple of kilometres east of Biniaraix along a quiet, signposted country road, is touted as the most attractive village on the island, and certainly has a superb location. Orange and lemon groves scent the valley as it tapers up towards the settlement, whose honey-coloured stone houses huddle against a mountainous backdrop. Fanning out from the minuscule main square, the centre of Fornalutx is a quaint affair of narrow cobbled streets, stepped to facilitate mule traffic, though nowadays you're more likely to be hit by a Mercedes than obstructed by a mule: foreigners love the place and own about half of the village's three hundred houses. This sizeable expatriate community sustains two excellent restaurants, the *Bella Vista*, just off the main square on the road back towards Sóller, and, further back down the road, the *Santa Marta* (closed Tues). Both enjoy fabulous views over the valley and concentrate on traditional Mallorcan cuisine, with full meals costing around 2500ptas. If your budget doesn't stretch that far, the *Café del Centro*, in the main square, serves inexpensive snacks.

By car, you can climb east from Fornalutx into the hills to meet, after 1.2km, the main coastal road near the Mirador Ses Barques – see p.124.

As for **accommodation**, the village boasts the charming *Hostal Fornalutx*, c/Alba 22 (closed July; ☎631997; ⑥), a relaxing and attractively furnished old house. If you've walked here and are heading back to Sóller, you might want to consider a taxi. The fare is just 650ptas – if you don't spot one hanging around, telephone ☎630571.

Port de Sóller

PORT DE SÓLLER is one of the most popular resorts on the west coast, and its horseshoe-shaped bay must be the most photographed spot on the island after the package resorts around Palma. The high jinks of the Badia de Palma are about the last thing imaginable down here, though – the place is almost stiflingly staid. There's no point in staying just for the swimming either, since, although the water is warm and calm, it's often surprisingly murky (courtesy of the yachts at anchor), and the sandy beach is overlooked on all sides – by the road, hotels and restaurants. About the best thing to do in town, apart from sampling one of the excellent seafood restaurants (see below), is to make the fifty-minute stroll out west to the **lighthouse**, which guards the cliffs above the entrance to Port de Sóller's inlet. From here, the views out over the wild and rocky coast are spectacular, especially at sunset. Directions couldn't be easier as there's a tarmac road all the way: from the centre of the resort, walk round the southern side of the bay past the beach and keep going along the seashore.

See p.109 for details of an excellent coastal walk from Deià to Port de Sóller.

If you're around here in the second week of May, be sure to catch the **Festa de Nostra Senyora de la Victòria**, which commemorates events of May 1561. A large force of Arab pirates surprised Sóller and sacked the town, but were then ambushed and massacred

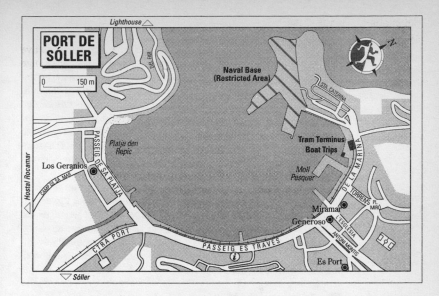

as they returned to their ships. The islanders took grisly revenge by planting the raiders' heads on stakes. The story – bar decapitations – is played out in chaotic, alcoholic fashion every year at the festival. The re-enactment begins with the arrival of the pirates by boat, and continues with fancy-dress Christians and Arabs battling it out through the streets of the port, to the sound of blanks being fired in the air from antique rifles. The tourist office can give you a rough idea of the schedule of events, plus details of the dances and parties that follow.

Port de Sóller practicalities

Trams from Sóller shadow the main road and clank to a full stop beside the waterfront, bang in the centre of town. En route, the road and the tramlines pass the **Oficina d'Informació Turística**, on Passeig es Través (May–Sept Mon–Fri 11.30am–3pm, Sat 9.30am–1.30pm; ☎633042), which carries a reasonable range of local information, including restaurant and accommodation lists, maps and boat-trip details.

Outside of peak season there's a chance of a reasonably priced room at the mundane *Hotel Miramar*, c/de la Marina 12 (April–Oct; ☎631350; ③), a standard-issue skyrise down by the waterfront in the centre, and at the equally unexciting, 100-room *Hotel Generoso*, nearby at c/de la Marina 4 (☎631450; ④). Moving upmarket, and just a few minutes' walk from the bay, the three-star *Hostal Es Port*, c/Antoni Montis 6 (☎631650; ⑤), boasts lovely gardens, a swimming pool, and a charming reception area set inside a renovated medieval manor house. The *hostal's* rooms are, however, far less endearing, occupying an unimaginatively modern concrete block. The string of one- and two-star hotels and *hostals* behind the Platja den Repic on the south side of the bay are worth considering too: the no-frills *Los Geranios*, Passeig de sa Platja 15 (mid-March to Oct; ☎631440; ④), offers the best deal here.

Port de Sóller has several fine **seafood** restaurants overlooking the bay. The pick of the bunch is the spick and span *Sa Llotja des Peix* on Moll Pesquer, the old fishing jetty, where a delicious *menú del día* will set you back a bargain 1200ptas. Other good alternatives are *El Pirata* and *Meson del Puerto*, both on c/Santa Caterina Alejandria, a narrow side street cutting up from the waterfront close to Moll Pesquer.

In the summer, **boats** leave the jetty by the tram terminus for day excursions along the coast: south to Sant Elm (1 weekly; 2200ptas) and Cala Deià (1 weekly; 1200ptas), and north to Sa Calobra (5 daily; 1700ptas). Cala Deià (see p.107) is the most diverting of the destinations, though each trip is a good way of seeing a chunk of coast. You pay for the round trip, but you don't, of course, have to come back.

The Jardins de Alfabia

Heading south from Sóller, the road towards Palma hairpins up into the mountains to reach, after about 8km, the **Coll de Sóller**, a rocky pass with a car park and lookout point offering splendid views out over the coast (note, however, that a tunnel to carry the main C711 through the mountains will soon be completed). It's downhill from here, with more twisting and turning until, just beyond the last hairpin (and the other end of the nearly finished road tunnel), you arrive at the **Jardins de Alfabia**, lush and beautiful terraced gardens surrounding a genteel hacienda. Shortly after the Reconquest, Jaume I granted the estate of Alfabia to a prominent Moor by the name of Benhabet. Seeing which way the historical wind was blowing, Benhabet, as governor of Pollença, had thrown his support behind Jaume, provisioning the Catalan army during the invasion. There was no way Jaume I could leave his ally in charge of Pollença (and anyway it was already pledged to a Catalan noble), but he was able to reward him with this generous portion of land. Benhabet planned his new estate in the Moorish manner, channelling water from the surrounding mountains to irrigate the fields and fashion oasis-like gardens. Generations of Catholic gentry added to the estate, but without marring Benhabet's original design, thus creating the homogenous ensemble that survives today.

The Jardins de Alfabia are open May–Oct Mon–Fri 9.30am– 6.30pm, Sat 9.30am–1pm; Nov–April Mon–Fri 9.30am– 5.30pm, Sat 9.30am–1pm; 500ptas.

From the roadside, visitors follow a stately avenue of plane trees towards the house, but, before reaching the gatehouse, they're directed up a flight of stone steps and into the **gardens**. Here, a footpath leads past ivy-covered stone walls, gurgling water courses and brightly coloured flowers cascading over narrow terraces.

Patterns of light and shade are created by trellises of jasmine and
wistaria, while palm and fruit trees jostle upwards, allowing only the
occasional glimpse of the surrounding citrus groves. At the end of
the path, the gardens' highlight is a verdant jungle of palm trees,
bamboo and bullrushes tangling a tiny pool. It's an enchanting spot,
especially on a hot summer's day, and an outdoor **bar** sells big
glasses of freshly squeezed orange juice, a snip at 175ptas. A few
paces away is the **house**, a rather mundane, verandahed hacienda
whose handful of rooms house an eccentric mix of antiques and
curios. Pride of place goes to a superb fourteenth-century **oak chair**
adorned with delightful bas-relief scenes honouring Mallorca's
royals. The chair was ordered by the uncrowned Jaume IV, though
he never had a chance to sit on it: after the Battle of Llucmajor in
1349, in which his father, Jaume III, was killed by the Aragonese, he
was captured and spent the rest of his days in exile.

At the front of the house, the cobbled **courtyard** is shaded by a
giant plane tree and surrounded by pretty, rustic outbuildings;
beyond lies the **gatehouse**, an imposing structure sheltering a fine
coffered ceiling of Mudéjar design, with an inscription praising Allah.

Orient and the Castell d'Alaró

About 4km south of Alfabia along the C711, a country road forks
east past the plane trees and sun-bleached walls of the unassuming
market town of **BUNYOLA**, before snaking across the forested foothills of the Serra de Tramuntana. It's a beautiful drive (the tarmac's
in good nick too, though some of the bends are nerve-jangling) that
brings you, after about 13km, to **ORIENT**. This remote hamlet of
ancient houses is scattered along the eastern side of the lovely Vall
d'Orient, with hills rising all around above olive and almond groves.
There's even somewhere to stay in the village, the simple, tiny
Hostal-residencia Muntanya at c/Bordoy 6 (☎613380; ⑨), but
this is as nothing compared to the romantic *Hotel L'Hermitage*
(mid-Dec to Oct; ☎613300; ⑨), a luxuriously renovated medieval
manor house roughly 1km beyond Orient on the PM210. The hotel
gardens are lovely, the scenery gorgeous and the **restaurant**, with
its mammoth antique olive press, excellent, even if the decor is a
little twee. Needless to say, advance reservations are pretty much
essential and, if you're paying this sort of money, try to get one of
the four rooms in the old manor house, rather than one of the
twenty in the modern annexe.

The Castell d'Alaró

Beyond *Hotel L'Hermitage*, the PM210 sticks to the ridge overlooking the narrow valley of the Torrent d'en Paragon for around 3km,
before veering south to slip between a pair of molar-like hills whose
bare rocky flanks tower above the surrounding forest and scrub.
The more westerly of the two sports the sparse ruins of the **Castell**

d'Alaró, originally a Moorish stronghold but rebuilt by Jaume I. Visible for miles around, the castle looks impregnable on its lofty perch, and it certainly impeded the Aragonese invasion of 1285. Indeed, Alfonso III was so irritated by the effort involved in capturing the place that he had the garrison's two commanders roasted alive. Not that the men concerned helped their own cause. When an Aragonese messenger suggested terms for surrender, they punned on Alfonso's name in Catalan, calling him "fish-face" (*anfos* means "perch"). Goodness knows what would have happened to them if they had thought of something really rude.

Access to the castle is from the south: coming from Orient, watch for the signposted right turn just beyond the "Kilometre 18" stone marker. There are plans to improve the quality of this side road, but at present its well-surfaced beginning flatters the rough track further along. About 4km up through terraced olive groves, you'll reach *Es Pouet* (closed Mon), a **restaurant** with a car park. It's tempting to linger here: the views down over the plain are sumptuous and the food delicious, particularly the house speciality, oven-baked lamb. From the restaurant it's about an hour's walk up a track to the stone gateway, beyond which lies an expansive wooded plateau accommodating the fragmentary ruins of the fortress, the tiny pilgrims' church of **Mare de Déu del Refugi**, and a simple hotel with a restaurant and bar, the *Hostal Castell d'Alaró* (☎510480; ①), where a handful of very basic rooms are available all year.

Back on the PM210, about 1km south of the turn-off for the castle, **ALARÓ** itself is a sleepy little town of shuttered stone houses, just 5km from tedious Consell on the main Palma–Port d'Alcúdia highway.

Down the coast from Deià to Port d'Andratx

The southwesterly reaches of the **Serra de Tramuntana** rise out of the flatlands around Palma, with the range's forested foothills and sheltered valleys soon giving way to the craggy, wooded mountains that crimp most of the seashore. Several fast roads link Palma with the coast – the prettiest runs the 20km to Valldemossa – and a delightful network of country roads patterns the foothills, but the key sights (and the best scenery) are most readily reached along the main coastal road, the C710.

From Sóller, this main road skirts the broad and wooded slopes of the Puig des Teix to reach, after 10km, **Deià**, an ancient mountain village which perches precariously high above the seashore, clinging to the fame brought by Robert Graves. Moving on, the next 20km of coastline boasts three of the island's star attractions – **Son Marroig**, the well-appointed mansion of the Mallorca-loving archduke, Ludwig Salvator; the hilltop monastery of **Valldemossa**, complete with its plush cells and choice examples of modern art; and the old grandee's mansion and estate of **La Granja**. Allied to some of the island's finest coastal scenery, this captivating trio is hard to beat, and, in comparison, the tiered hamlets that decorate the coast further down the road are something of an anticlimax. Nonetheless, both **Banyalbufar** and **Estellencs** occupy fine sites and are well worth at least a fleeting visit – or you can travel inland from La Granja, climbing the slopes of the leafy foothills and rambling through secluded valleys of almond, olive and carob trees, to reach the charming village of **Galilea**. Both the Galilea route and the C710 emerge from the Serra de Tramuntana at **Andratx**, a crossroads town with easy access to the tiny port of **Sant Elm** and the more commercialized harbour-cum-resort of **Port d'Andratx**.

Beach lovers have meagre pickings in this part of the island. There's a good sandy beach with safe swimming at Sant Elm, but further up the coast, shingle strips will have to suffice. The most impressive of these is **Cala de Deià**, set in the shadow of the mountains at the end of a narrow ravine. **Accommodation** can be hard to find, too. Each of the destinations mentioned above, with the exception of Galilea, has at least a couple of places to stay, but you're strongly advised to book well ahead from May to September, even October. With their clusters of hotels and *hostals*, Deià and Port d'Andratx represent the best bets for a last-minute vacancy, with Sant Elm the third favourite.

An excellent **bus** service runs regularly from Palma to Valldemossa and Deià, continuing on to Sóller and its port. There are also fast and frequent buses from Palma to Andratx, from where it's easy to get to either Port d'Andratx or Sant Elm. Along the C710 between Andratx and Valldemossa, however, you're limited to a Monday–Saturday once-daily service, which originates in Peguera (see p.90). Distances between destinations are short, so taxis can work out a reasonable proposition if you're in a group – the fare for the twenty-kilometre trip from Sóller to Valldemossa, for example, is 3000ptas, 2000ptas to Deià.

Deià

DEIÀ is beautiful. The mighty Puig des Teix meets the coast here, and, although its lower slopes are now gentrified by the villas of the well-to-do, the mountain retains a formidable, almost mysterious presence, especially in the shadows of a moonlit night. Doubling as the coastal highway, Deià's main street skirts the base of the Teix, showing off most of the village's hotels and restaurants. At times, this main street is too congested to be much fun, but the tiny heart of the village, tumbling over a high and narrow ridge on the seaward side of the road, still manages a surprising tranquillity. Labyrinthine alleys of old peasant houses curl up to a pretty country church, in the precincts of which stands the **grave of Robert Graves**, the village's most famous resident – marked simply *Robert Graves: Poeta, E.P.D. (En Paz*

*A fine walk
connects
Valldemossa
with Deià; see
p.115 for
details.*

Robert Graves in Deià

The English poet, novelist and classical scholar **Robert Graves** (1895–1985) had two spells of living in Deià, the first in the 1930s, and the second from the end of World War II until his death. During his earlier stay, he shared a house at the edge of the village with **Laura Riding**, an American poet and dabbler in the mystical. Riding had arrived in England in 1926 and, after she became Graves's secretary and collaborator, the two of them began an affair. The tumultuous course of their relationship created sufficient furore for them to decide to leave England, choosing to settle in Mallorca on the advice of Gertrude Stein in 1930. The fuss was not simply a matter of morality – many of their friends were indifferent to adultery – but more to do with the self-styled "Holy Circle", a cabalistic, literary-mystic group they had founded. The last straw came when Riding, in her attempt to control the group, jumped out of a window exclaiming "Goodbye, chaps", and the besotted Graves leapt after her. No wonder his mate T. E. Lawrence wrote of "madhouse minds" and of Graves "drowning in a quagmire".

They both recovered, but the dottiness continued once they'd moved to Deià, with Graves acting as doting servant to Laura, who he reinvented as a sort of all-knowing matriarch and muse. Simultaneously, Graves thumped away at his prose: he had already produced **Goodbye to All That** (1929), his bleak and painful memoirs of his army service in the World War I trenches, but now came his other best-remembered books, **I, Claudius** (1934) and its sequel **Claudius the God** (1935), historical novels detailing the life and times of the Roman emperor. To Graves however, these "pot-boilers", as he styled them, were secondary to his poetry, and indeed his verse works of this period, usually carefully crafted love poems of melancholic tenderness in praise of Riding, were well received by the critics.

At the onset of the Spanish Civil War, Graves and Riding left Mallorca, not out of sympathy for the Republicans – Graves was far too reactionary for that – but to keep contact with friends and family. During their exile, Laura ditched Graves, who subsequently took up with a mutual friend, **Beryl Hodge**. After Graves had returned to Deià in 1946, he worked on **The White Goddess**, a controversial study of prehistoric and classical myth which argued the existence of an all-pervasive, primordial religion based on the worship of a poet-goddess. In the midst of his labours (the book was published in 1948), Beryl joined him, and in 1950 they were married in Palma. However, they didn't live happily ever after. Graves had a predilection for young women, claiming the need for female muses to inspire his poetic vision; outwardly Beryl accepted this waywardness, but without much enthusiasm. While his novels became increasingly well-known and profitable, his poetry, with its preoccupation with romantic love, fell out of fashion, and his last anthology, *Poems 1965–1968*, was widely criticized by the literary establishment.

Nevertheless, Graves's international reputation as a writer attracted a steady stream of visitors to Deià from the ranks of the literati, with the occasional film star adding to the self-regarding stew. By the middle of the 1970s, however, he had begun to lose his mind, ending his days in sad senility.

Descanse: "Rest In Peace"). From the graveyard, the views out over the coast are truly memorable, with banks of carefully terraced fields tumbling down from the mountains towards the sea.

Graves put Deià on the international map, and nowadays the village is the haunt of long-term expatriates, mostly ex-flower children and artists living on ample trust funds, judging from the sorts of monthly rents charged. These inhabitants nourish a couple of **art galleries** and congregate at the **Cala de Deià**, the nearest thing the village has to a beach – some 200m of shingle at the back of a handsome rocky cove of jagged cliffs, boulders and white-crested surf. It's a great place for a swim, the water clean, deep and cool, and there's a ramshackle beach bar, but the cove often gets crowded, especially when the day-trippers arrive by boat from Port de Sóller (usually on Tuesdays). It takes about twenty minutes to walk from the village to the *cala*, a delightful stroll down a wooded ravine – for directions, see the first part of the "Coastal walk from Deià to Port de Sóller" box on p.109. Driving there takes about ten minutes: head north along the main road out of Deià and watch for the left turn marked "Depuradora" (water purification station) – a proper signpost is promised.

Practicalities

The Palma–Port de Sóller **bus** scoots through Deià five times daily in each direction. There's no tourist office, but the village's hotels and *hostals* will gladly provide local advice on walks and weather, and can fix you up with a **taxi** – or do it yourself on ☎639035.

Of the two places where there's a good chance of a moderately priced **room** in high season, the *Fonda Villa Verde* (usually April–Oct; ☎639037; ④) has lovely premises near the village church, while *Pension Miramar*, a no-frills second choice, is situated on the other side of the main road on the slopes of Puig des Teix (March–Oct; ☎639084; ④). Deià also possesses two of the finest hotels on Mallorca, both overlooking the main road. At the west end of the village, *Es Moli* (April–Oct; ☎639000; ⑨) occupies a grand, lavishly refurbished stone mansion, surrounded by lovely gardens and equipped with a swimming pool. Further into the village, *La Residencia* is also sited in a gracious old mansion (☎639011; ⑨), but its opulent furnishings and fittings probably have the edge over those of its rival.

If these options fail, you may have better luck at the hamlet of **Lluc Alcari**, a handful of houses dotted along the main road 3km northeast of Deià. The one-star *Costa d'Or* here is a bargain by island standards (May–Oct; ☎639025; ④), especially considering it has a pool and private access to a nearby beach. It is, however, frustratingly hard to find: look out for the sign on the left-hand side of the main road coming from Deià, prohibiting through traffic from a narrow lane that goes down to the village; go down the lane and you'll stumble across the hotel.

Down the coast from Deià to Port d'Andratx

As for **eating** in Deià, you're spoiled for choice. There's a concentration of cafés and restaurants along the main street towards the west end of the village. These include *Café La Fabrica*, which offers reasonably priced *tapas*, *bocadillos* and the traditional *pa amb oli* (bread rubbed with olive oil); and the *Restaurante Deià*, where you'll pay a little more for a light meal, but with the compensation of a terrace overlooking the countryside. Moving up the price range, the *Restaurant Vista Deià*, which is also at the west end of the village, a couple of minutes' walk up Puig des Teix, has a charming terrace, shielded by a lattice of passion flowers, and serves from a wide-ranging and moderately expensive menu.

A COASTAL WALK FROM DEIÀ TO PORT DE SÓLLER

KEY TO WALKS:
Primary Route
Secondary Route

MULETA GRAN

Port de Sóller

Foot Bridge

Rocamar

Muleta 222m

Large House With Tower

Bens d'Avall

Alconassar

C710

Can Prohom   Castell

Lluc Alcari

Cala de Deià

Son Coll

N

Valldemossa

C710

Residencia

Deià   Bus Stop

Es Molí

Sóller

Sóller

0   1 km

A coastal walk from Deià to Port de Sóller

12km, 4hr–4hr 30min.

Dotted with pine trees and abandoned olive terraces, the coast north of Deià slopes steeply down to the sea from the high massif of Sa Galera. On such steep terrain, run-off plays havoc with terrace walls and paths, so although this delightful walk is mainly easy, care is needed where erosion has taken place. All the way the views are superlative, from the overlook of the blue-green waters of Cala de Deià at the start, to the impressive 150-metre sea cliffs on the western edge of the Muleta Gran headland. The route, which sometimes drops almost to sea level and at other times rises to avoid difficult ground, is partially waymarked with red paint and cairns, although a certain amount of route-finding is required. There are stiles at all the boundary fences the path crosses. The walk starts in Deià village and ends at the *Rocamar* hotel in Port de Sóller; if you have your own transport, the best plan is to park at Port de Sóller and take the 9.30am bus to Deià before embarking on the hike. The views from the bus are outstanding, too: notice especially the picturesque hamlet of Lluc Alcari, which cannot be seen from the coastal path below.

From the bus stop in Deià, walk in the Palma direction to a sharp right bend in the main road. Turn right down the shallow steps and continue downhill, taking a right fork after a few minutes. When the lane ends a signposted footpath continues in the same direction; after about 5min turn right by a white painted sign. The path joins a surfaced road about 500m before reaching tiny **Cala de Deià**, with its cluster of small boats and, in summer, a beach bar serving meals.

The **coastal path** begins up a flight of steps some 20m before the road end. Ignore a left branch after about 5min, but 2min later turn left where the stepped path swings right. The coastal path immediately turns right along a terrace, crosses a low wall and then turns sharp left downhill at the side of the wall. One minute later it turns right again and leads to an attractive headland among pine trees, overlooking the sea and the photogenic white rocks of Cala de Deià.

Continue along the path to the north, passing a *mirador* (viewpoint) with a private path descending to it from an unseen house above. Later, after crossing two stiles, there are notices saying "No picnic" next to a large circular table with surrounding seats. This is a useful landmark, indicating a point where the path forks left downhill and leads to another stile. A few minutes later, below a stone enclosure, the path deteriorates and a way must be found up to a higher level – look for signs of where others have gone and occasional cairns. After passing some boats the path disappears again, another diversion uphill leading to a headland with a few almond trees growing in bare red earth.

Round a corner beyond the headland there's an eroded gully: go high to avoid the steepest parts, reaching a terrace with cairns. At the end of this terrace follow the lower path to reach the next stile and another terrace, quite low down near the sea. Next, go uphill by a fallen tree, cross a headland among boulders and heather, and then go fairly steeply upwards through terraces of olive trees. This part of the route is well marked and leads in about 15min to a path which contours left above a steep cliff to reach another stile.

continues overleaf

Down the coast from Deià to Port d'Andratx

A coastal walk from Deià to Port de Sóller (cont.)

The path then dips into and out of a stream bed and goes over a stile into a lane. Turn left and when the lane ends a minute later find the continuation of the footpath on the right. Four minutes later this reaches a concrete road near some houses. After a few minutes of steep uphill walking, cross another stream bed (normally dry) by means of the metal pegs in the enclosing dry-stone walls – a slightly awkward manoeuvre for the not-so-agile. Turn right along the wide road by the Bens d'Avall **restaurant** (closed in winter), and follow this uphill for 1500m to reach the Muleta road junction. Turn left, then right, to reach a cross-track near a large house with a square tower. The most direct route to Port de Sóller from here is to turn right and go through the gate towards the house, following a path to the right between the buildings. Continue through a gate to the mule track which leads down to the *Rocamar* hotel. Turn left for the seafront and the stop for trams to Sóller town.

An alternative ending to the walk is to cross the Muleta Gran headland to the **lighthouse**, from where there are outstanding views of Port de Sóller's natural circular harbour, and walk down the road to the port. To do this, turn left instead of right along the cross-track by the house with the tower, and climb over the wall on the right of the locked gate by means of inset metal bars. Follow the path ahead and after about 50m look for a blue arrow on the wall to the right. Cairns and more blue arrows show the way along a narrow path through abandoned terraces. The path descends a little, then rises across open ground strewn with wild flowers – look out for bright yellow hemispherical euphorbia bushes in spring. A track is met at the corner of a disused military building just before reaching the lighthouse.

Further east, *Ca'n Xeline*, in an attractively converted cellar close to *La Residencia* hotel at c/Archiduque Luís Salvador 19 (closed Wed), specializes in Mallorcan cuisine and fondues, while nearby at no. 24, *Sa Dorado* is the best place in town for fish. Both of Deià's top-notch hotels (see above) have excellent but expensive restaurants. At *Es Moli* it's the nearby *Restaurant Ca'n Quet*, with a *menú del día* for around 3500ptas, but that's only about half the price of a meal at *El Olivo*, in *La Residencia*.

Son Marroig

Son Marroig is open June–Sept Mon–Sat 9.30am–2pm & 3–7pm; Oct–May Mon–Sat 9.30am–2pm & 3–5.30pm; 350ptas.

Pressing on from Deià, the C710 snakes through the mountains for 3km to reach **Son Marroig**, an imposing L-shaped mansion perched high above the seashore (and just below the road). The house dates from late medieval times, but it was refashioned in the nineteenth century to become the favourite residence of the Hapsburg archduke **Ludwig Salvator** (1847–1915). Dynastically insignificant but extremely rich, the Austrian noble was a man in search of a hobby – and he found it in Mallorca. He first visited the island at the tender age of 19 and, falling head-over-heels in love with the place, returned to buy a chunk of the west coast between Deià and Valldemossa. In residence, Ludwig immersed himself in all things

Mallorquín, learning the dialect and chronicling the island's topography, archeology, history and folklore in astounding detail. He churned out no fewer than seven volumes on the Balearics and, perhaps more importantly, played a leading role as a proto-environmentalist, conserving the coastline of his estates and, amongst many projects, paying for a team of geologists to chart the Coves del Drac (see p.165).

The **house** boasts a handful of period rooms, whose antique furnishings and fittings are enlivened by an eclectic sample of Hispano-Arabic pottery. On display too are many of the archduke's manuscripts and pen drawings, as well as some interesting photographs of the man. It won't be long, however, before you're out in the **garden**, whose pretty terraces are graced by a Neoclassical belvedere of Carrara marble. The views out along the jagged, forested coast are gorgeous, and down below is a slender promontory where the archduke used to park his yacht, known as **Sa Foradada**, "the rock pierced by a hole" (the hole in question is a strange circular affair, sited high up in the rock face at the end of the promontory). It takes about forty minutes to walk the three kilometres down to the tip, a largely straightforward excursion to a delightfully secluded and scenic spot. A sign on the gate at the beginning of the path (up the hill and to the left of the house) insists you need to get permission at Son Marroig before setting out – it's worth asking, but don't be too concerned if no one at the house seems bothered. There should be few problems with direction-finding on this short jaunt: about 100m beyond the gate, keep right at the fork in the track; and as you approach the end of the promontory, think carefully before deciding to attempt the precarious climb beyond the old jetties. On your return, you can slake your thirst at the ugly, modern **café-bar** by the car park near the house.

Beyond Son Marroig, the C710 stays high above the coast, twisting through what was once the estate of the archduke and passing by the **Mirador de Ses Pites** en route to Valldemossa.

Valldemossa and around

The ancient and intriguing hill town of **VALLDEMOSSA** may at first appear disappointing if you're coming from Deià via the C710, as the western outskirts are a bore. The best approach is from the south, where, after squeezing through a narrow, wooded defile, the road from Palma enters a lovely valley, whose tiered and terraced fields ascend to the town, a sloping jumble of rusticated houses and monastic buildings backclothed by the mountains. The origins of Valldemossa date to the early fourteenth century, when the asthmatic King Sancho built a royal palace here in the hills where the air was easier to breathe. Later, in 1399, the palace was gifted to Carthusian monks from Tarragona, who converted and extended the original buildings into a **monastery**, which is now the island's most visited building after Palma cathedral. Besides the monastery, however, there's not much to Valldemossa. The narrow cobbled lanes of the oldest and prettiest part of town tumble down the hill around the dilapidated hulk of the church of **Sant Bartomeu**. Close by, along a narrow alley at c/Rectoria 5, is the humble birthplace of **Santa Catalina Thomás**, a sixteenth-century nun revered for her piety. The interior has been turned into a glitzy little shrine.

The monastery

*The monastery
at Valldemossa
is open
March–Oct
Mon–Sat
9.30am–1pm &
3–6pm;
Nov–Feb
Mon–Sat
9.30am–1pm &
3–5.30pm;
1000ptas.*

Remodelled on several occasions, most of the present complex of the **Real Cartuja de Jesús de Nazaret** (Royal Carthusian Monastery of Jesus of Nazareth) is of seventeenth- and eighteenth-century construction, its square and heavy church leading to the shadowy corridors of the cloisters beyond. The monastery owes its present notoriety almost entirely to the novelist and republican polemicist **George Sand**, who, with her companion, the composer **Frédéric Chopin**, lived here for four months in 1838–39. Just three years earlier the last monks had been evicted during the Liberal-inspired suppression of the monasteries, so the pair were able to rent a commodious set of vacant cells. Their stay is commemorated in Sand's *A Winter in Majorca*, a stodgy, self-important book that is considerably overplayed hereabouts, being available in just about every European language. Reading the book today, what comes through strongly is the couple's mean-spirited contempt for their Spanish neighbours: Sand explains that their nickname for Mallorca, "Monkey Island", was coined for its "crafty, thieving and yet innocent" inhabitants, who, she asserts, are "heartless, selfish and impertinent". What the villagers made of Sand is unknown, but her trouser-wearing, cigar-smoking image – along with her "living in sin" – could hardly have made the woman popular.

There's an obvious, though limited curiosity in looking around Sand and Chopin's old quarters, but the monastery boasts far more interesting diversions, and it's easy to follow the multilingual signs around. A visit begins in the gloomy, aisleless **church**, which is distinguished by its Late Baroque ceiling paintings and fanciful bishop's throne, though the lines of the nave are spoiled by the clumsy wooden stalls of the choir. In the adjoining cloisters, the first port of call is the **pharmacy**, which survived the expulsion of the monks to serve the town's medicinal needs well into the twentieth century. Its shelves are crammed with a host of beautifully decorated majolica jars, antique glass receptacles and painted wood boxes, each carefully inscribed with the name of the potion or drug.

The nearby **prior's cell** is, despite its name, a comfortable suite of bright, sizeable rooms, enhanced by access to a private garden with splendid views down the valley. The cell, together with the adjoining library and audience room, are graced by a wide assortment of religious *objets d'art*, including an exquisite medieval triptych. This degree of luxury – the other cells are of similar proportions – was clearly not what the ascetic St Bruno had in mind when he founded the Carthusian order in the eleventh century, but it's hard to blame the monks at Valldemossa for lightening what must have been a very heavy burden of privations. Bruno's rigorous regime, inspired by his years as a hermit, had his monks in almost continuous isolation, gathering together only for certain church services and to eat in the refectory on Sundays. At other times, lay brothers fed the monks through hatches along the cloister corridors, though this was hardly an onerous task: three days a week the monks had only bread and water, and they never ate meat. The diet and the mountain air, however, seemed to suit: the Valldemossa monks' longevity was proverbial.

Along the corridor, **Cell No. 2** exhibits miscellaneous curios relating to Chopin and Sand, from portraits and a lock of hair to musical scores and letters (it was in this cell that the composer wrote the *Raindrop Prelude*). There's more of the same next door in Cell **No. 4**, plus Chopin's piano, which only arrived after three months of unbelievable complications, just three weeks before the couple left for Paris. Considering the hype, these incidental mementoes are something of an anti climax. Neither do things improve much in the ground-floor galleries of the adjacent **Municipal Museum**, which feature local landscape painters and trace the pioneering endeavours of Archduke Ludwig Salvator (see p.110). But don't give up: upstairs, another part of the museum has a small but outstanding collection of **modern art**, including work by Miró and Picasso, not to mention Francis Bacon and Henry Moore. And be sure to take the doorway beside the prior's cell, which leads outside the cloisters to the **Palace of King Sancho**. It's not the original palace at all – that disappeared long ago – but it is the oldest part of the complex and its fortified walls, mostly dating from the sixteenth century, accommodate a string of handsome period rooms. Regular displays of folk dancing and piano concerts are held here too.

Practicalities

Along the modern bypass that skirts Valldemossa to the north there are several car parks; the biggest of these, at the west end of town, is where **buses** stop. Regular services arrive from Palma, 18km away, before continuing to Deià and Sóller; except on Sundays, one bus a day also comes from Peguera and points west. From the bus stop, it's just a couple of minutes' walk to the monastery – cross the bypass and keep going straight on. The town doesn't have a tourist office and maps of the place are impossible to come by, but orientation is easy – use the monastery, on the west side of the town centre, as your landmark.

Accommodation in Valldemossa itself is limited to the *Ca'n Mario*, c/Uetan 8 (☎612122; ④), an attractive *hostal* where an elegant, curio-cluttered foyer leads to comfortably old-fashioned

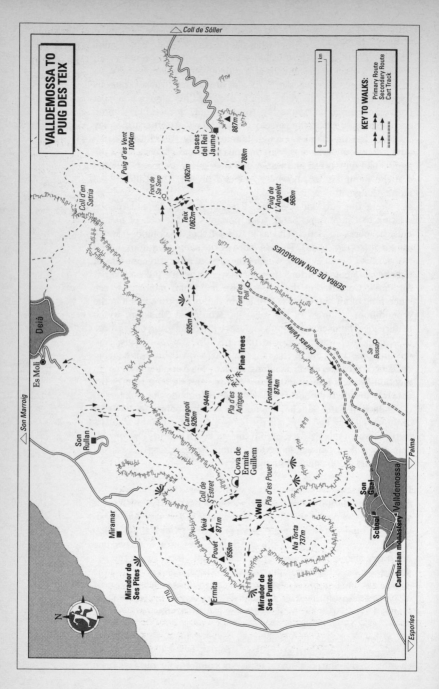

VALLDEMOSSA TO
PUIG DES TEIX

△ Coll de Sóller

KEY TO WALKS:
Primary Route
Secondary Route
Cart Track

1 km

0

Puig d'es Vent
1004m

Font de
Sa Serp ◌

1062m

Cases
del Rei
Jaume ■

887m ▲

788m ▲

Puig de
L'Angelet
968m ▲

Coll d'en
Satria

Teix
1062m ▲

SERRA DE SON MORAGUES

Deià

Es Moli ◌

△ Son Marroig

935m ▲

Font d'es
Poll ◌

Cairats Valley

Sa
Bussa ◌

Pine Trees

Pla d'es
Aritges

Fontanelles
874m ▲

Son
Rullan ■

Caragoli
926m ▲ 944m ▲

Cova de
Ermita
Guillem

Miramar ■

Coll de
S'Estret

Well

Pla d'es Pouet

Son
Gual ■

School

Carthusian monastery / Valldemossa

▽ Palma

Veià
Pouét
871m ▲   858m ▲

Na Torta
737m ▲

Mirador de
Ses Pites

Mirador de
Ses Puntes

Ermita

N

▽ Esporles

From Valldemossa to Puig des Teix by the Archduke's Path

12.5km, 674m of ascent, 4hr 30min–5hr.

Down the coast from Deià to Port d'Andratx

For more information about Ludwig Salvator, and for details on visiting his mansion at Son Marroig, see p.110.

As elsewhere in Mallorca, the mountains around **Valldemossa** are criss-crossed with paths made by charcoal-burners, hunters and other local people, but this area is particularly richly endowed because of the work of the nineteenth-century Austrian archduke **Ludwig Salvator**, who had some wonderful paths constructed so that he could ride on horseback to admire the scenery. Today walkers benefit from Salvator's efforts because his estate of Son Moragues was acquired by ICONA (the island's organization for nature conservation) in 1967. The country between Valldemossa and Deià is mountainous and wild, abounding in steep cliffs and rocky summits. The lower slopes are wooded but the tops are almost devoid of vegetation, with numerous dramatic viewpoints, many of them overlooking the sea. The terrain is rough and even the paths are stony, but the following circular walk – which can be lengthened or shortened to suit – is a classic, showing the best of the area.

From the back of the small car park at the edge of Valldemossa, opposite the road which forks left into the town from the Palma road, head uphill to the school. Go up the steps at the left-hand side of the school, then turn right and almost immediately left. Descend slightly then turn right and go uphill until the road swings right and ends at a house. Turn left up an old path that leads into the woods, entered by a stile over a gate. The stony path rises moderately steeply in numerous bends to reach an opening in the wall at the edge of the wooded plain, the **Pla d'es Pouet** (a short cut near the top is waymarked, but it makes little difference which way you go). From the wall go straight on across the level ground to reach an old **well** (polluted, alas) in a large clearing with a conspicuous fallen tree. This well is a vital reference point in a confusing area and it is essential to take your bearings carefully. The option to lengthen the walk, taking in Veià, begins here and is described overleaf.

For the main walk be careful to take the path bearing slightly right, northeast at first and then north and leading easily up to the **Coll de S'Estret de Son Gallard**. On the col is a barrier of brushwood set up by hunters who still practise the traditional *caza a coll* method, which you can observe: birds are lured to fly along artificial tunnels created by cutting passages through the trees, then captured in nets. From the nearby stone seats in the form of a "V", the path continues uphill to the right. **Cova de Ermita Guillem**, an interesting hermit's cave that offers excellent shelter if you are unlucky with the weather, can be visited to the south of the main path: look out for a branch path on the right, which leads to the enclosure in front of the cave. Rejoin the uphill main path, steep in places, to begin the most spectacular part of the walk, a wide and easy walkway on the edge of cliffs with a simply breathtaking view.

As you approach the hill of Caragoli, a path branching off left towards the cliffs offers the possibility of an adventurous **descent to Deià** by a thrilling, but surprisingly easy cliff path. If you're tempted to try this, find the start by making for the largest of the holm oaks on the horizon, growing out of a pothole. In the woods below, look out for a large *sitja* (charcoal-burning circle), with two stone shelters and a stone bread-oven: turn right here, join another track and turn left. Reaching a gate, double-back along terraces to a *caseta* (field-house), from where a path leads down to the *Es Moli* hotel in Deià. *continues overleaf*

From Valldemossa to Puig des Teix (cont.)

Following the main path, the views continue to delight at every step, but take the little diversion to the 926-metre summit of **Caragoli** to feast the eyes even more: among the mountains, Puig Major, Teix and Galatzó are prominent, while you can see Port de Sóller on the coast, and the Bay of Palma. After this the path climbs southeast to 944m, before descending gently over a sloping arid plain, the **Pla d'es Aritges** (*aritge* is smilax, the plant designed to tear walkers' legs to shreds if they are wearing shorts). A path junction at a lonely group of pine trees offers the possibility of shortening the walk by returning to Valldemossa *via* **Fontanelles**. To continue on the main route, take the left fork, which brings you over a 935-metre top and, shortly after, to a viewpoint overlooking Deià. After this the path swings east and begins to descend to the Teix path junction.

At the junction, branch left on a path which scrambles up a little gully and then over a stile perched on the edge of a cliff. It's an easy walk to the **Pla de Sa Serp**, a little plain where there is a spring. A well-used path leads up to the dip between the two tops and on to the main west **summit of Teix** (1062m), where the views are especially good to the northeast, looking over the Sóller valley to Mitx Dia, the western summit of Puig Major, with the tops of Cornadors, L'Ofre and the Alfabia ridge forming a fascinating skyline. Return to the Teix path junction by the same route (avoid the difficult-to-follow route southwest from Teix towards Sa Bassa) and turn left to follow the main track down the **Cairats valley**. First you'll come to an old "snowhouse" (a deep hole used for storing ice in winter), then a mountain hut and below that a spring and picnic site, the **Font d'es Poll** (Well of the Poplar). The wide track beyond is rather stony but there are no route-finding problems. On the way down you'll see reconstructions of a *sitja* and of a charcoal-worker's shelter, signposted and labelled. Keep on the main track down the Cairats valley, going through a gate and ignoring two branches left, before joining a road which leads down to Valldemossa by a house with a square tower, Son Gual.

Extension of the walk to Mirador de Ses Puntes and Veià

1.5km, 116m of ascent, 45min.

From the well in the clearing on the Pla d'es Pouet, take the path which leads northwest at first, before zigzagging uphill and swinging west. Fork left shortly after passing an old bread-oven, to reach the **Mirador de Ses Puntes**. From this superb viewpoint return to the fork and take the left branch, which rises through the trees to the top of **Pouet** (858m) and, after a little dip, **Veià** (871m). For much of the way the path is the wide bridleway built by Ludwig Salvator; from it you can look down on Sa Foradada, a rocky headland near his house at Son Marroig, pierced with an enormous hole. From the ruined shelter on Veià the path descends to the Coll de S'Estret de Son Gallard, where you rejoin the main path up from the well.

rooms; it's situated just five minutes' walk from the monastery – from the pedestrianized area between the church and the palace, go downhill and take the first turning on the right. The only other option nearby, off the C710 just over 2km west of town, is the solitary *Hotel Residencia Vistamar* (☎612300; ⑨), an opulently converted eighteenth-century *finca* (farmhouse) whose gardens and swimming pool abut a deep, green gully that plunges down towards the sea. It's a gorgeous place to stay, and the rooms are decorated in traditional style with dark wood and bright fabrics.

The centre of Valldemossa heaves with **restaurants and cafés**, mostly geared up for day-trippers – many offer dire fast food at inflated prices. Nonetheless, amongst the dross there are several quality places, including the unpretentious first-floor restaurant of the *Ca'n Mario* (closed Tues), where a small but mouthwatering selection of Mallorcan dishes cost around 1000ptas each; don't be deterred by the lack of a sign or menu posted outside the *hostal*. Another good if more tourist-clogged choice is *Ca'n Pedro* (closed Mon), a large café-restaurant beside the main car park, where tasty omelettes start at 600ptas. There's also the popular *Ca'n Costa* (closed Tues), which occupies a *finca* about 2km out of town on the Deià road; the decor is over the top – old farm equipment and other rusticated touches – but the shaded terrace is lovely, and the Mallorcan cuisine is excellent and affordable, with light meals from 800ptas.

Port de Valldemossa

The closest spot to Valldemossa for a swim is **Port de Valldemossa**, a hamlet set in the shadow of the mountains at the mouth of a narrow, craggy cove. The beach here is small and shingly, and prone to be battered by the surf, but the scenery is stunning and the village sports a handful of **restaurants**. The pick of the bunch is the busy *Es Port*, which has a well-deserved reputation for its superb seafood, with main courses from around 1400ptas. The drive down to the hamlet, once Valldemossa's gateway to the outside world, is stimulating: head west out of town along the C710, turn right near the *Hotel Vistamar* and follow the twisty, six-kilometre-long side road through the mountains. There's no public transport.

La Granja and Esporles

The hacienda of **La Granja** nestles in a tranquil wooded and terraced valley some 10km southwest from Valldemossa – follow the C710 for about 8.5km and take the signposted turn. The house and its grounds are a popular day trip (Palma–Estellencs **buses** stop by the entrance), but, despite the many visitors, the estate maintains a languorous air of old patrician comfort. There's hardly anything new or modern on view, but this doesn't come across as a contrived effect – La Granja was occupied until very recently by the Fortuny family, who took possession in the mid-fifteenth century, and it seems that modernization simply never crossed their minds after the 1920s.

La Granja is open daily 10am–7pm; 1000ptas.

A visit begins in the expansive **forecourt**, shaded by plane trees and edged by antiquated workshops where costumed "artisans" practise such traditional crafts as wood-turning and candle-making. This part of the visit is a bit bogus, but good fun all the same – and the home-made pastries and doughnuts are lip-smacking. From the forecourt, signs direct you up round the back of the house, past an incidental collection of well-weathered farming tackle and on into the tiny Renaissance-style **gardens**. Next door, a small courtyard leads to the main **house**, a ramshackle sequence of apartments strewn with domestic clutter – everything from childrens' games and mannequins, through old costumes, musical instruments and a cabinet of fans, to a fully equipped antique kitchen. There's also a delightful little theatre, where plays were once performed for the household in a manner common amongst Europe's nineteenth-century rural landowners. Likewise, the dining room, with its faded paintings and heavy drapes, has a real touch of country elegance, as does the graceful first-floor loggia. Look out also for the finely crafted, green-tinted Mallorcan chandeliers, and the beautiful majolica tile-panels that embellish several walls.

Tagged onto the house, a series of **workrooms** dustily recall the days when La Granja was a profitable and almost entirely self-sufficient concern. A wine press, almond and olive oil mills prepared the estate's produce for export, whilst plumbers, carpenters, cobblers, weavers and sail-makers all kept pace with domestic requirements from their specialized workshops. The Fortunys were one of Mallorca's more enlightened landowning families, and employees were well fed by the kitchen staff, who made cheeses, bread and preserves by hand. Beyond the workrooms, a footpath leads up the adjacent stream to several sheep and goat pens (closed at 2pm), but this is hardly riveting and you're better off proceeding back to the main entrance, where you may coincide with a mildly diverting display of Mallorcan **folk dancing** (summer Wed & Fri 3.30–5pm).

On the road from La Granja towards Palma, it's a couple of kilometres to **ESPORLES**, an unexciting town whose elongated main street follows the line of an attractive stone watercourse. There's no particular reason to stop, but if you're keen to find a **room**, you could try the one and only *hostal*, the simple *Central* (☎610202; ③), by the main church at Plaça Espanya 8. There's nowhere outstanding to eat, but the *Café Passeig*, on the main street, should suffice.

Puigpunyent and Galilea

Southwest of La Granja, a country road heads up a V-shaped valley before snaking through the foothills of the Serra de Tramuntana. After 10km you come to **PUIGPUNYENT**, a small, tidy farmers' village enhanced by a handsome seventeenth-century church with a mighty rectangular tower. Peaceful and quaint, the place is worth a brief stroll and the *English Rose* restaurant-bar, beside the church, serves reasonably priced snacks and meals. On the far side of the village, a signposted, 4.5-kilometre-long side road ducks and dips northwest through forested ravines to reach **La Reserva Puig de**

Galatzó (Wed–Sun daily 10am–6pm, till 8pm in summer; 1000ptas). Here, behind unseemly wire fences, a clearly defined three-kilometre footpath explores the lower slopes of Puig de Galatzó, at 1026m the highest peak for miles around. It's an easy walk through a dense forest of holm oak and pine, past a sequence of rather prepackaged attractions: a couple of modest waterfalls, uninspiring caves and a fig orchard. The *mirador* at the start of the trail offers a great view of the mountain, but, that apart, it's a humdrum outing, which you'll share with coachloads of day-trippers.

Travelling southwest from Puigpunyent, a benign valley of citrus groves and gnarled olive trees leads to **GALILEA**, 4km away, an engaging scattering of whitewashed farmsteads built in sight of a stolid hilltop church. There's a rusty old café-bar beside the church, but the best place to soak up the bucolic atmosphere is at the *Bar Galilea*, below the church and beside the through road, where the views from the terrace are gorgeous and the Mallorcan food is both delicious and cheap.

Beyond Galilea, the road wriggles its way through to the unremarkable settlement of Capdellà, before squeezing through the mountains – the most beautiful, and nerve-jangling, part of the drive – for a further 8km to enter Andratx (see p.120) from the east.

Port des Canonge and Banyalbufar

Back on the C710, just beyond the turning for La Granja, a narrow side road forks down to the coast at **PORT DES CANONGE**. The five-kilometre journey down through thickly forested hills is splendid, but the settlement itself is disappointing, a scrawny, modern *urbanització* flanking a shingle beach. Far better, in fact, to stay on the main coast road for a further 6km, as it weaves round to the attractive village of **BANYALBUFAR**, whose terraced fields cling gingerly to the coastal cliffs. The land here has been cultivated since Moorish times, with a spring above the village providing a water supply that's still channelled down the hillside along slender water-courses into open storage cisterns, the unlikely-looking home for a few carp. The village itself, little more than an elongated main street along the C710, is enhanced by old stone houses and a chunky medieval church. A rash of modern villas somewhat disfigures the scene, but it remains a likeable spot, with a rough and rocky beach ten minutes' walk away down the hill, past the *Hotel Sa Coma*.

Banyalbufar has two hotels and one hostal. Behind its antique exterior, the excellent *Hotel Mar y Vent*, on the main street in the centre of the village (☎618000; ⑨), features attractively furnished rooms with balconies looking out to sea, plus a rooftop swimming pool. There's probably more chance of a vacancy, however, at the *Hostal Baronia*, at the west end of the main drag (April–Oct; ☎618146; ④), an old-fashioned, laid-back sort of place whose forty balconied bedrooms occupy a tastefully refurbished manor house. The *Hotel Sa Coma* (April–Oct; ☎618034; ⑤), an unappealing concrete lump below the main street on the way to the beach, is the third choice.

The village has a good selection of **restaurants**. There's an enticing terrace bar-restaurant at the *Mar y Vent*, where you can enjoy traditional Mallorcan dishes as well as tasty seafood at reasonable prices. Nearby, the *Café Bellavista* (closed Sun) serves delicious salads, omelettes and light meals from a delightful garden terrace. Island cuisine is also available at the *Hostal Baronia*, though the quality here is less consistently high – and the same caution applies to the neighbouring *Son Tomas* (closed Tues), where you should stick to the seafood and the paella, a good deal at 1400ptas.

Estellencs

Some 2km west out of Banyalbufar stands perhaps the most impressive of the lookout points that dot the coastal road, the **Mirador de Ses Animes**, a sixteenth-century watchtower built as a sentinel against pirate attack, which provides stunning views along the coast. ESTELLENCS, 6km further on, is similar to Banyalbufar, with steep coastal cliffs and tight terraced fields, though if anything a tad prettier. There's almost no sign of tourist development in the village, its narrow, winding alleys adorned with old stone houses and a trim, largely eighteenth-century parish church – peep inside for a look at the exquisite pinewood reredos. A steep, but driveable, two-kilometre lane leads down from the village, past olive and orange orchards, to **Cala Estellencs**, a craggy, surf-buffeted cove that shelters a beach (of sorts – you won't spot any sand) and a summertime bar.

Estellencs has one **hotel**, the cosily furnished *Maristel*, with great views down over the coast (Jan–Oct; ☎618529; ④). Amongst a handful of **cafés**, the low-price *Cafeteria Estellencs*, opposite the *Maristel*, sells substantial and tasty snacks, and the nearby *Bar Pizzeria Giardini* is a safe, if predictable bet, offering pizzas and the like. Best of the **restaurants** is the *Montimar*, sited in a graceful old mansion near the church, which serves splendid traditional meals, including rabbit dishes for 1250ptas. Its principal, but less distinguished rival is the restaurant of the *Maristel*, where paella will set you back around 1300ptas per person.

Andratx

Heading southwest from Estellencs, the C710 threads along the littoral for 6km, before slipping through a tunnel and, immediately beyond, passing the **Mirador de Ricardo Roca**. At 400m above the sea, this lookout point offers some fine coastal views, and you can wet your whistle at the *Es Grau* **restaurant** next door.

Beyond the *mirador*, the C710 turns inland, cutting down through forested foothills to **ANDRATX**, a small and unaffected town 19km from Estellencs, where the main event is the Wednesday morning **market**, a tourist favourite. At other times there's not much to detain you, though the old houses and cobbled streets of the upper town form a harmonious ochre ensemble that culminates in the fortress-like walls of the thirteenth-century church of **Santa Maria**, built high and strong to deter raiding pirates.

Down the coast from Deià to Port d'Andratx

For information about Peguera, 7km southeast of Andratx see p.90.

Sant Elm and Illa Dragonera

From Andratx there's an easy and enjoyable seven-kilometre hike along a narrow country road to the dishevelled, low-key resort of **SANT ELM** (in Castilian, San Telmo). Directions couldn't be more straightforward – just follow the road (initially c/General Bernardo Riera) west from Andratx's church and keep going, out into the pretty, orchard-covered landscape that rolls around the hillside hamlet of S'Arracó (after 3km) and down to the sea.

Sant Elm is little more than one main street draped along the shore, with a sandy beach at one end and a harbour at the other. There are plans to expand the resort, but at present it's a quiet spot where there's a reasonable chance of a **room** in high season, either at the conspicuous *Hotel Aquamarín* (May–Oct; ☎109075; ④), a spectacularly unsuccessful concrete edifice built in the style of an old watchtower and equipped with depressingly spartan rooms; or, preferably, at the *Hostal Dragonera* (☎109086; ③), a simple modern building with clean and neat rooms, most of which offer sea views. For such a small place, there's a surprisingly wide choice of **cafés and restaurants**. The *Café Playas* serves filling snacks at low prices, while the set meal at the *Hostal Dragonera* costs a bargain 900ptas. Moving upmarket, the *Vistamar* has a mouthwatering paella for 1400ptas and, best of the lot, the *Na Caracola* specializes in seafood and has a charming terrace and ocean views – reckon on 4500ptas for a complete meal, including house wine.

If you've walked here, there's no need to trudge back. From May to October, **buses** ply between Sant Elm, Andratx and Peguera (see p.90) seven times a day Monday to Saturday, and once on Sundays (in winter, once daily). An alternative and far more enjoyable way out of Sant Elm is by boat, either for Port d'Andratx (May–Sept; 1 daily; 600ptas) or Port de Sóller (June–Sept; 1 weekly; 2000ptas; reservations essential on ☎630170).

Illa Dragonera

From Sant Elm's minuscule harbour, boats shuttle across to the austere offshore islet of **Illa Dragonera**. This uninhabited chunk of rock, some 4km long and 700m wide, lies at an oblique angle to the coast, with an imposing ridge of seacliffs dominating its north-western shore. Behind the ridge, a rough track travels the length of the island, linking a pair of craggy capes and their lighthouses. Most people visit for the scenic solitude, but the island is also good for birdlife – ospreys, shags, gulls and other seabirds are plentiful and there may be chance sightings of several species of raptor.

There are two ways of getting to the island. Seven times a day, four days a week, between April and November (usually Tues, Thurs, Sat & Sun), a **ferry** rattles across, dropping passengers about halfway up the east shore at a tiny cove-harbour. Arrangements for the return trip should be made on the way out; the return fare is 1100ptas. If, however, you're lukewarm about tramping the island, the better option is to take a two-hour **cruise**, which allows just thirty minutes on Dragonera and spends the rest of the time exploring the local coastline (twice daily on the other three days of the week, May–Sept only). This trip costs 1400ptas and reservations are a good idea, though not essential. For sailing times, ask at the harbour or telephone ☎470449 (mobile ☎908/532901).

Port d'Andratx

The picturesque port and fishing harbour of **PORT D'ANDRATX**, 5km southwest of Andratx, has been disfigured by low-rise shopping complexes and apartment blocks. However, it's not quite a classic case of overdevelopment: there's still no denying the prettiness of the setting, with the port standing at the head of a long and slender inlet that's flanked by wooded hills; and the heart of the old town, which slopes up from the south side of the bay, more than hints at former virtues in its cramped network of ancient lanes. Sunsets show the place to best advantage, casting long shadows up the bay, and it's then that the old town's gaggle of harbourside restaurants crowd with holidaymakers and expatriates, a genteel and rather blimpish crew, occasionally irritated by raucous teenagers.

Port d'Andratx may be a tad on the staid side (and the nearest sandy beach is over the hills at Camp de Mar – see p.91), but it's still an enjoyable place to spend a night or two and it's easy to reach. There are summer **boat trips** along the coast to and from Sant Elm (see p.121), and regular **buses** from Andratx and from Camp de Mar and Palma. The bus station is at the back of the bay, a brief walk from both the old town (on the left) and the big, modern marina (to the right). There's a reasonably good chance of finding an **inexpensive room**. Try along the harbourfront of the old town, where the no-frills *Hostal Las Palmeras* has simple rooms (☎672078; ④), or, further down the quay, at the pleasanter *Hotel Brismar* (☎671600; ④), a straightforward, modern hotel with plain and comfortable bedrooms. Better still, head one block up from the harbourfront to the quiet, relaxing *Hostal-residencia Catalina Vera*, c/Isaac Peral 63 (April–Oct; ☎671918; ④), a neatly shuttered and whitewashed building with frugal, tidy rooms, edged by a small orchard. Finally, the *Hostal Moderno* (April–Oct; ☎671650; ④), about five minutes' walk up from the harbourside on the road to

Camp de Mar, offers plain but serviceable rooms, though they're situated above a noisy restaurant-bar. Upmarket accommodation can be found at the *Villa Italia* (☎674011; ⑨), an opulent, 1920s twin-towered mansion set behind a steeply terraced garden. The hotel has luxuries such as a rooftop swimming pool, as well as gorgeous views out over the bay, and is a five-minute stroll west of the old part of town along c/San Carlos (the road that heads down the south side of the inlet to Cap de Sa Mola).

Along the harbourfront are the town's best and most expensive **restaurants**: at the far end of the quay, the *Rocamar* offers delicious seafood and a lovely waterside terrace, while the *Layn* (closed Mon), a few paces away, serves a wide range of wonderful fish dishes, including a superb paella for 1550ptas per person. Close by, just off the harbourfront at Plaça Almirante Oquendo 12, you'll find less expensive seafood, as well as tasty pizzas and pastas, at the extremely popular *La Piazzetta*. One block up from the waterside on c/Isaac Peral, there are several other good, low-cost places, including *Casa Vieja*, at no. 43, where monkfish, for instance, will cost you a bargain 1900ptas; and the bar-restaurant *Pina*, along the street at no. 51, which sells cheap and filling snacks. Amongst a handful of harbourside bars, *Mitj & Mitj* is the liveliest and youngest, while *Tim's* is more laid-back and likeable.

Beyond Sóller: Cala Tuent to the Cap de Formentor

Beyond a doubt, the most interesting approach to the northernmost tip of the island, the Cap de Formentor, is the continuation of the C710 beyond Sóller, slipping through the highest and harshest section of the Serra de Tramuntana. For the most part, the mountains drop straight into the sea, precipitous and largely unapproachable cliffs with barely a cove in sight. The accessible exceptions are the comely beach at **Cala Tuent** and the horribly commercial hamlet of **Sa Calobra** next door. The best place to break your journey, however, is inland at the monastery and pilgrimage centre of **Lluc**, which offers a diverting museum, ready access to excellent hiking trails in the mountains, a campground and a fairly reliable supply of inexpensive rooms.

There's more low-priced monastic accommodation at the hilltop **Ermita de Nostra Senyora del Puig**, just outside of **Pollença**, a beguiling old town of grandee mansions sitting at the foot of a beautiful Calvary. Nearby, at the end of the C710 and just 60km from Sóller, is **Port de Pollença**, a low-key, medium-sized resort whose long sandy beach drapes around the Badia de Pollença. A popular summertime retreat for the inhabitants of Palma, the resort abounds with places to stay, and is within easy striking distance of the dramatic seacliffs of the **Península de Formentor**.

Long-distance **buses** link Palma with Pollença and its port, while twice every weekday from May to October a bus runs along the C710 from Port de Sóller to Port de Pollença, and on to Port d'Alcúdia. These services are supplemented by more localized routings, which are itemized in "Travel details" on p.145.

Cala Tuent, Sa Calobra and Escorca

Heading northeast from Sóller, the C710 zigzags up into the mountains. After 7km there's a last lingering look over the coast from the **Mirador de Ses Barques**, but then the road snakes inland, tunnelling through the western flanks of **Puig Major**, the island's highest mountain at 1447m. Beyond the tunnel is the **Gorg Blau** (Blue Gorge), a wild and barren ravine that was a well-known beauty spot until a hydroelectric scheme created a trio of puddle-like reservoirs. And there's further bad news here: the dramatic trail which twists up Puig Major from the military base beside the main road remains off-limits because of the radar station on the summit. This makes **Puig de Massanella** (1367m), which looms over the gorge to the east, the highest mountain that can be climbed on Mallorca.

Puig de Massanella is best ascended from Lluc – see the recommended hike on p.127.

At the far end of the gorge the road tunnels into the mountains, to emerge just short of a left turn leading to Cala Tuent and Sa Calobra. An exhilarating, ear-popping detour to the seashore, this well-surfaced side road hairpins down the mountain slopes so severely that at one point it actually turns 270 degrees to run under itself. About 10km down the road, fork left over the hills for the four-kilometre journey to the **Ermita de Sant Llorenç**, a tiny medieval church perched high above the coast, and **CALA TUENT**, where a smattering of villas clings to the northern slopes of Puig Major as it tumbles down to the seashore. Ancient orchards temper the harshness of the mountain, and the gravel and sand beach is one of the quietest on the north coast. It's a lovely spot to while away a few hours and, provided you stay well inshore, the swimming is safe. There's nowhere to stay, but an excellent **restaurant** sits on the far side of the cove – the *Es Vergeret*, where lunch is the finest meal of the day, a wide range of fish and meat dishes best devoured at the terrace bar in sight of the ocean.

Sa Calobra

If you ignore the left fork to Cala Tuent, it's just 2km more to **SA CALOBRA**, a modern resort occupying a pint-sized cove in the shadow of the mountains. There's nothing wrong with the setting, but the place is an overvisited disaster. Almost every island operator deposits a busload of tourists here every day in summer, and the crush is quite unbearable – as is the overpriced and overcooked food at the local cafés. The reason why so many people come here is to visit the impressive box canyon at the mouth of the **Torrente de Pareis** (River of the Twins). It takes about ten minutes to follow the partly tunnelled walkway round the coast from the resort to the mouth of the canyon. Here, with sheer cliffs rising on every side, the milky-green river trickles down to the narrow bank of shingle that bars its final approach to the sea – though the scene is transformed after heavy rainfall, when the river crashes down into the canyon and out into the sea.

Escorca

ESCORCA, a poorly defined scattering of houses along the C710, a couple of kilometres northeast of the Sa Calobra turn-off, lays claim to the island's oldest church in the **Oratori de Sant Pere**, a modest structure dating from the middle of the thirteenth century. From the car park opposite the nearby *Restaurant Escorca*, signs indicate the start of the **descent of the Torrente de Pareis**, a famous, though testing hike, for which rock-climbing skills and ropes are recommended. The river drops from here to Sa Calobra through an awesome, seven-kilometre-long limestone gorge, which takes about five hours to negotiate. The descent is not practicable in winter, spring, or after rainfall, when the river may be waist-high and the rocks dangerously slippy.

The Monestir de Lluc

Tucked away in a remote valley about 35km east of Sóller, the austere, high-sided dormitories and orange-flecked roof tiles of the **Monestir de Nostra Senyora de Lluc** (Monastery of Our Lady of Lluc) stand out against the greens and greys of the surrounding mountains. It's a magnificent setting for what has been Mallorca's most important place of pilgrimage since the middle of the thirteenth century. The religious significance of the place, however, goes back much further: the valley's animistic prehistoric inhabitants deified the local holm oak woods, and the Romans picked up on the theme, naming the place from "lucus", the Latin for "sacred forest". After the Reconquest, however, the monks who settled here were keen both to coin a purely Christian etymology and to enhance their reputation. They invented the story of a shepherd boy named Lluc (Luke) stumbling across a tiny, brightly painted statue in the woods. Frightened by his discovery, the lad collared the nearest monk, and when the pair returned heavenly music filled their ears, bright lights dazzled their eyes, and celestial voices declared the statue an authentically heaven-sent image of the Virgin.

The monastery, including the museum, is open to non-residents April–Sept daily 10am–6.30pm; Oct–March daily 10am–5.30pm. Entry to the museum costs 275ptas.

The monastery complex

Home to this much-venerated statue, Lluc's present monastic complex is an imposing and formal-looking affair mostly dating from the eighteenth and early nineteenth centuries. At its centre is the main shrine and architectural highlight, the **Basilica de la Mare de Deu de Lluc**, graced by an elegant Baroque facade. To get there,

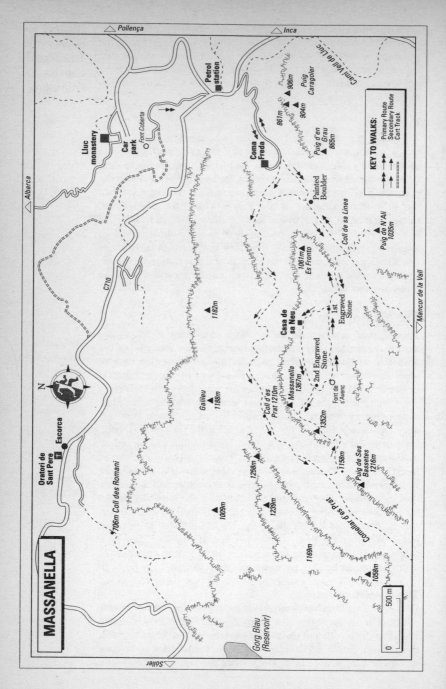

MASSANELLA

△ Pollença
△ Inca

Camí Vall de Lluc

△ Albarca

Lluc monastery

Car park

Font Coberta

Petrol station

Coma Freda

861m
906m
904m
Puig Caragoler

Puig d'en Grau 865m

Painted Boulder

Coll de sa Línea

Puig de N'Alí 1035m

KEY TO WALKS:
Primary Route
Secondary Route
Cart Track

C710

1182m

1061m
Es Fronto

Mancor de la Vall △

1st Engraved Stone

Casa de sa Neu

Massanella 1367m

Galileu 1188m

2nd Engraved Stone

Font de s'Avenc

Coll d'es Prat 1210m

1352m

N

Escorca

1158m

Oratori de Sant Pere

Puig de Ses Bassetes 1216m

706m Coll des Romani

1258m

1239m

1009m

Comellar d'es Prat

1169m

1058m

500 m

0

Gorg Blau (Reservoir)

△ Sóller

126   THE GUIDE: CHAPTER 2

From Lluc to Massanella

14km, 887m of ascent, 5hr 30min–6hr.

The large **Massanella massif** has eleven peaks over 1000m and is defended by many crags and steep rocky slopes. Since the construction of a military establishment put Puig Major out of bounds, it has become the best-loved high summit of the island. There are some well-defined paths and the classic **ascent from Lluc monastery**, with magnificent views, uses the best of these. Although quite strenuous, the route is not difficult and is deservedly popular. The top is all bare rock, although some small plants grow where moisture lingers in the crevices. Keep an eye open for black **vultures**, and for the friendly Alpine **accentors** who often appear on the summit or down by **Font de S'Avenc**, the spring on the southern flank.

From the front of the monastery, walk up through the vast car park to the **Font Coberta** and turn left behind the restaurant of the same name, following the road up to join the C710 at a junction on the Coll de Sa Batalla. Turn towards Inca and go past the service station, where walkers arriving by car may park.

Cross the bridge and turn right through the iron gates onto a wide track – ignore the Camí Vell de Lluc, a restored footpath to Caimari. Follow the track for 250m past a spring and watertrough, then leave it to swing sharp right uphill. Continue on the wide track and over an access stile into the cultivated area of the Coma Freda farm. Pause when you come to a wide opening into a field to look at the impressive **Es Fronto**, a high spur of Massanella with precipitous cliffs. At this point the track to the farm turns right and the path to Massanella goes straight on outside the wall enclosing the field. This path is well used and marked with paint signs and cairns. Rising through the woods, it joins a wide track by a **painted boulder**, a point which you should take note of for use in descent. Turn left to reach the **Coll de Sa Linea** at 822m, where there is a clearing among the trees and two engraved stones on the right. The main track begins to descend here towards the village of Mancor de la Vall. A possible diversion for strong walkers is to make the ascent of **Puig de N'Ali** by a winding route marked with some cairns and red paint signs; it's not easy to follow, especially at first because of the trees. The top is unusual, with an immense boulder supported in three places to form a sheltering cave with a southern outlook over the plain.

For Massanella, turn right up a clearly defined path rising in big swings at first, then twisting and turning to reach a junction where the two paths to the top diverge. At the junction, there's a stone engraved "Puig y Font" (mountain and spring) on the right-hand side and "Font y Puig" on the left, showing the order of arrival at these points; for the ascent, the route to the right is recommended, following an old track used to carry ice down on mules. Later on above the treeline, you'll see the old dry-stone walls of the Casa de Sa Neu, where the ice was stored until required, on the right.

After the path almost levels out, it meanders through boulders and clumps of *carritx* grass in a shallow valley, then veers left to join the other, southerly path coming up from Font de S'Avenc (described under the descent below) by a second engraved stone.

continues overleaf

From Lluc to Massanella (cont.)

Beyond here, several paths are visible: head towards the dip between the highest peak of **Massanella** (1367m) and the secondary peak to the southwest (1352m), then veer right to the main peak. Be careful how you go up here as there's a pothole some 20m deep not a stone's throw from the summit. On a good day the view from the top encompasses almost the entire island, from the Formentor headland in the northeast to the Bay of Palma. To the north, vertical cliffs plunge 150m to the **Coll d'es Prat** (1210m), above which lies the northern section of the Massanella massif. The Puig Major is readily identified by the radar domes on the summit and the splendid cliffs below.

To descend, retrace your steps to the second engraved stone, on the edge of a sloping shelf below the summit. An obvious rocky staircase leads down to the Font de S'Avenc, outside which is a red earth platform conspicuous in the grey rocky landscape. Steps lead down to an upper cave where a table and benches have been cut out of the rock, and a further set of steps leads down to a lower chamber with two basins of clear water (a torch is needed to go inside the lower cave).

The path from the spring runs horizontally to the east at first, dividing and rejoining again after a short distance. The route is marked, but pay careful attention to where you're going as there are many goat paths and natural ledges to lead walkers astray. Follow the marked path back into the trees and on to reach the first engraved stone, which signals the junction with the old mule track used on the ascent. Now it's a question of retracing your steps, turning left at the Coll de Sa Linea and right at the painted boulder, before passing through Coma Freda farm again.

Alternative ascent via Coll d'es Prat

With descent as above: 16km, 1022m of ascent, 6hr–6hr 30min.

An alternative and longer ascent can be made by following the old track from Coma Freda up the valley on the north side of Massanella to the high **Coll d'es Prat** (1210m), then descending the Comellar d'es Prat for about 1km, until a way is found up to the 1158-metre col between Puig de Ses Bassetes (1216m) and Massanella by a short easy scramble. From this col, a direct way up the southwest ridge to a secondary peak of Massanella (1352m) is for rock-climbers only, but a walkers' route is found by a rising traverse, east at first, then looking out for the cairns which show the way up the steep and rocky ground. These cairns are difficult to see in the grey rocky wilderness and a descent by this route is not recommended.

pass through the monastery's expansive double-doored entrance, turn right down the covered passage and keep going. Dark and gaudily decorated, the church is dominated by heavy jasper columns, whose stolidness is only partly relieved by a dome over the crossing. On either side of the nave, stone steps extend the aisles round the back of the Baroque high altar to a modest chapel. This is the holy of holies, built to display the statue of the Virgin, which has been commonly known as **La Moreneta** ("the Dark-Skinned One") ever since the original paintwork peeled off in the fifteenth century to reveal brown stone underneath. Just 61cm high, the Virgin looks innocuous, her face tweeked by a hint of a smile and haloed by a jewel-encrusted gold crown. In her left arm she cradles a bumptious baby Jesus, who holds the Book of Life open to reveal the letters alpha and omega. Every day at 11am, the **Escolania de Lluc** (nicknamed *Los Blauets*, "The Blues", for the colour of their cassocks), a boys' choir founded in the early sixteenth century with the stipulation that it must be "composed of natives of Mallorca, of pure blood, sound in grammar and song", performs in the basilica.

Just before the entrance to the basilica, a stairway climbs up one floor to the enjoyable **Museu de Lluc**. After a modest section devoted to archeological finds from the Talayotic and Roman periods come cabinets of intricate old vestments, exquisite gold and silver sacred vessels, medieval religious paintings, and an intriguing assortment of votive offerings – folkloric bits and bobs brought here to honour La Moreneta. The museum also boasts an extensive collection of **majolica**, tin-glazed earthenware whose characteristic shapes are two-handled drug jars and show dishes or plates, of which some two or three hundred are on display. The designs vary in sophistication – from broad and bold dashes of colour to carefully painted naturalistic designs – but the colours remain fairly constant, restricted by the available technology to iron red, copper green, cobalt blue, manganese purple and antimony yellow. It was the Italians who first used the term "majolica", a bastardized version of Mallorca, where they picked up the manufacturing skills that had been pioneered by the Moors. The last, disappointing section of the museum displays the paintings and drawings of the early twentieth-century artist José Coll Bardolet.

It doesn't take long to explore the rest of the monastery – or at least those sections open to the public. The narrow courtyard in front of the basilica's main facade features a dreary statue of Bishop Campins, who overhauled Lluc in the early part of this century, and the nearby natural history museum, with its stuffed birds and mounted animal horns, is eminently missable. Head instead for the **Camí dels Misteris del Rosari** (Way of the Mysteries of the Rosary), a broad pilgrims' footpath that winds its way up the rocky hillside directly behind the monastery. Dating from 1913, the solemn granite stations marking the way are of two types – simple stone pediments and, more intriguingly, rough-hewn trilobate columns of Gaudí-like design, each surmounted by a chunky crown and cross. It takes about ten minutes to reach the crucifix at the top of the hill, from where the views out over the Albarca valley are delightful. It's possible to stroll down into the valley by following the country road that begins to the left of the monastery's main entrance; for a longer hike into the mountains, see p.127.

Practicalities

Buses to Lluc, which is situated 2km off the C710, stop right outside the monastery. In addition to the Port de Sóller–Port de

Pollença–Port d'Alcúdia service, buses run to Lluc at least once a day from Palma via Inca – there's usually a departure at 9am or 10am, returning from Lluc at 5pm or 6pm, allowing you ample time to visit. For longer stays, **accommodation** at the monastery is highly organized, with simple, self-contained apartment-cells. In summer phone ahead if you want to be sure of space, but at other times simply book at the monastery's information office on arrival (☎517025; ②). The monastery also has a popular, first-come, first-served, all-year **campsite**, where the charge is a flat 300ptas per person – no additional costs for vehicles or tents.

For **food**, there's a café-bar and a restaurant beside the car park, but far preferable, even though it has become a little pricey, is the monks' former dining room, a grandly restored old hall of wooden beams and wide stone arches, where the food is traditional Spanish – and the meat dishes are much better than the fish. A more distinguished local choice is the *Restaurant Es Guix* (closed Tues), but you'll need your own transport to get there: from the monastery, head back to the C710, turn right and watch for the sign on the right-hand side of the road shortly before the Inca road. The restaurant, which occupies an enchanting oasis-like hollow, offers fine traditional dishes at reasonable prices – rabbit stew, for example, for 1100ptas.

Pollença and around

Founded in the thirteenth century, the tranquil little town of POLLENÇA nestles among a trio of hillocks, where the Serra de Tramuntana fades into coastal flatland. Following standard Mallorcan practice, the town was established a few kilometres from the seashore to militate against sudden pirate attack, with its harbour, Port de Pollença (see p.135), left an unprotected outpost. For once the stratagem worked. Unlike most of Mallorca's old towns, Pollença successfully repelled a string of piratical onslaughts, the last and most threatening of which was in 1550, when the notorious Turkish corsair Dragut came within a hair's breadth of victory. In the festival of *Mare de Déu dels Àngels* on August 2, the townspeople celebrate their escape with enthusiastic street battles, the day's events named after the warning shouted by the hero of the resistance, a certain Joan Más: *Mare de Déu dels Àngels, assistiu-mos* (Our Lady of Angels, help us).

The Town

Although Pollença avoided being destroyed by Dragut, not much of the medieval town remains today, and the severe stone houses that cramp the twisting lanes of the compact centre mostly date from the seventeenth and eighteenth centuries. In the middle, **Plaça Major**, the lazy main square, accommodates a cluster of laid-back cafés and the dour facade of the church of **Nostra Senyora dels Àngels**, a

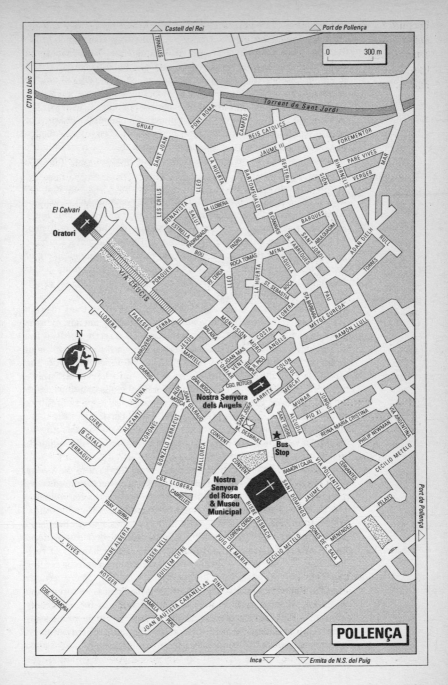

POLLENÇA

sheer cliff-face of sun-bleached stone pierced by a rose window. Dating from the thirteenth century but extensively remodelled in the Baroque style five centuries later, the church's gloomy interior has a mildly diverting sequence of ceiling and wall paintings, as well as a whopping, tiered and towered high altarpiece. The original church was built for the Knights Templar, a rich and secretive organization founded as a military order in support of the Crusades, but suppressed by the pope in 1312 following trumped-up charges of heresy, sorcery and bestiality. As elsewhere, the Templars' Pollença possessions passed to the Hospitallers of St John, a rival knightly order who struggled on until 1802 when the Spanish king appropriated all they owned.

Close by along c/Sant Domingo – and behind a tiny square housing an antique waterwheel and watchtower – stands the church of **Nostra Senyora del Roser**, outside of which stands a curious piece of modern sculpture, chiselled in the shape of a bookcase. Inside, the church has a barrel-vaulted ceiling and a flamboyantly Baroque high altar, whilst the **Museu Municipal** in the adjoining cloisters of Sant Domingo contains a modest collection of contemporary paintings and, amongst the ecclesiastical bric-a-brac, several good examples of Mallorcan Gothic art.

The Museu Municipal is open Tues, Thurs & Sun 10am–noon; 100ptas.

Pollença's pride and joy is its **Via Crucis** (Way of the Cross), a long, steep and beautiful stone stairway, graced by ancient cypress trees, which ascends **El Calvari** (Calvary hill) directly north of the town centre. At the top, a much-revered thirteenth-century statue of **Mare de Deu del Peu de la Creu** (Mother of God at the Foot of the Cross) is lodged in a simple, courtyarded **Oratori** (chapel), whose whitewashed walls sport some of the worst religious paintings imaginable. However, the views out over coast and town are sumptuous. On Good Friday, a figure of Jesus is slowly carried by torchlight down from the Oratori to the church of Nostra Senyora dels Àngels, in the **Davallament** (Lowering), one of the most moving religious celebrations on the island.

There are further magnificent views from the **Ermita de Nostra Senyora del Puig**, a rambling, mostly eighteenth-century monastery perched on top of the Puig de Maria, a 320-metre-high hump facing the south end of town. The monastic complex, with its fortified walls, courtyard, chapel, refectory and cells, has had a chequered history, alternately abandoned and restored by both monks and nuns. It's now a working monastery again, with a handful of resident Benedictines supplementing their collective income by renting out cells to tourists (see "Practicalities", below). There are no specific sights to see, but the setting is extraordinarily serene and beautiful, with the mellow honey-coloured walls of the monastery surrounded by ancient carob and olive trees, a million miles away from the tourist resorts visible far below. To get to the monastery, take the signposted turning left off the main Pollença–Inca/Palma road just south of town; head up this steep, 1500-metre-long lane until it fizzles out, to be replaced by a cobbled footpath which winds up to the monastery entrance. It's possible to drive to the top of the lane, but unless you've got nerves of steel, you're better off leaving your vehicle by the turning near the foot of the hill. Allow just over an hour each way if you're walking from the centre of town.

Practicalities

Regular **buses** from Palma, Inca and Port de Pollença halt immediately to the south of Plaça Major. The town doesn't have a tourist office, nor is there anywhere central to **stay** – until, that is, the *Hostal Juma*, on Plaça Major (☎530007; ③), reopens for business after its extended refurbishment. The nearest accommodation is at the Ermita de Nostra Senyora del Puig (☎530235; ①), just over 2km south of town on the summit of Puig de Maria (see above for directions), where the original monks' cells have been renovated to provide simple accommodation. Even in a monastery, however, there are degrees of frugality: as a rule of thumb, the most spartan rooms are rented to solitary travellers and those without reservations. Be warned also that it can get cold and windy at night, and the refectory food is mediocre.

Pollença does well for **cafés** and **restaurants**. On Plaça Major, the *Café Espanyol* offers filling snacks and a good strong cup of coffee, while the neighbouring *Can Olesa* (closed Wed) serves delicious Mallorcan cuisine at reasonable prices, in tastefully furnished ancient premises. On c/Montesión, in between the main square and El Calvari, you'll find the upbeat and fashionable *Bar Cantonet*, where excellent vegetarian snacks cost around 400ptas – or you can try the adjoining restaurant (closed Tues) with its wide-ranging but rather pricey international menu. Along the same street, *La Font del Gall* (closed Mon) also has vegetarian specialities and again the menu is international rather than local; it's a justifiably popular spot, where you should allow 4000ptas for a full meal including wine. Even more expensive, but with well-prepared food and a fine cellar setting, a short way up the El Calvari steps, is the *Daus* (closed Tues and all Jan), which emphasizes local ingredients in its Spanish menu; goat and wild boar are particular favourites.

The Castell del Rei

The battered ruins of the medieval **Castell del Rei** (Castle of the King) are glued to a remote and inhospitable crag, which rears high above the ocean about 7km north of Pollença. Founded by the Moors, this remote fastness was strengthened by Jaume I to guard the northerly approaches to Pollença against pirate attack. In this regard, however, it was something of a failure: the pirates simply ignored it, preferring to land at nearby Cala Sant Vicenç instead. More successfully, it held out for months against the Aragonese invasion of 1285 and was the last fortress to surrender to Pedro of Aragón, the supplanter of the Mallorcan king Jaume III, in 1343.

Subsequently, the castle was used as a watchtower, finally being abandoned in 1715.

It takes about two hours to walk there, an undemanding hike along a country lane, and then a forest footpath leading through the pretty Ternellas valley. The problem, however, is access: the castle is on a vast private estate, whose owner allows visitors in on most Saturdays, when hikers are instructed to arrive between 8.30am and noon, and to leave by 3pm (*Globespan* in Port de Pollença is the best place to ask for information about current opening times).

If these restrictions don't deter you, directions are as follows: on the northern edge of Pollença, a signposted turning off the C710 leads along a country road. This passes through orchards and farmland to reach, after 1.5km, a guarded gate set in the narrow defile at the entrance to the Ternellas valley. If you're driving, you have to park here. An easy-to-follow, rough and dusty track leads to another set of gates, beyond which the path starts to rise, climbing through oak woods to a stretch of mixed woodland dominated by pines. Further on, the trees thin out and the castle ruins can be spied in the distance. About 100m after the start of a fenced-off area on the right-hand side, fork left off the main track – which continues down to the shingly beach at **Cala Castell** – for the climb up to the ruins.

Cala Sant Vicenç

The mundane modernity of **CALA SANT VICENÇ**, a small resort 6km northeast of Pollença, is largely camouflaged by its attractive setting, with sharp escarpments and steep hills backdropping a narrow slice of rocky seashore. Nonetheless, it's the tediousness of the villas you'll probably remember, along with the overpowering *Hotel Don Pedro*, insensitively located on the minute headland that separates two small sandy beaches. The only real reasons to visit are for a swim or a stroll into the surrounding bleak limestone hills. There's an easy walk northeast along a coastal side road to **Cala Carbo**, an uninspiring *urbanització* a couple of kilometres away, while a far rougher, four-kilometre-long lane runs northwest – behind the hills edging the bay in front of the resort – to a coastal lookout point at **Punta de Covas Blancas**.

Buses from Port de Pollença stop on c/Temporal, a short walk from the **Oficina d'Informació Turistica** on Plaça Sant Vicenç (June–Aug Mon–Fri 9am–1pm; ☎533264): head along c/Temporal towards the seashore, turn left down c/Cala Clara and then left again. Vacant **rooms** are extremely thin on the ground in summer, but you could try the *Hotel Niu*, a comfortably old-fashioned, low-rise place next to the beach (April–Oct; ☎530100; ④), or the more secluded *Hostal Los Pinos*, which has spick and span rooms and its own pool (May–Oct; ☎531210; ④). The best **restaurant** is the *Cavall Bernat* (May–Oct), which specializes in traditional Mallorcan dishes; the adjoining pizzeria is a less expensive option, serving delicious pizzas from 700ptas.

Port de Pollença

Over at **PORT DE POLLENÇA** things are a little more lively, though still pleasantly low-key. With the mountains as a backcloth, the resort arches through the flatlands behind the Badia de Pollença, a deeply indented bay whose sheltered waters are ideal for swimming. The **beach** is the focus of attention, a narrow, elongated sliver of sand that's easily long enough to accommodate the crowds, though as a general rule you'll have more space the further southeast (towards Alcúdia) you walk. A rash of apartment buildings and hotels blights the edge of town, and the noisy main road to Alcúdia runs close to the seashore, but all in all the place is very appealing, especially in the centre behind the marina, where old narrow streets hint at the resort's origins as a small port and fishing harbour.

For a change of scene, **boat-taxis** shuttle between the marina and the Platja de Formentor, one of Mallorca's most attractive beaches (4 daily; 30min; 700ptas each way), whilst **boat trips** cruise the bay (Mon–Fri 2 daily; 2hr; 1100ptas), or work their way along to Cap de Formentor (Mon & Fri 1 daily; 2hr; 1150ptas). There's also the option of making a delightful three-kilometre **hike** across the neck of the Península de Formentor to **Cala Boquer**. On the seafront north of the marina, hang a left at Avgda Bocchoris and follow the signposted route up to the farm. From here an obvious path, beginning from an iron gate, leads through the mountainsheltered **Vall de Boquer** (Boquer Valley), a favourite of ornithologists, especially for its migrant **birds**, and of botanists for its **wild flowers and shrubs**. The valley's lower slopes, which have been heavily grazed, support a sparse, scrubby vegetation whose most common species are the mastic tree and the narrow-leafed cistus, though you'll also catch sight of the pink-flowered bush heather and St John's wort. As you approach the coast, Mediterranean buckthorn and broom take over, ideal cover for warblers, nightingales and other small songbirds, whilst up above, the rocky hill slopes accommodate blue rock thrush and red-legged partridge. The valley is also home to several birds of prey – peregrine and kestrel are the most common, but if you're lucky you may spot a black vulture. These residents are joined in the spring and autumn migrations by eagles, ospreys, kites, falcons and buzzards, which prey upon the many smaller birds, such as the thrush and sparrow, that use the valley as a feeding ground as they migrate through. After about 45 minutes you reach a small, shingly **beach** offering good swimming in clean water (though the shore is sometimes rubbish-strewn).

Practicalities

Buses to Port de Pollença from Palma, Alcúdia, Port d'Alcúdia and Port de Sóller stop by the marina right in the town centre. A couple of minutes' walk away is the **Oficina d'Informació Turistica**, one

Beyond Sóller: Cala Tuent to the Cap de Formentor

For more on the Platja de Formentor and Cap de Formentor, see p.138.

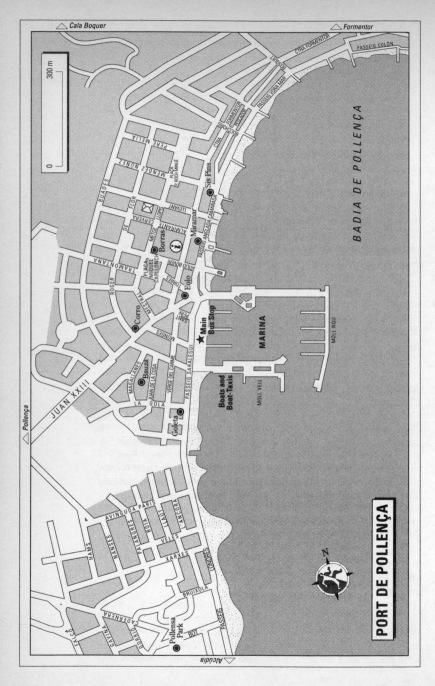

PORT DE POLLENÇA

block behind the seafront at Carretera Formentor 31 (May–Oct Mon–Fri 9am–1pm & 4–7pm; ☎865467), which has local information and accommodation lists. The flatlands edging the Badia de Pollença and stretching as far as Pollença and Alcúdia make for easy, scenic cycling. **Mountain bikes** can be rented for 1400ptas per day from *Cerda March*, c/Joan XXIII, 89 (☎864784), as can **mopeds** and **motorcycles**. Local **car** rental companies include *La Parra*, c/Joan XXIII, 20 (☎530721), and *Garau*, along the street at no. 88 (☎865871). On the same street at no. 9, *Viajes Iberia* (☎530262) are the **American Express** agents for this part of Mallorca. The walking holiday specialists *Globespan* (see p.5) also have an office here in Port de Pollença, at Passeig Saralegui 114 (☎864711), where you can pay to join one of their day-long guided walks (around 2000ptas per person). The office will provide all the details – you should book a minimum of 24 hours beforehand.

Beyond Sóller: Cala Tuent to the Cap de Formentor

Accommodation

There are several reasonably priced and convenient **accommodation** options, though getting a room in season may be difficult. Overlooking the tiny main square stands the delightful *Hostal-residencia Borras*, Plaça Miquel Capllonch 16 (☎531474; ③), a real bargain where most of the rooms are comfortably spacious and you can eat breakfast in the pretty little courtyard. On the seafront, the *Hotel Miramar*, Passeig Anglada Camarasa 39 (April–Oct; ☎531400; ⑤), is an attractive three-star hotel, with balconied rooms set behind a grand facade; and the equally agreeable *Hotel Residencia Sis Pins* occupies a handsome white-washed and balconied villa along the street at no. 77 (☎531050; ⑥). Also by the water is the friendly, unpretentious *Hostal-residencia Eolo*, a hikers' favourite at c/Torres 2 (☎531550; ④); and the workaday *Hostal-residencia Goleta*, Passeig Saralegui 64 (March–Oct; ☎865902; ④). At the south end of the resort, just off the seafront, the *Pollensa Park Hotel* is also worth a try (March–Nov; ☎865350; ⑥): a standard-issue high-rise, with a swimming pool and all mod cons, it's geared up for package tours, but may have one or two vacancies. Finally, if you're stuck, there are a couple of simple, low-priced places tucked away in the streets behind the marina, the *Hostal Corro*, c/Joan XXIII, 68 (☎531005; ②), and the *Hostal Bauza*, c/Juan de la Cosa 32 (mid-June to mid-Sept; ☎865474; ②).

Eating and nightlife

Among a plethora of **restaurants**, the best and most expensive is the *Bec-Fi*, at Passeig Anglada Camarasa 91, apparently visited by both Pete Townshend and King Juan Carlos. Other excellent choices include the *Restaurant Stay*, on the marina's Moll Nou jetty, a neat little place which features the freshest of seafood and charges about

4500ptas for a full à la carte meal; and the *El Pozo*, c/Joan XXIII, 25, where you can devour fine seafood on an attractive terrace. For something more informal and inexpensive, head for the seafront around the marina. Places come and go, but try *Andy's Bar and Grill* or *Pizzeria Tolo's* for filling snacks and meals.

Port de Pollença's **nightlife** is generally low-key, but there is a disco of sorts at the *Pollensa Park Hotel*, and another, the *Chivas*, on c/Metge Llopis off the main square, which has no entry charge (though drinks are expensive). The best place to hang out, though, is the *Bar Pascalinos* on Passeig Anglada Camarasa, which boasts a beachfront location, reasonable prices, and a young Palmese clientele who keep the place swinging until around 3am.

The Península de Formentor

Heading northeast out of Port de Pollença, the road clears the military zone at the far end of the resort, before weaving up into the craggy hills of the twenty-kilometre-long **Península de Formentor**, the final spur of the Serra de Tramuntana. At first, the road (which suffers a surfeit of tourists from mid-morning to mid-afternoon) travels inland, out of sight of the true grandeur of the scenery, but after about 6km the **Mirador de Mal Pas** rectifies matters with a string of lookout points perched on the edge of plunging, north-facing seacliffs. There are further stunning views, in this case over the south shore, from the **Talaia de Albercutx** watchtower viewpoint, but you'll have to be prepared to tackle the rough side road that climbs the hills opposite the Mirador de Mal Pas.

Continuing along the main road, it's another couple of kilometres to the short access road that leads down through the woods to the **Platja de Formentor**, a pine-clad beach of golden sand in a pretty cove. It's a beautiful spot, with views over to the mountains on the far side of the bay, though it can get a little crowded. In summer, you can get here from Palma and Port de Pollença on a once-daily **bus** service. At the end of the cove, opposite a tiny islet, stands the *Hotel Formentor* (☎865300; ⑨). Opened in 1930, this wonderful hotel – arguably the island's best – lies low against the forested hillside, its hacienda-style architecture enhanced by Neoclassical and Art-Deco features and exquisite terraced gardens. The place was once the haunt of the rich and fashionable – Charlie Chaplin and Scott Fitzgerald both stayed here – and although these socialite days are long gone, the hotel preserves an air of understated elegance. Stay here if you can afford it – there's a surprisingly good chance of a vacant room, even in high summer.

Beyond the turn-off for the beach, the main peninsula road runs along a wooded ridge, before tunnelling through Mont Fumat to emerge on the rocky mass of **Cap de Formentor**. This tapered promontory of bleak seacliffs and scrub-covered hills offers spectacular views and is a fruitful area for **birdwatching**, especially from the silver-domed lighthouse stuck on the windswept tip. The light-house itself is out of bounds, but you can wander round its rocky environs, where the sparse vegetation is a perfect habitat for lizards and small birds, especially the deep-blue feathered rock thrush and the white-rumped rock dove. From the lighthouse you can also view the steep, eastward-facing seacliffs, which shelter colonies of nest-ing Eleanora's falcons from April to October, whilst circling over-head there are often ravens, martins and swifts. During the spring and summer migrations, thousands of seabirds fly over the cape, Manx and Cory's shearwaters in particular. If you're ready for a snack before heading back from the cape, pop into the coffee bar next to the lighthouse.

Alcúdia and around

Moving south from Port de Pollença, it's just 10km round the bay to the compact old town of **Alcúdia**, whose main claims to fame are its imitation medieval walls and the battered ruins of the old Roman settlement of Pollentia. Within easy striking distance lies the mega-resort of **Port d'Alcúdia**, where glistening skyrises sweep around the Badia d'Alcúdia's glorious sandy beach. In summer the place is eminently missable – it's far too crowded to be much fun – but the shoulder seasons are more relaxing and the beach comparatively uncrowded. In the wintertime you'll barely see a soul, but almost all the hotels and restaurants are closed.

The resort stretches for 10km round the bay to the end of the beach at Ca'n Picafort. Most of the swampland that used to extend behind this coastal strip has been drained, but a small area of marsh has been left to form the **Parc Natural de S'Albufera**, a real bird-watchers' delight. Further behind the coast lies a tract of fertile farmland dotted with country towns, amongst which **Muro**, with its ethnological museum and old grandee mansions, is the most diverting.

Accommodation is concentrated in Port d'Alcúdia, but it's nearly all reserved for package tourists in the summertime. As a possible alternative, both of Mallorca's official **campgrounds** border the Badia d'Alcúdia – one on the edge of Ca'n Picafort, the other outside Colònia de Sant Pere (see p.157) – though advance reserva-tions are advised.

Transport connections, particularly from May to October, are excellent. Frequent **buses** link Port de Pollença, Alcúdia, Port d'Alcúdia and Ca'n Picafort. There are also regular services to Alcúdia and its port from Palma, and fairly regular summertime connections from Port de Sóller, Pollença and the major resorts of the east coast. Port d'Alcúdia also boasts a **ferry port**, with car ferries running to Barcelona, and both car ferries and summer-only hydrofoils shuttling over to Menorca.

Palma to Alcúdia

Alcúdia is best seen in conjunction with a visit to Pollença and the
Serra de Tramuntana, but if you're in a hurry to get there from
Palma, there's a more direct, though far less memorable route over
the island's central plain. Between three and ten **buses** a day run
along the C713 from the capital to Alcúdia, and a **rail line** covers
about half the distance, shunting through the wine-producing centre
of Binissalem to arrive at its terminus in INCA. This industrialized
town is heavily promoted for its distilleries, leather factories and
Thursday market, but it's an ugly place that's best avoided unless
you're a devotee of leather goods. Beyond Inca, the main road
continues towards Alcúdia, cutting between Campanet, home to an
uninspiring cave complex, and the country town of Sa Pobla, which
accommodates a very modest contemporary art museum. At least
there's a more attractive look to the landscape around here – arable
land liberally scattered with broken-down windmills – and at Muro,
5km southeast of Sa Pobla but easily accessible from Ca'n Picafort,
is one of Mallorca's more interesting folkloric museums (see p.144).

Alcúdia

To pull in the day-trippers, pint-sized **ALCÚDIA** wears its history on
its sleeve. The crenellated wall that encircles much of the town is
mostly a modern imitation of the medieval original, and, although
the sixteenth- to eighteenth-century houses behind it are genuine
enough, the whole place is overly spick and span. In fact, little can
be seen today which reflects the town's true historical importance.
Situated on a neck of land separating two large, sheltered bays, the
site's strategic value was first recognized by the Phoenicians, whose
scant remains have been unearthed here, and later by the Romans,
who built their island capital, Pollentia, here in the first century AD,
on top of the earlier settlement. In 426, the place was destroyed by

*The Museu
Monogràfic is
open Tues–Sat
10am–1.30pm
& 5–7pm, Sun
10.30am–
1.30pm;
200ptas. Sant
Jaume is open
Tues, Wed,
Thurs & Fri
10am–1pm,
Sun
10am–noon;
100ptas.*

the Vandals and lay neglected until the Moors built a fortress in
about 800, naming it *Al Kudia* (On the Hill). After the Reconquest,
Alcúdia prospered as a major trading centre, a role it performed
well into the nineteenth century, when the town slipped into a long
and gentle decline – until tourism refloated the economy.

It only takes an hour or so to walk around the antique lanes of
Alcúdia's compact centre, and to explore the town walls and their
fortified gates. This pleasant stroll can be extended by a visit to four
specific sights, though none of them is compelling. The **Museu
Monogràfic**, at c/Sant Jaume 2, is no more than a single room
stuffed with archeological bits and bobs, primarily Roman artefacts
from Pollentia, including amulets, miniature devotional objects and
tiny oil-burning lamps. A few paces away, dominating the southwest
corner of the old town, the heavyweight, neo-Gothic church of **Sant
Jaume** houses a modest religious museum. Across the road from the
church, just outside the town walls, are the broken pillars and

mashed-up walls that constitute the meagre remains of Roman Pollentia (open access; free). Nearly all the stone has been looted by the townsfolk over the centuries, so it's no longer possible to discern the layout of the former capital. The remains of Pollentia's theatre, the **Teatre Roma** (open access; free), are slightly less skimpy – signs from the town centre will take you there, about 1km south along the old main road to Port d'Alcúdia. Dating from the first century BC, this is the smallest of the twenty Roman theatres to have survived in Spain. Despite its modest proportions, the builders were able to stick to the standard type of layout: eight tiers of seats were carved out of the rocky hillside, divided by two gangways. The stage area, which was constructed of earth and timber, has, however, disappeared.

Buses to Alcúdia halt beside the town walls on Plaça Carles V; there's no tourist office. The only **rooms** in town are at the no-frills *Fonda C'an Llabres* (☎545000; ③), on Plaça Constitució, the main square. For **food**, there are several mundane cafés on Plaça Constitució, but these are best avoided in favour of the cosy café-bar of *Ca's Capella*, at the foot of c/Serra.

The Santuari de la Victòria

The northwest shore of the forested promontory beyond Alcúdia offers fine views of the Badia de Pollença. Here you'll find the barracks-like *Albergue Juvenil de Alcúdia* (mid-June to Aug; ☎545395; ①), a 120-bed **youth hostel**, 4km from town along the well-surfaced side road that shadows the seashore (there's no public transport). Vacant rooms are a rarity – school parties predominate – so turning up on the off-chance is pretty pointless and reservations need to be made well in advance.

About 1km further along the headland, a turning on the right climbs up the wooded hillside to the **Santuari de la Victòria**, a fortress-like church in a lovely spot, sheltering a crude but much-venerated statue of the Virgin. The adjacent **restaurant** (closed Mon), a cavernous affair named after the sanctuary, has splendid views from its terrace bar and serves excellent food – guinea fowl and chicken are the specialities.

Port d'Alcúdia

PORT D'ALCÚDIA, 2km south of Alcúdia, is the biggest and busiest of the resorts on the Badia d'Alcúdia, its clutch of restaurants and café-bars attracting crowds from a seemingly interminable string of high-rise hotels and apartment buildings. This is not, however, to equate this resort with some of its seamier rivals, for the tower blocks are relatively well distributed, the streets are neat and tidy and there's a prosperous and easy-going air, with families particularly well catered for. Predictably, the daytime focus is the **beach**, a superb arc of pine-studded golden sand, which stretches south for

*For full details
of ferry and
hydrofoil
services out of
Port d'Alcúdia,
see p.30.*

10km from the two purpose-built jetties of Port d'Alcúdia's combined marina and fishing harbour. About half a kilometre east of the marina along the headland lies the **commercial port**, reached along c/Moll Comercial. It's Mallorca's second port (after Palma), with car ferries for Barcelona and both car ferries and summertime hydrofoils for Ciutadella, on Menorca. *Flebasa* operate all these services from their dockside **kiosk** (☎546454).

A tourist **"train"** (on wheels, with clearly marked roadside stops) runs up and down the length of the resort at hourly intervals (summer 9am–10pm; free), transporting sunbaked bodies from one part of the beach to another. Not that there's very much to distinguish anywhere from anywhere else – the palm-thatched *balnearios* (beach-bars) are a great help in actually remembering where you are. A walkway runs along the back of the beach, which is usually more crowded to the north. A kilometre or so inland, reached along Avgda del Tucan, the much-vaunted **Hidropark** is a gigantic pool complex with all sorts of flumes and chutes (daily 10am–6pm; 1600ptas); special buses leave for the park every 15min from hotels along the main street, Carretera d'Artà.

Practicalities

Port d'Alcúdia acts as northern Mallorca's summertime transport hub, with **bus** services to and from Palma, Port de Sóller, Artà, Cala Millor and Cala Rajada, as well as neighbouring towns and resorts. All these buses stop in the town centre beside the **Oficina d'Informació Turistica** (Mon–Sat 9am–7pm; ☎892615), which is situated on Carretera d'Artà, the main drag. The office can supply all sorts of information, most usefully free maps marked with all the resort's hotels and apartments.

In season, vacant rooms are few and far between, but there's a vague chance amongst the low-priced **hostals** clustered behind the marina. The least expensive rooms here – basic, no-frills affairs – are provided by the mundanely modern *Calma*, c/Teodor Canet 41 (March–Dec; ☎545343; ③), the equally modest *Puerto*, just down the street at no. 47 (April–Oct; ☎545447; ②), and *Vista Alegre*, which at least has the advantage of being on the seafront, at Passeig Marítim 10 (☎547347; ②). In winter almost all the hotels and *hostals* close down, but in the shoulder seasons it's sometimes possible to get a good deal at one of the plusher **hotels**. Try along the seafront at the *Hotel Platja d'Or*, an attractive 230-bedroom complex about 1.5km south of the marina, with its own swimming pools and balconied bedrooms looking out to sea (April–Oct; ☎890052; ⑦); or at the *Hotel Condesa*, a few metres further along the beach, a huge L-shaped complex with all the facilities you can think of, from bike rental to a children's playground (April–Nov; ☎890120; ⑦).

There's also the possibility of **camping**, at *Platja Blava*, 9km southeast of Port d'Alcúdia, an all-year site with a great location, just a stone's throw from the beach (summer ☎537863, winter ☎717116). It has 500 pitches, as well as its own swimming pool, tennis courts, supermarket, nightclub and restaurant. Watersports equipment can be rented, as can mobile homes, though these usually need to be booked well in advance. In high season (mid-June to mid-Sept) campers pay 500ptas each, plus 700–2275ptas for a site, depending on size; cars (650ptas) and IVA (7 percent) further add to the bill and there are small supplementary charges for electrical hook-ups and hot water. Off-season rates are around 25 percent less.

For **food** you're spoiled for choice, though most of the resort's eating places are identikit pizzerias and tourist-style restaurants. Try the *Miramar*, Passeig Marítim 2, or *Ca'n Toni*, along the waterfront at no. 8, which both serve delicious seafood. The well-established *Bar Lovento*, on c/Gabriel Roca behind the fishing port, is a justifiably popular spot, and again fish is the big deal.

There's a superabundance of **car, moped and bicycle rental** companies strung out behind the beach. *Avis*, for example, have an office at Passeig Marítim 56 (☎545468); many outlets offer mountain bikes for around 1000ptas per day, 5600ptas for the week. Summer **boat trips**, leaving from the marina at the north end of the beach, explore the rocky, mountainous coastline to the east of Port d'Alcúdia: the shorter excursion travels as far as the tip of the headland, the Cap des Pinar, without venturing into the Badia de Pollença (April–Oct 3 daily; 3hr; 1400ptas); the longer version continues round this headland and across the bay to the Platja de Formentor (May–Oct 1 daily; 7hr; 3370ptas).

The Parc Natural de S'Albufera

Port d'Alcúdia lies at the beginning of an intensively developed tourist zone, which takes advantage of a great swathe of pine-studded sandy beach around the Badia d'Alcúdia. Some lessons have been learnt from earlier developments – there are more recreational facilities and at least some of the coast has been left unscathed – but first impressions are primarily of concrete and glass. The beach and the skyrises end on the western outskirts of **Ca'n Picafort**, once an important fishing port – the old town still preserves vestiges of its earlier function – but today an uninteresting suburban sprawl.

*The Parc
Natural de
S'Albufera is
open
April–Sept
daily
9am–7pm;
Oct–March
daily
9am–6pm; free.*

In this unpromising environment, the 2000-acre **Parc Natural de S'Albufera**, a segment of pristine wetland on the west side of Ca'n Picafort, makes a wonderful change. Swampland once extended round much of the bay, but large-scale reclamation began in the nineteenth century, when a British company dug a network of channels and installed a steam engine to pump the water out. These endeavours were prompted by a desire to eradicate malaria – then the scourge of the local population – as much as by the need for more farmland. Further drainage schemes accompanied the frantic tourist boom of the 1960s, and only in the last decade has the Balearic government recognized the ecological importance of the wetland and organized a park to protect what little remains.

Access to the park is straightforward, but if you're driving you'll need to be alert: heading southeast from Port d'Alcúdia on the C712, watch for the *Hotel Esperanza* after about 6km, and the signposted entrance is on the right about 200m further on, just after a small hump-backed bridge. **Buses** from Port d'Alcúdia to Ca'n Picafort and points east stop by the entrance. From the entrance, a country lane leads to the reception centre, **Sa Roca**, just over 1km away, where you can pick up a free map and permit; an adjacent building houses a useful identity parade of local wildlife.

*The reception
centre is open
daily 9am–1pm
& 2–5.30pm.*

Footpaths leave the reception area to explore the reedy, watery tract beyond. It's a superb habitat, where four well-appointed hides – more are planned – allow excellent **birdwatching**. Over 200 species have been spotted, resident wetland-loving birds such as the crake, warbler, tern and hoopoe; autumn and/or springtime migrants, like the heron, crane, plover and godwit; and wintering species such as the egret, sandpiper and wagtail. Such rich pickings attract birds of prey in their scores, especially kestrels, marsh harriers and ospreys. The open ground edging the reed beds supports many different wild flowers, the most striking of which are the orchids that bloom during April and May.

Muro

From the west side of Ca'n Picafort, a gentle country road crosses the pancake-flat, windmill-studded hinterland, to reach **MURO** after 10km. There's a big bash here on January 16 for the *Revetla de*

Sant Antoni Abat (Eve of St Antony's Day), when locals gather round bonfires to drink and dance, tucking into specialities like sausages and eel pies (*espinagades*) – the eels from the marshes of S'Albufera. Otherwise, Muro is a sleepy little place, dotted with big old town houses built by wealthy landowners.

One of these villas now houses the **Museu Etnològic**, c/Major 15, which showcases an enjoyable miscellany of folkloric items. There's everything from traditional costumes, nativity figures and clay whistles to an old country kitchen. Agricultural equipment includes an example of a mule- or donkey-driven waterwheel, a *noria*. Introduced by the Moors, these were a common feature of the Mallorcan landscape for hundreds of years, though there are few of them left today. Amongst the pottery, look out for the medieval *siurels*, miniature green- and red-painted figurines in a naive style. Now debased as a mass-produced tourist trinket, they were originally made as whistles – hence the spout with the hole.

In the main square, the domineering church of **Sant Joan** is a real hotchpotch of architectural styles, its monumental Gothic lines uneasily modified by the sweeping sixteenth-century arcades above the aisles. A slender arch connects the church to the adjacent **belfry**, an imposing seven-storey construction partly designed as a watchtower; sometimes it's possible to go to the top, where the views out over the coast are superb. That's just about it for Muro, though you could walk straight down from the main square to the sixteenth-century church of **Santa Anna**, a more homogenous edifice cheered by a large rose window and an attractive Baroque doorway.

Off the main square, opposite the church, the *Ca'n Costitx* **café-bar** serves reasonable snacks and light lunches. Local buses, arriving by the main square, link Muro with Ca'n Picafort, Sa Pobla, Inca and Palma.

The Museu Etnològic is open Tues–Sat 10am–2pm & 4–7pm, Sun 10am–2pm; 300ptas.

Travel details

Buses

From **Ca'n Picafort** to: Cala Millor (May–Oct Mon–Sat 3 daily; 1hr); Cala Rajada (May–Oct Mon–Sat 5 daily; 35min); Muro (May–Oct 2–3 daily; 10min); Porto Cristo (May–Oct Mon–Sat 3 daily; 55min).

From **Palma** to: Alaró (Mon–Sat 3 daily, 2 on Sun; 25min); Alcúdia (May–Oct Mon–Sat 10 daily, 5 on Sun; Nov–April 3 daily; 1hr); Andratx (Mon–Sat every 30min; 11 on Sun; 35min); Banyalbufar (Mon–Sat 3 daily, 1 on Sun; 35min); Camp de Mar (May–Oct every 15min, Nov–April every hour; 40min); Ca'n Picafort (2–3 daily; 1hr); Deià (5 daily, except Oct–March Sun 3 daily; 45min); Esporles (Mon–Sat 4 daily, 2 on Sun; 20min); Estellencs (Mon–Sat 3 daily, 1 on Sun; 45min); Inca (Mon–Sat 8 daily, 4 on Sun; 30min); La Granja (Mon–Sat 3 daily, 1 on Sun; 25min); Lluc (Mon–Sat 2 daily, 1 on Sun; 1hr); Muro (2–4 daily; 50min); Platja de Formentor (May–Oct Mon–Sat 1 daily; 1hr

15min); Pollença (3–5 daily; 1hr); Port d'Alcúdia (May–Oct Mon–Sat 10 daily, 5 on Sun; Nov–April 3 daily; 1hr 10min); Port d'Andratx (May–Oct every 15min, Nov–April every hour; 45min); Port de Pollença (3–5 daily; 1hr 10min); Port de Sóller (5 daily, except Oct–March 3 on Sun; 1hr 15min); Sóller (5 daily, except Oct–March 3 on Sun; 1hr 10min); Valldemossa (5 daily, except Oct–March 3 on Sun; 30min).

From **Peguera** to: Andratx (May–Oct Mon–Sat 15 daily, 3 on Sun; Nov–April 2 daily; 10min); Port d'Andratx (May–Oct Mon–Sat 8 daily, 1 on Sun; 15min); Sant Elm (May–Oct Mon–Sat 7 daily, 1 on Sun; Nov–April 1 daily; 15min); Valldemossa (1 daily; 1hr 5min).

From **Pollença** to: Cala Sant Vicenç (3–5 daily; 15min).

From **Port d'Alcúdia** to: Alcúdia (May–Oct every 15min; Nov–April 3 daily; 5min); Artà (May–Oct Mon–Sat 5 daily; 30min); Cala Millor (May–Oct Mon–Sat 3 daily; 1hr); Cala Rajada (May–Oct Mon–Sat 2 daily; 40min); Ca'n Picafort (May–Oct every 15min; Nov–April 3 daily; 10min); Platja de Formentor (May–Oct 2 daily; 25min); Pollença (3–5 daily; 20min); Port de Pollença (May–Oct every 15min; Nov–April 3 daily; 15min); Port de Sóller (May–Oct Mon–Sat 2 daily; 1hr 10min).

From **Port de Pollença** to: Alcúdia (May–Oct every 15min; Nov–April 3 daily; 10min); Ca'n Picafort (3 daily; 25min); Platja de Formentor (May–Oct 2 daily; 20min); Pollença (3–5 daily; 10min); Port d'Alcúdia (May–Oct every 15min; Nov–April 3 daily; 15min); Port de Sóller (May–Oct Mon–Sat 2 daily; 55min); Sóller (May–Oct Mon–Sat 2 daily; 50min).

From **Port de Sóller** to: Deià (5 daily; 20min); Pollença (May–Oct Mon–Sat 2 daily; 50min); Port d'Alcúdia (May–Oct Mon–Sat 2 daily; 1hr 10min); Port de Pollença (May–Oct Mon–Sat 2 daily; 55min); Sóller (5 daily; 5min); Valldemossa (5 daily; 30min).

From **Valldemossa** to: Andratx (Mon–Sat 1 daily; 1hr); Banyalbufar (Mon–Sat 1 daily; 30min); Estellencs (Mon–Sat 1 daily; 45min); Peguera (Mon–Sat 1 daily; 1hr 10min).

Trains

From **Palma** to: Binissalem (hourly; 30min); Inca (hourly; 40min); Sóller (5 daily; 1hr 15min).

Chapter 3

Southeast Mallorca

For most visitors, the hinterland of **southeast Mallorca** is simply a monotonous interlude between airport and resort. However, it was this fertile central plain – **Es Pla** as it's known to the islanders, stretching from the Serra de Tramuntana in the west to the **Serres de Llevant**, the hilly range which shadows the east coast – that defined Mallorca until the twentieth century. The majority of the island's inhabitants lived here, it produced enough food to meet almost every domestic requirement, and Palma's gentry were reliant on Es Pla estates for their income. To defend "The Plain" from marauding pirates, Mallorca's medieval kings constructed hilltop fortresses along the Serres de Llevant, leaving the eastern shoreline an unprotected area fit only for a smattering of insignificant fishing villages and tiny ports. And so matters remained until the tourist boom stood everything on its head: from the 1960s onwards, the developers simply bypassed Es Pla to focus on the picturesque coves of the east coast, where they constructed a long string of brash resorts.

In truth, the towns of Es Pla do not put themselves out to attract visitors. There's hardly anywhere to stay, and restaurants are thin on the ground, while tourist offices simply don't exist. As a consequence, visiting the region is mostly a matter of day trips. The softly hued landscape, patterned with olive orchards, chunky farmhouses and country towns of low, whitewashed houses huddled beneath outsized churches, is appealing, though there's precious little to distinguish one settlement from another – **Sineu** is by far the most diverting. Other sights worth making a beeline for are the impres-

---

Accommodation price symbols

The symbols used in our accommodation listings denote the following price ranges:

① Under 2000ptas	④ 4000–6000ptas	⑦ 10,000–14,000ptas
② 2000–3000pta	⑤ 6000–8000ptas	⑧ 14,000–20,000ptas
③ 3000–4000ptas	⑥ 8000–10,000ptas	⑨ Over 20,000ptas

For more details see p.31.

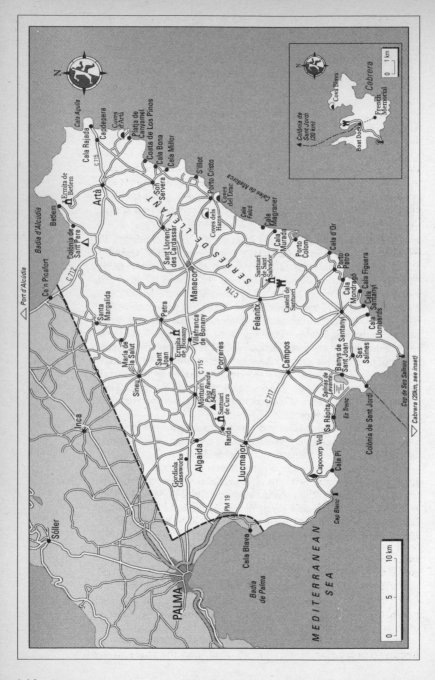

sive monastery perched on the summit of **Puig Randa** and, in the Serres de Llevant, the hilltop shrine at **Artà** and the delightful medieval castle at **Capdepera**. All these destinations are accessible from the C715, which runs the 70km from Palma to Artà.

The ancient fishing villages of the **east coast** have mostly been transformed into mega-resorts, but there are a couple of manageable, enjoyable seaside places which have avoided the worst excesses of concrete and glass: **Cala Rajada**, a lively holiday spot bordered by fine beaches and a beautiful pine-shrouded coastline, and **Cala Figuera**, which surrounds a lovely, steep-sided cove. This coast also boasts the cave systems of **Coves d'Artà** and **Coves del Drac**, justifiably famous for their extravagant stalactites and stalagmites. On the **south coast**, the scenery changes again with hills and coves giving way to sparse flatlands, whose only star turn is the port-cum-resort of **Colònia de Sant Jordi**. From there boat trips leave for the scrubby remoteness of the fauna-rich island of **Cabrera**.

On Puig Randa the monastery offers simple **accommodation**, as does the Santuari de Sant Salvador, outside Felanitx, and the Ermita de Nostra Senyora de Bonany, near Petra. In view of the general dearth of accommodation in the interior, and the difficulty of finding a room in the coastal package resorts, these are well worth bearing in mind – especially as there's usually space and the rates are low.

Travelling by **bus** presents problems. Palma has direct links with almost every resort and town, but services between the towns of Es Pla are virtually non-existent while those along the coast are patchy. Broadly speaking, you'll manage to get around most easily in the north between Cala Rajada, Artà and Cala Millor, and to the south between Cala d'Or, Cala Figuera and Colònia de Sant Jordi. Elsewhere, you'll be struggling without a car.

East from Palma to Artà

Whisking through the agricultural landscape to the east of Palma, the C715 is lined with roadside tourist attractions. The most successful of these is the **Gordiola Glassworks**, which houses a superb museum; as second choice, the pearl-making factory of **Perlas Majorica**, at Manacor, lags some way behind. By far the most interesting detours from the highway are to the monastery surmounting **Puig Randa**, and to **Sineu**, once the site of a royal palace and now the prettiest town on the plain. Neither should Artà, tucked away amongst the Serres de Llevant, be overlooked, not only for its delightful location, but also for its proximity to the fascinating Talayotic settlement of **Ses Paisses** and the laid-back mini-resort of **Colònia de Sant Pere**.

Buses from Palma to Petra, Manacor and Artà are fast and frequent, but there are no services to Sineu. Apart from the spartan rooms at the monasteries on Puig Randa and near Petra, the only places to stay in this area are at Manacor, Sineu and Colònia de Sant Pere.

Gordiola Glassworks

*The Gordiola
Glassworks is
open May–Sept
daily
9am–8pm;
Oct–April
Mon–Sat
9am–1.30pm &
3–7pm, Sun
9am–1pm; free.*

Some 19km east of Palma along the C715, just beyond the awful plastic dinosaurs of the Prehistoric Park, the **Gordiola Glassworks** (*Ca'n Gordiola*) occupies a conspicuous castle-like building whose crenellated walls and clumsy loggias date from the 1960s. However, don't be put off by its appearance – or the herd of tourist coaches parked outside. For a start, you can watch highly skilled **glassblow**ers in action, practising their precise art in a gloomy hall, designed to resemble a medieval church, that's illuminated by glowing furnaces. Guides explain the techniques involved – the fusion of silica, soda and lime at a temperature of 1100°C – and you can hang around for as long as you like. It is, of course, all part of a public relations exercise intended to push you towards the adjacent gift shops. Here, amongst a massive assortment of glass and ceramic items, you'll find everything from the most abysmal tourist tat to works of great delicacy, notably green-tinted chandeliers of traditional Mallorcan design priced at around 190,000ptas.

It is, however, the **museum**, tucked away on the top floor, which really grabs the attention. The owners of the glassworks, the Gordiola family, have been in business in Mallorca since the early eighteenth century, when the first of the line, Gordiola Rigal, arrived from the Spanish mainland. Since then, seven successive generations have accumulated an extraordinary collection of glassware: each of the fifty-odd cabinets is devoted to a particular theme or country and each is labelled, though if you've more than a general interest it's worth investing in a guidebook from the gift shop (950ptas).

On display are examples of the earliest Gordiola work, green-coloured jugs and jars of a frothy consistency, where both the shade and the trapped air bubbles were entirely unwanted. Heated by wood and coal, the original hoop-shaped furnaces had tiny windows through which works-in-progress could be rotated. With such limited technology, however, it was impossible to maintain a consistently high temperature, so the glass could neither be clarified nor cleared of its last air bubbles. Aware of these deficiencies, the next of the line, Bernardo Gordiola, spent years in Venice cultivating the leading glassmakers of the day, and the results of what he learnt can be seen in the same display case. He developed a style of Mallorcan-made jugs decorated with *laticinos*, glass strips wrapped round the object in the Venetian manner, and, in general, improved the quality of the glass. Amongst later Gordiola work, kitchen- and tableware predominate – bottles, vases, jugs and glasses – in a variety of shades, of which green remains the most distinctive. There's also a tendency to extrapolate functional designs into imaginative, ornamental pieces, ranging from hideous fish-shaped receptacles designed for someone's mantlepiece to the most poetic of vases.

Yet Gordiola glassware is just a fraction of the collection. Other cabinets feature pieces from every corner of the globe, beginning with finds from classical Greece, the Nile and the Euphrates. There's also an exquisite sample of early Islamic glassware, Spanish and Chinese opalescents, and superb Venetian vases dating to the seventeenth and eighteenth centuries. More modern stuff includes goblets from Germany and Austria, devotional pieces from Poland, traditional Caithness crystal from Scotland, and a striking melange of Norwegian Art Nouveau glasswork. The museum also exhibits decorative items from cultures where glass was unknown: an eclectic ensemble of pre-Columbian pieces worked in clay, quartz and obsidian, along with the zoomorphic and anthropomorphic basalt figures characteristic of the Sahara.

Algaida and Puig Randa

ALGAIDA, just off the main highway 2km east of the glassworks, is typical of the small agricultural towns that sprinkle Mallorca's central plain – low, whitewashed houses fanning out from an old Gothic church. It's hardly inspiring, but if you're travelling the C715, you'll need to pass through here to reach **Puig Randa**, the highest of a slim band of hills on the north side of Llucmajor. Beginning around 3km south of Algaida, the road to the 542-metre summit – a well-surfaced but serpentine affair, some 5km long – starts by climbing through the hamlet of **RANDA**, a pretty little place of old stone houses harbouring a comfortable **hotel**, *Es Reco de Randa* (☎660997; ⑤). The hotel, with only eight rooms and an outdoor swimming pool, is usually booked up months in advance, but it's a good spot to take a break – the terraced **restaurant** serves delicious food, especially roast lamb and suckling pig.

The top of the hill is flat enough to accommodate a substantial walled complex, the **Santuari de Nostra Senyora de Cura** ("Hermitage of Our Lady of Cura" – Cura is the name of the upper part of Puig Randa). Entry is through a seventeenth-century portal, but most of the buildings beyond are plain and modern, the work of the present incumbents, Franciscan monks who arrived in 1913 after the site had lain abandoned for decades. The original hermitage was founded by the scholar and missionary Ramon Llull in the thirteenth century, and it was here that he prepared his acolytes for their missions to Asia and Africa. Succeeding generations of Franciscans turned the site into a centre of religious learning, and the scholastic tradition was maintained by a grammar school, which finally fizzled out in 1826. The Llull connection makes the monastery an important place of pilgrimage, especially for the *Bendición*

For more on Ramon Llull, see p.72.

de los Frutos (Blessing of the Crops) held on the fourth Sunday after Easter.

Nothing remains of Llull's foundation and the oldest surviving building is the quaintly gabled chapel, parts of which date from the 1660s. Reached via the loggia in the right-hand corner of the complex, the chapel interior is dark and gloomy, its stunted nave spanned by a barrel-vaulted roof. Next door, in the old school, there's a modest museum with an incidental collection of ecclesiastical bric-a-brac – not much to delay a visit to the nearby terrace café, which offers average food and excellent views out across the island. There are a couple of other belvederes on the hilltop, plus an information desk where you can get free maps and fix yourself up with a room in the guest quarters – a self-contained, modern block of basic bedrooms (advance bookings on ☎660994; ①).

The sanctuaries of Sant Honorat and Gràcia

There are two other, less significant sanctuaries on the lower slopes of Puig Randa. Heading back down the hill, past the radio masts, it's a couple of kilometres to the easily missable sharp left turn for the Santuari de Sant Honorat, which comprises a tiny church and a few conventual buildings of medieval provenance. Back on the main summit road 1.2km down the hill, is the more appealing third and final monastery, the Santuari de Gràcia, which is approached through a signposted gateway on the left and along a short, gravelled road. Founded in the fifteenth century, the whitewashed walls of this tiny sanctuary are tucked underneath a severe cliff face, which throngs with nesting birds. The simple barrel-vaulted church boasts some handsome majolica tiles, but it's the panoramic view of Es Pla's rolling farmland that holds the eye.

Montuiri

Travelling east of Algaida on the C715, you'll soon reach the first of several turnings for MONTUIRI, and, immediately afterwards, the new Perlas Orquidea factory, where artificial pearls are made up from glass globules, an industry for which Mallorca is internationally famous. The sales rooms are extensive and you can glimpse aspects of the production process. Similar pearl plants can be found at Manacor, the next point of interest on the main road (see below), though it's more enjoyable to detour north to Sineu and Petra via Montuiri itself, a gentle sweep of pastel-shaded stone houses on a low hill. In the heart of town, it's worth taking a peek at the Baroque retables of the largely Gothic church of Sant Bartomeu, an imposing pile next to the small main square.

Sineu

SINEU, 11km north of Montuiri, is undoubtedly the most interesting of the ancient agricultural towns of Es Pla. Glued to a hill at the geographical centre of the island, the town had obvious strategic advantages for the independent kings of fourteenth-century Mallorca. Jaume II built a royal palace here; his asthmatic successor, Sancho, came to take the upland air; and the last of the dynasty, Jaume III, slept in Sineu the night before he was defeated and killed at the battle of Llucmajor by Pedro of Aragon. The new Aragonese monarchs had no need of the Sineu palace, which disappeared long ago, but former pretensions survive in the massive stone facade of **Nostra Senyora de los Angeles**, one of the grandest parish churches on the island. Built in the thirteenth century, the church was extensively remodelled three hundred years later, but the majestic simplicity of the original Gothic design is still plain to see – though it's in a dreadful state of repair. At the side a single-span arch connects with the colossal free-standing belltower, and in front stands a big, modern and aggressive statue of a winged lion, the emblem of the town's patron, St Mark.

Walking under the arch, you enter the unassuming main square, Sa Plaça. Here you'll find the first of two excellent, traditional Mallorcan **restaurants** in Sineu, the *Celler Ca'n Font* (closed Thurs), whose cavernous interior doubles as a wine vault, hence the enormous wooden barrels. The decor is similar at the nearby *Celler Es Crup*, c/Major 18 (closed Mon), but the atmosphere is more welcoming, and the food, if anything, even better. Both restaurants are at their busiest on Wednesdays, when the town fizzes with one of Mallorca's biggest fresh produce markets. Sineu also has (and this is something of a surprise) a very good hotel, the *Leon de Sineu*, c/Bous 129 (☎520211; ⑤), set in an attractively refurbished mansion five minutes' stroll from Sa Plaça: walk down the hill from the square, turn first right and keep going.

Petra

Nothing very exciting happens in **PETRA**, 10km east of Sineu, but it was the birthplace of **Junipero Serra**, the eighteenth-century Franciscan friar who played an important role in the settlement of Spanish North America. Serra's missionary endeavours began in 1749 when he landed at Veracruz on the Gulf of Mexico. Despite a particularly unpleasant voyage, he and his band of monks promptly walked 500km to Mexico City, thereby completing the first of many mind-boggling treks. For eighteen years Serra thrashed around the remoter parts of Mexico until, entirely by chance, political machinations back in Europe saved him from obscurity. In 1768, Carlos III claimed the west coast of the North American continent for Spain, and, to substantiate his claim, dispatched a small expeditionary force of soldiers and monks north. Serra happened to be in the right place at the right time, and was assigned to lead the priests. Even by Serra's standards, the walk from Mexico City to California was a hell of a trek, but almost all the force survived to reach the Pacific

Ocean somewhere near the present US-Mexico border in early 1769. Over the next decade, Serra and his small party of priests set about converting the Native Americans of coastal California to the Catholic faith, and established a string of nine missions along the Pacific coast, including San Diego and San Francisco. Serra was beatified by Pope Paul II in 1988.

Petra makes a reasonable hand of its connection with Serra. In the upper part of town on c/Major is the chunky church of **Sant Bernat**, beside which – down a narrow alley – lies a modest sequence of majolica panels honouring Serra's life and missionary work. This simple tribute is backed up by a minuscule **museum** at the end of the alley and, next door to the museum, the **house** where Serra was born, which contains a series of mildly diverting displays outlining the priest's life and times. Both can be visited between 9am and 8pm, Monday to Friday, but you have to collect the key from the custodian – to do this follow the instructions posted outside.

Other than that, there's little reason to hang around – the C715 is just 5km away to the south – though the hilltop **Ermita de Nostra Senyora de Bonany**, on the south side of Petra, does offer great views. To get there, take the signposted, four-kilometre country lane which begins on the town's main street. Simple **rooms** are available for rent at the monastery (reservations on ☎561101; ①), but there's no hot water or food for guests.

Manacor

MANACOR declares its business long before you arrive: vast roadside hoardings promote its furniture and artificial pearl factories. On the strength of these, the city has risen to become the second urban centre of Mallorca, far smaller than Palma but large enough to have sprawling suburbs on all sides. It's not exactly compelling, but Manacor does have an industrial independence distinctly lacking elsewhere.

In a rather half-hearted attempt to catch the passing tourist trade, the town also musters several modern attractions, situated beside the C715 as you approach from the west. Next door to each other, the first two are paragons of bad taste: the **Deformed Animal Museum** is plain disgusting, while the **Olive Wood Shop and Museum** is more shop than museum, churning out thousands of household ornaments – oversized ashtrays and the like – stained in a sticky-looking brown. Sometimes it verges on the kitsch, but mostly it's just ugly.

The Perlas Majorica factory is open Mon–Fri 9am–1pm & 3–7pm, Sat & Sun 10am–1pm.

Next door again is the first of the town's several *Perlas Majorica* **artificial pearl** shops, but skip it in favour of the company's factory, only 1km further east along the main road and well signposted. At this main complex, you can go on a free **factory tour**, a somewhat perfunctory cruise giving just a general insight into the

manufacturing process. The core of the imitation pearl is a glass glob-
ule on to which are painted many layers of a glutinous liquid primarily
composed of fish scales. The finished item – anywhere between soft
yellow and metallic grey – is gently polished and then included within
many different types of jewellery. Artificial pearls last longer than and
are virtually indistinguishable from the real thing, but consequently
they're expensive – as you'll discover at the end of the tour when
you're shepherded into the adjacent showroom and gift shop.

It's unlikely that you'll want to stay in industrial Manacor, but if
you do – perhaps with a view to commuting to the coast – you'll find
a couple of reasonably priced and pretty basic possibilities: *Hostal
Jacinto*, across from the main church at c/Weyler 1 (☎550124; ①),
and *Can Guixa*, c/Alfareros 15 (no phone; ①). Be warned, though,
that even here rooms are in short supply in the height of the season.
For food, try the local speciality, spicy, black pork sausage (*sobra-
sada de cerdo negro*) in one of the town's cafés; or, for something
more substantial, head for *Fonda Marc*, c/Valencia 7, which serves
traditional Mallorcan cuisine at very reasonable prices.

Artà and around

Beyond Manacor the C715 veers north to run parallel to the coast,
with the flatlands soon left behind for the peaks of the Serres de
Llevant. The top end of this mountain range bunches to fill out
Mallorca's northeast corner, thus providing a dramatic backdrop to
ARTÀ, an ancient hill town of sun-bleached roofs clustered beneath
a castellated chapel-shrine. It's a delightful scene, though at close
quarters the town is something of an anticlimax – the cobweb of
cramped and twisted alleys doesn't quite match the setting.
Nonetheless, the ten-minute trek to the Santuari de Sant Salvador,
the panoramic shrine at the top of Artà, is a must. It's almost impossible to get lost: just keep going upwards, from the main square,
Plaça Conqueridor, via Plaça Espanya, site of the town hall, and up
through streets of gently decaying grandee mansions to the gargantuan parish church. From this unremarkable pile, steep stone steps
and cypress trees lead up the *Via Crucis* (Way of the Cross) to the
santuari, which, in its present form, dates from the early nineteenth century, though the hilltop has been a place of pilgrimage for
much longer. The Catalans of the Reconquest demolished the
Moorish fort that once stood here, and replaced it with a shrine
accommodating an image of the Virgin Mary which they had
imported with them. This edifice was, in its turn, knocked down in
1820 in a superstitious attempt to stop the spread of an epidemic
that was decimating the region's population. Built a few years later,
the interior of the present chapel is hardly awe-inspiring – the paintings are mediocre and the curious seventeenth-century statue
behind the high altar has Jesus smiling like an imbecile – but the
views out over eastern Mallorca more than compensate.

Practicalities

Arriving from several directions, including Palma, Cala Rajada Ca'n Picafort and the Coves d'Artà, **buses** to Artà stop outside the *Bar Ca'n Balague* on c/Ciutat, the town's main street which leads directly off the C715 as it skirts the southern edge of town. If you've driven here, finding somewhere handy to **park** can be a bit of a hassle: try along c/Ciutat and the adjoining Plaça Conqueridor. There's nowhere great to **eat**, but the *Ca'n Balague* is reasonable enough, as is the nearby *Cafe Parisien*, which has daily specials for 1000ptas. Artà has no hotels, but you stand a fairly good chance of finding a room in nearby Colònia de Sant Pere (see below).

Ses Paisses

Ses Paisses is open Mon–Fri 9am–1pm & 3–7pm, Sat 9am–1pm; 200ptas. For more information on Talayotic culture, see p.221.

One kilometre to the south of Artá lie the substantial and elegiacally rustic remains of the Talayotic settlement of **Ses Paisses**. To get there, walk to the bottom of c/Ciutat, turn left along the main through-road and watch for the signposted (and well-surfaced) country lane on the right. A clear footpath explores every nook and cranny of the village, its numbered markers thoroughly explained in the English-language **guidebook** available at the entrance (300ptas).

Tucked away in a grove of olive, carob and holm-oak trees, the village is entered through a monolithic **gateway**, whose heavyweight jambs and lintel interrupt the Cyclopean **walls** that still encircle the site. These outer remains date from the second phase of the Talayotic culture (*c.* 1000–800 BC), when the emphasis was on consolidation and defence; in places, the walls still stand at their original size, around 3.5m high and 3m wide. Beside the gate, there's also a modern monolith erected in honour of Miquel Llobera, a local writer who penned romantic verses about the place. Beyond the gateway, the central **talayot** is from the first Talayotic period (*c.* 1300–1000 BC), its shattered ruins flanked by the foundations of several rooms of later date and uncertain purpose. Experts believe the **horseshoe-shaped room** was used, at least towards the end of the Talayotic period, for cremations, whilst the three **rectangular rooms** were probably living quarters. In the rooms, archeologists discovered various items such as iron objects and ceramics imported from elsewhere in the Mediterranean, some of which were perhaps brought back from the Punic Wars (264–146 BC) by mercenaries – the skills of Balearic stone slingers were highly prized by the Carthaginians, and it's known that several hundred accompanied Hannibal and his elephants over the Alps in 218 BC.

The Ermita de Betlem

A longer excursion from Artà will bring you to the **Ermita de Betlem**, a remote and minuscule hermitage hidden away in the hills 10km northwest of town. The road begins just below the Santuari de Sant Salvador, though the start is poorly signed and tricky to find.

Its rough surface and snaking course make for a difficult drive, so it's far better to **walk** the route (2–3hr one way). The first portion is an easy stroll up along the wooded valley of the Torrent d'es Cocones. After about 3km, the road squeezes through the narrowest of defiles, with the hills rising steeply on either side, and beyond begins to climb into the foothills of the Serra de Llevant (here classified as the Massís d'Artà). A signposted left turn about 3km beyond the defile signals the start of the strenuous part of the journey, as the track wriggles up the steep hillside, finally reaching the Ermita de Betlem after a further 4km. The buildings, which date from the hermitage's foundation in 1805, arc quite unassuming – although, if you've come this far, you'll undoubtedly want to peep into the tiny church, where the walls are decorated with crude religious frescoes – but the views over the Badia d'Alcúdia are magnificent. The hermitage doesn't offer accommodation or food, just picnic tables, so you'll soon be moving on. Rather than retracing your steps, it's possible to make the 350-metre descent down to the coast, bringing you out about 2km east of Colònia de Sant Pere (see below) on the road to the seaside *urbanització* of Betlem. The descent takes about an hour and the footpath is fairly clear and easy, beginning beside a roofed spring, five minutes' walk below the gates of the hermitage. From the spring, a wide cart track zigzags downwards to meet a footpath which continues down to the seashore.

Colònia de Sant Pere

West of Artà the C712 weaves through the hills to pass the turning for **COLÒNIA DE SANT PERE**, a downbeat resort and fishing village overlooking the Badia d'Alcúdia. There were plans to build a mammoth villa complex on this part of the coast, but they appear to have been postponed, and, although developers have scratched away here and there, the village itself has been left alone. Not that there's much to the place. Founded in 1881, Colònia de Sant Pere is no more than a few blocks across, its plain, low-rise, modern buildings set behind a small sandy beach on an otherwise bare and rocky shoreline. It's all very low-key and laid-back, and this, along with the setting, is the place's charm. Behind are the jagged flanks of the Massís d'Artà, where a popular footpath, its trailhead some 2km east of Colònia de Sant Pere, connects the coast with the Ermita de Betlem. If you're tackling the walk from the Colònia de Sant Pere end, you'll find the trailhead at a roadside cairn, about 300m west of the roundabout that marks the start of the *urbanització* of Betlem; to check you've got the right track, watch out for the deep, stone-walled well near the start.

Colònia de Sant Pere has just one convenient **hostal**, the *Rocamar*, c/Sant Mateu 9 (☎589312; ②), an unassuming white-washed and green-shuttered building right in the centre, with a restaurant on the ground floor and a handful of simple rooms up above. Alternatively, several of the village's cafés rent fairly basic and inexpensive **rooms and apartments** on a more casual basis – *Sa Xarxa*, on the seafront, is a promising place to start, but most of the cafés concerned advertise in their windows. About 1km west of the village is one of Mallorca's few **campsites**, the *Camping Club San Pedro* (April–Sept; ☎589023), which occupies an isolated and landscaped location behind a pebble and sand beach. It has 500 pitches, as well as a swimming pool, bar, restaurant and sports facilities. Pitch prices start from 1200ptas, added to which is the cost per person, 470ptas, and per car, 625ptas; try to book ahead in summer. You can eat well in Colònia de Sant Pere at *El Pescador*, a restaurant serving the freshest of fish and a tasty *menú del día* at c/Sant Joan 58, and cheaply at *Sa Xarxa* on the seafront.

The east coast

Mallorca's **east coast**, stretching for about 60km south from Cala Rajada to Cala Figuera, is fretted by narrow coves, the remnants of prehistoric river valleys created when the level of the Mediterranean was much lower. All of these inlets have accrued at least some tourist development, ranging from a mild scattering of second homes to intensive chains of tower blocks. An attractive minor road links the resorts, running, for the most part, a few kilometres inland along the edge of the Serres de Llevant, a slim band of grassy hills which rises to over 500m at its two extremities – south outside Felanitx and north around Artà. If you have your own transport, this coastal road enables you to pick and choose destinations with the greatest of ease, dodging the crassest examples of overdevelopment – principally Cala Millor, Cales de Mallorca and Cala d'Or – altogether. Among resorts that are worth seeking out, **Cala Rajada**, a boisterous place surrounded by excellent, sandy beaches, is particularly enjoyable, as well as being handy for the lovely medieval fortress of **Capdepera**. For a quiet day on the beach, however, you'll probably do better at the much smaller resort of **Platja de Canyamel**, while, moving south, you can get far more isolation at the relatively untouched beaches of **Cala Mondragó** and **Cala Llombards**. In between these last two is another lively and scenic resort, **Cala Figuera**, the site of some fine restaurants and a top-notch diving centre. The east coast is also famous for its limestone cave systems: the most impressive formations are to be found at the **Coves d'Artà** in the north, closely followed by the **Coves del Drac** at Porto Cristo.

It would be lovely to work your way down the coast, stopping for a couple of nights here and there, but the problem is **accommodation**. In the height of the season, locating a vacant room in one of the more attractive resorts can be a real tribulation – if you do find somewhere reasonable, you'll probably want to stay put. An alternative is to select a less appealing resort, such as dilapidated **Porto**

Cristo or dishevelled **Porto Colom**, where there's far more chance of a bed. Naturally, in the shoulder season, things ease up, but in winter many hotels and *hostals* close down.

To explore the east coast thoroughly you'll need your own transport. All the larger resorts have regular **bus** links with Palma and, in summer, there are good connections to Port d'Alcúdia from Porto Cristo and points north, but services up and down the coast are generally inadequate.

Capdepera

Spied across the valley from the west, the crenellated walls dominating **CAPDEPERA**, a tiny village 7km east of Artà, look too pristine to be true. Yet the triangular fortifications are genuine enough, built in the fourteenth century by the Mallorcan king Sancho to protect the coast from pirates. Nestling below the walls, the village contains a pleasant medley of old houses, its slender main square – Plaça L'Orient – acting as a prelude to the steep steps up to the **Castell de Capdepera**. Flowering cactuses give the fortress a special allure from late May, but it's a beguiling place at any time, with over 400m of wall equipped with a parapet walkway and sheltering neat terraced gardens. At the top of the fortress, **Nostra Senyora de la Esperança** (Our Lady of Good Hope) is the quaintest of Gothic churches: its aisle-less, vaulted frame is furnished with outside steps leading up, behind the bell gable, to a flat roof, from which the views are superb.

The Castell de Capdepera is open April–Sept Tues–Sun 10am–1pm & 4–7pm; Oct–May Tues–Sun 10am–1pm & 3–5pm; 200ptas.

On the way down from the castle, a good spot to break the journey is *PJ's*, c/Major 37, an English-owned **café-bar** where the food isn't brilliant, but the views out from the terrace are; it's just a couple of minutes' walk downhill from the castle entrance, along the street that cuts across the head of the steps down to the main square. There's also a very good **restaurant** in the town centre, the *Ca's Padri*, c/Ponent 5 (closed Mon), whose speciality is charcoal-grilled meat (stick to the lamb). To get there, turn right at the foot of c/Major, then first right and it's on the left. There's nowhere to **stay** in Capdepera, but it's easy enough to visit by **bus** from Artà, Cala Rajada, Cala Millor or even Palma.

Cala Rajada

Awash with cafés, bars and hotels, lively **CALA RAJADA** lies on the southerly side of a stubby headland in the northeast corner of Mallorca, just 3km beyond Capdepera. The town centre, an unassuming patchwork of low-rise modern buildings, is hardly prepossessing, but all around is a wild and rocky coastline, backed by pine-clad hills and sheltering a series of delightful beaches. The resort was once a fishing village, but there's little evidence of this today, and the old **harbour**, at the far end of the main drag, c/Elíonor Servera, is now used by pleasure boats and overlooked by restau-

rants. From the harbour, walkways extend along the headland's
south coast. To the southwest, past the busiest part of town, it takes
about five minutes to stroll round to **Platja Son Moll**, a slender arc
of sand overlooked by goliath-like hotels. More rewarding is the ten-
minute stroll east to **Cala Gat**, a narrow cove beach tucked tight up
against the steep, wooded coastline. The beach is far from undiscov-
ered – there's a beach bar and at times it gets decidedly crowded –
but it's an attractive spot all the same.

Up above the footpath to Cala Gat you can glimpse some of the
modern sculptures that embellish the gardens of the **Parc Casa
March**, a privately owned open-air museum which also contains a
beautiful orchid house. Most of the exhibits are Spanish, but there's
also a bronze by Rodin and examples of the work of three British
sculptors, Henry Moore, Barbara Hepworth and Anthony Caro. The
entrance is on c/Joan March, a turning off c/Elíonor Servera just
beyond the harbour, though opening times are at the discretion of
the family, and visits – at 400ptas per person – can only be arranged
via the *oficina d'informació turística*. Beyond the gardens, continuing east along c/Elíonor Servera, the road twists steeply up through
the pine woods to reach, after about 1km, the bony headlands and
lighthouse of the **Cap de Capdepera**, Mallorca's most easterly point
– the views out along the coast are a treat.

On the northern side of Cala Rajada, c/L'Agulla crosses the
promontory to hit the north coast at **Platja Cala Agulla**, the nearer
reaches of which are often known as **Cala Guya**. The approach road
– some 2km of tourist tackiness – is of little appeal, but the beach, a
vast curve of bright golden sand, is big enough to accommodate
hundreds of bronzing pectorals with plenty of space to spare. The

further you walk – and there are signed and shaded footpaths
through the pine woods to assist you – the more isolation you'll get.
Consider also **Cala de Sa Font**, a cove beach about 5km south of
town; there is development here as well, but it isn't too overpowering and the beach is a beauty.

Practicalities

Most **buses** to Cala Rajada stop right in the town centre, one block
behind the main square, Plaça dels Pins, where you'll find the
Oficina d'Informació Turística (March–Oct Mon–Fri 9.30am–
1.30pm & 4–7pm, Sat 9.30am–1.30pm; Nov–Feb Mon–Fri 9.30am–
1.30pm & 2.30–5pm; ☎563033). The office can supply an excellent
range of local information including restaurant lists, bus schedules,
details of car and bicycle rental firms, and free town maps marked
with all the accommodation. They also have a popular, though not
very detailed, pamphlet on "Hiking Tours" (300ptas), and will
advise you on entry to the Parc Casa March (see above). The town
centre is easy to explore on foot, but for the outlying beaches you'll
probably want a **local bus**. Among several summertime services
from the bus stops along c/Castellet, the most useful are to Cala
Agulla, Cala de Sa Font, the Coves d'Artà and Platja de Canyamel.

The major drawback is that in high season you'll be lucky to
find a **room**, as Cala Rajada is a favourite German package resort.
The best place to try is among the **hostals** dotted around the pleasant residential streets just up from the harbour. Reasonable bets
here are the *Vista Pinar*, a large, comfortable *hostal* with its own
swimming pool at c/Reis Catòlics 11 (April–Oct; ☎563751; ③); the
Casa Bauza, which has attractively furnished rooms as well as a
pool at c/Méndez Núñez 61 (April–Oct; ☎563844; ②); and the
Bellavista, c/Miquel Garau 30 (mid-March to Oct; ☎563194; ④), a
modern, air-conditioned place with motel-style rooms. In the shoulder season, it's probably worth paying a bit extra to stay in one of
Cala Rajada's **hotels**. Particularly good-value choices are the two-
star *Ses Rotges*, c/Rafael Blanes 21 (April–Oct; ☎563108; ⑤), a
delightful place in an elegantly restored antique villa just out of
earshot of the main square; and the *Hotel Cala Gat* (April–Oct;
☎563166; ④) which, although it isn't as plush, does offer a
secluded location in the pine woods above Cala Gat. A more workaday option, the *Hotel Son Moll*, overlooking the Platja Son Moll
(April–Oct; ☎563100; ⑤), has light and airy rooms, most with
balconies, and magnificent views out to sea.

The *Hotel Ses Rotges* boasts the best **restaurant** in town, but
it's expensive and there are scores of cheaper rivals. It's hard to
make specific recommendations as there's not much to choose
between most of them, and you could try anywhere down by the
harbour where the fish is usually mouthwateringly fresh. Here,
squeezed together on c/Gabriel Roca, you'll find the *Restaurant
Escorcat*, a chic and attractive spot specializing in fish – seafood

main courses from 1800ptas – and also serving superb steaks; the *Restaurant El Puerto*, with its neat cane furniture, offering quality pizzas from 600ptas; and the similar *Pizzeria Negresio* cafeteria, a popular and cheerful place with low-price pizzas, sandwiches, steaks and spaghetti. **Boats** leave the harbour for regular summer excursions down the east coast and back. They venture as far as Cala Millor (2 daily except Sun; 1400ptas) and Porto Cristo (1 daily except Sun; 1900ptas), last all day and offer side trips to the Coves d'Artà (see below) and Drac (see p.165).

The Coves d'Artà

Guided tours of the Coves d'Artà run April–Oct daily 10am–7pm; Nov–March daily 10am–5pm; 800ptas.

The succession of coves, caves and beaches notching the seashore between Cala Rajada and Cala Millor begins promisingly with the **Coves d'Artà** (in Castilian, Cuevas de Artá), reached along the first turning off the main coastal road from Capdepera. The caves are linked by **bus** with Artà and Cala Rajada four times daily in summer except on Sundays. The approach to the caves is stunning, with a majestic stairway straight out of a Hammer Horror movie leading up to the yawning entrance, which beckons like the mouth of Hell, high in the cliffs above the bay. This is the pick of the numerous cave systems of eastern Mallorca, its sequence of cavernous chambers, studded with stalagmites and stalactites, extending 450m into the rock face. Artificial lighting exaggerates the bizarre shapes of the caverns and their concretions, especially in the **Hall of Flags**, where stalactites up to 50m long hang in the shape of partly unfurled flags. Visiting the caves for their scientific interest became fashionable amongst the rich and famous – including Jules Verne – at the end of the nineteenth century, and nowadays they feature prominently on package-tour itineraries. It wasn't, however, much of a treat to be here during the Reconquest, when a thousand Moors – refugees from Artà – holed up inside the caves, until they were literally smoked out to be slaughtered by the Catalan soldiers waiting outside.

The guides give a complete geological description in tedious detail and in several languages (including English), as you wander the illuminated abyss. Allow about an hour for the visit – more if there's a queue, as there often is.

Platja de Canyamel

PLATJA DE CANYAMEL is the prettiest of this area's cove resorts, with neat modern villas draped around a pine-backed sandy beach in sight of a pair of rocky headlands. It's situated about 1km south around the bay from the Coves d'Artà, but there's no direct route between the two – you have to retrace your steps inland to pick up the signposted turnings (don't confuse Platja de Canyamel with the tedious Costa de Canyamel *urbanització*, which lies at the southern end of this same bay). Platja de Canyamel's only **hostal** is the appealing *Laguna* (May–Oct; ☎563400; ④), whose trim white-washed and shuttered frame is situated right on the beach. However, you'll be lucky to get a room – it's almost always block-booked by German package tour operators. Local **buses** from Cala Rajada and Artà stop beside the *Laguna*. For **food**, try the *Isabel* restaurant, where the seafood is fresh and well prepared, or head back down the access road for about 3km until you reach the excellent *Porxada de Sa Torre* (closed Mon & Nov–April; ☎563044), a stone watchtower converted into a restaurant, which specializes in traditional Mallorcan cuisine.

Cala Millor and around

Continuing south along the main coast road, several turnings lead to the well-heeled villas of **COSTA DE LOS PINOS**, the most northerly and prosperous portion of a gigantic resort conurbation centred on **CALA BONA** and **CALA MILLOR**. This is development gone quite mad, a swathe of apartment buildings, sky-rise hotels and villa-villages overwhelming the contours of the coast as far as the eye can see. The only redeeming feature – and the reason for all this frantic construction in the first place – is the beach, a magnificent two-kilometre stretch of sand fringed by what remains of the old pine woods. The principal **Oficina d'Informació Turistica**, at Parc de la Mar 2, just behind the beach at the south end of Cala Millor (Mon–Fri 9am–1pm & 3–7pm, Sat 9am–1pm; ☎585409), has all the usual information, including free maps.

South of Cala Millor, the main coastal road passes by the **Auto-Safari-Park**, where a motley assortment of African animals roams open countryside. Visitors can either drive through or take one of the Safari Buses (for an extra 1500ptas). Beyond, there are yet more acres of concrete and glass at **S'ILLOT**, though the main road, set back from the coast, cuts a rustic route through vineyards and almond groves, before reaching the multicoloured billboards which announce the cave systems of Porto Cristo.

The Auto-Safari-Park is open April–Oct daily 9am–7pm; Nov–March daily 9am–5pm; 1400ptas.

Porto Cristo

Although **PORTO CRISTO** prospered in the early days of the tourist boom, sprouting a string of hotels and *hostals*, it's fared badly since mega-resorts such as Cala Millor and Cala d'Or were constructed. Don't be deceived by the jam of tourist buses clogging the town's streets on their way to the nearby caves – few of their occupants will actually be staying in Porto Cristo. Consequently, this is one of the very few places on the east coast where you're likely to find a room in July and August – and it's not too bad a spot to spend a night either. Porto Cristo's origins are uncertain, but it was definitely in existence by the thirteenth century, serving as the fishing harbour and seaport of the inland town of Manacor. Nothing remains of the medieval settlement, and today the centre, which climbs the hill behind the harbour, consists of high-sided terraced buildings, mostly dating from the late nineteenth and early twentieth centuries.

At the bottom of the hill, right in front of the main square-cum-promenade, is the **beach**, a small sliver of sand, poor for sunbathing, which cannot compete with the long, flat strands of the new mega-resorts. The beach is tucked inside the **harbour**, a narrow V-shaped channel entered between a pair of humpy promontories. Beyond the beach, the harbour accommodates a large marina and then meets the oily-green Es Rivet river, which forms the town centre's southern perimeter. Long a naval base, the harbour is one of the most sheltered on Mallorca's east coast and was the site of the **Republican landing** in August 1936 to try to capture the island from the Falangists. The campaign, however, was a fiasco: the Republicans disembarked over 7000 men and quickly established a long and deep bridgehead, but their commanders, completely surprised by their initial success, quite literally didn't know what to do next. The Nationalists did. They counter-attacked and, supported by the Italian air force, soon had the Republicans dashing back to the coast. Barcelona radio put on a brave face, announcing, "The heroic Catalan columns have returned from Mallorca after a magnificent action. Not a single man suffered from the effects of the embarkation."

Practicalities

The main coastal road passes along Porto Cristo's seafront, and a healthy number of long-distance **buses**, principally from Palma and Port d'Alcúdia, terminate in the centre beside the harbour and the beach. The town's **Oficina d'Informació Turistica** is at c/Gual 31 (Mon–Fri 8am–2pm; ☎820931): take c/Concepció up from the beach and make the fifth turning on the left. There are a dozen or so modern **hotels and hostals** in and around the town centre, though they're an undistinguished lot. For starters, try the very basic one-star *Hostal-residencia Aurora*, at c/Villalonga 3, the third turning left up c/Concepció (April–Oct; ☎821642; ③), or the much bigger but equally tatty *Hotel Felip*, overlooking the beach at c/Bordils 41 (☎820750; ④). There's also a string of places south of the river on or near Carretera Coves (the main coastal road) as it nears the Coves del Drac. The best options here are the simple *Hotel Estrella*, which occupies an old and slightly frayed house off the road to the right at c/Curricà 16 (May–Oct; ☎820833; ④); and, close by, the two-star *Hotel Drach*, Carretera Coves (May–Oct; ☎820818; ④), a massive and mildly dishevelled establishment catering for the cheapest of British package tours.

With most of Porto Cristo's **restaurants and cafés** geared up for the passing tourist trade, getting a decent meal is difficult. There are only a couple of places of any quality: your best bet is the family-run *Sa Carrotje*, a low-key spot just north from the beach along c/Bordils, at Avgda Joan Amer 45, where a tasty fish dish will set you back around 1000ptas; slightly more expensive, but a good second choice all the same, is the *Siroco*, whose cosy terrace abuts the harbour a few metres south from the beach on c/Veri. The pizza bars and cafés directly behind the beach are considerably less expensive than either of these restaurants, but their food is mediocre at best.

Around Porto Cristo

Across the river, about fifteen minutes' walk south of the centre along the coastal road, lies Porto Cristo's pride and joy, the **Coves del Drac** (Cuevas del Drach in Castilian). Locals had known of the "Dragon's Caves" for hundreds of years, but it was the Austrian archduke Ludwig Salvator who recruited French geologists to explore and map them in 1896. The French discovered four whopping chambers that penetrated the coast's limestone cliffs for a distance of around 2km. In the last cavern they found one of the largest subterranean lakes in the world, some 177m long, 40m wide and 30m deep. The eccentric shapes of the myriad stalactites and stalagmites adorning each chamber immediately invited comparison with more familiar objects. As the leader of the French team, Edouard Martel, wrote, "On all sides, everywhere, in front and behind, as far as the eye can see, marble cascades, organ pipes, lace draperies, pendants of multi-faceted gems hang suspended from the walls and roof".

Hourly guided tours of the Coves del Drac run daily in summer 10am–5pm, in winter 10.30am–4pm; 800ptas. For more on Ludwig Salvator, see p.110.

Since the French exploration, the caves have been thoroughly commercialized. The present complex accommodates a giant car park, ticket office and restaurant, behind which lurk the gardens that lead to the flight of steps down to the caves: you may come to know each step well, as, especially on the weekend, you can wait in line for ages. Inside, the myriad concretions of calcium carbonate, formed by the dissolution of the soft limestone by rainwater, are shrewdly illuminated. Shunting you through the hour-long, multilingual tour, the guides invite you to gawp and gush at formations such as "the Buddha", "the Pagoda" and "the Snowy Mountain", and magnificent icicle-like stalactites, some of which are snowy white, while others pick up hints of orange and red from the rocks they pass through. The *tour de force* is the larger of the two subterranean lakes, whose translucent waters flicker with reflected colours, the effects further enhanced by musicians drifting about in boats playing harmoniums (performances begin on the hour). At the end of the tour, most visitors walk out, but there's also the option of a brief and disappointing boat ride across part of the lake.

The Acuàrium is open daily 10am–5.30pm; 600ptas. Guided tours of the Coves des Hams run daily 10.30am–1.15pm & 2.15–5.30pm; 1100ptas.

Leaving the caves, it's a short walk from the car park (away from the caves) to the well-stocked **Acuàrium**, where the glass tanks magnify such exotic horrors as electric eels, piranhas and stinging fish – kids love it. Though you'd hardly want to visit both, there's another cave system situated 2km west of Porto Cristo on

the road to Manacor. The **Coves d'es Hams** (Cuevas de Hams)
follow the same format as their rival, with a sequence of (somewhat
smaller) caverns lit to emphasize the beauty of the stalagmites and
stalactites. As at the Coves del Drac, musicians are rowed across an
underground lake (every 20min till 4.30pm).

South to Porto Colom

The modern resorts swarming the pint-sized coves to the **south of
Porto Cristo** reach a crescendo at the **CALES DE MALLORCA**, the
collective name for a band of tourist settlements extending from
Cala Magraner in the north to Cala Murada in the south. This part of
the shoreline didn't have much charm in the first place – the coves
are mostly scrawny and shadeless – and it's even less compelling
now. Inland, however, the main coast road gives little hint of these
aesthetic atrocities, as it wends its pastoral way past honey-coloured
dry-stone walls and a smattering of ancient farmhouses in the lee of
the Serres de Llevant.

PORTO COLOM straggles round a long and irregular bay some
20km south of Porto Cristo. Originally a fishing village supplying
the needs of the neighbouring town of Felanitx, the port boomed
throughout most of the nineteenth century from the export trade in
wine to France. The good times, however, came to an abrupt end
when, in the 1870s, phylloxera (a greenfly-like aphid) wiped out the
region's vines. The villagers returned to fishing, which is still a
significant part of the local economy today – the boats they use, as
well as some interesting old boat sheds, litter the kilometre-long
quay on the southwest side of the bay. The quayside, along with the
modest settlement immediately behind it, constitute the heart of the
present village – there's little to grab your attention, but it's an
enjoyably low-key spot. It's not the oldest part of the village – that
can be found by walking 300m from the west end of the quay round
the back of the harbour, to a small patch of pastel-shaded cottages
shadowing a dinky little square. The area around Porto Colom has
much less to grab your attention: the headlands overlooking the
entrance to the inlet host a lighthouse and a scrawny mix of villas
and hotels, while over the hill behind the village (about 1km to the
south) is **Cala Marsal**, a crowded, shadeless wedge of sand overlooked by the concrete flanks of the eponymous hotel.

Porto Colom practicalities

Bus services to Porto Colom, principally from Palma, arrive at the
quayside. Towards the quay's eastern end you'll probably find a
vacant room at the no-frills *Hostal Porto Colom*, c/Pescadors 5
(April–Oct; ☎825323; ②), whose thirty-odd rooms are stashed
away above a cavernous café-bar. The café is popular with locals, a
rare slice of Mallorcan life that makes this *hostal* preferable to the
more tourist-oriented accommodation on the headland to the east,

such as the basic *Hostal-residencia César*, c/Llaud (April–Oct; ☎825302; ③), and the equally undistinguished *Hostal Bahía Azul*, Ronda Creuer Baleares 88 (☎825280; ④). For something rather more comfortable, especially in the shoulder season, try the three-star *Hotel Cala Marsal* (April–Oct; ☎825225; ⑤), a package-tour favourite with sea-facing rooms and all the usual facilities from swimming pools to tennis courts. Dotted along the quayside are several quality **restaurants**. The cream of the crop is the *Celler Sa Sínia* at the west end of the quay (closed Mon), whose fish dishes are both reasonably priced and lip-smackingly fresh. At the other end of the quay, just along Ronda Creuer Baleares, the smart *Celler Ses Portadores* is an excellent alternative; it's a bit pricier, but the fish is just as fresh and there's a wider selection.

Felanitx and around

FELANITX, the main town of the southeastern corner of the island and 14km inland from Porto Colom, is an industrious place, producing wine, ceramics and pearls. It's short on specific sights, though the honey-gold, Baroque facade of the church of **Sant Miquel** gives an elegant air to the mostly modern main square. Nor are there many facilities – no tourist office, accommodation or noteworthy restaurant – but strolling the old streets and alleys is an agreeable way to pass the odd hour, and you can sample local wines at the *Celler Ca'ntia*, near the church at c/Pou de la Vila 5. **Buses**, linking the town with Palma, stop by the main square.

The Santuari de Sant Salvador and the Castell de Santueri

From Felanitx the Serres de Llevant are within easy striking distance. The best approach is to head back along the road to Porto Colom for about 2km and take the signposted, four-kilometre byroad that snakes up the mountain to the **Santuari de Sant Salvador**, recognizable from miles around by its conspicuous stone cross and enormous statue of Christ. Long an important place of pilgrimage, the monastery occupies a splendid position near the summit of the highest mountain in these parts, the 510-metre Puig Sant Salvador, with sumptuous views out over the east coast. The sanctuary was founded in the mid-fourteenth century, but the original buildings were razed by raiding pirates and most of today's complex is Baroque. The heavy gatehouse is its most conspicuous feature while, inside the compound, the eighteenth-century church shelters a much-venerated image of the Virgin Mary. You can usually get a meal at the monastery, and can rent simple **rooms** (☎827282; ①) – with a car this could make an interesting base for a couple of days.

The monks will be able to point you toward the footpath to the **Castell de Santueri**, about 4km away across the hills to the south, which is also accessible by car along a rough four-kilometre-long lane from the Felanitx–Santanyí road. The hiking route is fairly easy to follow and the going isn't difficult, although it's still advisable to have a walking map and stout shoes. The path meanders through a pretty landscape of dry-stone walls, flowering shrubs and copses of almond and carob trees, bringing you to the castle after about an hour and a half. Glued to a rocky hilltop, the battered ramparts date from the fourteenth century, though it was the Moors who built the first stronghold here. Getting inside the ruins is pot luck – sometimes you can, when a small entry fee is levied at the main gate, and sometimes you can't.

Cala d'Or and around

Down the coast from Porto Colom, the pretty little fishing villages that once studded the discrete coves between Cala Serena and Porto Petro have been blasted by development. The interconnected resorts that now stand in their place are largely indistinguishable, a homogenously designed strip of whitewashed, low-rise villas, hotels, restaurants and bars in a sort of pueblo style. Confusingly, this long string of resorts is now usually lumped together under the name CALA D'OR, though in fact this particular cove is one of the smallest. For simplicity's sake, the "Cala d'Or" we refer to in this account is the original cove and not the whole development.

To be fair, the pseudo-Mexican style of the new resorts blends well with the ritzy haciendas left by a previous generation of sunseekers, the latter largely concentrated on the humpy, pint-sized headland which separates Cala d'Or from its northerly neighbour CALA GRAN. These two pretty little coves, tucked between the cliffs and edged by narrow golden beaches, are the highlights of the area. The beaches are jam-packed throughout the season, but the swimming is perfect and the wooded coastline here is far preferable to the more concentrated development all around. A ten-minute walk north beyond Cala Gran are the densely packed villas of uninspiring CALA ESMERALDA. In the opposite direction, the headland on the south side of Cala d'Or is genteel and leafy, but this is a flattering and brief preamble to the massive marina and endless villas of CALA LLONGA.

Practicalities

Buses to Cala d'Or stop on the crowded and charmless main drag, Avinguda Fernando Tarrago, two minutes' walk from the beach. Under various designations, this same street links the main cove-resorts, from Cala Esmeralda in the north to Cala Llonga in the south, about a twenty-minute walk. The area's Oficina d'Informació Turistica is situated a few metres up from the Cala Llonga waterside (May–Dec Mon–Fri 8.15am–2pm; Jan–April Tues & Wed 8.15am–2pm; ☎657463). They provide free maps marked with all the hotels and *hostals*, though finding a room is well-nigh impossible in the summer – for inexpensive accommodation, your best bet is to try the hotels of Porto Petro (see below). The most luxurious place to stay – where you'll almost certainly need an advance reservation – is the luxurious *Hotel Cala d'Or*, right above Cala d'Or's beach on Avinguda Belgica (April–Oct; ☎657249; ⑨). The hotel has a hundred balconied bedrooms, each furnished in an attractive modern style with fine sea views, while the equally appealing public areas include a bar, restaurant and an outside swimming pool. Cala Gran also has a good upmarket hotel, the *Cala Gran* (April–Oct; ☎657100; ⑦), a much bigger and brisker affair at the back of the beach, where the modern bedrooms have balconies and sea views, and there's every convenience including a swimming pool. There are myriad **cafés and restaurants** around Cala d'Or and Cala Llonga, especially on the main street, Avgda Fernando Tarrago. One that's worth going out of your way for is the popular *Ca'n Trompé*, Avgda Belgica 4 (closed Dec–Feb), which serves delicious meals, with the emphasis on Mallorcan mainstays, from around 2500ptas.

Porto Petro

Only recently swallowed into the Cala d'Or conurbation, **PORTO PETRO** rambles round a twin-pronged cove a couple of kilometres south of Cala Llonga. There's no beach here, so the development has been fairly restrained. The old fishing harbour has been turned into a marina, and a handful of villas dot the gentle wooded hillsides edging the coast, but it remains a quiet and tranquil spot – the only real activity is the promenade round the crystal-watered cove. The minuscule centre of the village perches on the headland above the marina. Here you'll have a reasonable chance of getting a room at either the two-star *Hotel Nereida* (May–Oct; ☎657223; ④), a comfortable and neat little place with its own pool and rooftop sun terraces; or at the nearby, but somewhat tattier, one-star *Hotel Porto Petro* (April–Oct; ☎657002; ⑤). If you do find a vacancy, the village has all the amenities to make for a good base: there's car and cycle rental; daily **boat trips** around the neighbouring coast (1hr 30min; 1200ptas); and regular *mini tren* connections up and down the coast to all the resorts between Cala Serena and Cala Mondragó. Furthermore, there are a couple of fine harbourside **restaurants**: the *Ca'n Martina*, at the head of the marina, boasts a paella to die for and a sweet outside terrace, whilst the nearby *Restaurant Porto Petro* serves delicious and reasonably priced seafood from first-floor premises overlooking the bay.

Cala Mondragó

The *mini tren* shuffles to its terminus at **CALA MONDRAGÓ**, about 4km south of Porto Petro. There's some development here, but it's not so intensive as to destroy the cove's pelagic beauty: low, pine-clad cliffs frame a pair of sandy beaches, which are linked along a concrete footpath. However, the cove's "unspoilt" reputation and

A tourist "train" on wheels, the mini tren, *shuttles up and down the coast from Cala Serena in the north to Porto Petro and Cala Mondragó in the south, with stops along the main street and beside all the beaches (6 daily in each direction; 400ptas per trip).*

safe bathing acts as a magnet for sun-lovers from miles around. To
escape the crowds, come early in the morning, or else stay the night
(if there's space), either at the beachside *Hostal Playa Mondragó*,
an ugly, modern concrete block with forty plain but adequate rooms
(April–Oct; ☎657752; ③), or the rather more attractive *Hostal
Condemar*, about 300m from the beach, where most of the rooms
have balconies (May–Oct; ☎657756; ③).

Santanyí and around

The crossroads town of SANTANYÍ, 17km from Porto Colom, was
once an important medieval stronghold guarding the island's southeastern approaches. It was ransacked by corsairs on several occasions, but one of the old town gates, **Sa Porta**, has survived along
with the occasional chunk of masonry extant from the old city walls.
However, it's Santanyí's narrow alleys, squeezed between high-sided
stone houses, that are the town's main appeal. Several pavement
cafés edge the main square, but these should not detain you long,
whether you're making the fast, fifty-kilometre journey west along
the C717 to Palma or heading east to the coast. *Autocares Grimalt*
operate the bus network in and around Santanyí. Between two and
four times daily their buses link Palma, Llucmajor and Colònia de
Sant Jordi with Santanyí, and there are less regular services to Cala
Santanyí, Cala Figuera and Cala d'Or.

Cala Figuera and Cala Santanyí

Travelling southeast from Santanyí, a five-kilometre side road cuts a
pretty, rustic route through to CALA FIGUERA, whose antique
harbour sits beside a fjord-like inlet below the steepest of coastal
cliffs. Local fishermen still land their catches and mend their nets
here, but nowadays it's to the accompaniment of scores of photo-
snapping tourists. Up above, the pine-covered shoreline heaves with
villas, hotels and *hostals*, although, the absence of high-rise buildings means the development is never overbearing.

Cala Figuera is extremely popular, and there are few vacant
rooms at its dozen or so establishments, even in the shoulder
seasons. If you do chance your arm, the obvious place to start is on
the steep pedestrianized ramp – c/Verge del Carmen – which leads
up from the harbour. In this prime location, at no. 50, is the unassuming *Hostal Cala*, whose twenty rooms are stashed above a
restaurant (April–Oct; ☎645018; ④). Close by at no. 58, the all-
year *Hostal Ca'n Jordi* has just six simple bedrooms, also over a
restaurant (☎645035; ③). Up the hill, overlooking the cove from a
wide ridge, stands the modern and comfortable *Hotel Rocamar*
(April–Oct; ☎645125; ④). In dire emergencies, try the unprepossessing *Hostal Oliver*, stuck at the back of the resort, which has a
few rooms that aren't booked by package operators in summer
(May–Oct; ☎645127; ③). Of Cala Figuera's many **restaurants**, the

most distinguished are the seafood eateries lining c/Verge del Carmen. It's difficult to select – and hard to go wrong – but *La Marina*, *Ca'n Jordi* and *Cala* are all excellent and not too pricey.

In terms of amenities, the resort has car and cycle rental outlets, and, down by the harbour, a prestigious, German-run **diving school**, the *Albatros* (☎645300), which hires out a wide range of subaqua gear to experienced divers, and arranges novice courses – three days of tuition for around 45,000ptas. The resort also has several lively **music bars** – try *Hero's* or *Bananas* – and discos dotted along its main street.

What you won't get is a **beach**. The nearest is 4km away at **CALA SANTANYÍ**, a busy little resort with a medium-sized (and frequently crowded) beach at the end of a steep-sided, heavily wooded gulch. To get there, head back towards Santanyí for about 2km and take the signposted turning on the left.

Cala Llombards

The next bay down from Cala Santanyí is little-developed **CALA LLOMBARDS**, a beautiful pine-forested cove of gleaming sand, turquoise sea and sheer cliffs. There's a scrawny villa-village behind, not visible from the beach, a beach-bar and a dirt car park, but otherwise it's pristine stuff. As you'd expect, you won't have the beach to yourself, but it's rarely crowded; a handful of campers often sleep rough in the woods behind, to the chagrin of many locals. Cala Llombards is only accessible from the Santanyí–Colònia de Sant Jordi road; **buses** from Colònia de Sant Jordi, Santanyí and Cala Figuera drop passengers at the village of Llombards on the main road, leaving a signposted four-kilometre walk to the beach.

The south coast

Mallorca's **south coast**, stretching from the rim of the Bay of Palma to the island's most southerly point, Cap de ses Salines, has hardly been developed at all, but the reasons behind this lack of interest are pretty obvious when you come here. Most of the shoreline is unenticingly spartan, a long and low rocky shelf that meets the sea almost as an afterthought – with barely a decent beach in sight. Behind is a flat, sparsely populated hinterland of little shade or variety. Villages are few and far between, and in places the land has an eerie sense of desolation – especially at the wind-buffeted **Cap de ses Salines** – which some assert as its fascination.

A smattering of modern resorts gamely make the most of these disheartening surroundings. The pick of the crop is undoubtedly **Colònia de Sant Jordi**, a curious amalgamation of plush tourist settlement and old seaport which thoroughly deserves a visit, not least because it's situated near the region's best beach – **Es Trenc** –

and offers boat trips to the remote islet of **Cabrera**. The other resort
you might consider is **Cala Pi**, where a deep ravine frames a sandy
beach, but only if you're dropping in on the substantial remains of
prehistoric **Capocorp Vell** just up the road. East of Cala Pi, through
the grim and untidy resorts of Valgornera, S'Estanyol and Sa Rapita,
clumps of mundane second homes decorate the treeless shore.

Planning an itinerary is straightforward. The best advice is to
use the C717, which runs from Santanyí to the Platja de Palma, as
your baseline, branching off as you wish. The following account is
written east to west, but it doesn't make much difference in which
direction you're travelling. As ever, **accommodation** is at a
premium. Throughout the season, your best chance, by a long
chalk, is in Colònia de Sant Jordi; from November to March, nearly
everything is closed and you'll almost certainly have to visit on a
day trip. **Bus** services are adequate if you're heading somewhere
specific from Palma, or between Colònia de Sant Jordi and Cala
d'Or, but are dreadful when you attempt to move between other
resorts.

Colònia de Sant Jordi and around

Heading southwest from Santanyí, a gentle country road drifts
through a landscape of old dry-stone walls and straggling fields
towards Colònia de Sant Jordi. After 4km, a left turning leads down
through coastal pine woods to the lighthouse on **Cap de ses Salines**,
a bleak, brush-covered headland that is Mallorca's most southerly
point. The lighthouse itself is closed to the public, but there are fine
views out to sea and a two-kilometre footpath wends its way northwest to the tiny beach of **Es Caragol**, though the trail is sometimes
difficult to discern. **Thekla larks** and **stone curlews** are often to be
seen on the cape, whilst gulls, terns and shearwaters glide about offshore, benefiting from the winds which, when they're up, can make
the place intolerable.

*Botanicactus is
open daily
9am–7pm;
500ptas.*

Back on the road to Colònia de Sant Jordi, billboards welcome
you to **Botanicactus**, a huge botanical garden mostly devoted to
indigenous and imported species of cactus. A surprise here is the
artificial lake, which encourages the growth of wetland plants – a
welcome splash in arid surroundings – but otherwise the place has
all the atmosphere of a garden centre and is definitely missable.

Beyond, just 13km from Santanyí, is **COLÒNIA DE SANT
JORDI**, whose wide streets pattern a substantial and irregularly
shaped headland. It's a confusing place, at least at first, and you'll
need to get your bearings. The main approach road is the Avinguda
Marqués del Palmer, at the end of which – roughly in the middle of
the headland – lies the principal square, the vacuous **Plaça
Constitució**. From here, c/Sa Solta and then, across another square,
Avinguda Primavera lead west, with the surprisingly pleasant main
tourist zone appearing on the left, the domineering lines of its flashy

hotels broken by low-rise villas and landscaped side streets. To the right are the **Salinas de S'Avall**, saltpans which once provided the town with its principal source of income. At the end of the avenue, the polished *Hotel Marqués del Palmer* sits tight against the **Platja d'Estanys**, whose gleaming sands curve round a dune-edged cove.

East from Plaça Constitució along c/Major, and then left down c/ Gabriel Roca, is the old **harbour**, the most diverting part of town. Framed by an attractive, early twentieth-century ensemble of balconied mansions, the port makes the most of a handsome, horseshoe-shaped bay. There's nothing special to look at, but it's a relaxing spot with a handful of restaurants, a pocket-size beach and a marina.

Practicalities

Buses to Colònia de Sant Jordi from Palma, Cala d'Or, Cala Figuera and Santanyí stop at several downtown locations, including the harbour. The **Oficina d'Informació Turistica** is in the town hall at c/Doctor Barraquer 5 (May–Oct Mon–Sat 8am–2pm; ☎656073): follow c/Gabriel Roca from the harbour and take the first road on the right. Staff have free town maps to hand out and information about local **bike rental** shops (cycling in the flatlands around the resort is a popular and enjoyable pastime), as well as details of local **accommodation**. In the **budget** range, there's a handful of undistinguished *hostals* behind the harbour, and these are your best chance if you're looking for a last-minute room in high season. Try the clean and frugal, one-star *Hostal Colonial*, c/ Gabriel Roca 9 (March–Oct; ☎655278; ③); or the slightly down-at-heel, two-star *Hostal Playa*, c/Major 25 (May–Oct; ☎655256; ④). Moving **upmarket**, Colònia de Sant Jordi boasts some of the flashiest hotels in southeast Mallorca, glistening towers of air-conditioned, balconied bedrooms with lovely sea views. Rooms, however, are very hard to come by at the height of summer, though you should have a decent chance in the shoulder seasons. The cream of the crop are the opulent *Tres Playas*, which looms over the seashore on c/Esmeralda in the main resort area, and has lovely gardens and outside pools among many other facilities (April–Oct; ☎655150; ⑧); and the nearby *Hotel Cabo Blanco*, c/ Carabella, a smooth and polished three-star which also has pools and attractive gardens (April–Oct; ☎655075; ⑥). The *Hotel Marqués del Palmer*, at the end of Avgda Primavera, isn't quite as new and glitzy, but it's still a good-quality, comfortable hotel and right beside the town's best beach (May–Oct; ☎655100; ⑤).

There's a cluster of decent **restaurants** beside the harbour: the workaday *El Puerto* offers bargain-basement pizzas and spaghetti, whilst the *La Mar* nearby serves delicious seafood, costing from around 1400ptas for a main course. Another fine seafood place, marginally more expensive, is the *Pep Serra*, c/Gabriel Roca 87, which has a lovely seashore terrace.

Cabrera

Beside Sant Jordi harbour a tiny kiosk (daily 8am–1pm & 5–9pm;
☎649034) has information on, and takes reservations for, boat trips
to the island of **Cabrera** (late April–Sept 1 daily; 8hr; 2600ptas).
Easily the largest of a clustered archipelago, Cabrera ("Goat Island")
is a bumpy, scrub-covered chunk lying 20km offshore. Bare, almost
entirely uninhabited, and no more than 7km wide and 5km long, the
only significant hint of its eventful past is the protective castle above
its supremely sheltered harbour. Pliny claimed the island to have
been the birthplace of Hannibal; medieval pirates hunkered down on
it to plan future raids; and, during the Napoleonic Wars, the Spanish
stuck nine thousand French prisoners of war out here and tried to
forget about them – during their three-year captivity, two thirds of
Napoleon's men died from hunger and disease.

The day-trip itinerary starts with a two-hour voyage, including a
visit to Cabrera's **Cova Blava** (Blue Grotto). The boat sails right into
the cave, through the fifty-metre-wide entrance and on into the
yawning chamber beyond. The grotto reaches a height of 160m and
is suffused by bluish light, from which it gets its name. Afterwards,
the boat bobs across the bay and rounds a hostile-looking headland
to enter the harbour – Es Port – a narrow finger of calm water, edged
by hills and equipped with a tiny jetty. From here, you're shepherded
up the lung-wrenching path to the battered and unadorned ruins of
the fourteenth-century **castle** up above. Perched on the island's west
coast, the views from the fortress back across to Mallorca are
magnificent, and all sorts of **birds** can be viewed gliding round the
seacliffs, including Manx and Cory's shearwaters, herring gulls and
the far rarer Audouin's gulls, as well as peregrine falcons and shags.
It is, however, the blue-underbellied **Lilfords wall lizard** that really
takes the naturalists' biscuit. After you've completed the walk to the
castle and back (which takes about an hour each way), there's time
to have a drink down by the jetty, where you can tempt the lizards
out from the scrub with pieces of discarded fruit.

Unless you happen to have your own vessel, these boat trips are
the only way to reach Cabrera. There's also a very good reason for
the guided tour: the island has been used as a military base since
1916 and there's a real danger from discarded, unexploded arma-
ments. This is the main reason why the **memorial** to the dead
French prisoners of war in the centre of Cabrera is out of bounds to
day-trippers.

Es Trenc

One of Colònia de Sant Jordi's attractions is its proximity to **Es
Trenc**, a 4km strip of sand that extends as far as the eye can see.
It's neither unknown, nor unspoilt, but the crowds are easily
absorbed and the development only scratches away at the edges. To
get there, head north from Colònia de Sant Jordi and turn left
towards Campos; 4.5km along this road take the left turn and then

follow the signposted country lanes down to the beach – a total distance of around 12km.

The scrawny hamlet of Ses Covetes lies at the west end of the beach. Along the seashore, about 2km to the east, several footpaths track the 1km inland to the **Salinas de Levante**, saltpans which support a wide variety of **birdlife**. You can also approach the pans from the east (though this access may soon be closed by the owners because of overuse): on the road to Campos, about 3km out of Colònia de Sant Jordi, watch for the distinctive **Banys de Sant Joan** building, marking both the site of curative hot springs and the start of a footpath that cuts across the saltpans. This path is, in fact, one of many in the area, so, for more than a fleeting visit, you should take a hiking map. The *salinas*, and the surrounding farm- and scrubland, boast a broad range of resident birds including marsh harriers, kestrels, spotted cranes, fan-tailed warblers and hoopoes. This makes a visit at any time of year enjoyable, though the best season to come is the spring when hundreds of migrants arrive from Africa. Commonly seen at this time are avocets, little-ringed plovers, little egrets, black-tailed godwits, collared pratincoles and black terns.

Campos, Llucmajor, Capocorp Vell and Cala Pi

On the C717, 14km west of Santanyí, the unassuming town of **CAMPOS** will hardly fire the imagination, though the immaculately restored sixteenth-century town hall does merit a quick gander for its fine facade. Neither will **LLUCMAJOR**, the next settlement along, delay your progress, despite its medieval foundation as a market town and its long association with the island's shoemakers. It was here, just outside the old city walls, that Jaume III, the last of the independent kings of Mallorca, was defeated and killed by Pedro IV of Aragon.

For information on Puig Randa, 9km northeast of Llucmajor, see p.151.

Llucmajor is just 12km from the teeming hotel strip at S'Arenal; it's also at the head of the byroad leading south to Cap Blanc and Cala Pi. About 12km along this road lies **Capocorp Vell** (in Castilian, Capicorp Vey), whose extensive remains date from around 1000 BC. Surrounded by arid scrubland and enclosed within a modern dry-stone wall, this prehistoric village incorporates the battered ruins of five *talayots* and twenty-eight dwellings. A footpath weaves round the haphazard remains, but most of what you see is hardly inspiring and gives little idea of how the village was arranged. The most impressive features are the Cyclopean walls, which reach a height of 4m in places. To make more sense of what you see, pick up the free leaflet, in English, at the entrance.

Capocorp Vell is open daily except Thurs 10am–5pm; 250ptas. For more information on talayots, see p.221.

Just beyond the village there's a choice of routes: straight on for **Cap Blanc**, a desultory cape with a lighthouse, or left for the four-kilometre trip to **CALA PI**. Spreading over a scrawny headland, this resort is the remote setting for the glitzy *Club Cala Pi*, a self-contained resort complex that's a favourite with French tourists. In the cove, there's a lovely beach, a tiny finger of sand wedged between high, pine-studded cliffs and fringed by ramshackle fishing huts. You won't find anywhere to stay on spec, but you can refresh your palate at the *Miguel* restaurant, where the grilled fish is very tasty, or snack at the bar next door.

Travel details

Buses

From **Artà** to: Cala Rajada (Mon–Sat 9 daily, 1–2 on Sun; 10min); Coves d'Artà (May–Oct Mon–Sat 4 daily; 15min); Palma (Mon–Sat 4 daily, 1–2 on Sun; 1hr 25min); Platja de Canyamel (May–Oct Mon–Sat 4 daily; 10min).

From **Cala d'Or** to: Colònia de Sant Jordi (Mon–Sat 1 daily; 45min); Palma (2–4 daily; 1hr 10min); Santanyí (2–4 daily; 15min).

From **Cala Figuera** to: Cala Santanyí (May–Oct Mon–Sat 2 daily; Nov–April Mon–Sat 1 daily; 5min); Colònia de Sant Jordi (Mon–Sat 2 daily; 40min); Palma (Mon–Sat 1–2 daily; 1hr 20min); Santanyí (Mon–Sat 2 daily; 15min).

From **Cala Millor** to: Cala Rajada (May–Oct Mon–Sat 11 daily; Nov–April Mon–Sat 1 daily; 25min); Palma (Mon–Sat 5–7 daily, 1–2 on Sun; 1hr 15min); Port d'Alcúdia (May–Oct Mon–Sat 3 daily; 1hr).

From **Cala Rajada** to: Artà (Mon–Sat 9 daily, 1–2 on Sun; 10min); Cala Agulla (May–Oct Mon–Sat 4 daily; 5 min); Cala de Sa Font (May–Oct Mon–Sat 4 daily; 10 min); Cala Millor (May–Oct Mon–Sat 11 daily; Nov–April Mon–Sat 1 daily; 25min); Capdepera (Mon–Sat 9 daily, 1–2 on Sun; 5min); Coves d'Artà (May–Oct Mon–Sat 4 daily; 25min); Palma (Mon–Sat 4 daily, 1–2 on Sun; 1hr 30min); Platja de Canyamel (May–Oct Mon–Sat 4 daily; 20min); Port d'Alcúdia (May–Oct Mon–Sat 2 daily; 45min).

From **Colònia de Sant Jordi** to: Cala d'Or (Mon–Sat 1 daily; 45min); Cala Figuera (Mon–Sat 2 daily; 40min); Palma (2–4 daily; 1hr); Santanyí (2–4 daily; 25min).

From **Felanitx** to: Palma (3–4 daily; 50min); Porto Colom (2–3 daily; 15min).

From **Palma** to: Algaida (3–5 daily; 20min); Artà (Mon–Sat 4 daily, 1 on Sun; 1hr 25min); Cala d'Or (2–4 daily; 1hr 10min); Cala Figuera (Mon–Sat 1–2 daily; 1hr 20min); Cala Millor (Mon–Sat 5–7 daily, 1–2 on Sun; 1hr 15min); Cala Pi (May–Oct 2 daily except Thurs; 45min); Cala Rajada (Mon–Sat 4 daily, 1–2 on Sun; 1hr 30min); Cales de Mallorca (May–Oct Mon–Sat 3 daily; 1hr); Colònia de Sant Jordi (2–4 daily; 1hr); Coves del Drac (Mon–Sat 2–4 daily, 1 on Sun; 1hr); Felanitx (3–4 daily; 50min); Inca (Mon–Sat 8 daily, Sun 4 daily; 30min); Manacor (Mon–Sat 7 daily, 2 on Sun; 55min); Petra (2–3 daily; 45min); Porto Colom (1–3 daily; 1hr); Porto Cristo via Manacor (Mon–Sat 7 daily, 1–2 on Sun; 1hr 10min); Porto Petro (2 daily; 1hr 10min); Santanyí (2–4 daily; 1hr); Ses Covetes (for Es Trenc beach; May–Oct 1 daily; 1hr).

From **Porto Colom** to: Palma (1–3 daily; 1hr).

From **Porto Cristo** to: Ca'n Picafort (May–Oct Mon–Sat 3 daily; 1hr); Palma via Manacor (Mon–Sat 7 daily, 2 on Sun; 1hr 10min); Port d'Alcúdia (May–Oct Mon–Sat 3 daily; 1hr).

From **Santanyí** to: Cala Santanyí (May–Oct Mon–Sat 2 daily; Nov–April Mon–Sat 1 daily; 10min).

Menorca

S econd largest of the Balearics, boomerang-shaped MENORCA stretches from the enormous natural harbour of Maó in the east to the smaller port of **Ciutadella** in the west, a distance of just 45km. These two towns, boasting over sixty percent of the population, are the only points of arrival (Menorca's airport lies on the outskirts of Maó). Each has preserved much of its eighteenth- and early nineteenth-century appearance, though Ciutadella's labyrinthine centre, with its grandee mansions and Gothic cathedral, has the aesthetic edge over Maó's plainer, more mercantile architecture. Running through the little-developed interior between the two, the main C721 highway forms the island's backbone, linking a trio of modest market towns – **Alaior**, **Es Mercadal** and **Ferreries** – and succouring what little industry Menorca enjoys, a few shoe factories and cheese-making plants. Branching off the highway, the best of the side roads lead to the resorts that notch the north and south coasts. Mercifully, however, the tourist development is largely confined to individual coves and bays, and only amongst the sprawling villa-villages of the southeast and on the west coast has it become overpowering. What's more, there are still many remote cove beaches with not a speck of concrete in sight, though access to them is usually along rough and dusty lanes.

The main highway also acts as a rough dividing line between Menorca's two distinct geological areas. In the north, sandstone predominates, giving a red tint to the low hills and the fretted coastline, which shelters the lovely fishing village and resort of **Fornells**. To the south all is limestone, with a range of bulging hills flanked by a pair of low-lying plateaux and fringed by a cove-studded coastline. Straddling the two zones, **Monte Toro**, Menorca's highest peak and site of a quaint little convent, offers panoramic views which reveal the topography of the whole island. Clearly visible from here are the wooded ravines that gash the southern zone, becoming deeper and more dramatic as you travel west – especially around **Cala Santa Galdana**, a handsome resort set beneath severe, pine-clad seacliffs.

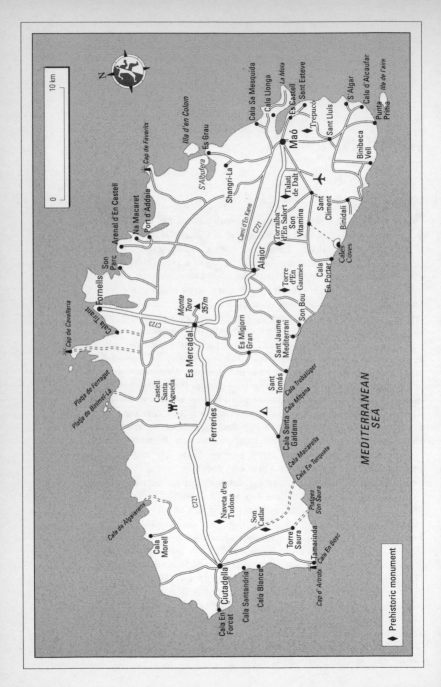

This varied terrain supports a smattering of minuscule villages and solitary farmsteads, present witnesses to an **agriculture** that had become, before much of it was killed off by tourism, highly advanced. Every field was protected by a dry-stone wall (*tanca*) to prevent the Tramóntana, the vicious north wind, from tearing away the topsoil. Even olive trees had their roots individually protected in little stone wells, while compact stone ziggurats (*ponts*) sheltered cattle from both the wind and the blazing sun. Nowadays, apart from a few acres of rape and corn, many of the fields are barren, but the walls and ziggurats survive, as do many of the old twisted gates made from olive branches.

The landscape is further cluttered by hundreds of crude stone memorials, mostly dating from the second millennium BC. Yet, despite this widespread physical evidence, little is known of the island's prehistory. The most common monuments are thought to be linked to those of Sardinia and are attributed to the so-called Talayotic culture, which reached a peak of activity here in Menorca in around 1000 BC. **Talayots** are the rock mounds found all over the island. Popular belief has it that they functioned as watchtowers, but it's a theory few experts accept: they have no interior stairway, and only a few are found on the coast. Even so, no one has come up with a more convincing explanation. **Taulas** – huge stones topped with another to form a T, around four metres high – are unique to Menorca and even more puzzling. They have no obvious function, and they are almost always found alongside a *talayot*. The best-preserved *talayot* and *taula* remains are on the edge of Maó at the **Trepucó** and **Talatí de Dalt** sites. The third kind of prehistoric monuments found on Menorca are **navetas**, stone-slab constructions, dating from 1400 to 800 BC, shaped like an inverted loaf tin. Many have false ceilings, and although you can stand up inside, they were clearly not living spaces, but rather communal tombs, or ossuaries. The prime example is **Naveta d'es Tudons**, near Ciutadella.

All of Menorca's prehistoric sights have free, open access. For more information on Talayotic culture, see p.221.

In more recent times, the deep-water channel of the port of Maó promoted Menorca to an important position in European affairs. The **British** saw its potential as a **naval base** during the War of the Spanish Succession and had the island ceded to them under the Treaty of Utrecht in 1713, five years after they had first occupied it. Spain regained possession in 1783, but with the threat of Napoleon in the Mediterranean, a new British base was temporarily

---

Accommodation price symbols

The symbols used in our accommodation listings denote the following price ranges:

① Under 2000ptas	④ 4000–6000ptas	⑦ 10,000–14,000ptas
② 2000–3000ptas	⑤ 6000–8000ptas	⑧ 14,000–20,000ptas
③ 3000–4000pta	⑥ 8000–10,000ptas	⑨ Over 20,000ptas

For more details see p.31.

---

established under admirals Nelson and Collingwood. The British influence on Menorca, especially its architecture, is still manifest: the sash windows so popular in Georgian design are even now sometimes referred to as *winderes*, locals often part with a fond *bye-bye*, and there's a substantial expatriate community. The British also introduced the art of distilling juniper berries, and Menorcan **gin** (*Xoriguer, Beltran* or *Nelson*) is now world-renowned.

Maó and around

Despite its status as island capital, **MAÓ** (in Castilian, **Mahón**) has a comfortable, small-town feel. Wandering around the ancient centre, with its long-established cafés and old-fashioned shops, is a relaxing and enjoyable way to pass some time, though it's hard to keep your bearings among the narrow streets and plazas. Nowadays most visitors approach Maó from its landward side, but this gives the wrong impression. The town has always been a **port** and it's only from the water that the logic of the place becomes apparent, with its centre crowding a steeply inclined ridge set tight against the south side of the harbour – which, in turn, marks the westerly limit of a narrow five-kilometre-long inlet that stretches to the Mediterranean. From this angle Maó is extraordinarily beautiful, its well-worn, pastel-shaded houses tumbling down the hillside, interrupted by bits and pieces of the old city walls, and the occasional church. Indeed, the town's main churches constitute notable artistic attractions, though it's the general flavour that really appeals, particularly as the **architecture** is a striking and unusual hybrid: tall, monumental Spanish mansions shade the streets alongside classical Georgian sash-windowed town houses, reminders of the British occupation.

Port it may be, but there's no seamy side to Maó, and the harbourfront is home to a string of excellent **restaurants** and **cafés** that attract tourists in their droves. Few, however, stay the night, preferring the purpose-built resorts and villa complexes which fill much of Menorca's southeast corner. As a result, Maó has surprisingly few *hostals* and hotels, though it's a very enjoyable, if somewhat staid place to base yourself – reserving in advance is strongly recommended in July and August.

Arrival, orientation and information

Menorca's **airport** (☎369015), just 5km west of Maó, is short on amenities, with just a handful of car rental outlets and a **tourist information desk**, which has a good selection of free literature (May–Oct daily 8.30am–11pm; ☎157115). There are no buses into the town, but the taxi fare will only set you back about 1000ptas. **Ferries** from Barcelona and Palma sail right up the inlet to Maó harbour, mooring next to the *Trasmediterranea* offices

Details of ferries and flights to Maó are given in Basics.

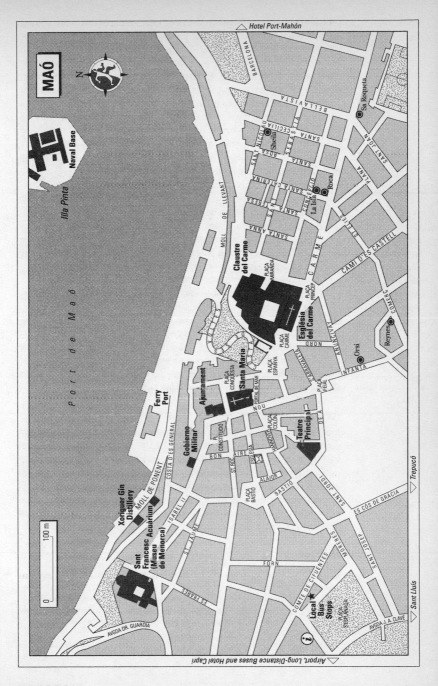

△ Hotel Port-Mahón

MAÓ

N

Illa Pinta

Naval Base

Port de Maó

Sa Roqueta

Sheila

Roca

La Isla

Claustre
del Carme

PLAÇA
MIRANDA

PLAÇA
PRINCEP

Església
del Carme

PLAÇA
CARME

Reynés

Orsi

PLAÇA
ESPANYA

INFANTA

PLAÇA
CONQUESTA

Santa Maria

PORTAL DE MAR

Ferry
Port

Ajuntament

Gobierno
Militar

PL.
CONSTITUCIO

PLAÇA
COLON

Teatre
Principal

MOLL DE LLEVANT

COSTA D'ES GENERAL

BON AIRE

ST. ROC

ISABEL II

PLAÇA
BASTIO

Xoriguer Gin
Distillery

MOLL DE PONENT

Sant
Francesc Acuárium
(Museu
de Menorca)

ST. JAUME

ES ERARES

AVGDA. DR. GUARDIA

100 m

0

FORN

COMTE DE CIFUENTES

Local
Bus
Stops

PLAÇA
ESPÀNYA

AVGDA. J. A. CLAVÉ

i

MORRES

SANT JOSEP

ES COS DE GRACIA

△ Trepucó

△ Sant Lluís

△ Airport, Long-Distance Buses and Hotel Capri

MENORCA

181

(☎366050) directly beneath the town centre. From behind the ferry dock, it's a two-minute walk up the wide stone stairway of Costa de ses Voltes to **Plaça Espanya**. The oldest part of Maó runs east and west of this small square, rolling along the clifftop above the harbour for roughly 1km. Behind, to the south, the predominantly nineteenth-century town climbs up the hill. Its complicated pattern of tiny squares and short lanes is bisected by the principal shopping street and pedestrianized main drag, which goes under various names, with c/Hannover and c/Moreres being the longest individual strips. A fairly steep five- to ten-minute walk from one end to the other, this street leads directly to **Plaça S'Esplanada**, billed as the main square but more a car park and bus terminus.

The **Oficina d'Informació Turistica** in Plaça S'Esplanada (Mon–Fri 8am–3pm & 5–7pm, Sat 9am–2pm; ☎363790) will provide maps of the island and free leaflets giving the lowdown on almost everything you can think of, from archeological sites and beaches to bus timetables, car rental, accommodation and banks. **Island-wide buses** arrive at the stands along Avgda Quadrado, round the corner from the tourist office; **local buses**, which shuttle up and down the southeast coast, stop on the square, just across from the tourist office.

Further information about Menorca's bus routes can be found on p.217.

Exploring Maó on foot doesn't require much effort, but driving in the centre is well-nigh impossible and you're better off **parking** on the edge. Plaça S'Esplanada has an underground car park, as well as on-street parking, which is free except during shopping hours (Mon–Fri 9am–2pm & 4.30–7.30pm, Sat 9am–2pm) when you should take a ticket from a meter. The maximum stay of two hours costs 200ptas; note that if the time allowed overlaps into a free period, your ticket is still valid when the next restricted time begins.

Accommodation

Maó has a limited supply of **accommodation** and excessive demand tends to inflate prices at the height of the season. However, along with Ciutadella, it remains the best Menorcan bet for bargain lodgings, with a small concentration of **hostals** among the workaday streets near Plaça Princep, a few minutes' walk east of the town centre. None of these places is inspiring, but they're reasonable enough and convenient – unlike Maó's two quality **hotels**, which are stuck out on the edge of town.

Hostals

Hostal La Isla, c/Santa Caterina 4, at the corner of c/Concepció; ☎366492. Recently refurbished, comfortable one-star with 25 rooms, and its own bar and restaurant. ③.

Hostal-residencia Orsi, c/Infanta 19; ☎364751. The most agreeable *hostal* in town, English-owned and a couple of minutes' walk from Plaça Reial; pleasant, spick-and-span old rooms with large windows and green shutters. Closed Dec & Jan. ③.

Hostal Reynes, c/Comerç 26, just off c/Infanta; ☎364059. Undistinguished modern block with basic rooms. ③.

Hostal-residencia Roca, c/Carme 37, at the corner of c/Santa Caterina;
☎364763. Fourteen no-frills rooms in a plain but quite cheerful modern
block with a ground-floor café. ③.

Hostal-residencia Sa Roqueta, c/Carme 122, at the corner of c/Sant Joan;
☎364335. Modern, four-storey block, painted in painful shades of orange and
green, with basic, rather unwelcoming rooms. ③.

Hostal Sheila, c/Santa Cecília 41, at the corner of c/Sant Nicolau; ☎364855.
An old terraced house scheduled for reopening in 1996 after extensive refurbishment. Probably ④.

Hotels

Hotel del Almirante, Carretera de Maó, nearly 2km from Maó by the coastal
road to Es Castell; ☎362700. Once the residence of British admiral Lord
Collingwood, this maroon and cream Georgian house has a delightful,
antique-crammed interior, though some of the bedrooms are modern affairs
overlooking the swimming pool round the back. The package-tour operators
Thomson use the place, but there are often vacancies. ⑥.

Hotel Capri, c/Sant Esteve 8; ☎361400. Characterless, modern, three-star
hotel in the centre of Maó, a brief walk west of the tourist office along Avgda
Quadrado. ⑦.

Hotel Port-Mahón, Avgda Fort de L'Eau 13; ☎362600. Elegant colonial-
style hotel of columns, pediments and circular windows, in a superb location
overlooking the Maó inlet. There's a swimming pool and all mod cons,
though some of the rooms are rather dilapidated – refurbishment is planned.
Room prices vary enormously, with the top whack a hefty 27,000ptas. The
hotel is a 20-min walk east of the town centre along either c/Carme or the
harbourfront. ⑧.

The Town

Maó's setting and architecture are delightful, but it musters few
sights of specific interest. The highlights are the exquisite
Churrigueresque chapel in the church of **Sant Francesc** and the
monumental Neoclassicism of the church of **Santa Maria**, which is
also the home of a mammoth nineteenth-century Austrian organ.
Both these attractions are in the town centre above the **harbour**,
where you can sample as much of the island's liquors as you like at
the fascinating **Xoriguer gin distillery**.

Plaça Espanya and Plaça Carme

The stone stairway from the harbourfront – Costa de ses Voltes –
brings you first to **Plaça Espanya**, which offers fine views back
down over the port. Immediately to the left, **Plaça Carme** is over-
shadowed by the massive facade of the **Església del Carme**, a
Carmelite church whose airy interior is almost entirely devoid of
embellishment. The adjoining cloisters, the **Claustre del Carme**,
have been adapted to house the town's fresh meat, fruit and vegetable market (*mercat*), a rather eccentric arrangement pitting the
stalls against sculpted angels designed for a more spiritual environment. The fish market occupies more ordinary premises next door,
while at the back of the cloisters a modest **museum** features temporary exhibitions devoted to local themes.

*The cloisters
museum is
open Mon–Fri
10am–1pm;
200ptas.*

Plaça Conquesta and Plaça Constitució

North of Plaça Espanya lies **Plaça Conquesta**, whose full-length
statue of Alfonso III was donated by Franco. The narrow confines
of the adjacent **Plaça Constitució** are dominated by the church of
Santa Maria, founded in 1287 by Alfonso III to celebrate the
island's reconquest, but thoroughly remodelled in the late eighteenth century to create the broadly Neoclassical structure of
today. The interior boasts a cavernous, aisle-less nave with an
eye-catching high altar, whose larger-than-life Baroque excesses
shoot up to the roof flanked by spiral columns. Several side chapels exhibit similar Baroque flourishes, but the church's pride and
joy is its **organ**, a monumental piece of woodwork filling out the
elevated gallery above the south entrance. The organ, with its
trumpeting angels, four keyboards and three thousand pipes, was
made in Austria in 1810 and lugged across half of Europe at the
height of the Napoleonic wars. Britain's Admiral Collingwood
helped with the move, probably as a crafty piece of appeasement:
defiance of their new Protestant masters had played a large part
in the locals' decision to rebuild the church during the British
occupation.

Next door, the genteel arcades and wrought-iron balconies of
the **Ajuntament** (Town Hall) also date from a late eighteenth-
century refurbishment. There's another example of British goodwill
here too, for the clock was presented to the town by the island's
first British governor, Sir Richard Kane.

*For a brief
biography of
Richard Kane,
see p.217.*

Carrer Isabel II

Georgian doors and fanlights, sash windows and fancy ironwork
distinguish **Carrer Isabel II** as it runs west from Plaça Constitució.
Backing onto the cliffs above the harbour, this narrow, elongated
street accommodates a string of fine patrician mansions that once
lay at the heart of the British administration. Halfway along, the
present **Gobierno Militar** (military governor's house) is the prime
example, decked out in colonial style with shaded balconies framing
an expansive courtyard.

At the end of the street the Baroque facade of **Sant Francesc**
appears as a cliff-face of pale golden stone set above the rounded,
Romanesque-style arches of its doorway. The church was a long
time in the making, its construction spread over the seventeenth
and eighteenth centuries, following the razing of the town by
Barbarossa in 1535 as part of the Ottoman Empire's piratical
campaign to control the Mediterranean. Now deconsecrated, the
church has recently been turned into the **Museu de Menorca**,
with exhibits tracing the history of the island through its
archeology on display in the adjoining monastic buildings. But it's
the interior of the church which remains the main event, the
mighty nave, with its lofty, arching roof, enclosing a flamboyant
high altar flanked by spiral columns and enormous panels of

*The Museu de
Menorca is
open Tues–Fri
10am–1pm &
6–9pm, Sat &
Sun 10am–
1pm; free.*

Biblical scenes. Tucked away on the north side of the church is the **Chapel of the Immaculate Conception**, an octagonal wonderland of garlanded vines and roses in the Churrigueresque style. The chapel is attributed to Francesc Herrara, who trained in Rome and worked in Menorca before moving on to Palma's church of Sant Miquel.

From the museum, you can either work your way uphill through the town centre, or return to the harbour direct via **Costa d'es General**, a narrow alley that cuts through the old city walls before snaking its way down to the waterside.

Plaça Bastió and Plaça S'Esplanada

From the museum, it's a few minutes' walk along narrow side streets to **Plaça Bastió**, the site of Maó's one remaining medieval gateway. A short stroll up c/Moreres through the town's commercial centre leads to the flowerbeds and fountains of the principal square, **Plaça S'Esplanada**. The square's large military barracks is edged by an unpleasant reminder of Fascist days, a monumental Civil War memorial endowed with Francoist insignia and inscribed with the old fable, *Todos los que dieron su vida por Espanya* (To all those who gave their life for Spain). The only excitement here is on Sunday, when the square becomes the social hub, with crowds converging on its bars and ice-cream parlours, and street entertainers playing to the strolling multitudes.

The quayside

Below the town, Maó's ferry port is situated in the middle of the two-kilometre-long quayside. To the west a partly abandoned industrial area overlooks the murky waters at the head of the inlet. To the east, fishing jetties precede the town's elongated marina, where flashy chrome yachts face a string of restaurants, bars and cafés. Heading this way you'll end up on the eastern peripheries of Maó below the *Hotel Port-Mahon*. By day, the half-hour stroll along the quayside is tame verging on boring; at night, with the tourists converging on the restaurants, it's slightly more animated, but not that much. There are, however, two popular tourist attractions a couple of minutes' walk west of the ferry dock. The eminently missable **Acuàrium**, which doubles as a bar at night, features local fish bottled up in tanks that look too small for comfort. Far more appealing is the neighbouring showroom of the **Xoriguer gin distillery**, where you can help yourself to free samples of gin, various liqueurs and other spirits. Multilingual labels give details on all the different types, and there are some pretty obscure examples, such as *calent*, a sweet, brown liqueur with aniseed, wine, saffron and cinnamon, and *palo*, a liquorice-tasting spirit supposedly of Phoenician provenance. The lime-green *hierbas*, a favourite local tipple, is a sweet and sticky liqueur, partly made from camomile collected on the headlands of La Mola outside of Maó. In all its

The Acuàrium is open daily June–Aug 9am–8pm; Sept–May 10am–6pm; 225ptas. For the bar see p.187. The distillery is open Mon–Fri 8am–7pm, Sat 9am–1pm; free.

Maó and
around

*The distillery
runs a sideline
in boat trips –
see p.189.*

guises, it is, however, **gin** which remains the main product, and *pomada*, a gin cocktail with lemonade, is now near as damn it Menorca's national drink. Gin was first brought to the island by British sailors in the late eighteenth century, but a local businessman, a certain Beltran, obtained the recipe in obscure circumstances and started making the stuff himself. Nowadays, *Xoriguer* is the most popular island brand, mostly sold in modern versions of the earthenware bottles once used by British sailors, which are known locally as *canecas*.

Eating, drinking and nightlife

Maó has a place in culinary history as the eighteenth-century birthplace of **mayonnaise** (*mahonesa*). Various legends, all of them involving the French, claim to identify its inventor: take your pick from the chef of the French commander besieging Maó; a peasant woman dressing a salad for another French general; or a housekeeper disguising rancid meat from the taste buds of a French officer. The French also changed the way the Menorcans bake their bread, while the British started the dairy industry and encouraged the roasting of meat. Unfortunately, traditional Balearic food is not very much in evidence these days, as most of Maó's **restaurants** specialize in Spanish, Catalan or Italian dishes. These tourist-oriented establishments are mainly spread out along the harbourside – the Moll de Ponent west of the main stairway, the Moll de Llevant to the east. There's also a smattering of cheaper restaurants and **coffee bars** in the centre of town, though surprisingly few **tapas bars**. The mundane snack bars lining Plaça S'Esplanada are your best bet for an early **breakfast**.

Nightlife is not Maó's forte, but some fairly lively **bars** dot the harbourfront – mostly near the ferry port, staying open till around 2am on summer weekends – and one or two **nightclubs** pound the ears till early in the morning.

Cafés and tapas bars

American Bar, Plaça Reial 8. Big-windowed, expansive café-bar that was once the most fashionable place in town, and is still a good spot to nurse a coffee or tuck into unexceptional but filling snacks.

Cafeteria La Bocha, c/S'Arravaleta 27. Spick-and-span café in the heart of the downtown shopping area, serving tasty *tapas* and pizzas at reasonable prices.

Cafeteria La Bombilla, c/Sant Roc 31, adjoining Plaça Bastió. Unenticing decor, but good, cheap food: sardines, for example, cost just 800ptas.

La Farinera, Moll de Llevant 84. Spruce and modern café-bar offering excellent snacks near the ferry port. Open from 6am.

La Morada, Plaça Bastió 12. A good range of traditional *tapas*.

Sa Parada, Plaça S'Esplanada 64. Among the string of mundane cafés on the main square, this place stands out for its above-average *tapas* and snacks at reasonable prices.

Sa Placeta, Plaça Bastió 14. Unexciting but filling meals at bargain-basement prices (pizzas 700ptas).

Restaurants

L'Arpó, Moll de Llevant 124. Cosy and initimate restaurant featuring a superb selection of fish dishes from 1600ptas.

Ca'n Pau, Moll de Llevant 200. Pint-sized French restaurant with delicious daily specials from as little as 1500ptas.

Gregal, c/Martires Atlante 43. Chic little establishment at the east end of the harbourfront serving the best of Greek cuisine as well as excellent seafood.

Il Porto, Moll de Llevant 225. Enjoyable place to eat with a fountain and an arcaded terrace. The cooks perform in full view, turning out tasty fish and meat dishes from a wide-ranging menu.

Mos i Glop, off Plaça Bastió at c/Alaior 10. Most of the food here is mediocre, but the pizzas are cheap and substantial and the seafood is better than average.

Pilar, c/Forn 61. Family-run place featuring traditional Menorcan cuisine, near Plaça S'Esplanada: leave the square along c/Moreres, take the first left and then the first right. Closed in winter.

Roma, Moll de Llevant 295. Popular, fast-service eatery specializing in well-prepared Italian food at bargain prices. The decor is a tad old-fashioned, but that seems to suit the *Daily Express*-reading clientele.

Bars and nightclubs

Acuàrium, Moll de Ponent 73. At night the aquarium becomes a deep and dark bar (free admission); drink while the fish look on.

Bar Akelarre, Moll de Ponent 41. Relaxed, fashionable bar set in an imaginatively refurbished old stone vault, close to the ferry terminal.

Café Baixamar, Moll de Ponent 17. Modernist decor, great atmosphere and music to suit most tastes.

Nou Bar, c/Nou 1, at the corner of c/Hannover. Trendy, youthful first-floor bar in an attractive old building (the downstairs café, with its ancient armchairs and gloomy lighting, is a real old-fashioned place much favoured by locals).

Pacha, just before Sant Lluis about 3km along the main road from Maó. Big, flashy nightclub, popular with locals and tourists alike. Open, in high season only, till 3am.

Salsa Music Pub, Moll de Ponent 20. Lively bar playing mostly Latin sounds.

Si, c/Virgen de Gràcia 16, at c/Santiago Ramón y Cajal. Low-key nightspot south of Plaça Reial. From 11.30pm to around 3am.

Listings

Airport information Central switchboard ☎360150.

American Express At *Viajes Iberia*, c/Nou 35 (☎362848).

Banks *Banco de Credito Balear*, Plaça S'Esplanada 2; *Banca March*, c/ S'Arravaleta 7; *Banco de Santander*, c/Moreres 46.

Bicycle rental *Just Bicicletas*, c/Infanta 19 (☎364751), has mountain bikes for around 1000ptas per day, 5000ptas per week.

Car rental *Avis* (☎361838) and *Atesa* (☎366213) have branches at the airport, while downtown there's another *Avis* outlet, at Plaça S'Esplanada (☎364778), plus many smaller concerns – the tourist office has an exhaustive list.

Emergencies *Creu Roja* (Red Cross) for an **ambulance** ☎361180; **firefighters** ☎351011; **police** (*Policia Municipal*) ☎092.

Ferries The tourist office has ferry schedules and tariffs. Tickets can be purchased at larger travel agents or direct from the ferry line, *Trasmediterranea* (☎366050), whose office is next to the ferry port.

Hospital *Hospital Municipal*, Es Cós de Gràcia 26.

Library The well-stocked *English Lending Library*, c/Vassallo 48 (Mon–Sat 9am–1pm, plus Mon, Wed, Fri 5–7pm), accepts temporary members and makes a minimal charge for each book borrowed. C/Vassallo runs west from Plaça S'Esplanada.

Maps and books *Libreria Catolica*, adjoining Plaça Colón at c/Hannover 14 (☎363543), has a good selection of guidebooks and general maps of Menorca, as well as a reasonable, though far from exhaustive, assortment of island walking maps.

Mopeds *Motos Gelabert*, Avgda J. A. Clavé 12 (☎360614).

Pharmacies Among several downtown pharmacies, there's one at c/ S'Arravaleta 5.

Post office The central *correus* is at c/Bon Aire 15, near Plaça Bastió (Mon–Fri 9am–5pm, Sat 9am–1pm).

Taxis There are taxi ranks on Plaça S'Esplanada and Plaça Espanya. Alternatively, telephone *Radio Taxis* (☎367111).

Travel agencies There's a full list in the yellow pages under *viajes agencias*; *Viajes Iberia*, c/Nou 35 (☎362848), is one of the most reliable.

Trepucó and Talatí de Dalt

Two notable prehistoric monuments are located close to Maó, both with open access and no entry charge. By far the easier to get to is **Trepucó**, twenty minutes' walk south of Plaça S'Esplanada: follow Es Cós de Gràcia to the ring road, cross the traffic island and follow the twisting lane that leads past the cemetery. Surrounded by olive trees and dry-stone walls, the tiny site is dominated by its 4.2-metre-high and 2.75-metre-wide *taula* (T-shaped monolith), the largest and best-preserved monument of its kind on Menorca. The *taula* stands on the edge of a circular compound containing the scant remains of several broadly circular buildings. These were thoroughly excavated by a team of archeologists from Cambridge University in the late 1920s, but even they couldn't work out how the village was structured. There are two cone-shaped *talayots* close by, though the lines of the larger one were mucked up by the French – during the invasion of 1781, they increased the width of the walls and mounted their guns on them.

Another illuminating Talayotic remnant, **Talatí de Dalt**, lies 4km from Maó, just south of the main C721 highway: if you're driving, take the short and clearly signposted country lane on the left, then it's a five-minute walk from the car park; by public transport, take any Alaior bus, though it's best to check first that the driver is prepared to let you off. Much larger than Trepucó, the site is enclosed by a Cyclopean wall and features an imposing *taula* set within a circular precinct. The *taula* here appears to be propped up by a T-shaped pillar, though it's generally agreed that this is the result of an accidental fall, rather than by prehistoric design. Next to the *taula* are the heaped stones of the main *talayot* and all around are the scant remains of prehistoric dwellings. The exact functions of these are not known, but there's no doubt that the *taula* was the village centrepiece, and probably the focus of religious ceremonies. The rustic setting is charming – olive and carob trees abound and a tribe of hogs roots around the undergrowth.

Port de Maó

Port de Maó, as Menorcans term the whole of the extended inlet that links Maó with the Mediterranean, is one of the finest natural harbours in the world. No less than 5.4km long and a maximum of 900m wide, the channel also boasts the narrowest of deep-sea entrances, strategic blessings that have long made it an object of nautical desire. The high admiral of the Holy Roman Emperor, Charles V, opined, "June, July, August and Mahon are the best ports in the Mediterranean", and after Barbarossa's destruction of Maó in 1535, his master finally took the point and had the harbour fortified. Later, the British eyed up the port as both a forward base for Gibraltar and a lookout against the French naval squadron in Toulon. Using the War of the Spanish Succession as their excuse, they occupied Menorca in 1708 and, give or take occasional French and Spanish interventions, stayed in control until 1802, pouring vast resources into the harbour defences. Since the departure of the Brits, the fortifications have been repeatedly reinforced by the Spanish.

Nowadays, both shores, and a trio of mid-channel islets, carry the marks of all this military interest. Sights include the garrison town of **Es Castell**, purpose-built by the English in the 1770s, and a string of mostly ruined **fortifications**, thick-walled affairs hugging the contours of the coast to counteract the effects of hostile artillery fire. To explore the harbour thoroughly you'll need your own transport, though there is a frequent **bus** service from Maó to Es Castell. Boat trips leave both these places for hour-long harbour tours, costing 800ptas. In Maó, the boats leave six to eight times daily from the *Xoriguer* gin distillery, where tickets can be bought (see p.185). The excursion comprises a dash down to La Mola and back, with guides pointing out the sights in several languages. The boats from Es Castell leave four times daily, with tickets available at the kiosk on the quayside. Es Castell is halfway down the inlet, so the cruises are more circular than those departing from Maó, but they still cover all the sights from Maó to La Mola.

The north shore

Port de Maó's remaining fortifications are at their most impressive on the north shore. Here, a narrow byroad leaves the west end of the inlet to twist up across the coastal hills, passing after 3km the **Golden Farm** (no entry), a fine old mansion that was at one time the headquarters of Admiral Nelson. He barely visited it, however, being more concerned with his mistress, Emma Hamilton, who was ensconced at Naples, than with the possibility of a French attack on his Menorcan base.

East of Golden Farm, the road skirts the wealthy suburb of
Cala Llonga and offers fine panoramas of both the harbour and its
smaller islands – **Illa del Rei**, whose buildings once accommodated a military hospital, and **Illa Plana**, a pancake-flat islet that's
variously been a quarantine station, a US and now a Spanish navy
base. At the end of the promontory stands the formidable headland fastness of **La Mola**, still in use by the military, so visitors
can't get in. The view from the road, however, is daunting, tier
upon tier of complementary gun emplacements designed to resist
prolonged bombardment. To the right lies the island of **Latzaret**
(no access), a former leper colony which was made more secure
when it was cut off from the peninsula by a canal in 1900.
Lazareto's massive walls are a tribute to superstition rather than
military necessity: the Menorcans were convinced that contagion
could be carried into town by the wind, so they built the walls to
keep the germs inside.

Returning from La Mola, a signposted turning (west of Golden
Farm) heads north for 2km to **SA MESQUIDA**, which possesses the
nearest beach to Maó. Flanked by a rough and rocky shoreline, the
beach is a popular strip of dark red sand, but all in all it's not an
endearing spot – the village is a tatty affair which sprawls along the
coast in the shadow of a ruined fortress.

Es Castell and the south shore

Tucked in tight against the shore just 3km from Maó, the gridiron
streets of **ES CASTELL** (Villa Carlos) have a militaristic and very
English air. Originally called Georgetown, the town is ranged
around the old parade ground-cum-plaza, an expansive square that
bears elegant witness to the British in its Georgian-style town hall,
with soaring clock tower, and the elongated facades of its barracks.
Elsewhere, sash windows, doors with glass fanlights, and wrought-
iron work adorn many of the older houses, though nowadays the
centre looks rather bedraggled. As a garrison town, the fortunes of
Es Castell have always been tied to those of the military; with
Franco gone, the army no longer has the same prestige, and this is
reflected in the town's general demeanour.

Nevertheless, Es Castell is still worth a brief wander, beginning
in the main square, **Plaça S'Esplanada**. One of the barracks in the
square now houses a modest **military museum**, which displays a
motley collection of old rifles and uniforms (Sat & Sun 11am–1pm;
free). From the plaza, it's a couple of minutes' walk east down c/
Stuart to the harbour, a pretty spot occupying the thumb-shaped
cove of Cales Fonts. Besides several bars, the waterside is lined with
a string of **restaurants**, two of the best being the *Vell Parrander*,
Moll de Calles Fonts 52, and the *Siroco* at no. 40; both serve tasty
seafood at reasonable prices. Walking round the Cales Fonts
harbour, you'll come to the scant remains of the town's fortifications at the foot of c/Bellavista, which leads back towards the main

*For
information
about boat
tours of Port de
Maó from Es
Castell, see
p.189.*

square – hang a left at either c/Sant Ignasi or c/Victori. In the
unlikely event you decide to stay, the basic *Hostal-residencia Toni*,
c/Castillo 3 (☎365999; ②), is just off the main square at the corner
of c/Stuart. **Buses** from Maó stop on c/Gran, footsteps away from
the plaza along c/Victori.

Beyond Es Castell, the coastal road runs down towards the
mouth of the harbour, where the *zona militar* (no access) incorporates the site of **Fort Sant Felip**. Once the island's grandest
fortification, the fort was levelled by the Spanish in 1807, and
nothing survives except ruins – though rumours persist of secret
tunnels. To extend the excursion, you can follow the signposted
road round to **SANT ESTEVE**, a tiny village strung out along a
narrow cove that was close enough to the harbour entrance to be
extensively fortified: very little has survived, but on the coast
beyond the end of the road you'll spy the encrusted ruins of the
Marlborough Redoubt earthworks and a solitary, broken-down
corner tower.

*From Sant
Esteve, it's
possible to
drive on down
country lanes
to Sant Lluís,
described
overleaf.*

Southeast Menorca

The **southeastern corner** of Menorca, delineated by the road
between Maó and Cala En Porter, consists of a low-lying limestone
plateau fringed by a rocky shoreline with a string of craggy coves.
In recent years this stretch of coast has been extensively developed and today thousands of villas cover what was once empty
scrubland. The result is not pretty and, although many prefer this
low-rise architecture to the high-rise hotels of the 1960s, it's difficult to be enthusiastic, especially in **Cala En Porter**, the biggest
and perhaps the ugliest *urbanització* of the lot. That said, the
coast itself can be beautiful and the resort of **Cala d'Alcaufar**, one
of the earliest developments, fringes a particularly picturesque
cove. Inland lies an agricultural landscape criss-crossed by country
lanes and dotted with tiny villages, plus one town – unassuming
Sant Lluís.

Most of the district is devoted to villa-style accommodation, and
there are just five **hotels** and five **hostals**, which are only open from
April or May to October. As a consequence, advance reservations
are pretty much essential. It's best to stay in Cala d'Alcaufar, but
Punta Prima, a plain modern resort with a wide, windy beach in the
southeast corner of the island, is a reasonable second choice.

Getting around without your own transport is fairly easy. There
are hourly **buses** from Maó to Sant Lluís, Punta Prima and Cala En
Porter, as well as regular services to Cala d'Alcaufar. Bear in mind,
however, that with the exception of compact Cala d'Alcaufar, all of
these resorts spread for miles, and, if you've hired a villa and arrive
by bus, you could be facing a very long, hot and confusing trek –
taxis are generally available in the resorts.

Sant Lluís and Cala D'Alcaufar

Heading south from Maó along the main road, it's just 4km to SANT LLUÍS, a trim, one-square, one-church town of brightly white-washed terraced houses. As at Es Castell, the town's grid plan betrays its colonial origins. A French commander, the Duc de Richelieu, built Sant Lluís to house his Breton sailors in the 1750s, naming the new settlement after the thirteenth-century King Louis IX, who was beatified for his part in the Crusades. The French connection is further recalled by the trio of coats of arms carved on the west front of the church – those of the royal household and two French governors. Buses from Maó stop at the north end of town beside Plaça Nova; there are no *hostals*.

Beyond Sant Lluís you can reach the east coast after 5km, at either S'ALGAR, where rank upon rank of suburban-looking villas sprawl along the coast, or – a far better option – at the neighbour-ing resort of CALA D'ALCAUFAR. The development here is restrained, a smattering of holiday homes and old fishermen's cottages set beside a handsome inlet of flat-topped limestone cliffs and turquoise sea. You can stroll out across the surrounding head-lands, one of which has a Martello tower, or enjoy the sandy beach, a deep and narrow affair backed by an expensive stone bridge that, oddly enough, has been waiting for a connecting road for years. The main footpath down to the beach runs through the *Hostal Xuroy* (May–Sept; ☎151820; ⑥), a pleasant two-star establishment with forty modern rooms – though most of them are booked up months in advance for *Thomson* package tours.

Punta Prima to Binidali

Directly south of Sant Lluís lies PUNTA PRIMA, a large, standard-issue resort whose villas and supermarkets back onto a wide, sandy beach at the island's southeastern tip. Just offshore is the Illa de L'Aire, an inaccessible and uninhabited chunk of rock equipped with an automatic lighthouse. The sea, funnelled between the island and the shore, can make swimming dangerous from the beach – watch for the green or red flags. Windsurfing and sailing equipment is available for rent, as are pedaloes and sunbeds. Of the two hotels, the comfortable *Xaloc* is a one-star establishment with its own swimming pool and mini-golf course (May–Oct; ☎150106; ⑨), while the nearby 500-room *Pueblo Menorca* also has its own pools, plus sports facilities and disco (April–Oct; ☎151850; ⑦).

Travelling Menorca's south coast from Punta Prima to Binidali, a distance of around 10km, is a depressing experience: poorly sign-posted roads drift across the coastal scrubland encountering patches of undistinguished tourist development. On maps, it looks as if there are about half a dozen resorts, but on the ground it's impossible to determine where one settlement ends and another begins. The only vague light in the architectural gloom is

BINIBECA VELL, a purpose-built settlement of second homes which, with its narrow whitewashed alleyways, wooden balconies and twisting flights of steps, was designed to resemble an old Mediterranean fishing village. At the end of the coastal road is scrawny, unfinished BINIDALI, from where you can head inland to Sant Climent, on the main road between Maó and Cala En Porter.

Cales Coves and Cala En Porter

It's hard to understand why anyone thought the projected villa complex of SON VITAMINA, off the main road 4km west of Sant Climent, would prosper – it's simply too far from the ocean. Nonetheless, ambitious plans were laid and a wide access road was constructed. But the plot buyers failed to materialize and now it's the most forlorn of places, an untidy smattering of villas surrounded by waste ground. It's only of use if you fancy the 2.5-kilometre hike down to the coast to see the remote prehistoric caves of Cales Coves (or Ses Coves). The walk starts at the three-way intersection in Son Vitamina. Take the lane on the right – it's too rough to drive in an ordinary car – and proceed down through the scrubland to the seashore, where a pair of pebbly beaches edge an attractive forked inlet; a sketchy footpath climbs the rocks to link the two. The surrounding cliffs are punctured by over one hundred caves, the earliest of which date to neolithic times when they served as both funerary chambers and troglodytic dwellings, equipped with circular living quarters. Later, in the Talayotic period, the caves were used exclusively as burial chambers and, though the necropolis was abandoned long before the end of the Iron Age, several engraved stones discovered here indicate a continued interest well into Roman times, when the caves were visited during pagan festivals. It's easy and fun to explore the caves by clambering around the cliffs, though there's nothing specific to see once you're inside.

Returning to the main road, it's a short haul west to CALA EN PORTER. This shabby, sprawling *urbanització* has engulfed a bumpy plateau with hundreds of villas of such similar appearance and proportions that it soon becomes disorientating. Neither is there any focus to the development, which is limited in the west by a steep, marshy ravine and to the south by steep cliffs towering above a wide strip of pale gold sand. Access to the beach is either by road along the ravine or by flights of steps running down the cliffside. Restaurants and bars back onto the beach, and the bathing is safe. The resort does boast one noted attraction, the Cova d'En Xoroi, a large cave stuck in the cliff-face high above the beach. A stairway from the entrance on the cliff-top wriggles down to the cave, offering stirring views along the coast. You can also visit at night, as a local businessman has installed a boisterous bar and disco in the cave, which warms the place up from about midnight onwards.

The Cova d'En Xoroi is open daily 11am–1pm & 4–9pm; 375ptas. The bar-disco is open nightly from 10pm until around dawn, with entry about 1000ptas.

Fornells and the northeast coast

North of Maó, the 25-kilometre minor road to Fornells takes in some of Menorca's finest scenery, running alongside cultivated fields protected by great stands of trees, on the fringe of the bulging hills that form the backbone of the island. There's little to stop for along the way, but at regular intervals you can turn off towards beachside communities on what is, generally speaking, a harsh and rocky shoreline. Renowned for the excellence of its restaurants, **Fornells** itself boasts a delightful bayside location, and is, with its measured development, one of the most appealing resorts on the island. None of the village's three *hostals* is used by package-tour operators, so there's a reasonable chance of a room, and, although there's no beach at Fornells itself, it's a good base for visiting some of the remote cove beaches of the north coast – providing you're up to tackling the access roads, which require sturdy cars and good nerves.

Buses leave Maó for Fornells and the bigger resorts of the northeast coast twice a day from Monday to Saturday, and once on Sunday.

Es Grau and Cap de Favaritx

Just outside Maó, the first turning off the Fornells road leads to ES GRAU, a tidy hamlet overlooking a horseshoe-shaped bay that's fringed by dunes and an unenticing arc of greyish sand. The shallow waters here are ideal for children, and on weekends the handful of bars and **restaurants** – the best of them is the waterside *Tamarindos* – are crowded with holidaying Mahonese. Also popular is the quick boat trip over to the **Illa d'en Colom** (Pigeon Island), a rocky, one-kilometre-square islet with jagged cliffs and a couple of beaches. You can get off the boat at either beach, and there are sailings roughly every hour – either wait around at the jetty, between the beach and the fishing harbour, or ask at the beachside *Ca'n Bernat* bar for precise departure times. The return fare will set you back 500ptas.

The grassy dunes behind Es Grau's beach form the periphery of an expanse of wetland that encircles the freshwater lake of **S'Albufera**. The marshland is rich in migrant birdlife – all sorts of waders and terns are especially common in the springtime – and has, as a consequence, recently been designated a nature reserve. This has, however, come a little late for the protection of the lake's southern shore, now blighted by the villas of Shangri-La – but at least the resort provides easy access to the lake.

Returning to the Maó–Fornells road, the next fork along takes you to **Cap de Favaritx**, whose lighthouse shines out over an extraordinary, almost lunar landscape: a series of jagged inlets surrounded by tightly layered slate rocks, stubbled with red and green shrubs.

Port d'Addaia to Son Parc

"I shall ever think of Adaia, and of the company I enjoyed at that charming little Retirement, with the utmost Complacency and Satisfaction", wrote John Armstrong, an engineer in the British army, in the 1740s. If he could only see it now. The old **PORT D'ADDAIA**, at the mouth of a long, wooded inlet, has mushroomed dreary holiday homes, supermarkets and a marina, and as if that wasn't bad enough, the neighbouring headlands now heave with the villas and apartment buildings of two oversized resorts, low-key **NA MACARET** and the more boisterous **ARENAL D'EN CASTELL**. A redeeming feature is the latter's wide and sandy beach, set within a circular, cliff-edged cove, but otherwise you'll probably be keen to move on, by returning along the access road that's shared by all three resorts.

The next turning along the main road leads to **SON PARC**, a leafy grid of holiday homes surrounding a golf course. One of the more upmarket resorts, Son Parc is pleasantly arboreal with thick pine woods extending down to a beautiful pink-tinged sandy beach, equipped with a restaurant and beach bar. For a tad more isolation, walk the 1km west to **Cala Pudent**, where a peaceful sandy beach fringes a narrow inlet. The stony footpath begins at the wooden gate in the wall at the northwest end of Son Parc beach, before crossing a headland and skirting another tiny cove on the way.

Fornells

FORNELLS, a low-rise, classically pretty fishing village at the mouth of a long and chubby bay, has been popular with tourists for years, above all for its **seafood restaurants**, whose speciality, *caldereta de llagosta* (*langosta* in Castilian), is a fabulously tasty – and wincingly expensive – lobster stew. Nevertheless, there's been little development, just a slim trail of holiday homes extending north from the village in a suitably unobtrusive style. Behind the village and across the bay lie rockily austere headlands where winter storms and ocean spray keep vegetation to a minimum. This bleak terrain envelops a quartet of ruined **fortifications**, evidence of the harbour's past importance, of which two are easy to reach: an old watchtower peering out over the coast on the headland beyond Fornells and a shattered fort in the village itself. Built to protect the inlet from Arab and Turkish corsairs in the late seventeenth century, the fort was refurbished by the British, who constructed another on an island in the middle of the bay and posted a garrison. In a controversial piece of early tourist development, one of the commanders turned a local chapel into a tavern, incurring the disapproval of fellow officer John Armstrong: "In the Temple of Bacchus, no bounds are set to their [the soldiers'] Debauches and such a quantity of Wine is daily swallowed down, as would stagger Credulity itself."

Practicalities

Nowadays, nightlife is confined to the expensive **restaurants** that
edge the waterfront on either side of the minuscule main square,
Plaça S'Algaret. Such is their reputation that King Juan Carlos regularly drops by on his yacht, and many people phone up days in
advance with their orders. The royal favourite is the harbourside *Es
Pla* (☎376655), whose sedately bourgeois dining room offers a
superb paella for two for 7000ptas as well as the traditional lobster
stew. More relaxed alternatives include *Sibaris*, Plaça S'Algaret 1,
and *El Pescador*, next door, which concentrates on a magnificent
caldereta de llagosta – as does the *Es Port*, nearby at c/Rosario
17. Also consider *Es Cranc*, Escoles 29, a smooth and polished
restaurant offering a wide variety of fish dishes a couple of minutes'
walk north of Plaça S'Algaret. As a general rule, reckon on about
2000–2500ptas for a seafood main course, twice that for paella or
lobster stew.

Fornells has three reasonably priced and quite comfortable
hostals. The two-star *S'Algaret* is a neat little place, with slightly
old-fashioned furnishings and plain but cheerful rooms, at Plaça
S'Algaret 7 (☎376674; ⑤), and the nearby *Bar La Palma* is very
similar (☎376634; ④). The *Hostal Fornells*, c/Major 17
(☎376676; ⑤), is slightly smarter, a sprucely modern three-star
with a swimming pool.

Fornells' sweeping inlet provides ideal conditions for **windsurfers**; *Windsurf Fornells* (☎376458), situated 1km south of the
village, offers tuition to both novices and more experienced hands
(lessons include the use of their wetsuits and boards). The town has
no **beach** to speak of, but there is a strip of sand 2km back down
the main road beside the modest apartment complex of Ses Salines
(more interesting beaches in the area are detailed below). If you
need a **bike or car**, try *Roca-Rosello*, c/Major 57 (☎376540).

Beyond Fornells

The wild and rocky coastline west of Fornells boasts several **cove
beaches** of outstanding beauty. Getting to them, however, can be a
problem: this portion of the island has barely been touched by the
developers so the coast can only be reached along gravel or dirt
tracks, often poorly signposted. These usually branch off from the
narrow but metalled country lanes which cross the lovely pastoral
hinterland. Public transport around here is, as you might expect,
non-existent.

Cala Tirant

From Fornells, the obvious starting point for a coastal excursion is
the stepped crossroads about 3km south of the village. Here, just
north of the junction of the Maó and Es Mercadal roads, a signposted turning leads west down a country lane to pass, after 2km,

the clearly marked turning to Cala Tirant. This side road is unmade, so it's a rough and dusty two-kilometre drive down to the cove, where a thick arc of ochre-coloured sand lies trapped between bumpy headlands, with grassy dunes and marshland to the rear. It's a pleasant spot, but not a perfect one – there are villa developments on both sides of the cove and the beach is exposed to the north wind. To serve the villa residents, facilities include a beach **bar** and **windsurfing**.

Cap de Cavalleria
West of the turn-off to Cala Tirant, the country lane continues through a charming landscape of old stone walls and scattered farmsteads. After about 2km, keep an eye out for the gated road-cum-track that leads north for 8km to **Cap de Cavalleria** and its lighthouse (there is a sign, but it's hard to spot). The rocky and wind-buffeted cape, Menorca's most northerly point, pokes out into the ocean at the end of a slender promontory and offers great views of the island's north shore. However, you're well advised to park by the gate and walk the 8km, as the track is a nightmare to drive and turning the car round for the return journey can be a real headache.

Beach-seekers won't have so far to walk as the cape has a couple of lovely, westward-facing beaches near its base. These, **Platja de Ferragut** and **Platja de Cavalleria**, occupy the same wide and expansive cove, separated only by a low-lying sliver of rock. Get there via the main Cap de Cavalleria track: almost exactly 2km from the gate, take the left fork along an easy-to-follow but unsignposted trail that drops down to the cove after about 1.5km. Fringed by a thick band of dunes, the beaches are tinted deep yellow and, although they're popular at the weekend, most of the time you'll have the place pretty much to yourself. There are no facilities, so bring a picnic.

Platja de Binimel-Là
Back on the country lane, it's a further 2km west to the signposted turning for **Platja de Binimel-Là**. At first the access road is wide, sandy and fairly easy to negotiate, but, after 1.5km, you hang a left and the last bit of road deteriorates dramatically – 500m of bone-jangling motoring. Once you've arrived, you'll spy a tiny freshwater lake set behind a narrow band of dark red dunes which in turn gives onto a beautiful sand and pebble beach. This is a popular spot, though there are several more secluded and much smaller beaches on the east side of the cove, reached by clambering along the seashore. In the summer, there's usually an ad hoc beach **bar** and it's possible to rent **pedaloes** and **windsurfing boards**. The beach lacks trees and shade, so you may be confronted with the odd sight of bathers plastered in mud from the stream running across the beach.

One significant problem at Binimel-Là is the seaweed and detritus that sometimes get driven onto the beach by a northerly wind. If

this has happened, and if you've come equipped with reasonably
stout shoes and a hiking map, move on to **Cala Pregonda**, a splendid, seastack-studded bay with pine woods and a sandy beach, thirty
minutes' walk away to the west. The terrain isn't difficult, though
there's no clear route except at the start: you should climb the little
hill above the west end of Binimel-Là beach, clamber over a wall
just to the right of a large stone inscribed "1915" and follow the
wide track beyond, but this soon fizzles out as it approaches an
expanse of salt flats.

Central Menorca

Richard Kane, Menorca's first British governor, devoted much time
and energy to improving the island's communications, and his principal achievement was the construction of a highway between Maó
and Ciutadella – funded by a tax on alcohol. The only surviving
stretch of this original road makes a good alternative route, for
those with their own transport, from Maó to Alaior and central
Menorca. To reach it, take the Fornells road out of Maó and, after a
couple of kilometres, watch for the **Camí d'En Kane** sign on the
left. The old road follows the agricultural contours of the island,
passing ancient haciendas and dry-stone walls to approach Alaior
from the north. Most of Kane's original road, however, has disappeared beneath the modern highway, the C721. This runs from Maó
to Alaior across a flattish agricultural district that's liberally sprinkled with prehistoric remains: the Talayotic complex of Talatí de
Talatí de Dalt is Dalt, 4km from Maó, is the most diverting, but of the others, the
described on twin *navetas* of Rafal Rubí Nou, 3km further on, are the most
p.188. substantial, though they're far from awe-inspiring.

Alaior is the home of a couple of cheese-making factories where
you can sample local brands, and signals a change in scenery, from
the plains of the southeast to the limestone hills of central Menorca.
These culminate, just outside the antique village of **Es Mercadal**, in
the highest peak of the lot, **Monte Toro**, home to both a military
lookout point and a convent. The road to the summit is excellent and
the views are superb, making this an essential detour – unlike the
excursions south to the seaside resorts of **Son Bou** and **Sant Tomás**,
grimly modern affairs only redeemed by their sandy beaches. Back
on the main road, you'll soon reach the third and last market town on
the C721, **Ferreries**, a mildly industrialized shoemaking centre.
From here, a short excursion south leads to **Cala Santa Galdana**, an
attractive resort of manageable proportions that's within easy hiking
distance of several superb and isolated cove beaches.

Getting around is no problem: **buses** along the C721 are fast
and frequent, and from Monday to Saturday, there's one service a
day from Maó to Sant Tomás, five to Son Bou, and two to Cala Santa
Galdana; in the opposite direction, one bus a day from Monday to

Richard Kane

Born in Ulster in 1666, **Richard Kane** was the quintessential military man. His long career in the British army included service in Canada and campaigns with the Duke of Marlborough, experiences which he crystallized in a much-lauded pamphlet on infantry tactics. In 1713, following the Treaty of Utrecht, Kane was appointed Lieutenant-Governor of Menorca. He was transferred in 1720, but returned a decade later for a second stint, staying until 1736, the year of his death.

When Kane arrived in Menorca, he found a dispirited and impoverished population, governed from Ciutadella by a reactionary oligarchy. Kane's initial preoccupation was with the island's food supply, which was woefully inadequate. He promptly set about draining swampland near Maó and introduced new and improved strains of seed corn. The governor also had livestock imported from England – hence the Friesian cattle that remain the mainstay of the island's cheese-making industry. Meanwhile, a tax on alcohol provided the cash to develop Menorca's infrastructure, resulting in improved port facilities at Maó and the construction of the first road right across the island.

These were innovative times, not at all to the taste of the Menorcan aristocracy, who, holed up in Ciutadella, were further offended when Kane arranged for the capital to be moved to Maó. They bombarded London with complaints, eventually inducing a formal governmental response in an open letter to the islanders entitled *A Vindication of Colonel Kane*. Most Menorcans, however, seem to have welcomed Kane's benevolent administration – though not in the matter of religion. Here, the governor created genuine offence by holding Protestant services for his troops in Catholic churches. That apart, there's little doubt that, by the time of his death, Kane was a widely respected figure, whose endeavours were ill served by the colonial indifference of some of his successors.

Friday links Ciutadella with Sant Tomás and Cala Santa Galdana. Accommodation, on the other hand, is difficult for independent travellers. The resorts are dominated by the package-tourist industry, though you can, of course, try pot luck. Of the three inland towns, only Ferreries and Es Mercadal have *hostals* – just one each.

Alaior and around

Cheese is the main reason to stop at **ALAIOR**, an old market town 12km from Maó, which has long been the nucleus of the island's dairy industry. There are two major companies, both of which have factory shops near to – and clearly signposted from – the main road, as it cuts across the western periphery of the town centre (though a bypass will soon be completed). Approaching from Maó, the first shop is owned by *La Payesa* (Mon–Fri 9am–1pm & 4–7.30pm), while the second is the bigger and better outlet of *Coinga* (Mon–Fri 9am–1pm & 5–8pm, Sat 9am–1pm). Both companies sell a similar product, known generically as *Queso Mahon*, after the port from which it was traditionally exported. It's a richly textured, white, semi-fat cheese made from pasteurized cow's milk with a touch of ewe's milk added for extra flavour. The cheese is sold at four different stages of maturity, either *tierno* (young), *semi-curado* (semi-mature), *curado* (mature) or *añejo* (very mature). Both shops have the full range and, although quite expensive, their prices are the best you'll see.

The centre of Alaior is a tangle of narrow streets and bright white houses tumbling down the hillside beneath the imposing church of Santa Eulalia, a seventeenth-century edifice stuck on a rise behind the main square, Plaça Nova. There's nowhere to stay, but for food, *The Cobblers Garden*, in a fine old town house at c/ Sant Macari 6, close to Plaça Nova, has tasty snacks and light meals at reasonable prices. Apart from a bite to eat and a quick gambol up and down the hill, however, there's not much reason to hang around – unless you happen to be here in the second weekend of August. This is when Alaior lets loose for the Festa de Sant Llorenç, a drunken celebration and display of horsemanship. As its highlight, with the tiny town square packed, a procession of horses tears through the crowd, bucking and rearing, with their riders clinging on for dear life. Although no one seems to get hurt, you'd probably do best to join the privileged townspeople and witness the spectacle from the safety of an overlooking balcony.

Torralba d'En Salort

One of the better-preserved Talayotic settlements, Torralba d'En Salort, lies 3km southeast of Alaior – the road towards Cala En Porter and Sant Climent bisects the site, with the most significant remains located behind the modern stone wall on the right. Beside the entrance, the rectangular shrine surrounding the taula is in particularly good condition and has been the subject of minute examination and much conjecture by archeologists. They discovered that several of the recesses had large fireplaces, which may well have been used for the ritual slaughter of animals. It was, however, the unearthing of a tiny bronze bull that really got the experts going, the suggestion being that, just as the bull was venerated by other prehistoric Mediterranean peoples, so it was worshipped here in Menorca, with the *taula* a stylized representation of a bull's head. Circumnavigated by a footpath, the rest of the site contains a confusion of stone remains, none of them especially revealing, while across the road in the middle of a field lurk the remains of a *talayot* and, about 30m to the north, an underground chamber roofed with stone slabs.

Son Bou and around

On the west side of Alaior along the main road, take the Son Bou turning for the beaches of the south coast and, if you still have the enthusiasm, the Talayotic settlement of Torre d'En Gaumes. The drive to the seashore is easy enough, but the prehistoric site can only be reached via a rough country lane: 2.5km from the C721, fork left and bump down the lane for another 2km. Perched on a hilltop, the sprawling site contains three well-preserved *talayots* and a *taula*, which together form what is presumed to have been the public part of the village. It's impossible to interpret precisely the surrounding remains, as the site was inhabited – and continually modified – well into Roman times. That said, you can pick out the broadly circular outlines of a sequence of private dwellings dating from the Talayotic period.

At **SON BOU**, 8km south of Alaior, the antiquarian interest is maintained by an extensive cave complex, cut into the cliff-face above the approach road, and the foundations of an early Christian basilica, set behind the beach at the east end of the resort. They're hardly popular attractions, however, when compared with the beach, a whopping pale-gold strand some 3km long and 40m wide. This is Menorca's longest beach, and behind it has mushroomed a massive tourist complex of skyscraper hotels and villa-villages that spreads west into the twin resort of **SANT JAUME MEDITERRANI**. The sand shelves gently into the sea, but the bathing isn't quite as safe as it appears: particularly when the wind picks up, ocean currents are hazardous, and you should watch for the green or red flags. The beach accommodates several beach bars, and watersports equipment is widely available – everything from jet-skis, snorkels and windsurfing boards to sunbeds and pedaloes. The development is at its crassest – and the crowds at their worst – towards the east end of the beach, where the foreshore is dominated by two huge sky-rise hotels, the *Sol Milanos* (May–Oct; ☎371175; ⑦) and the *Sol Pinguinos* (May–Oct; ☎371075; ⑦). These hotels, with their spruce, modern, balconied bedrooms, share facilities, including sun terraces, outside pools, bars and restaurants. Further west, a strip of dune-fringed, marshy scrubland runs behind the beach, pushing development a kilometre or so inland. Bathing is more secluded here, and in the pine woods overlooking the seashore stands the *San Valentin Menorca* (May–Oct; ☎372748; ⑧), a four-star hotel with comfortable, air-conditioned apartments, a cafeteria, sauna, swimming pools and a gymnasium.

Es Mercadal and Monte Toro

Nine kilometres northwest of Alaior you arrive at **ES MERCADAL**, squatting amongst the hills at the very centre of the island. Another old market town, it's an amiable little place of whitewashed houses and trim allotments whose antique centre straddles a quaint water-course. Tucked down c/Major is a Ruritanian town hall, and the minuscule main square, a few paces away, has a couple of sleepy cafés. The town also boasts two top-notch restaurants, popular with tourists, near the main road on the edge of town. The *Ca N'Aguedet*, at c/Lepanto 30, and the *Es Moli d'Es Recó*, located in a windmill, both serve up excellent traditional Menorcan cuisine, with suckling pig, for instance, costing around 1600ptas, and snails with mayonnaise 1000ptas. Es Mercadal has a one-star **hostal-residencia** too, the spick-and-span *Jeni*, in a modern building at Mirada del Toro 81 (☎375059; ④). Rooms here are comfortable, with attractive modern furnishings, there's a rooftop swimming pool, and the bar, though a little glum, is a pleasant enough spot to nurse a drink. To get there, walk south from the main square – Sa Plaça – along c/Nou and take the first left and then the first right. Buses from Maó, Ciutadella and Sant Tomás stop on the south side of town, just off Avgda Metge Camps, which leads on to c/Nou.

Monte Toro

From Es Mercadal you can set off on the ascent of **Monte Toro**, a steep 3.4-kilometre climb along a serpentine road. At 357m, the summit is the island's highest point and offers wonderful vistas: on a good day you can see almost the whole island, on a bad one to Fornells, at least. From this lofty vantage point, Menorca's geological division becomes apparent: to the north, Devonian rock (mostly reddish sandstone) supports a rolling, sparsely populated landscape edged by a ragged coastline; to the south, limestone predominates in a bumpy plain that boasts both the island's best farmland and, as it approaches the south coast, its deepest valleys.

It's likely that the name of the hill is derived from the Moorish *El Tor* (the height), but Christians have invented an alternative etymology, involving villagers spotting a mysterious light on the mountain, and, on closer investigation, being confronted by a bull (*toro*) who, lo and behold, leads them to a miracle-making statue of the Virgin. Whatever the truth, Monte Toro has been a place of pilgrimage since medieval times, the highlight of the year being the first Sunday in May when the local bishop blesses the land.

The Augustinians plonked a monastery on the summit in the seventeenth century and bits of the original construction survive in the **convent**, which shares the site today with an army outpost bristling with all sorts of aerials and radar dishes, and a monumentally ugly statue of Christ. Much of the convent is out of bounds, but the public part, approached across a handsome courtyard, encompasses a couple of gift shops, a delightful terrace café and a cosy, Neoclassical **church**. The simple white lines of its porch, accommodating an ancient well girt with bright flowers and deep green shrubs, provides a hospitable introduction, while inside, the truncated nave showcases a Baroque high altar with a much-venerated image of the Virgin.

Es Migjorn Gran and Sant Tomás

Es Mercadal is an important crossroads: the road north meanders through gentle wooded hills and red-soiled fields to reach the coast at Fornells; a similarly attractive route leads south to unassuming **ES MIGJORN GRAN** (sometimes called San Cristóbal or San Cristofól), an elongated hillside village flanked by intricate terraced fields. These scenic pleasures continue with the wooded ravine that leads south to the seashore, but here they end abruptly in the crass hotel and apartment buildings of **SANT TOMÁS**. The three-kilometre-long sandy **beach**, however, is superb, very similar to that of Son Bou, a couple of headlands away to the east – though all is not quite as it seems. A thunderous storm stripped the existing sand away in 1989, and what you see has been imported. The beach looks very inviting as it slopes gently into the ocean, but there are sometimes dangerous undercurrents so you should observe the green or red flags. The access road reaches the shore halfway along the beach, which is called Platja Sant Adeodat to the west and Platja Sant Tomás to the east. The latter is easily the more congested and it's here you'll find all the high-rise **hotels**, amongst which the air-conditioned, ultra-modern *Santo Tomás* is the most lavish (May–Oct; ☎370025; ⑨), whilst the less expensive *Sol Cóndores* will do almost as well, though there's no air conditioning (☎370050; ⑦). Both have pools, restaurants, night-time entertainment and many types of sports facility. Windsurfers, jet-skis and pedaloes can all be rented on the beach nearby. By contrast, the Platja Sant Adeodat has barely been touched by the developers and is still backed by an old dry-stone wall and farmland.

Central
Menorca

Fornells is described on p.195.

Ferreries and around

Tucked into a hollow beneath a steep hill, the narrow, sloping streets of **FERRERIES**, 8km from Es Mercadal on the C721 and 7km from Es Migjorn Gran on a minor road, are framed by terraced fields. A surprise here is the pagoda-like piece of modern sculpture in the Plaça Espanya, whilst the palm trees in front of the neatly shuttered town hall, primly facing the old parish church across the square, present a more traditional aspect. There's not much to detain you, though you could spare time either to watch or to buy from one of the self-employed **shoemakers** who ply their craft from tiny workshops in the town centre – despite competition from the *Rubrica* shoe factory, a kilometre or so back along the C721, whose shop promises made-to-measure footwear within 24 hours. The factory shoes are less expensive, but the quality is nowhere near as high.

One definite plus in town is the *Vimpi* café-bar, beside the main road on Plaça Joan Carles, which serves some of the tastiest **tapas** on the island; the adjoining restaurant, *Ca'n Aleja*, is, however, only mediocre. You probably wouldn't choose to stay in Ferreries – it's just too quiet – but there is a **fonda**, the no-frills *Loar*, off the Plaça Espanya at Avgda Verge de Monte Toro 2 (☎373888; ②).

Castell Santa Agueda

A lattice of rough country roads covers the sparsely inhabited hills and farmland in between Ferreries and the north coast. The district's main attraction is the **Castell Santa Agueda**, whose scant remains perch atop the peak of the same name, Menorca's second highest at 268m. The Romans were the first to recognize the hill's strategic value, fortifying the summit in the second century BC, but it was the Moors who developed the stronghold, and it was here that they made their final stand against Alfonso III's invasion in 1287. Fresh from their defeat at Maó, the demoralized Moors didn't put up much of a fight – though they would certainly have been more determined if they had known of their ultimate fate. After the surrender, the Catalans demanded a heavy ransom for every captive. Those who couldn't pay were enslaved and those who weren't fit to work as slaves were shoved onto ships, taken out to sea and thrown overboard.

To get to the castle, take the C721 west out of Ferreries. At about 3km, turn right down the reasonably well-surfaced (and signposted) lane towards Binisuesets. Go straight down the lane for around 3km, ignoring the Binisuesets turning, and you'll spy the footpath up the hill to the right, starting on the right-hand side of the deserted white schoolhouse beside the lane. The lung-bursting hike up the rocky mountainside, flanked by ancient olive trees bent by the gusts of the *Tramuntana*, takes at least an hour. At the top, there's little besides the sparse ruins of the fortress and an abandoned farmhouse, but you'll be rewarded with superb views.

Cala Santa Galdana

South from Ferreries, an excellent eight-kilometre road through a picturesque pastoral landscape leads down to CALA SANTA GALDANA. Once a much-loved beauty spot, the bay has experienced a rash of development since the building of the road; on arrival, the first thing you'll see is a twelve-storey hotel, *Hotel Sol Gavilanes*, built high above the beach. Although it's become a busy resort, the place preserves a semblance of its original charm, its curving sandy strand framed by pine-studded, limestone cliffs and intercepted by a rocky promontory adjacent to a narrow river. Early in the morning or out of season is the best time to appreciate the scene – or you can escape the crowds by hiking round the headland beside the *Hotel Audax* at the west end of the bay. Alternatively, it's possible to hire out all sorts of watersports equipment – from pedaloes and water scooters to windsurfing boards and snorkelling tackle; and small boats ply regularly to other more secluded beaches (see below).

Among the resort's three high-rise **hotels**, you're most likely to find a vacant room at the luxurious, four-star *Audax* (May–Oct; ☎373125; ⑦), though if you're prepared to pay this much, make sure you get a sea-facing balcony. The *Cala Galdana*, set just back from the beach (May–Oct; ☎373000; ⑦), and the *Sol Gavilanes* (April–Oct; ☎373175; ⑦) both have spick-and-span modern rooms, but lack style or interest. At the other end of the market, Menorca's one and only official **campsite**, *S'Atalaia*, is located about 3km

back down the road towards Ferreries (open all year; ☎373095).
Pine trees shade much of the site, which has an outdoor swimming
pool and a restaurant-bar. It can accommodate about 100 guests
but advance reservations are strongly advised. Charges are 525ptas
for a site, 525ptas for a vehicle, and 525ptas per person.

Back in the resort, there's a good-quality seafood restaurant, *El
Mirador*, built into the beachside promontory, though you do pay
over the odds for the view out over the bay. Among several less
expensive choices stuck behind the *Hotel Audax*, *Sa Lluna* offers
reasonably priced Italan food, with pizzas for around 850ptas. Close
by, there's an *Avis* car rental outlet (☎374163).

Around Cala Santa Galdana

Several exquisite cove beaches lie within easy reach of Cala Santa
Galdana, the most obvious choice being Cala Mitjana, just 1km to
the east. The footpath to the cove begins behind the *Hotel Sol
Gavilanes* at the Plaça Na Gran, where a gate leads onto an easy-
to-follow path through coastal pine woods. Once you get there
you'll be rewarded with a broad strip of sand set beneath wooded
cliffs at the end of a beguiling bay – though sometimes there's an
unpleasant smell from an accumulation of seaweed. A favourite
sport here is jumping into the crystal-clear water from the
surrounding cliffs.

Equally beautiful but also afflicted with periodic seaweed problems is Cala Trebalúger, a further 2.5km east and best reached by
boat from Cala Santa Galdana (1–2 daily; 400ptas). Cala Trebalúger
boasts a beautiful arc of sand flanked by steep cliffs and crossed by
a stream which emerges from the gorge behind. There are no beach
facilities, so take your own food and drink.

Walking west from Cala Santa Galdana on the footpath starting opposite the *Hotel Audax*, it takes about forty minutes to
reach Cala Macarella, where severe, partly wooded limestone
cliffs surround a band of white sand that shelves gently into the
Med. It's a beautiful spot, with ideal conditions for swimming –
unlike the other beaches around Cala Santa Galdana, seaweed is
never a problem here. There's a touch of development in the form
of a summertime beach bar, and sunbeds and pedaloes for hire,
but it's nothing excessive.

Ciutadella and around

Like Maó, CIUTADELLA sits high above its harbour. Here,
though, navigation is far more difficult, up a narrow channel too
slender for all but the smallest of cargo ships. Despite this nautical inconvenience, Ciutadella has been at the centre of affairs as
the island's capital for most of its history. The Romans chose it,
the Moors adopted it as *Medina Minurka*, and the Catalans of

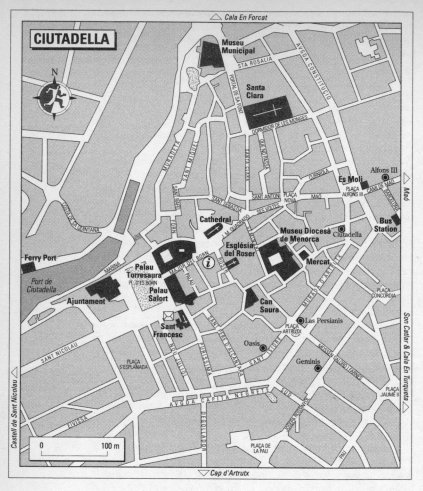

△ Cala En Forcat

CIUTADELLA

N

Museu Municipal

STA ROSALIA

Santa Clara

DORMIDOR DE LES MONGES

AVGDA CONSTITUCIÓ

Alfons III ◉

Es Moli

PLAÇA ALFONS III

▷ Maó

SANT MIQUEL

SANT RAFEL

QUE NO PASSA

PORTAL DE SA FONT

SANT ANTONI

CURNIOLA

CAMI DE MAÓ

BARCELONA

Bus Station

SANT SEBASTIA

SES VOLTES

PLAÇA NOVA

MAÓ

J.M. QUADRADO

COSTA DE SA QUINTANA

SANT PAU

Cathedral

Església del Roser

Museu Diocesà de Menorca ◉ Ciutadella

Ferry Port

MARINA

Palau Torresaura

PL. D'ES BORN

Palau Salort

Mercat

MIRADOR D'EN MARTI

PLAÇA CONCORDIA

Port de Ciutadella

MAJOR DEL BORN

PALAU

Ajuntament ⊠

Can Saura

Las Persianis ◉

PLAÇA ARTRUTX

Sant Francesc

SANT PERE D'ALCÂNTARA

PURISSIMA

SANT ISIDRE

SANT CLIMENT

MISSER

Oasis

Geminis ◉

MISSION SALORO FABREGUES

PLAÇA JAUME II ▷

SANT NICOLAU

PLAÇA S'ESPLANADA

SUD

Son Catlar & Cala En Turqueta ▷

Castell de Sant Nicolau ◁

EIVISSA

AVGDA CAPITÀ NEGRETE

DEGOLLADOR

ROSER MORAGUES

PAU

PLAÇA DE LA PAU

0   100 m

▽ Cap d'Artrutx

The story of the Turkish raid of 1558 is told on p.209.

the *Reconquista* flattened the place and began all over again. In 1558, the Catalan-built town was, in its turn, razed by Turkish corsairs. Several thousand captives were carted off to the slave markets of Istanbul, but the survivors determinedly rebuilt Ciutadella in grand style, its compact, fortified centre brimming with the mansions of the rich. To the colonial powers of the eighteenth century, however, Ciutadella's feeble port had no appeal when compared with Maó's magnificent inlet. In 1722 the British moved the capital to Maó, which has flourished as a trading centre ever since, whilst Ciutadella has stagnated – a long-lasting economic reverie that has, by coincidence, preserved its old and beautiful centre as if in aspic.

The bulk of the Menorcan aristocracy remained in Ciutadella, where the colonial powers pretty much left them to stew – an increasingly redundant, landowning class far from the wheels of mercantile power. Consequently, there's very little British or French influence in Ciutadella's **architecture**; instead, the narrow, cobbled streets boast fine old palaces, hidden away behind high walls, and a set of Baroque and Gothic churches very much in the Spanish tradition. Essentially, it's the whole ensemble, centred on stately **Plaça d'es Born**, that gives Ciutadella its appeal rather than any specific sight, though the mostly Gothic **cathedral** is a delight, as is the eclectic **Museu Diocesà de Menorca**. An ambitious renovation programme has further enhanced the town, restoring most of the old stone facades to their honey-coloured best. Added to this are some excellent restaurants, especially on the harbourfront, and an adequate supply of *hostals* and hotels. It's a lovely place to stay, and nothing else on Menorca rivals the evening *passeig* (promenade), when the townsfolk amble the narrow streets of the centre, dropping in on pavement cafés as the sun sets. Allow at least a couple of days, more if you seek out one of the beguiling cove beaches within easy striking distance of town: **Cala En Turqueta** is the pick of the bunch.

Arrival, information and orientation

Ciutadella's compact centre could hardly be more convenient. **Buses** from Maó and points east arrive at the station on c/ Barcelona, just south off the end of the Camí de Maó, an extension of the main island highway, the C721. **Local buses** shuttle up and down the west coast from Plaça S'Esplanada, on the west side of the town centre next to the main square, Plaça d'es Born. **Ferries** from Port d'Alcúdia, on Mallorca, dock in the harbour right below the Plaça d'es Born. If you're **driving** in, there's no missing the ring road which, under various names, encircles the old town. Approaching from the east, turn left when you hit it and keep going until you reach its conclusion beside the Plaça S'Esplanada; if you can't find a parking spot actually on this square, turn left at the top of the square near the bus stops and drive down Camí Sant Nicolau, where there's always space.

The **Oficina d'Informació Turistica** (May–Oct Mon–Fri 8am–3pm & 5–7pm, Sat 9.30am–1pm; Nov–April Mon–Fri 9am–2pm, Sat 9.30am–1pm; ☎382693) has buckets of information on Menorca as a whole and Ciutadella in particular, including bus timetables, ferry schedules, lists of *hostals* and hotels, and free maps. It's opposite the cathedral on Plaça Catedral, bang in the middle of the old town, which can only be explored on foot. Keeping your bearings here is straightforward – the main square and harbour are on the west side of the centre, the ring road on the east.

Further information about Menorca's bus routes can be found on p.217.

Full details of ferries and hydrofoils to Ciutadella are given on p.30.

Accommodation

There's hardly a plethora of **accommodation** in Ciutadella, but the
town does have two quality hotels that aren't booked up by package-tour operators – the *Patricia* and the *Geminis* – and a handful
of fairly comfortable and reasonably priced *hostals* dotted in and
around the centre, with a concentration in the vicinity of Plaça
Alfons III and Plaça Artrutx.

Inexpensive

Hostal Oasis, c/Sant Isidre 33, footsteps away from Plaça Artrutx; ☎382197.
Attractive one-star with nine simple rooms set around a courtyard-restaurant. ③.

Casa de Huéspedes Las Persianis, Plaça Artrutx 2; ☎381445. Simple rooms
occupying two storeys above a popular café-bar, in a square adjoining the
ring road: take earmuffs, especially at the weekends. ③.

Hostal Sa Prensa, Plaça Madrid; ☎382698. Somewhat dishevelled lodgings
with six spartan bedrooms above a café-bar. It's a 15-min walk west of the
centre, close to the rocky seashore at the end of c/Madrid; follow Camí de
Sant Nicolau from the Plaça S'Esplanada, take the third turning on the left (c/
Saragossa) and c/Madrid is the first major turn on the right. ③.

Moderate

Hotel-residencia Alfons III, Camí de Maó 53; ☎380150. Brashly modern
hotel with 50 simple one-star rooms. Located beside the main road from Maó,
a couple of minutes' walk from the ring road; try to get a room at the back
away from the noisy road. ④.

Hostal-residencia Ciutadella, c/Sant Eloi 10; ☎383462. Unassuming yet
comfortable two-star, in an old terraced house down a narrow side street off
Plaça Alfons III. ⑤.

Hotel-residencia Geminis, c/Josepa Rossinyol 4; ☎385896. Painted bright
pink and white, with blue awnings to add to the effect, this well-tended,
comfortable one-star certainly hits the eye. To get there on foot, walk a few
paces down c/Mossèn Salord i Farnès from the ring road and watch for the
archway on the right; proceed through the arch and the hotel's on the right at
the bottom of a prosperous, suburban street. Closed Jan. ④.

Hotel Madrid, c/Madrid 60; ☎380328. Fourteen quite comfortable rooms in
a well-maintained, villa-style building with its own ground-floor café-bar.
Located near the ocean a 10-min walk west of the town centre, halfway along
c/Madrid (directions as for *Hotel Sa Prensa* above). Open May–Oct. ④.

Hostal-residencia Menurka, c/Domingo Savio 6; ☎381415. Tidy two-star
establishment of 21 rooms, some with balconies, though they overlook a
modern, boring street. C/Domingo Savio (sometimes called c/Fred) is east of
the town centre and one block up from Camí de Maó. ⑤.

Expensive

Hotel-residencia Esmeralda, Camí de Sant Nicolau 171; ☎ 380250. The
sweeping curves of this four-storey hotel are a classic example of 1960s
design, with a swimming pool and private gardens out front. Most of the
bedrooms have balconies and face out to sea, but most are booked up by
package-tour operators. At the west end of the street, a 15-min walk from the
centre. Open April–Oct. ⑦.

Hotel-residencia Patricia, Camí de Sant Nicolau 90; ☎385511. The best hotel
in town, popular with business folk and handy for the centre. Extremely
comfortable, ultra-modern rooms with all facilities, the only downer being the
lack of a sea view – though the best rooms have rooftop balconies with panoramic vistas. ⑧.

The Town

Ciutadella's centre crowds around the fortified cliff shadowing the south side of the harbour. The main plazas and points of interest are within a few strides of each other, on and around the expansive Plaça d'es Born.

Plaça d'es Born

Primarily a nineteenth-century creation, **Plaça d'es Born** is easily the finest main square in the Balearic islands. In the middle is a soaring **obelisk** commemorating the futile defence against the Turks in 1558, a brutal episode that was actually something of an accident. The Ottomans had dispatched 15,000 soldiers and 150 warships west to assist their French allies against the Habsburgs. With no particular place to go, the Turks rolled around the Mediterranean for a few weeks and, after deciding Maó wasn't worth the candle, they happened on Ciutadella, where the garrison numbered just a few hundred. For the Menorcans, the results were cataclysmic. The one-sided siege ended with the destruction of the town and the enslavement of its population – there was so much damage that when the new Spanish governor arrived, he was forced to live in a cave. The obelisk's Latin inscription, penned by the nineteenth-century historian Josep Quadrado, reads, "Here we fought until death for our religion and our country in the year 1558".

To the north of Plaça d'es Born, steep steps lead down to the harbour, where the waterside restaurants (see p.213), pleasure boats and sturdy remains of the city walls comprise one of Menorca's most attractive scenes.

On the western side of the square stands the **Ajuntament**, whose nineteenth-century arches and crenellations mimic Moorish style, purposely recalling the time when the site was occupied by the Wali's Alcázar (palace). Tucked away in the southeast corner, the church of **Sant Francesc** is a clean-lined, airy structure of Gothic design, though the chancel and the dome were added later. Most of the town's churches were looted during the Civil War, but this one survived pretty much intact, preserving its carved wood altars, embossed ceiling and polychromatic saints. In the square's northeast corner, the massive **Palau Torresaura**, built in the nineteenth century but looking far older, is the grandest of several aristocratic mansions edging the plaza. Embellished by self-important loggias, its frontage proclaims the family coat of arms above a giant wooden door leading to the patio. The impressively luxurious interior, however, is off limits, because the house is still owner-occupied, like most of its neighbours. An exception is the adjacent **Palau Salort**, which is entered round the corner on c/Major del Born. The admission fee is steep, but the house, built in the same style as Palau Torresaura, is worth a brief look for its high-ceilinged rooms and smattering of family bygones, redolent of nineteenth-century bourgeois life.

The Palau Salort is open Mon–Sat 10am–2pm; 300ptas.

The cathedral

Beyond Palau Salort, c/Major del Born leads to the **cathedral**, built by Alfonso III at the end of the thirteenth century on the site of the

The cathedral is open Mon–Sat 9am–1pm & 6–8pm; free.

chief mosque. So soon after the Reconquest, its construction is fortress-like, with windows set high above the ground – though the effect is somewhat disturbed by the flashy columns of the Neoclassical west doorway, the principal entrance. Inside, light from the narrow, lofty windows bathes the high altar in an ethereal glow, the hallmark of the Gothic style. There's also a wonderfully kitschy, pointed altar arch, and a sequence of glitzily Baroque side chapels. Most of the church's original furnishings and fittings, however, were destroyed in a frenzy of anticlericalism when the Republicans took control of Menorca during the Civil War. Despite losing its status as the island capital, Ciutadella had remained Menorca's ecclesiastical centre. Its resident Catholic hierarchy were, by and large, rich and reactionary in equal measure, and they enthusiastically proclaimed their support for the officers of Maó garrison when the latter declared for Franco in July 1936. This insurrectionary gesture was, however, a miserable failure: the bulk of the garrison stayed loyal to the Republic and, allied with local left-wing groups, captured the rebels, shot their leaders and ransacked Ciutadella's main churches as retribution.

The Museu Diocesà de Menorca and around
Cutting down c/Roser from the cathedral, you'll pass the tiny **Església del Roser**, whose striking Churrigueresque facade, dating from the seventeenth century, boasts a quartet of pillars engulfed by intricate tracery. The church was the subject of bitter controversy when the British commandeered it for Church of England services – not at all to the liking of the Dominican friars who owned the place.

At the end of c/Roser, turn left past the palatial, seventeenth-century mansion of **Can Saura**, now an antique shop, and then left again for c/Seminari and the **Museu Diocesà de Menorca** (Diocesan Museum), housed in an old and dignified convent. Before you go in, take a look at the elongated perimeter wall, a sober affair cheered by the delicate flutings of a Neoclassical **portal** with a bizarre sculpted cameo stuck on top. This is certainly the town's most unusual sight, with the Virgin Mary, armed with a hammer and cudgel, standing menacingly over a cat-like dragon-devil. The museum itself is entered through a far more modest, late medieval doorway. Inside, the conventual buildings surround an immaculately preserved Baroque **cloister**, whose vaulted aisles sport coats of arms and religious motifs. The museum and its layout are still being developed, but at the moment the first room you visit (in the top right-hand corner of the cloister) is devoted to an enjoyable collection of prehistoric finds. These incorporate a ragbag of Talayotic remains including an intriguing assortment of lead pendants, a rare Punic plate recovered in Ibiza, and, amongst various classical artefacts, an exquisite Greek bronze of a mermaid.

Subsequent rooms around the cloister concentrate on matters ecclesiastical, with fancy vestments, macabre reliquaries, gold and

The Museu Diocesà is open Tues–Sun 10am–1.30pm; 300ptas.

silver chalices and various processional items. It's the general glitter that impresses, but if you want to dig beneath the gaudy surface, a leaflet issued at reception gives more detailed information than the inadequate labels. Spare time too for the room in the bottom left-hand corner of the cloister. The models are a bit of a bore, but there are also several fascinating photos of the anticlericalists in action in Ciutadella during the Civil War.

Behind the museum lies the **mercat** (market), on Plaça Llibertat, another delightful corner of the old town, where fresh fruit, vegetable and fish stalls mingle with lively and inexpensive cafés selling the freshest of *ensaimadas*.

East to Plaça Alfons III
Just north of the museum, c/Seminari intersects with the narrow, pedestrianized main street through the old town, c/J. M. **Quadrado** (though it goes under various names along its route). To the east of this intersection, it boasts a block of whitewashed, vaulted arches, **Ses Voltes**, distinctly Moorish in inspiration and a suitable setting for several attractive period shops and busy cafés. Carrer J. M. Quadrado then leads into **Plaça Nova**, a minuscule square edged by some of the most popular pavement-cafés in town. Nearby, off c/Sant Antoni, a narrow, balconied little street passes through arches where once ran the city wall – hence the name *Que no Passa* (The one that doesn't go through). Continuing east along c/Maó, you leave the cramped alleys of the old town at Plaça Alfons III, where a big old windmill, the **Molí d'es Comte**, accommodates a dreary museum explaining how the thing once worked, as well as a boisterous bar.

The Museu Molí d'es Comte is open Tues, Thurs & Sat 10am–1pm & 4–7pm; free. For details of Bar Es Molí, see p.212.

The Museu Municipal
From c/J. M. Quadrado near the junction with c/Seminari, a long, straight street, c/Santa Clara, shoots off north hemmed in by the walls of old aristocratic palaces. At the top is the convent of **Santa Clara**, a mundanely modern incarnation of a centuries-old foundation. In 1749, this was the site of a scandal that had tongues clacking from Ciutadella to Maó. During the night, three young women hopped over the convent wall and placed themselves under the protection of their British boyfriends. Even worse, as far as the local clergy were concerned, they wanted to turn Protestant and marry their men. In this delicate situation, Governor Blakeney had the room where the women were staying sealed up by a priest every night. But he refused to send them back to the convent and allowed the weddings to go ahead, thereby compounding a religious animosity – Catholic subject against Protestant master – which had begun in the days of Richard Kane.

Beyond, at the end of c/Portal de Sa Font, the **Museu Municipal** inhabits part of the old city fortifications, a massive honeysuckle-clad bastion overlooking a slender ravine that once had, until it was redirected, a river running along its base and into

The Museu Municipal is open Tues–Sat 10am–1pm & 7–9pm; free.

the harbour. Inside the museum, a long vaulted chamber is given over to a wide range of archeological finds, amongst which there's a substantial collection of Talayotic remains, featuring artefacts garnered from all over the island and covering the several phases of Talayotic civilization. These Bronze Age people moved from an initial period of agrarian colonization, through precarious times when they fortified their villages, to increasingly peaceful and commercial contacts with their neighbours. The earlier pieces, dating from around 1400 to 700 BC, include many examples of crudely crafted beakers and saucers. Later work – down to around 120 BC – reveals a far greater degree of sophistication, both in terms of kitchenware, with urns and amphoras particularly common, and weaponry, notably several finely chiselled arrowheads. From this later period comes most of the jewellery, whose fine detail and miniature size reveal a marked Carthaginian influence. A leaflet detailing the exhibits in English is available free at reception. Temporary exhibitions take place downstairs.

The Castell de Sant Nicolau is open Mon–Sat 7.30pm–9.30pm free.

The Castell de Sant Nicolau

West from Plaça d'es Born, Camí de Sant Nicolau runs along the northern edge of Plaça S'Esplanada and reaches, after about fifteen minutes' walk, the **Castell de Sant Nicolau**. This seventeenth-century watchtower is a dinky little thing, equipped with a drawbridge, oil holes and turrets, all stuck on unwelcoming rocks. The interior, however, is disappointingly bare and, indeed, is only open in the evening, when people visit to watch the sun set out beyond Mallorca.

Eating, drinking and nightlife

For an early **breakfast** make your way to the *mercat* on Plaça Llibertat, where a couple of simple cafés serve coffee and fresh pastries. Later in the day, aim for c/J. M. Quadrado, which is jam-packed with tiny **café-bars** offering reasonably priced snacks and light meals. More ambitious and expensive food is available at a string of excellent **restaurants** down by the harbourside, or at several good places tucked away near Plaça d'es Born.

People don't come to Ciutadella for the **nightlife**. There are a few late-night bars, mostly down by the harbour, though this is very much a tourist zone. If you want the flavour of the town, you're better off nursing a drink and watching the early-evening crowds on, or in the vicinity of, Plaça Nova.

Cafés and bars

Bar El Arco, Plaça Nova 17. One of several pleasant, and largely indistinguishable, café-bars on this tiny square.

Bar Es Moli, Camí de Maó 1. Big and attractive café-bar, with a young crowd, in the old windmill across the street from Plaça Alfons III. Open late at night for some serious drinking.

Bar Sa Clau, c/Marina. Busy and polished bar at the foot of the steps linking the harbour with the old town. Open till late.

Bar Ulises, Plaça Llibertat. No-frills café-bar next to the market. Their *ensaimadas*, a snip at 200ptas each, are probably the best in town.

Café Balear, c/Marina. Popular and attractive spot for a drink, but don't expect too much from the *tapas*. Down on the harbourside near the bridge.

Café Central, Plaça Catedral. Busy little place next to the cathedral's main entrance, serving traditional Menorcan *tapas*, including various sausages and cheeses.

Cafeteria Ses Voltes, c/J. M. Quadrado 22. Reasonably tasty and inexpensive snacks and light meals, at a down-to-earth eatery in the town centre.

Pastelería Mol, c/Roser 2. Delicious takeaway pizza slices and mouthwatering cakes from this little pastry shop off Plaça Catedral.

La Torre de Papel, Camí de Maó 46. The most urbane coffee house in town, all polished wood floors, with a bookshop at the front, and a tiny terrace café at the back.

Restaurants

El Bribón, c/Marina 115. Excellent harbourside restaurant specializing in Menorcan cuisine: substantial and delicious *tapas* from as little as 900ptas; 1700ptas for the *menú del día*. Next door to *Casa Manolo*.

Casa Manolo, c/Marina 117. Fabulous seafood, with main courses averaging around 2500ptas, at the end of the long line of restaurants flanking the south side of the harbour.

Ca's Quinto, Plaça Alfons III, 3. Open all day for both *tapas* and full meals, with the emphasis on traditional Menorcan cuisine. Next to the ring road on the eastern edge of the old town.

Sa Figuera, c/Marina 99. Flashy harbourside restaurant serving a wide range of quality seafood dishes, including *caldereta de langosta* for 5000ptas.

El Horno, c/Forn 10. French-style basement restaurant, where the food is good and reasonably priced. Near the northeast corner of Plaça d'es Born. Evenings only.

Oristano, c/Sant Rafel 10. Tasty pizzas at easy-to-afford prices, near the top of the steps leading down to the harbour.

La Payesa, c/Marina 65. Chic restaurant where the menu is wide-ranging and the seafood is usually a treat.

Racó d'es Palau, c/Palau 35. Comfortable spot with low, beamed ceilings off c/Major del Born. A good *menú del día* costs just 1100ptas, pizzas from around 700ptas.

Listings

Banks *Banco de Credito Balear*, c/J. M. Quadrado 3; *Banca March*, Plaça d'es Born 10.

Bicycle and moped rental *Bicicletas Tolo*, c/Sant Isidre 28, off Plaça Artrutx (☎381576).

Car rental Ciutadella has about 20 car rental firms, almost all of them small local companies. Amongst these are *Friend Cars*, Plaça d'es Born 27 (☎386067), and *Motos Genestar*, near the main bus station at c/Barcelona 24 (☎382282). There's also an *Avis* outlet on the ring road at Avgda Jaume el Conqueridor 81 (☎381174).

Emergencies *Creu Roja* (Red Cross) for an **ambulance** ☎361180; **firefighters** ☎351011; **police** (*Policia Municipal*) ☎092.

Ferries and hydrofoils Tickets can be purchased direct from the ferry line, *Flebasa* (☎480012), whose kiosk is down by the harbour next to the jetty.

You can't make advance reservations for your vehicle (so turn up early) and neither can you take rental cars from island to island.

Maps and books Both *Punt i Apart*, c/Roser 14, and *Libreria Pau*, c/Nou Juliol 11, have a good selection of travel books, general maps and Menorcan walking maps (*IGN* and *Mapa Militar*). They also have limited supplies of the best guides for walkers, Dodo Mackenzie's series of pamphlets which detail a wide variety of Menorcan hikes.

Pharmacies Amongst several downtown options, there's one at c/J. M. Quadrado 15.

Post office The central *correus* is on Plaça d'es Born (Mon–Fri 8.30am– 2.30pm, Sat 9.30am–1pm).

Taxis There are taxi ranks on Plaça d'es Born and Plaça Alfons III. Alternatively, telephone *Radio Taxis* (☎382896).

Around Ciutadella

The pristine cove beaches southeast of Ciutadella make delightful day trips, particularly beautiful **Cala En Turqueta**, though you do have to negotiate rough country tracks to get there. East of town, on the road to Maó, you could also consider the quick excursion to the **Naveta d'es Tudons**, the most complete prehistoric monument of its type on the island, or make a short jaunt northeast to the exclusive villa-village of **Cala Morell**, which occupies a singularly bleak and barren cove. Entirely different is the intensively developed west coast, where long lines of villas carpet the flat and treeless seashore on either side of Ciutadella, from Cala En Forcat in the north to the Cap d'Artrutx, 14km away to the south. By and large, this is all pretty dreadful – especially to the north of town in the dreary *urbanitzacions* of Cala En Blanes, Los Delfines and Cala En Forcat, and in the far south where interminable Tamarinda is ugly and dull in equal measure. Here and there, however, the villas bunch round a narrow cove to form reasonably pleasant resorts: amongst these, **Cala Santandría** and neighbouring **Cala Blanca** possess a fair degree of charm, sandy beaches and several comfortable hotels.

Buses leave Plaça S'Esplanada in Ciutadella for the tourist settlements of the west coast hourly. There are no services from town northeast towards Cala Morell or southeast towards Cala En Turqueta; buses to Maó pass by the Naveta d'es Tudons regularly, but check with the driver before you depart that he is prepared to stop there.

South along the coast from Ciutadella

After a couple of kilometres, the asphalt main road running south from Ciutadella skirts CALA SANTANDRÍA, where a jangle of high-rises dominates the rocky shoreline. At the back of the long, slender inlet lies a band of bright white sand, and the sheltered waters provide safe swimming, though sometimes the place gets too crowded for comfort. Pedaloes and sunbeds can be rented and there are a handful of beach bars. The *Ses Voltes* is the best hotel here, its forty comfortably modern bedrooms occupying a splendid position overlooking the inlet (April–Oct; ☎380400; ⑤). The much bigger *Prinsotel La Caleta*, one of the few hotels on Menorca to open all year, is also a pleasant place to stay, with modern, air-conditioned and balconied bedrooms overlooking the beach from the north (☎385911; ⑥).

A further 2km south along the coast is **CALA BLANCA**, where low limestone seacliffs frame a narrow cove and its small beach. Here too, the swimming is safe and pedaloes can be hired. For somewhere to stay, there's little to choose between a trio of sky-rise hotels, but the *Riu Mediterrani* probably just has the edge, with spacious balconied and air-conditioned rooms just footsteps away from the beach (☎384203; ⑦). In both Cala Santandría and Cala Blanca, most visitors eat wherever they stay, but it's worth trying the *Grill Es Caliu*, beside the main road in between the two, a big, popular place which serves delicious charcoal-grilled meats.

From Cala Blanca, the main road continues for 5km to the utterly dreary resort of Tamarinda.

Southeast of Ciutadella

The cross-country routes running **southeast from Ciutadella** to the remote coves of the south coast begin in town at Plaça Jaume II, just off the ring road. From here, head southeast along Camí Sant Joan de Missa; after about 4km, just beyond the farm of Son Vivó, the road branches into two seven-kilometre-long tracks which both lead through leafy countryside to unspoiled beaches. The going gets rougher, and the routes harder to discern, as you approach the south coast, so if you've hired a moped be prepared for a bumpy ride and watch out for the dust and muck churned up by passing cars.

The prime objective along the more easterly track is **Cala En Turqueta**, a lovely cove backed by wooded limestone cliffs. The beach, a sheltered horseshoe of white sand, slopes gently into the sea, making ideal conditions for bathing. There are no facilities, and it's most unusual to find a crowd, though boat trips do occasionally drop by in the afternoon. To get there, continue for around 2.5km beyond the Son Vivó fork, past the hermitage of Sant Joan de Missa, until you reach a junction; veer right along the Camí de Son Camaró and keep going to the end of the road at the farm of Sant Francesc, where the gate is usually locked; park here, clamber over the wall, and follow the track for the last 1km down to the beach.

The rather rougher, westerly track from the Son Vivó fork runs past **Son Catlar**, the largest prehistoric settlement on Menorca, though its scattered and largely incomprehensible remains are not especially diverting. Key features of the site are the battered remains of five *talayots* and 800m of rampart, exhibiting both Talayotic and classical workmanship. About 2.5km beyond Son Catlar skirt to the left of the fortified farmhouse of Torre Saura

along a rough, unsurfaced track; some 700m further on, keep right
at the junction and press on to the coast, opening and closing the
gates as you proceed. From the end of the track, it's a short walk to
the twin beaches of **Platges Son Saura**, a beautiful and – except on
summer weekends – sparsely populated spot, whose bright white
sands fringe a pine-clad, semicircular cove.

East of Ciutadella

The best-preserved *naveta* on the island, the **Naveta d'es
Tudons**, can be found to the **east of Ciutadella**, 6km along the
C721, then five minutes' walk from the roadside car park. Seven
metres high and fourteen long, the structure is made of massive,
stone blocks slotted together in a sophisticated dry-stone tech-
nique. The narrow entrance on the west side leads into a small
antechamber, which was once sealed off by a stone slab; beyond
lies the main chamber where the bones of the dead were stashed
away after the flesh had been removed. Folkloric memories of the
navetas' original purpose survived into modern times, for the
Menorcans were loathe to go near these odd-looking and solitary
monuments well into the eighteenth century. If your enthusiasm
for prehistory has been fired, you might consider extending your
trip to take in **Torrellafuda**, 3km east of the Naveta d'es Tudons
car park. A signposted dirt trail (beginning 300m west of the
37km marker stone) leads through a farm to reach, after 700m,
the scattered remains of the settlement, principally a *talayot*,
bits and pieces of a rampart and, hidden away in a copse, a
broken *taula*.

Northeast of Ciutadella

To the **northeast of Ciutadella**, and signposted from the ring road,
a well-surfaced country lane carves across a pastoral landscape
towards **CALA MORELL**, 8km from town at the end of a bumpy
side road. This small tourist settlement is one of the more refined
urbanitzacions, its streets – named in Latin after the constellations
– hugging a narrow and rocky bay. Besides swimming off the gritty
beach, you can visit some of the man-made caves for which Cala
Morell is noted, visible beside the road as you approach the village.
Dating from the late Bronze and Iron Ages, the caves form one of
the largest prehistoric necropolises known and are surprisingly
sophisticated, with central pillars supporting the roofs, and, in some
instances, windows cut into the rock and classical designs carved in
relief.

Back on the country lane, about 4km beyond the Cala Morell
turning, the road reaches a guarded gate where the landowner levies
500ptas for the one-kilometre onward drive down to **Cala de
Algaiarens**. Backed by attractive dunes and pine forests, the two
sandy cove beaches here offer excellent swimming in sheltered
waters.

Travel details

Details of ferries, hydrofoils and flights to Menorca are given in *Basics*.

Buses

From **Ciutadella** to: Alaior (Mon–Sat 6 daily, 4 on Sun; 40min); Cala En Forcat (hourly; 20min); Es Mercadal (Mon–Sat 6 daily, 4 on Sun; 30min); Ferreries (Mon–Sat 8 daily, 5 on Sun; 20min); Maó (Mon–Sat 6 daily, 4 on Sun; 1hr); Santandría (hourly; 10min); Sant Tomás (Mon–Fri 1 daily; 40min); Tamarinda (hourly; 15min).

From **Ferreries** to: Alaior (Mon–Sat 6 daily, 4 on Sun; 20min); Cala Santa Galdana (6 daily; 35min); Ciutadella (Mon–Sat 8 daily, 5 on Sun; 20min); Es Mercadal (Mon–Sat 6 daily, 4 on Sun; 10min); Maó (Mon–Sat 6 daily, 4 on Sun; 40min).

From **Fornells** to: Es Mercadal (Mon–Fri 1 daily; 15min); Maó (1–2 daily; 35min).

From **Maó** to: Alaior (Mon–Sat 11 daily, 9 on Sun; 20min); Cala d'Alcaufar (6 daily; 25min); Arenal d'En Castell (1–2 daily; 20min); Cala En Porter (7 daily; 25min); Ciutadella (Mon–Sat 6 daily, 4 on Sun; 1hr); Es Castell (every 30min; 10min); Es Mercadal (Mon–Sat 6 daily, 4 on Sun; 30min); Ferreries (Mon–Sat 6 daily, 4 on Sun; 40min); Fornells (1–2 daily; 35min); Punta Prima (hourly; 20min); Sant Lluís (hourly; 10min); Sant Tomás (Mon–Sat 1 daily; 35min); Cala Santa Galdana (1–2 daily; 1hr); Son Bou (5 daily; 35min); Son Parc (1–2 daily; 35min).

Contexts

A history of Mallorca and Menorca

Earliest peoples

The earliest inhabitants of the Balearics seem to have reached the islands from the Iberian peninsula, and carbon-dating of remains from both Menorca and Mallorca indicates that human occupation was well established by 4000 BC. The discovery of pottery, flint tools and antelope horns fashioned into tools suggests that these early people were **neolithic pastoralists**, who supplemented their food supplies by hunting, particularly the now-extinct Balearic mountain antelope.

Why, or how, these peoples moved to the islands is unknown. Indeed, the first landfall may have been accidental, made by early seafarers travelling along the shores of the Mediterranean – part of the wave of migration that is known to have taken place in the neolithic period. Many of the oldest archeological finds have been discovered in natural **caves**, where it seems likely these early settlers first sought shelter and protection. Later, cave complexes were dug out of the soft limestone that occurs on both islands, comprising living quarters, usually circular and sometimes with a domed ceiling, as well as longer, straighter funerary chambers; the best example is at **Cales Coves**, near Cala En Porter, on Menorca, a complex which contains no less than 145 excavated chambers.

The Mediterranean Sea, with its relatively calm and tide-free waters, has always acted as a conduit of civilization, and so regular contact with other cultures was inevitable in the Balearics. The discovery of Beaker ware at Deià, in Mallorca, indicates one of the earliest of these cultural influences. The **Beaker People**, whose artefacts have been found right across Western Europe, are named after their practice of burying their dead with pottery beakers. They had knowledge of the use of bronze, an alloy of copper and tin, a skill which they introduced to the islanders. The arrival of bronze-working, at around 1400 BC, marked the end of the Balearic Cave Culture and the beginning of the Talayotic period.

The Talayotic period

The megalithic remains of the **Talayotic period**, which extended almost to the Christian era, are strewn all over Mallorca and more particularly Menorca – though, surprisingly, there's no evidence of them on Ibiza. The structure which gives its name to the period is the **talayot** (from *atalaya*, Arabic for "watchtower"), a cone-shaped tower with a circular base, between five and ten metres in height, built without mortar or cement. There are literally hundreds of *talayots* on Mallorca and Menorca and the detail of their design varies from site to site: some are solid, others contain one or more chambers; most are found in settlements, but there are solitary examples too. This diversity has helped to generate considerable debate about their original purpose, with scholars suggesting variously that they were built for defence, as dwellings for chieftains, as burial sites or as storehouses. The mystery of the *talayots* is compounded by their unusualness. The only Mediterranean structures they resemble are the Nuragh towers found on Sardinia. A Sardinian connection would support the view that this phase in the Balearics' development was the result of contact with other cultures, though Egypt,

Crete and Greece have also been touted as possible influences. Whatever the origins, it is clear that by 1000 BC a relatively sophisticated, largely pastoral society had developed on Mallorca and Menorca, with at least some of the islanders occupying walled settlements, like **Capocorp Vell**, south of Llucmajor on Mallorca, where you can still inspect four *talayots* and the remains of up to thirty houses, and **Ses Paisses**, a settlement of comparable proportions outside Artà.

Talayotic culture reached its highest level of development on Menorca, and here you'll find the most enigmatic remains of the period. These are the **taulas** ("tables" in Catalan), T-shaped structures standing as high as four metres and consisting of two massive dressed stones. Their purpose is unknown, though many theories have been advanced. One early nineteenth-century writer suggested that they were altars used for human sacrifice. Unfortunately for this lurid theory, however, the height of most *taulas* makes it very unlikely. Other writers have noted that many *taulas* are surrounded by enclosures and have argued that the "T" formed the centre of a roofed structure, thatched in some way. Another theory is that the "T" was a stylized head of a bull, an animal that was venerated in many parts of the ancient Mediterranean, most notably in Crete. That these enclosures had a religious purpose is supported by Professor Fernandez Mirando's excavations of the *taula* enclosure of **Torralba d'En Salort**. There he found animal remains and pottery in side recesses of fireplaces, and concluded that these must have been ritual offerings. He also found a bronze sculpture of a bull, suggesting that cattle were, indeed, worshipped.

The other distinctive structure to be found on Menorca is the **naveta**. Referring to its resemblance to the upturned hull of a boat, the name was first given to the **Naveta d'es Tudons**, near Ciutadella, which was built at the beginning of the Talayotic period. Like the other thirty-five *navetas* on the island it was a collective tomb, or, more correctly, an ossuary. The bones of the dead, once the flesh had been removed, were placed in the *navetas* along with some personal possessions such as jewellery, pottery and bone buttons. Several Talayotic settlements have also survived in relatively good condition, primarily Menorca's **Talatí de Dalt**, which incorporates a *talayot*, a *taula* and several columned chambers or hypostyles. Partly dug out of the ground and roofed with massive slabs of stone, these hypostyles must have taken considerable effort to build, and would have been used for important gatherings, possibly of communal leaders. Dating from around 1400 BC, Talatí de Dalt, like other Menorcan settlements of this time, was occupied well into the Roman period.

Phoenicians, Greeks and Carthaginians

Fearful of attack from the sea, the Talayotic peoples of Mallorca and Menorca built their walled settlements a few kilometres inland. This pattern was, however, modified during the first millennium BC when the islands became a staging post for the **Phoenicians**, maritime traders from the eastern Mediterranean whose long voyages reached as far as Cornwall for supplies of tin. According to the Roman historian Pliny, the Phoenicians established the settlement of Sanisera on Menorca's north coast, and archeologists have discovered Phoenician artefacts at **Alcúdia** on Mallorca. In general, however, very few Phoenician remains have been found on the Balearics – just a handful of bronze items and pieces of coloured glass.

The Phoenicians were displaced by **Greeks** from around 800 BC, as several city-states explored the western Mediterranean in search of trade and potential colonies. Like the Phoenicians, the Greeks appear to have used the Balearics primarily as a staging post, for no Greek buildings have survived either on Mallorca or on Menorca – which the Greeks called *Meloussa*, "Cattle Island", an indication of the preoccupations of its inhabitants. The absence of metal apparently made the islands unsuitable for long-term colonization, and the belligerence of the native population may have played a part too: the Greeks coined another name for the islands, the **Balearics**, which they derived from *ballein*, meaning "to throw from a sling". The islanders were adept at this form of warfare, and many early visitors were repelled with showers of polished sling-stones. Some historians dispute this theory, claiming rather that the name comes from the Baleri tribe of Sardinia.

The Greeks were also discouraged from colonization by the growth of the **Carthaginian** empire across the western Mediterranean. The Phoenicians had established Carthage, on the North African coast, under the leadership of the princess Elissa, better known as Dido, the tragic hero of Virgil's Aeneid. According to the Greek historian Diodurus Siculus, the Carthaginians began to colonize the Balearics in the early seventh century BC, and certainly by the beginning of the third century BC, the islands were firmly under their control. Little is known of the Carthaginian occupation except that they established several new settlements, including Jamma (Ciutadella) and Maghen (Maó). It is also claimed that the famous Carthaginian general, Hannibal, was born on Mallorca, though Ibiza and Malta claim this honour too.

In the third century BC, the expansion of the Carthaginian empire across the Mediterranean and up the Iberian Peninsula precipitated the first two **Punic Wars** with Rome. In both of these wars the Balearics proved extremely valuable, firstly as stepping stones from the North African coast to the European mainland and secondly as a source of mercenaries. Balearic slingers were highly valued and accompanied Hannibal and his elephants across the Alps in the Second Punic War, when (for reasons that remain obscure) the islanders refused gold and demanded payment in wine and women instead. After Hannibal's defeat by the Romans at the battle of Zama in 202 BC, Carthaginian power began to wane and they withdrew from Mallorca and Menorca, although they continued to have some influence over Ibiza for at least another seventy years.

Romans, Vandals and Byzantines

As the Carthaginians retreated so the **Romans** advanced, incorporating Ibiza within their empire after the final victory over Carthage in 146 BC. On Mallorca and Menorca, the islanders took advantage of the prolonged military chaos to profit from piracy, until finally, in 123 BC, the Romans, led by the consul Quintus Metellus, restored maritime order by occupying both islands. These victories earnt Metellus the title "Balearico" from the Roman senate and the islands were given new names, Balearis Major (Mallorca) and Balearis Minor (Menorca).

For the next five hundred years the Balearics were part of the **Roman empire**. Amongst many developments, Roman colonists introduced viticulture, turning the Balearics into a wine-exporting area, and initiated olive oil production from newly planted groves. As was their custom, the Romans consolidated their control of the islands by building roads and establishing towns: on Mallorca they founded Pollentia (Alcúdia) in the northeast and Palmaria on the south coast, near the site of modern Palma; on Menorca, Port Magnum (Maó) was developed as an administrative centre. Initially, the Balearics were part of the Roman province of Tarraconensis (Tarragona), but in 404 AD the islands became a province in their own right with the name Balearica.

By this time, however, the Roman empire was in decline, its defences unable to resist the westward-moving tribes of central Asia. One of these tribes, the **Vandals**, swept across the Balearics in around 425 AD, thereby ending Roman rule. So thorough going was the destruction they wrought that very few signs of the Romans have survived - the only significant remains are those of Pollentia.

Christianity had taken root in the Balearics during the Roman occupation. The Vandals had themselves been Christianized long before they reached the Mediterranean, but they were followers of what was denounced as the **Arian** heresy. This interpretation of Christianity, founded by Arius, an Alexandrian priest, insisted that Christ the Son and God the Father were two distinct figures, not elements of the Trinity, along with the Holy Ghost. To orthodox Christians this seemed dangerously close to the pagan belief in a multiplicity of gods. Arianism had largely been eliminated within the Roman empire by the end of the fourth century AD, but Arian missionaries had enjoyed considerable success converting the Germanic peoples outside the empire. Armed with their "heretical" beliefs, the Vandals subjected the orthodox islanders to severe persecution and destroyed their churches. As a consequence, only a handful of Christian remains from this period have survived, most notably the ruins of the basilica at **Son Bou**, Menorca.

In 533 the Vandals were defeated in North Africa by the Byzantine general, Count Belisarius (who was the subject of a novel by one of Mallorca's adopted sons, Robert Graves). This brought the Balearics under **Byzantine** rule and, for a time, restored prosperity and stability. However, the islands were too far removed from Constantinople to be of much imperial importance and, when the empire was threatened from the east at the end of the seventh century, they were abandoned in all but name.

The Moors

As the influence of Byzantium receded, so militant Islam moved in from the south and east to fill the power vacuum. In 707-8 the **Moors** of

North Africa conducted an extended raid against Mallorca, destroying its entire fleet and carrying away slaves and booty. By 716 the Balearics' position had become even more vulnerable with the completion of the Moorish conquest of Spain. In 798 the Balearics were again sacked by the Moors – who were still more interested in plunder than settlement – and in desperation the islanders appealed for help to **Charlemagne**, the Frankish Holy Roman Emperor. As emperor, Charlemagne was the military – the Pope the spiritual – leader of Western Christendom, so the appeal signified the final severance of the Balearics' links with Byzantium.

Charlemagne's attempt to protect the islands from the Moors met with some success, but the respite was only temporary. By the middle of the ninth century, the Christian position had deteriorated so badly that the Balearics were compelled to enter a non-aggression pact with the Moors, and to add to the islanders' woes, the Balearics suffered a full-scale Viking raid in 859. Finally, at the beginning of the tenth century, the **Emir of Cordoba** conquered both Menorca and Mallorca. Moorish rule lasted over three hundred years, though internal political divisions among the Muslims meant that the islands experienced several different regimes. In the early eleventh century, the emirate of Cordoba collapsed and control passed to the Wali (governor) of Denia, on the Spanish mainland. This administration allowed the Christians – who were known as **Mozarabs** – to practise their faith, and the islands prospered from their position at the heart of the trade routes between North Africa and Islamic Spain.

In 1085 the Balearics became an independent emirate with a new dynasty of *walis*, from **Amortadha**, who pursued a more aggressive foreign and domestic policy, raiding the towns of the mainland and persecuting their Christian citizens. These actions, however, blighted trade and thereby enraged the emergent city-states of Italy at a time when Christendom was fired by crusading zeal. Anticipating retaliation, the Amortadhas fortified Palma, which was known at this time as Medina Mayurka, and other principal towns. The Christian attack came in 1114 when a grand Italian fleet – led by the ships of Pisa and supported by the Pope as a mini-crusade – landed an army of 70,000 Catalan and Italian soldiers on Ibiza. The island was soon captured, but Mallorca, the crusaders' next target, proved a

much more difficult proposition. Medina Mayurka's landward lines of defence had to be overcome separately in a number of bloody engagements, the coastal defences proving impregnable. When the city finally fell, most of the surviving Muslim population was slaughtered. Despite their victory, however, the Christians had neither the will nor the resources to consolidate their position and, loading their vessels with freed slaves and loot, they returned home.

It took the Moors just two years to re-establish themselves on the islands, this time under the leadership of the **Almoravids**, a North African Berber tribe who had previously controlled southern Spain. The Almoravids proved to be tolerant and progressive rulers, their most distinguished emir a certain Abu Ibrahim-Ashak (1152–85). The Balearics prospered: agriculture improved, particularly through the development of irrigation, and trade expanded as commercial agreements were struck with the Italian cities of Genoa and Pisa. The Pisans, Crusaders earlier in the century, defied a papal ban on trade with Muslims to finalize the deal – consciences could, it seems, be flexible even in the "devout" Middle Ages, when access to the precious goods of the east (silks, carpets and spices) was the prize.

Jaume I and the Reconquest

In 1203 the Almoravids were supplanted by the **Almohad** dynasty, who forcibly converted the islands' Christian population to Islam and started raiding the mainland. This was an extraordinary miscalculation as the kingdoms of Aragón and Catalunya had only recently been united, changing the regional balance of power, at a time when the momentum of the *Reconquista* was picking up right across Spain. In 1228 the Emir of Mallorca antagonized the young **King Jaume I** of Aragón and Catalunya by seizing a couple of his ships. The king's advisers, with their eyes firmly fixed on the wealth of the Balearics, determined to capitalize on the offence. They organized the first Balearic publicity evening, a feast at which the king was presented with a multitude of Mallorcan delicacies and Catalan sailors told of the islands' prosperity. And so, insulted by the emir and persuaded by his nobility, Jaume I committed himself to the invasion that was to end Moorish rule in the Balearics.

Jaume's expedition of 150 ships, 16,000 men and 1500 horses set sail for Mallorca in September 1229. The king had originally planned to land at Pollença, in the northeast, but adverse weather conditions forced the fleet further south, and it eventually anchored off Sant Elm. The following day, the Catalans defeated the Moorish forces sent to oppose the landing and Jaume promptly moved on to lay siege to Medina Mayurka. It took three months to breach the walls, but on December 31 the city finally fell and Jaume was hailed as "El Conqueridor".

The cost of launching an invasion on this scale placed an enormous strain on the resources of a medieval monarch. With this in mind, Jaume subcontracted the capture of Ibiza, entering into an agreement, in 1231, with the Crown Prince of Portugal, Don Pedro, and the Count of Roussillon. In return for the capture of the island, the count and the prince were to be allowed to divide Ibiza between themselves, provided they acknowledged the suzerainty of Jaume. This project initially faltered, but was revived with the addition of the Archbishop of Tarragona. The three barons captured Ibiza in 1235 and divided the spoils, although Don Pedro waived his rights and his share passed to Jaume.

In the meantime, Jaume had acquired the overlordship of Menorca. Unable to afford another full-scale invasion, the king devised a clever ruse. In 1232 he returned to Mallorca with just three galleys, which he dispatched to Menorca carrying envoys, while he camped out in the mountains above Capdepera, on Mallorca. As night fell and his envoys negotiated with the enemy, Jaume ordered the lighting of as many bonfires as possible to illuminate the sky and give the impression of a vast army. The ruse worked and the next day, mindful of the blood-bath of the invasion of Mallorca, the Menorcan Moors capitulated, informing the envoys – according to the king's own account – that "they gave great thanks to God and to me for the message I had sent them for they knew well they could not long defend themselves against me". The terms of submission were generous: the Moors handed over Ciutadella and a number of other strongpoints, but Jaume acknowledged the Muslims as his subjects and appointed one of their leaders as his *rais* (governor).

This retention of Moorish government, albeit under the suzerainty of the king, was in marked contrast to events on Mallorca. Here, the land was divided into eight blocks, with four passing to the king and the rest to his most trusted followers, who leased their holdings in the feudal fashion, granting land to tenants in return for military service. In 1230 Jaume issued the **Carta de Poblacio** (People's Charter), guaranteeing equality before the law, a very progressive precept for the period. Mallorca was exempted from taxation to encourage Catalan immigration, and special rights were given to Jews resident on the island, a measure designed to stimulate trade. Twenty years later, Jaume also initiated a distinctive form of government for Mallorca, with a governing body of six **jurats** (adjudicators) – one from the nobility, two knights, two merchants and one peasant. At the end of each year the *jurats* elected their successors. This form of government remained in place until the sixteenth century.

From a modern perspective, the downside of the Reconquest in Mallorca was the wholesale demolition of almost all Moorish buildings, with mosques systematically replaced by churches (at a later date the same policy was followed on Menorca). The main compensation is the architectural magnificence of **Palma Cathedral**, which was consecrated in 1269. Shortly afterwards, Jaume I died at Valencia. In his will he divided his kingdom between his two sons: Pedro received Catalunya, Aragón and Valencia, whilst Jaume was bequeathed Montpellier, Roussillon and the Balearics. Jaume II was crowned in Mallorca on September 12, 1276.

The Kingdom of Mallorca

Jaume I's division of his kingdom infuriated **Pedro**, as Mallorca stood astride the shipping route between Barcelona and Sicily, where his wife was queen. He forced his brother to become his vassal, but in response Jaume II secretly schemed with the French. When Pedro discovered this treachery, he promptly attacked his brother's territories, but died before the planned assault on Mallorca could be launched. Pedro's son, **Alfonso III**, carried out the invasion plans and, late in 1285, his army speedily captured Palma. Other strongholds, especially Alaró (see p.103), held out for longer; when he finally managed to take them, Alfonso brutally vented his frustation on their defenders. For his atrocities, the king was excommunicated by the Pope for a brief period.

When Mallorca was secured and Jaume deposed, Alfonso turned his attention to Menorca where he suspected the loyalty of the Moorish governor: rumour had it that the *rais* was in conspiratorial contact with the Moors of North

Africa. Alfonso's army landed on Menorca in January 1287 and decisively defeated the Moors just outside Maó; the whole island surrendered four days later. The king's treatment of the vanquished islanders was savage: those Muslims who were unable to buy their freedom were enslaved, and those who couldn't work as slaves – the old, the sick and the very young – were taken to sea and thrown overboard by the boatload. Alfonso rewarded the nobles who had accompanied him with grants of land and brought in hundreds of Catalan settlers. The capital, Medina Minurka, was renamed **Ciutadella**, and the island's mosques were converted to Christian usage, before being demolished and replaced.

Alfonso's brutal career was cut short by his death in 1291 at the age of 25. He was succeeded by his brother, Jaume, who was king of Sicily. A more temperate man, Jaume conducted negotiations through the Papacy that eventually led, in 1298, to the restoration of the partition envisaged by Jaume I: he himself presided over Catalunya, Aragón and Valencia, while his exiled uncle, **Jaume II**, ruled as king of Mallorca. Restored to the crown, Jaume II devoted a great deal of time to improving the commerce and administration of the Balearics. To stimulate trade, he established a weekly market in Palma, reissued the currency in gold and silver, and founded eleven towns in inland Mallorca, including Manacor, Felanitx, Llucmajor and Binissalem.

Jaume II attended to God as well as Mammon, and this period saw the building of many churches and monasteries. The king patronized the Mallorcan poet, scholar and Franciscan Friar, **Ramon Llull** (see p.72), providing him with the finance to establish a monastic school near Valldemossa. Jaume also established new settlements on Menorca – most notably Alaior – and divided the island into seven parishes, ordering the construction of churches for each of them. Perhaps his most important act, though, was to grant Menorca its own Carta de Poblacio, which bestowed the same legal rights as the Mallorcans enjoyed.

On his death in 1311 Jaume was succeeded by his son, **Sancho**, who spent most of his time in the mountains – he is thought to have been asthmatic – in the palace of Valldemossa. The new monarch continued with the successful economic policies of his father, whilst, internationally, he worked hard to avoid entanglement in the antag-

onism between Aragón and France. He also built up his fleet to protect the islands from North African pirates. Sancho died without issue in 1324 and, theoretically, the islands should have passed to the crown of Aragón. The Balearic nobility, however, crowned Sancho's ten-year-old nephew as **Jaume III** and, to forestall Aragonese hostility, had him rapidly betrothed to the king of Aragón's five-year-old daughter.

In the long term this marriage did Jaume III little good. After he came of age, his relations with his brother-in-law, Pedro IV of Aragón, quickly deteriorated, and Pedro successfully invaded the Balearics in response to an alleged plot that was hatching against him. Jaume fled to his mainland possessions and sold Montpellier to the French to raise money for an invasion. Having landed on Mallorca in 1349 however, he was defeated and killed, and his son captured. Although the uncrowned Jaume IV eventually escaped from prison, he was never able to drum up sufficient support to retake his throne from the Aragonese monarchy.

Unification with Spain

For a diversity of reasons the **unification** of the Balearics with Aragón – and their subsequent incorporation within Spain – proved a disaster. The mainland connection meant that the islands' nobility tended to gravitate towards the Aragonese court, regarding their local estates as little more than sources of income to sustain their expensive lifestyles. The neglect and exploitation inherent in this arrangement led to an uprising on Mallorca in 1391. Crowds marched on Palma and massacred most of the Jewish population, mainly because many landowners had delegated their authority to Jewish agents. In Menorca, the discontent of the period was manifested in terms of rivalry between Ciutadella and Maó: for a decade from 1426 to 1436 there was intermittent warfare between the two, reflecting the mainland conflict between the Aragonese king, supported by Ciutadella, and his nobles, favoured by Maó.

Discontent was also fuelled by economic trends. After the fall of Constantinople to the Islamic Turks in 1453, the lucrative overland trade routes from the eastern Mediterranean to the Far East were blocked. Worse still as far as the Balearics were concerned, the Portuguese discovered the way around the Cape of Good Hope to the Indies and, in 1492, Columbus reached the

Americas. As a consequence, the focus of European trade moved from the Mediterranean to the Atlantic seaboard. Meanwhile, **Fernando of Aragón** married **Isabella of Castile** in 1479, thereby uniting the two largest kingdoms in Spain. This increased the tendency towards centralization, rendering the islands a remote provincial backwater – a trend compounded by a royal decree that forbade Catalunya and the Balearics from trading with the New World. By the start of the sixteenth century, the Balearics were starved of foreign currency and the islands' merchants had begun to leave, signalling a period of long-term **economic decline**.

These problems led to an **armed uprising** of Mallorcan peasants and artisans in 1521. Organized in a *germania*, or armed brotherhood, they seized control of Palma when their complaints about the neglectful nobility and the high rate of taxation fell on deaf ears. Resident nobles tried either to flee the island or to beat a hasty retreat to the safety of the Bellver or Alcúdia citadels; those who didn't move fast enough were slaughtered on the streets. A massacre of blue bloods also followed the fall of the Castell de Bellver three months later, though Alcúdia held out until relieved. It was a long wait: only in 1523 did the forces of authority return under the command of **Emperor Charles V**, king of Spain (he was the grandson of Fernando and Isabella) and Hapsburg Holy Roman Emperor – a powerful union of crowns that was to last until 1713. Charles negotiated generous terms for the surrender of Palma, but once in possession of the city, promptly broke the agreement and ordered the execution of five hundred of the rebels, who were duly drawn and quartered.

Mallorca witnessed other sixteenth-century horrors with the arrival of the **Holy Office of the Inquisition**. The Inquisitors focused their attention on the Jewish community, which had earlier been confined within the Palma ghetto, El Call. Many Mallorcan Jews chose the course of least resistance and converted to Christianity, but scores of others were burnt to death. As late as the 1970s, the descendants of the converts still formed a distinct group of gold- and silversmiths in Palma.

The Balearics were also troubled by the renewal of large-scale maritime raids from North Africa. This development was partly stimulated by the final expulsion of the Moors from Spain in 1492, and partly by the emergence of the Ottoman Turks as a Mediterranean superpower.

Muslim raiders ransacked Pollença (1531 and 1550), Alcúdia (1551), Valldemossa (1552), Andratx (1553) and Sóller (1561), attacks which are still commemorated each year by these communities. In 1535 the Ottoman admiral Kheir-el-Din, better known as **Barbarossa**, landed on Menorca, taking Maó after a three-day seige. Hundreds of Menorcans were enslaved and carted away, prompting Charles V to construct the fort of Sant Felip to guard the Maó harbour. A few years later, the Turks returned and sacked Ciutadella, taking a further three thousand prisoners. Muslim incursions continued until the seventeenth century, but fell off in frequency and intensity after the Turkish fleet was destroyed by a combined Italian and Spanish force at Lepanto in 1571.

British and French occupation

The Balearics' woes continued throughout the seventeenth century. Trade remained stagnant and the population declined, a sorry state of affairs that was exacerbated by internal tensions. In Palma, the Canavall and Canavant factions engaged in a long-running vendetta, while on Menorca there remained friction between the rival towns of Maó and Ciutadella. By the 1630s the population problem had become so critical that Philip IV exempted the islands from the levies that raised men for Spain's armies – though this gain was offset by the loss of 15,000 Mallorcans to the plague in 1652.

A new development was the regular appearance of **British** vessels in the Mediterranean, a corollary of Britain's increasing share of the region's seaborne trade and the Royal Navy's commitment to protect their country's merchantmen from Algerian pirates. The British first put into Maó harbour to take on water in 1621 and were impressed by this secure, deep-water anchorage. In 1664 Charles II of England formalized matters by instructing his ambassador to Spain to "request immediate permission for British ships to use Balearic ports and particularly Port Mahon". The Spanish king granted the request, and the advantages of using Port Mahon (Maó) were noted by a poetic British seaman, a certain John Baltharpe:

Good this same is upon Minork
For shipping very useful 'gainst the Turk.
The King of Spain doth to our King it lend,
As in the line above to that same end.

For a time the British were simply content to "borrow" Maó, but their expanding commercial interests prompted a yearning for a more permanent arrangement. It was the dynastic **War of the Spanish Succession**, fought over the vacant throne of Spain, which gave them their opportunity. A British force invaded Menorca in 1708 and, meeting tepid resistance, captured the island in a fortnight. Apart from the benefits of Maó harbour, Menorca was also an ideal spot from which to blockade the French naval base at Toulon, thereby preventing the union of the French Atlantic and Mediterranean fleets. Indeed, so useful was Menorca to the English that they negotiated its retention at the **Treaty of Utrecht**, which rounded off the War of the Spanish Succession in 1713.

The island's first British governor, **Sir Richard Kane**, was an energetic and capable man who strengthened Menorca as a military base, and worked hard at improving the administration of the island, civilian facilities and the local economy. He built the first road across the island from Maó to Ciutadella and introduced improved strains of seed and livestock. During the first forty years of British occupation, the production of wine, vegetables and chickens increased by 500 percent. Relations between the occupying power and the islanders were generally good – though the Catholic clergy no doubt found it difficult to stomach the instruction to "pray for His Britannic Majesty".

The first phase of British domination ended when the island was captured by the **French** in 1756 at the start of the **Seven Years War**. Admiral Byng was dispatched to assist the beleaguered British force, but after a lacklustre encounter with a French squadron, he withdrew leaving Menorca to its fate. Byng's indifferent performance cost him his life: he was court-martialled and executed for cowardice, prompting Voltaire's famous aphorism that the English shoot their admirals "pour encourager les autres". The new French governor built the township of Sant Lluís to house his Breton sailors, and once again, the Menorcans adjusted to the occupying power without too much difficulty. In 1763, Britain regained Menorca in exchange for the Philippines and Cuba, which it had captured from Spain during the war.

The **second period of British occupation** proved far less successful than the first. The governor from 1763 to 1774, General Johnston,

was an authoritarian and unpopular figure, who undermined the Menorcans' trust in the British. The crunch came in 1781 when, with Britain at war with both Spain and France, the Duc de Crillon landed on the island with a force of 8000 men. With a total of only 2692 men, the new British governor, General John Murray, withdrew to the fort of Sant Felip, where he was besieged for eight months. Succoured by the Menorcans, the Franco-Spanish army finally starved the British into submission; Murray's men were badly stricken with scurvy, and only 1120 survived. The third and final period of British rule ran from 1778 to 1802, when the island was occupied for its value as a naval base in the Napoleonic Wars. The British relinquished all claims to Menorca in favour of Spain under the terms of the Treaty of Amiens in 1802.

Meanwhile, Mallorca, lacking a harbour of any strategic importance, was having a far quieter time. The Mallorcans chose the wrong side in the War of the Spanish Succession – most of Spain favoured the French candidate, Philip of Anjou, but Catalunya and Mallorca preferred the Austrian archduke Charles, who was supported by Britain and the Netherlands. After Philip had won the war, the Mallorcans paid for their choice: the new king stripped the island of its title of kingdom and many of its historic rights were removed. For the rest of the eighteenth century, Mallorca was left untouched by the European conflicts that rippled around it, though there was one major change imposed by Madrid: Castilian replaced the local dialect of Catalan as the official language.

The nineteenth century and the Spanish Civil War

For both Menorca and Mallorca, the nineteenth century brought difficult times. Neglected outposts, the islands were extremely poor and subject to droughts, famines, and epidemics of cholera, bubonic plague and yellow fever. The islanders were preoccupied with the art of survival rather than politics, and stayed out of the Carlist wars between liberals against conservatives that bitterly divided the Spanish mainland. Many islanders emigrated, some to Algeria after it was acquired by the French in 1830, others to Florida and California. However, the use of Maó as a training base by the American navy between 1815 and 1826 brought the Menorcans some measure of economic relief.

Matters began to improve towards the end of the nineteenth century, when agriculture, particularly Mallorcan almond cultivation, boomed. Menorca developed a thriving export industry in footwear, largely as a result of the efforts of Don Jeronimo Cabrisas, a Menorcan who had made his fortune in Cuba, and supplied many of the boots worn by troops in World War I. Modern services, like gas and electricity, began to be installed and a regular steam packet link was established between the islands and the mainland. Around this time too, a **revival of Catalan culture**, led by the middle class of Barcelona, stirred the Mallorcan bourgeoisie. In Palma, Catalan novelists and poets were lauded, nationalist political groupings were formed, and the town was adorned with a series of magnificent *Modernista* buildings.

During the **Spanish Civil War** (1936-39), Mallorca and Menorca supported opposing sides. General Goded made Mallorca an important base for the fascists, but when General Bosch attempted to do the same on Menorca, his NCOs and men mutinied and, with the support of the civilian population, declared their support for the Republic. In the event – apart from a few bombing raids and an attempted Republican landing at Mallorca's Porto Cristo – the Balearics saw very little actual fighting. Nevertheless, the Menorcans were dangerously exposed towards the end of the war, when they were marooned as the last Republican stronghold. A peaceful conclusion was reached largely through the intervention of the British, who brokered the surrender of the island aboard HMS *Devonshire*. Franco's troops occupied Menorca in April 1939 and the *Devonshire* left with 450 Menorcan refugees.

Recent times

Since World War II the most significant development has been the emergence of **mass tourism** as the principal economic activity, though the islands' charms had been discovered by the privileged long before. Frédéric Chopin and George Sand spent the winter of 1838 at Valldemossa, and Edward VII and the German Kaiser cruised the Balearics before World War I. The high-water mark of this elitist tourist trade was reached in the 1930s when the Argentinian poet Adan Diehl opened the *Hotel Formentor*, overlooking the bay of Pollença. Diehl advertised the hotel in lights on the Eiffel Tower and attracted guests such as Edward VIII, the Aga Khan and Winston Churchill. From such small and privileged beginnings, the Balearics' tourist industry has mushroomed in the latter part of this century. In 1950 Mallorca had just one hundred registered hotels and boarding houses; by 1972 the total had risen to 1509. Menorca experienced a similar rate of growth: in 1961 the total number of tourists was only 1500, but by 1973 it had reached over half a million each year.

The pace of development accelerated after the death of Franco in 1975, thereby further strengthening the economies of Mallorca and Menorca. The Balearics now have one of the highest per capita incomes in Spain, twice that of Extremadura for instance, and in 1989 received nearly five million holidaymakers, compared to a resident population of just 700,000. For as 'ng as the islands remain popular holiday destinations, their economic future seems secure, though the Balearic government isn't resting on its laurels: aware of its somewhat tacky image, Mallorca, in particular, is doing its best to move upmarket, greening its resorts, imposing strict building controls and spending millions of pesetas refurbishing the older parts of Palma.

The Balearics have also benefited from the recent political restructuring of Spain. In 1978, just three years after Franco's death, the *Cortes* passed a new constitution, which reorganized the country on a more federal basis and allowed for the establishment of Autonomous Communities in the regions. In practice however, the demarcation of responsibilities between central and regional governments has proved problematic, leading to interminable wrangling, not least because the Socialists, who have been in power since 1983, have waivered in their commitment to decentralization. Nonetheless, the Balearics, constituted as the **Comunidad Autónoma de las Islas Baleares** in 1983, have used their new-found independence to assert the primacy of their native Catalan language – now the main language of education – and to exercise a tighter local control of their economy.

A chronology of Spanish history

C11th–5th BC	Phoenicians, Greeks and Celts invade Spain and intermingle with the native (Iberian) population.
C3rd BC	Carthaginians conquer southeast Spain, incorporating the region within their Mediterranean empire.
C3rd–2nd BC	Carthage and Rome wrestle for control of the Iberian Peninsula in the three Punic Wars. Rome wins all three and their final act is the destruction of Carthage (in present-day North Africa) in 146 BC.
C2nd BC	Spain becomes part of the Roman empire, its administrative capital established at Córdoba in 151 BC. The region's mines and granaries bring unprecedented prosperity, and roads, bridges and aqueducts are built to network the peninsula.
C1st AD	Christianity makes rapid progress across Roman Spain.
264–76	Barbarian tribes, the Franks and the Suevi, ravage the peninsula.
414	The Visigoths reach Spain and become the dominant military force, with their capital at Toledo.
711	Islamic Moors (Arabs and Berbers from North Africa) invade and conquer the Visigoths' kingdom in a whirlwind campaign that lasts just seven years. However, a Christian victory at the battle of Covadonga (722) halts the Moorish advance and leads to the creation of the kingdom of the Asturias – a Christian toehold south of the Pyrenees.
756	Abd ar-Rahman I proclaims the Emirate of Córdoba, confirming Moorish control over almost all of Spain.
778	The Holy Roman Emperor Charlemagne invades Spain from France, but is defeated. In the dash back across the Pyrenees, the Christian rearguard – led by Roland – is hacked to pieces at Roncesvalles, inspiring the epic poem the *Chanson de Roland*. Charlemagne's subsequent endeavours meet with more success and undermine Moorish control of Navarra and Catalunya.
C9th	The Christian kingdoms of Catalunya and Navarra are founded.
C10th–early 11th	The Emirate of Córdoba flourishes, its capital becoming the most prosperous and civilized city in Europe. Abd ar-Rahman III breaks with Baghdad to declare himself Caliph of an independent western Islamic empire.
C11th	The Caliphate disintegrates into squabbling *taifas*, or petty fiefdoms. A local chieftain, El Cid, leads Christian forces against the Moors of Valencia, but his victories have no lasting effect. Independent Catalunya expands.
1037	Fernando I unites the kingdoms of Castile and León-Asturias.
1162	Alfonso II unites the kingdoms of Aragón and Catalunya.
C13th	The pace of the Christian Reconquest accelerates after the kings of Navarra, Castile and Aragón combine to defeat the Muslims at the crucial battle of Las Navas de Tolosa in 1212. Subsequent Christian victories include the capture of the Balearics

(1229), Valencia (1238), Córdoba (1236) and Sevilla (1248). The reconquered territories are mostly distributed amongst the Christian nobility in great estates, the *latifundia*. Men from the ranks also receive land, forming a lower, larger landowning class, the *hidalgos*.

1479   Castile and Aragón, the two pre-eminent Christian kingdoms, are united under Isabella I and Fernando V, the so-called Catholic Monarchs (Los Reyes Católicos). Subsequent emergence of Spain as a single political entity, with the Inquisition acting as a unifying force. The Inquisitors concentrate their attention on the Jews, expelling around 400,000 from Spain for refusing Christian baptism.

1492   The fall of Granada, the last Moorish kingdom. Columbus reaches the Americas.

1494   At the Treaty of Tordesillas, under the approving eye of the Pope, Spain and Portugal divide the New World between them. Portugal gets Brazil and Spain takes the rest of modern-day Latin America.

1516–56   On the death of Fernando, his grandson Carlos I succeeds to the Spanish throne. Three years later Carlos also becomes Holy Roman Emperor – as Charles V – adding Germany, Austria and the Low Countries to his kingdom. Throughout his reign, he wages almost incessant war against his many enemies, principally the French, the Protestants and the Muslims of North Africa. He funds his campaigns with the gold and silver bullion that is pouring into Spain from the New World, where Spanish adventurers have conquered, colonized and exploited a vast new empire.

1519   Cortés lands in Mexico, seizing its capital two years later.

1532   Pizarro "discovers" Peru, capturing Cuzco the next year.

1539   Hernando de Soto stakes out Florida.

1541   Pedro de Valdivia founds Santiago, Chile.

1555   Charles V finally accepts he is unable to suppress the German Reformation and agrees to a compromise peace with the Protestants at the Treaty of Augsburg.

1556   Charles V abdicates. His son, Felipe II, becomes king of Spain and its colonies, Naples, Milan and the Low Countries. His brother, Ferdinand I, becomes Holy Roman Emperor, ruling Germany and Austria. An ardent and autocratic Catholic, Felipe continues the militaristic policy of his father, but concentrates his efforts against the Protestants.

1567   The Protestants of the Low Countries rise against Felipe II, beginning a protracted conflict that will drain Spanish resources and exhaust the Low Countries.

1571   Spain wins control of the Mediterranean after defeating the Turkish fleet at Lepanto.

1588   The English defeat Felipe II's Armada, thereby eliminating Spain as a major sea power.

1598   Felipe II dies. His legacy is an enormous but bankrupt empire: Spain's great wealth, so ruthlessly extracted from its colonies, has been squandered in over seventy years of continuous warfare.

C17th   The decline. Spain's international credibility is undermined by the loss of Portugal (1640) and the Netherlands (1648), emphasizing her military degeneration. Domestically, the poverty and suffering of the mass of the population – as compared with the opulence of the royal court – fuels regional discontent and insurrection. Cervantes publishes *Don Quixote* in 1605.

1701–14	Europe's nation states slug it out in the War of the Spanish Succession. The Bourbon (French) claimant – as opposed to that of the Holy Roman Emperor – wins out to become Felipe V. The British pick up Gibraltar and Menorca. As Spain declines, so it moves into the French sphere of influence.
1804	Napoleon crowned Emperor of France. Spain assists him in his war against England.
1805	The British navy, under Nelson, destroys the Franco-Spanish fleet at the Battle of Trafalgar.
1808	Napoleon arrests the Spanish king and replaces him with his brother, Joseph. This starts the War of Independence (otherwise know as the Peninsular War) in which the Spaniards fight the French army of occupation with the help of their new-found allies, the British.
1811 onwards	The South American colonies take advantage of the situation to assert their independence, detaching themselves from Spain one by one.
1815	The end of the Napoleonic Wars.
C19th	Further Spanish decline. The nineteenth century is dominated by the struggle between the forces of monarchist reaction and those of liberal constitutional reform. There are three bitter Carlist wars – "Carlist" after one of the claimants to the throne. The progressives finally triumph in the 1870s, but the new government's authority is brittle and Spanish society remains deeply divided. Elsewhere, Puerto Rico, the Philippines and Cuba shake off Spanish control with the help of the US. Spain's American empire is at an end.
1900–31	Liberals and conservatives fail to reach a secure constitutional consensus, keeping the country on a knife's edge. Working-class political movements – of anarchist, Marxist and socialist inclination – grow in strength and stir industrial and political discontent. Spain stays neutral in World War I, but the success of the Russian Bolsheviks terrifies King Alfonso XIII and the bourgeoisie, who support the right-wing military coup engineered by General Primo de Rivera in 1923. Rivera dies in 1930 and the king abdicates in 1931 when anti-monarchist parties win the municipal elections.
1932–36	The new Republican government introduces radical left-of-centre reforms, but separatists (in Catalunya, Galicia and the Basque country), revolutionaries and rightists undermine its authority. Spain polarizes to the political left and right. Chaos and confusion prevail.
1936–39	The Spanish Civil War. General Francisco Franco leads a right-wing military rebellion against the Republican government. His Nationalists receive massive support from Hitler and Mussolini. The Republicans get sporadic help from the Soviet Union and attract thousands of volunteers, organized in the International Brigades. The Civil War is vicious and bloody, ending in 1939 with a Fascist victory. Franco becomes head of state and massive reprisals follow. Pope Pius XII congratulates the dictator on his "Catholic victory".
1939–75	Franco establishes a one-party state, backed up by stringent censorship and a vigorous secret police. By staying neutral during World War II, he survives the fall of Nazi Germany. In 1969, Franco nominates the grandson of Alfonso XIII, Juan Carlos, as his successor, but retains his vice-like grip on the country until his death in 1975.
1976–82	Juan Carlos recognizes the need for political reform and helps steer the country towards a parliamentary system. He reinforces his democratic credentials by

opposing the attempted coup of 1981, when Colonel Tejero of the *Guardia Civil* storms the *Cortes* (parliament) along with other officers loyal to Franco's memory. The coup fails.

1982–96   In 1982, Felipe González's Socialist Workers' Party – the PSOE – are elected to office with the votes of nearly ten million Spaniards. It's an electoral landslide and the PSOE, buoyed up by the optimism of the times, promises change and progress. But González finds it hard to deliver and loses the enthusiasm of the left, his electoral power base. The left feels that González has followed a semi-monetarist policy, putting economic efficiency above social policies and rating the control of inflation as more urgent than the reduction of unemployment. Nevertheless, Spain's economy has grown dramatically since 1982, the country is now a respected member of the EC, and the PSOE have attempted to deal with Spain's deep-seated separatist tendencies by permitting a large degree of regional autonomy.

Flora and fauna

Despite their reputation as package-holiday destinations, Menorca and more especially Mallorca have much to offer birders and botanists alike. Separated from the Iberian Peninsula some fifty million years ago, the Balearic archipelago has evolved (at least in part) its own distinctive flora and fauna, with further variations between each of the islands. Among the wildlife, it's the raptors inhabiting the mountains of northwest Mallorca – particularly the black vulture – which attract much of the attention. But there are other pleasures too, especially the migratory birds of the islands' saltpans and marshes, who congregate here in April and May and from mid-September to early October. The islands are also justifiably famous for their fabulous range of wild flowers and flowering shrubs.

Some of the islands' most important habitats have, however, been threatened by the developers. This has spawned an influential conservation group, **GOB** (*Grup Balear d'Ornitologia i Defensa de la Naturalesa*), which has recently launched several successful campaigns. It helped save the S'Albufera wetlands from development, played a leading role in the black vulture re-establishment programme, and successfully lobbied to increase the penalties for shooting protected birds. GOB provide the latest environmental news in its quarterly periodical *Socarrell*, which is available from larger bookshops. The group has offices in Palma (c/Verí 1-3), Maó (c/Isabel II, 42) and Ciutadella (c/ Bisbe 7). Another useful contact is Graham Hearle, Aptdo 83, Sa Pobla (☎971/862418), the GOB/ RSPB (Royal Society for the Protection of Birds)

representative in Mallorca; he organizes birders' meetings in Port de Pollença.

The account of the islands' flora and fauna given below serves as a general introduction and includes mention of several important birding sites, cross-referenced to the descriptions given in the *Guide*. For more specialist information, some recommended **field guides** are listed on p.239.

Habitats

The Balearic Islands are a continuation of the Andalucian mountains of the Iberian Peninsula, from which they are separated by a submarine trench never less than 80km wide and up to 1500m deep. Mallorca, the largest of the islands, comprises three distinct geographical areas with two ranges of predominantly limestone hills falling either side of a central plain, **Es Pla**. Mallorca's northwest coast is dominated by the **Serra de Tramuntana** (in Castilian, *Sierra del Norte*), a slim, ninety-kilometre-long range of wooded hills and rocky peaks, fringed by tiny coves and precipitous seacliffs, that reaches its highest point at Puig Major (1447m). Also edged by steep seacliffs is the **Serres de Llevante**, a range of more modest hills that runs parallel to the island's east shore and rises to 509m at San Salvador.

Menorca has less topographical diversity, dividing into two distinct but not dramatically different zones. The rolling sandstone uplands of the northern half of the island are punctuated by wide, shallow valleys and occasional peaks, the highest of which is Monte Toro at 357m. To the south lie undulating limestone lowlands and deeper valleys. Both parts of the island are trimmed by dramatic seacliffs and scores of rocky coves.

Mallorca and Menorca have a temperate Mediterranean climate, with winter frosts a rarity, but there are significant differences between the two. The Serra de Tramuntana both protects the rest of Mallorca from the winds that blow from the north and catches most of the rain. Menorca, on the other hand, has no mountain barrier to protect it from the cold dry wind (the *tramuntana*) which buffets the island, giving much of its vegetation a wind-blown look and prompting the island's farmers to protect their crops with stone walls.

Mallorcan flora

The characteristic terrain of Mallorca up to around 700m is **garigue**, partly forested open scrubland where the island's native trees – Aleppo pines, wild olives, holmoaks, carobs and dwarf palms – intermingle with imported species like ash, elm and poplar. Between 700m and 950m, *garigue* is gradually replaced by **maquis**, a scrubland of rosemary, laurel, myrtle and broom interspersed with swathes of bracken. Higher still is a rocky terrain that can only support the sparsest of vegetation, such as an assortment of hardy grasses and low-growing rosemary.

Across much of the island, this indigenous vegetation has been destroyed by cultivation. However, the **Aleppo pine** and the evergreen **holm oak** – which traditionally supplied acorns for pigs, wood for charcoal and bark for tanning – are still common, as is the **carob tree**, which prefers the hottest and driest parts of the island. Arguably the archipelago's most handsome tree, the carob boasts leaves of varying greenness and conspicuous fruits – large pods which start green, but ripen to black-brown. The **dwarf palm**, with its sharp lance-like foliage, is concentrated around Pollença, Alcúdia and Andratx. The **wild olive** is comparatively rare (and may not be indigenous), but the cultivated variety – which boasts silver-grey foliage and can grow up to 10m in height – is endemic and has long been a mainstay of the local economy. There are also **orange** and **lemon** orchards around Sóller and literally millions of **almond** trees, whose pink and white blossom adorns much of Mallorca in late January and early February.

Mallorca has a wonderful variety of **flowering shrubs**. There are too many to list in any detail, but look out for the deep blue flowers of the **rosemary**, the reddish bloom of the **lentisk** (or mastic tree), the bright yellow **broom** which begins blossoming in March, the many types of **tree heather** and, especially around C'an Picafort, the autumn-flowering **strawberry tree**. **Rockroses** are also widely distributed, the most common members of the group being the spring-flowering grey-leafed cistus, with its velvety leafs and pink flowers, and the narrow-leafed cistus whose bloom is white.

In spring and autumn the fields, verges, woods and cliffs of Mallorca brim with **wild flowers**. There are several hundred species and only in the depths of winter – from November to January – are all of them dormant. Amongst well-known species there are marigolds, daisies, violets, yellow primroses, gladioli, poppies, hyacinths, several kinds of cyclamen, the resinous St John's wort with its crinkled deep green leaves and, abundant in the pinewoods near the sea and in the mountains, many types of orchid. Two common mountain plants are the pampas-like grass **ampelodesmus mauritanica**, giant clumps of which cover the hillsides, and a local variety of the sarsaparilla, **smilax balearica**, which flourishes in limestone crevices where its sharp thorns are something of a hazard for walkers. Other common and prominent plants are the giant-sized **agave** (century plant), an imported amaryllid with huge spear-shaped, leathery leaves of blue-grey coloration, which produces a massive flower spike every ten years (just before it dies). There's also the distinctive **asphodel**, whose tall spikes sport clusters of pink or white flowers from April to June. The asphodel grows on over-grazed or infertile land and its starch-rich tubers were once used by shoemakers to make glue. Another common sight is the **prickly pear**, traditionally grown behind peasants' houses as a windbreak and toilet wall. A versatile plant, the smell of the prickly pear deflects insects (hence its use round toilets) and its fruit is easy to make into pig food or jam.

Finally, many islanders maintain splendid **gardens** and here you'll see species that flourish throughout the Mediterranean, most famously bougainvilleas, oleanders, geraniums and hibiscus.

Mallorcan birds

The diverse **birdlife** of Mallorca has attracted ornithologists for decades. The island boasts a whole batch of resident species and these are supplemented by migrating flocks of north European birds that descend on the island in spring and autumn. The Serra de Tramuntana is a haven for **predatory birds**, such as ospreys, red kites, Eleanora's falcons, kestrels, peregrines, several sorts of eagle and, rarest of all, **black vultures**. The last-mentioned, with their three-metre wingspan, breed on the seacliffs in November and, although there are only about fifty of them remaining, there's a reasonable chance of a sighting in the vicinity of Puig Massanella (see p.124) or the Boquer valley (Vall de Boquer – see p.135). The seacliffs of the Cap de Formentor (see p.138) are a good area to spot nesting colonies of **seabirds**, including shearwaters and shags.

Characteristic birds of the lower wooded slopes include wood pigeons, crossbills, firecrests and blue tits, whilst the island's scrubland provides excellent cover for a variety of **warblers** and **small songbirds**, such as nightingales and larks. These two types of terrain – and their associated birdlife – are seen to their best advantage in the **Boquer valley**, near Port de Pollença.

Two other areas of special note are the S'Albufera wetlands, part of which has recently been designated a nature reserve, and the saltpans – Salinas de Levante – near Colònia de Sant Jordi. The marsh of **S'Albufera** and its surrounds (see p.144) is the most important birdwatching spot in the whole of the Balearics, its resident species augmented by hundreds of migrating birds, which find fresh water here after their long journey north or south. Amongst scores of species, the shorter grasses shelter moorhens, coots and crakes, while the reeds hide herons, egrets, flamingoes, green sandpipers, the occasional kingfishers, and the distinctive hoopoe (though this relatively common bird prefers cultivated fields), with its long beak and punkish orange and black head-feathers. On the opposite side of Mallorca are the **Salinas de Levante** (see p.175), where the saltpans are especially attractive to waders and terns, including the black-tailed godwit, little egret, black and whiskered tern, sandpiper, redshank, heron and avocet. In both areas, the abundance of prey attracts raptors, most frequently marsh harriers, kestrels and ospreys.

Other Mallorcan fauna

Mallorca's surviving **mammals** are an uninspiring bunch. The wild boar and red fox were eliminated early this century, leaving a motley crew of mountain goats, wild sheep, pine martens, genets, weasels and feral cats, as well as such commonplace smaller mammals as hedgehogs, rabbits, hares and shrews. As far as **reptiles** go, there are four types of snake – all hard to come by – and two species of gecko (or broad-toed lizard), the lowland-living wall gecko and the mountain-dwelling disc-fingered version. With any luck, you'll spot them as they heat up in the sun, but they move fast since warm gecko is a tasty morsel for many a bird. Off the south coast of Mallorca, the desolate island of Cabrera has a large concentration of the rare, blue-undersided **Lilfords wall lizard**.

Among **amphibians**, Mallorca has a healthy frog population, concentrated in its marshlands but also surviving in its mountain pools (up to around 800m). There are also three types of toad, of which the **Mallorcan midwife toad**, hanging on in the northern corner of the island, is the rarest. With no natural predators, its evolution involved a reduction in fecundity (it produces only a quarter of the number of eggs laid by its mainland relative) and the loss of its poison glands. However, with the introduction of the viperine snake, the resident midwife toads were all but wiped out – only about 500 pairs remain.

Common **insects** include grasshoppers and cicadas, whose summertime chirping is so evocative of warm Mediterranean nights, as well as over 200 species of moth and around 30 types of **butterfly**. Some of the more striking butterflies are red admirals, which are seen in winter, and the clouded yellow and painted ladies of spring. One of the more unusual species is the two-tailed pasha, a splendidly marked gold-and-bronze butterfly that flits around the coast in spring and late summer, especially in the vicinity of strawberry trees.

Menorcan flora and fauna

Far flatter than its neighbour, Menorca's indigenous vegetation is almost all **garigue**, though intensive cultivation has reduced the original forest cover to a fraction of its former size – nowadays only about fifteen percent of the island is wooded. Native trees are the holm oak, the dwarf palm, the carob and, commonest of all, the **Aleppo pine**, which has bright green spines, silvery twigs and ruddy-brown cones. Olive trees are endemic and dramatically illustrate the effects of the *tramuntana*, with grove upon grove bent almost double under the weight of the wind.

Menorca's soils nourish a superb range of **flowering shrubs** and **wild flowers**. There is less variety than on Mallorca, but the islands have most species in common. Menorca also boasts a handful of species entirely to itself, the most distinguished of them being the dwarf shrub **daphne rodriquezii**, a purple-flowering evergreen present on the cliffs of the northeast coast. In addition, the cliffs of much of the coast have a flora uniquely adapted to the combination of limestone yet saline soils. Here, **aromatic inula**, a shrubby perennial with clusters of yellow flowers, grows beside the **common caper**, with its red pods and purple seeds, and the **sea aster**.

The mammal, amphibian and insect populations of Mallorca and Menorca are very similar, but Menorca does excel in its **reptiles**. Of the four species of lizard which inhabit the Balearics, Menorca has populations of three. There are two types of wall lizard – Lilfords, a green, black and blue version, and the olive green and black-striped Italian lizard – as well as the Moroccan rock lizard, with olive skin or reticulated blue-green coloration. The **birds** of Menorca are less inspiring than those of Mallorca and, in particular, there are very few species of raptor – the marsh harrier is the most common. The island's best birdwatching spot is the marshland round the lake of S'Albufera, near the village of Es Grau (see p.194).

Books

Most of the books listed below are available in Great Britain, some in Ireland, North America and Australasia too. Others are available on the Balearic Islands only. For all books in print, the publisher's name is given in brackets after the title; o/p means out of print.

Impressions and travel accounts

Tom Crichton *Our Man in Majorca* (Robert Hale, o/p). The American sailor, adventurer and journalist Tom Crichton was briefly a package-tour representative on Mallorca in the early 1960s. With the encouragement of Robert Graves, he published this account of a comical, disaster-filled fortnight. A book for the sunbed.

Paul Richardson *Not Part of the Package* (Pan). Richardson spent a year observing and enjoying the razzle-dazzle of Ibiza. His idiosyncratic tales are diverting and revealing in equal measure – and, by implication, throw light on the way mass tourism works in the Balearics as a whole.

George Sand *A Winter in Majorca* (OMNISA, Mallorca). Accompanied by her lover, Frédéric Chopin, Sand spent the winter of 1838–39 resident in the monastery of Valldemossa, on Mallorca. These are her recollections, ponderous in style and very critical of the islanders. Readily available in Valldemossa and Mallorca's better bookshops.

Gordon West *Jogging round Majorca* (Black Swan). This gentle, humorous account of an extended journey round Mallorca by Gordon and Mary West in the 1920s vividly portrays the island's pre-tourist life and times. The trip had nothing to do with running, but rather "jogging" as in a leisurely progress. West's book lay forgot-

ten for decades until a BBC Radio 4 presenter, Leonard Pearcey, stumbled across it in a second-hand bookshop and subsequently read extracts on air. The programmes were very well received, and the book was reprinted in 1994.

History

David Abulafia *Mediterranean Emporium: the Catalan Kingdom of Majorca* (Cambridge University Press). Serious-minded, detailed study of medieval Mallorca.

Raymond Carr *Spain 1808–1975* and *Modern Spain 1875–1980* (Oxford University Press). Two of the best books available on modern Spanish history – concise and well-considered narratives.

J. H. Elliott *Imperial Spain 1469–1716* (Penguin). The best introduction to Spain's "Golden Age" – academically respected as well as being a gripping yarn.

Desmond Gregory *Minorca, the Illusory Prize: History of the British Occupation of Minorca between 1708 and 1802* (Fairleigh Dickinson University Press). Exhaustive, scholarly and well-composed narrative detailing the British colonial involvement with Minorca.

Bruce Laurie *Life of Richard Kane: Britain's First Lieutenant Governor of Minorca* (Fairleigh Dickinson University Press). Detailed historical biography providing an intriguing insight into eighteenth-century Menorca.

Hugh Thomas *The Spanish Civil War* (Penguin). Exhaustively researched, brilliantly detailed account of the war and the complex political manoeuvrings surrounding it with sections on Mallorca and Menorca. First published in 1961 and now in its third edition, it remains easily the best book on the subject.

Fiction and general background

William Graves *Wild Olives* (Hutchinson). The son of Robert Graves, William was born in 1940 and spent much of his childhood in Palma and Deià, sufficient inspiration for mildly diverting accounts of his Mallorcan contemporaries. The book's real focus, however, is his troubled family life and his difficult relationship with his father. Published in 1995, the centenary of Robert's birth.

John Hooper *The New Spaniards: A Portrait of the New Spain* (Penguin). Well-constructed portrait of post-Franco Spain; an excellent general introduction.

Ramon Llull *Blanquerna* (Dedalus, o/p). The Mallorcan scholar and philosopher Ramon Llull wrote this lengthy and heavy-going treatise on mysticism and Christian zeal in the thirteenth century. It's one of the first books written in Catalan.

Juan Masoliver (ed.) *The Origins of Desire: Modern Spanish Short Stories* (Serpent's Tail). Enjoyable selection of short stories from some of Spain's leading contemporary writers, including Mallorca's own Valenti Puig and Carme Riera.

Ana María Matute *School of the Sun* (Quartet, UK; Columbia University Press, US). The loss of childhood innocence on the Balearics, where old enmities are redefined during the Civil War.

Manuel Vazquez Montalban *Murder in the Central Committee, The Angst-ridden Executive* and others (Serpent's Tail). Riveting tales by one of Spain's most popular crime thriller writers, a long-time member of the Communist Party and now a well-known journalist resident in Barcelona.

Miranda Seymour *Robert Graves: Life on the Edge* (Doubleday). Lengthy account of Robert Graves's personal life with lacklustre commentary on his poetry and novels. Much detail on Graves's residence in Deià, Mallorca. Published in 1995, to mark the centenary of Graves's birth.

Llorenç Villalonga *The Doll's Room* (o/p). Nobility in decline in nineteenth-century Mallorca, lyrically depicted by a local writer.

Specialist guidebooks

Giles Barnabe *Railways and Tramways of Majorca* (Plateway). Lavishly illustrated railway enthusiasts' guide to every bend in the line.

Marc Dubin *Trekking in Spain* (Lonely Planet). A detailed trekking guide with a chapter giving easy-to-follow and accurate accounts of half a dozen arduous hikes in Mallorca's Serra de Tramuntana.

Patricia Fenn *Entrée to Mallorca* (Quiller Press). Very good restaurant guide, though the prose can be painful.

Herbert Heinrich *Twelve Classic Hikes through Mallorca* (Editorial Moll, Mallorca). Heinrich has published a number of Mallorcan hiking guides in German. This was his first English volume, a compilation of some of the best and less demanding one-day hikes in the mountains of northwest Mallorca. The descriptions are a bit patchy, but the topographical sketches are extremely helpful. Widely available in Mallorca. Also available is the same author's *Walking in Southwest Mallorca* (Sigma, UK).

Dodo Mackenzie *Walks in Menorca* (Frans Lindsen, Netherlands). A series of booklets detailing a range of Menorcan walks, from short strolls to stiff hikes, with thorough and accurate descriptions. The booklets can be difficult to track down, although the better bookshops on Menorca (detailed in Maó and Ciutadella "Listings") should have copies.

Gaspar Martí *Walking Tours around the Historical Centre of Palma* (Ajuntament de Palma, Mallorca). Detailed and enjoyable exploration of Palma's historical nooks and crannies. Beautiful sketches illuminate the text. Published by Palma Town Hall and available in all leading Palma bookshops.

June Parker *Walking in Mallorca* (Cicerone). Highly recommended: detailed and accurate accounts of over seventy Mallorcan hikes, to suit almost all levels of fitness.

Flora and fauna

John Busby *Birds in Majorca* (Christopher Helm). Well-illustrated catalogue of Mallorcan birdlife.

John and Margaret Goulding *Menorca* (Windrush). A general travel guide with detailed and informative lists describing Menorca's flora and fauna.

Oleg Polunin and Anthony Huxley *Flowers of the Mediterranean* (Chatto). Useful if by no means exhaustive field guide.

Ken Stoba *Birdwatching in Mallorca* (Cicerone). An excellent introduction to Mallorca's birdlife and major birdwatching sites.

Language

Most of the inhabitants of Mallorca and Menorca are bilingual, speaking Castilian (ie Spanish) and their local dialect of the Catalan language (either *Mallorquín* or *Menorquín*) with equal facility. *Català* (Catalan) has been the islanders' everyday language since the Reconquest and absorption into the Kingdom of Aragón and Catalunya in the thirteenth century, whereas Castilian was imposed much later from the mainland as the language of government – and with special rigour by Franco. As a result, Spain's recent move towards regional autonomy has been accompanied by the islanders' assertion of Catalan as their official language. The most obvious sign of this has been the change of all the old Castilian town and street names into Catalan versions. On paper, Catalan looks like a cross between French and Spanish and is generally easy to understand if you know those two, although when spoken, it has a very harsh sound and is far harder to come to grips with.

Some background

When Franco came to power in 1939, publishing houses, bookshops and libraries were raided and *Català* books destroyed. While there was some relaxation in the mid-1940s, the language was still banned from the radio, TV, daily press and, most importantly, schools, which is why many older people today cannot read or write *Català* (even if they speak it all the time) – in the Balearics, the best-selling Catalan-language news-papers sell less than a fifth of the figure for the most popular Castilian-language daily papers. The linguistic picture has been further muddied by the emigration of hundreds of mainland Spaniards to the islands, and nowadays it's estimated that Castilian is the dominant language in around forty percent of island households.

Català is spoken by over six million people in total in the Balearics, Catalunya, part of Aragón, most of Valencia, Andorra and parts of the French Pyrenees; it is thus much more widely spoken than several better-known languages such as Danish, Finnish and Norwegian. It is a Romance language, stemming from Latin and more directly from medieval Provençal. Spaniards in the rest of the country belittle it by saying that to get a *Català* word you just cut a Castilian one in half (which is often true!), but in fact the grammar is much more complicated than Castilian and there are eight vowel sounds, three more than in Castilian.

Getting by in Mallorca and Menorca

Although Catalan is the preferred language of most islanders, you'll almost always get by perfectly well if you speak Spanish, as long as you're aware of the use of Catalan in timetables and so forth. Once you get into it, Spanish is one of the easiest languages there is, the rules of pronunciation pretty straightforward and strictly observed. You'll find some basic pronunciation rules below for both *Català* and Spanish, and a selection of words and phrases in both languages. The Spanish is certainly easier to pronounce, but don't be afraid to try *Català*, especially in the more out-of-the-way places – you'll generally get a good reception if you at least try communicating in the local language.

Castilian/Spanish: a few rules

Unless there's an accent, words ending in d, l, r, and z are **stressed** on the last syllable, all others on the second last. All **vowels** are pure and short; combinations have predictable results.

A somewhere between the A sound of back and that of father.

E as in get.

I as in police.

O as in hot.

U as in rule.

C is lisped before E and I, hard otherwise: *cerca* is pronounced "thairka".

CH is pronounced as in English.

G works the same way, a guttural H sound (like the *ch* in loch) before E or I, a hard G elsewhere – *gigante* becomes "higante".

H is always silent.

J the same sound as a guttural G: *jamón* is pronounced "hamon".

LL sounds like an English Y: *tortilla* is pronounced "torteeya".

N as in English unless it has a tilde (accent) over it, when it becomes NY: *mañana* sounds like "man-yarna".

QU is pronounced like an English K.

R is rolled, RR doubly so.

V sounds more like B, *vino* becoming "beano".

X has an S sound before consonants, normal X before vowels.

Z is the same as a soft C, so *cerveza* becomes "thairvaitha".

Català: a few rules

With *Català*, don't be tempted to use the few rules of Spanish pronunciation you may know – in particular the soft Spanish Z and C don't apply, so unlike in the rest of Spain it's not "Barthelona" but "Barcelona", as in English.

A as in hat if stressed, as in alone when unstressed.

E varies, but usually as in get.

I as in police.

IG sounds like the "tch" in the English scratch; *lleig* (ugly) is pronounced "yeah-tch".

O varies, but usually as in hot.

U somewhere between the U sound of put and rule.

Ç sounds like an English S; *plaça* is pronounced "plassa".

C followed by an E or I is soft; otherwise hard.

G followed by E or I is like the "zh" in Zhivago; otherwise hard.

H is always silent.

J as in the French "Jean".

LL sounds like an English Y or LY, like the "yuh" sound in million.

N as in English, though before F or V it sometimes sounds like an M.

NY replaces the Castilian Ñ.

QU before E or I sounds like K; before A or O as in "quit".

R is rolled, but only at the start of a word; at the end it's often silent.

T is pronounced as in English, though sometimes it sounds like a D, as in *viatge* or *dotze*.

TX is pronounced like English CH.

V at the start of a word sounds like B; in all other positions it's a soft "F" sound.

W is pronounced like a B/V.

X is like SH in most words, though in some, like *exit*, it sounds like an X.

Z is like the English Z in zoo.

Phrasebooks, dictionaries and teaching yourself

Spanish

Numerous **Spanish phrasebooks** are available in Britain, the most user-friendly of which is the *Rough Guide Spanish Phrasebook*. Harrap's small **dictionaries** are reliable. For **teaching yourself** the language, the BBC tape series *España Viva* and *Digame* are excellent.

Many of the books available in North America are geared to New World, Latin American usage; more old-fashioned publications may be better for Spain itself. Cassells, Collins and Langenscheidt all produce useful dictionaries; Berlitz publishes separate Spanish and Latin American Spanish phrasebooks.

Català

It's much harder to track down books that can help you with **Català**. In Britain, there's only one English–Catalan **phrasebook** in print, *Parla Català* (Pia), and for a **dictionary** you're limited to the version published by Routledge. For **teaching yourself** the language, the reasonably proficient *Teach Yourself Catalan* (Hodder & Stoughton) is a useful introduction, while *Catalan Grammar* (Dolphin Book Company) adopts a more academic approach. Spanish speakers can also use a total immersion course called *Digui Digui*, a series of books and tapes published by L'Abadia de Montserrat.

Words and phrases

Basics	Spanish	Catalan
Yes, No, OK	*Sí, No, Vale*	*Sí, No, Val*
Please, Thank you	*Por favor, Gracias*	*Per favor, Gràcies*
Where, When	*Dónde, Cuando*	*On, Quan*
What, How much	*Qué, Cuánto*	*Què, Quant*
Here, There	*Aquí, Allí, Allá*	*Aquí, Allí, Allá*
This, That	*Esto, Eso*	*Això, Allò*
Now, Later	*Ahora, Más tarde*	*Ara, Mès tard*
Open, Closed	*Abierto/a, Cerrado/a*	*Obert, Tancat*
With, Without	*Con, Sin*	*Amb, Sense*
Good, Bad	*Buen(o)/a, Mal(o)/a*	*Bo(na), Dolent(a)*
Big, Small	*Gran(de), Pequeño/a*	*Gran, Petit(a)*
Cheap, Expensive	*Barato, Caro*	*Barat(a), Car(a)*
Hot, Cold	*Caliente, Frío*	*Calent(a), Fred(a)*
More, Less	*Más, Menos*	*Mes, Menys*
Today, Tomorrow	*Hoy, Mañana*	*Avui, Demà*
Yesterday	*Ayer*	*Ahir*
Day before yesterday	*Ante ayer*	*Abans-d'ahir*
Next week	*La semana que viene*	*La setmana que ve*
Next month	*El mes que viene*	*El mes que ve*

Greetings and responses	Spanish	Catalan
Hello, Goodbye	*Hola, Adiós*	*Hola, Adéu*
Good morning	*Buenos días*	*Bon dia*
Good afternoon/night	*Buenas tardes/noches*	*Bona tarda/nit*
See you later	*Hasta luego*	*Fins després*
Sorry	*Lo siento/disculpéme*	*Ho sento*
Excuse me	*Con permiso/perdón*	*Perdoni*
How are you?	*¿Cómo está (usted)?*	*Com va?*
I (don't) understand	*(No) Entiendo*	*(No) Ho entenc*
Not at all/You're welcome	*De nada*	*De res*
Do you speak English?	*¿Habla (usted) inglés?*	*Parla anglès?*
I (don't) speak Spanish/Catalan	*(No) Hablo Español*	*(No) Parlo Català*
My name is . . .	*Me llamo . . .*	*Em dic . . .*
What's your name?	*¿Como se llama usted?*	*Com es diu?*
I am English	*Soy inglés(a)*	*Sóc anglès(a)*
Scottish	*escocés(a)*	*escocès(a)*
Australian	*australiano/a*	*australian(a)*
Canadian	*canadiense/a*	*canadenc(a)*
American	*americano/a*	*americà/ana*
Irish	*irlandes(a)*	*irlandès(a)*

Hotels and transport	Spanish	Catalan
I want	*Quiero*	*Vull (pronounced "fwee")*
I'd like	*Quisiera*	*Voldria*
Do you know . . . ?	*¿Sabe . . . ?*	*Vostès saben . . . ?*
I don't know	*No sé*	*No sé*
There is (is there?)	*(¿)Hay(?)*	*Hi ha(?)*

Hotels and transport (continued)

	Spanish	Catalan
Give me ...	Deme ...	Doneu-me ... (a bit brusque)
Do you have ...?	¿Tiene ...?	Té ...?
... the time	... la hora	... l'hora
... a room	... una habitación	... alguna habitació
... with two beds/double bed	... con dos camas/cama matrimonial	... amb dos llits/ llit per dues persones
... with shower/bath	... con ducha/baño	... amb dutxa/bany
for one person (two people)	para una persona (dos personas)	per a una persona (dues persones)
for one night (one week)	para una noche (una semana)	per una nit (una setmana)
It's fine, how much is it?	¿Está bien, cuánto es?	Esta bé, quant és?
It's too expensive	Es demasiado caro	És massa car
Don't you have anything cheaper?	¿No tiene algo más barato?	En té de més bon preu?
Can one ...?	¿Se puede ...?	Es pot ...?
... camp (near) here?	¿ ... acampar aqui (cerca)?	... acampar a la vora?
Is there a hostel nearby?	¿Hay un hostal aquí cerca?	Hi ha un hostal a la vora?
It's not very far	No es muy lejos	No és gaire lluny
How do I get to ...?	¿Por donde se va a ...?	Per anar a ...?
Left, right, straight on	Izquierda, derecha, todo recto	A la dreta, a l'esquerra, tot recte
Where is ...?	¿Dónde está ...?	On és ...?
... the bus station	... la estación de autobuses	... l'estació de autobuses
... the bus stop	... la parada	... la parada
... the railway station	... la estación de ferrocarril	... l'estació
... the nearest bank	... el banco más cercano	... el banc més a prop
... the post office	... el correos/la oficina de correos	... l'oficina de correus
... the toilet	... el baño/aseo/servicio	... la toaleta
Where does the bus to ... leave from?	¿De dónde sale el autobús para ...?	De on surt el autobús a ...?
Is this the train for Barcelona?	¿Es este el tren para Barcelona?	Aquest tren va a Barcelona?
I'd like a (return) ticket to ...	Quisiera un billete (de ida y vuelta) para ...	Voldria un bitlet (d'anar i tornar) a...
What time does it leave (arrive in ...)?	¿A qué hora sale (llega a ...)?	A quina hora surt (arriba a...)?
What is there to eat?	¿Qué hay para comer?	Què hi ha por monjar?
What's that?	¿Qué es eso?	Què és això?

Days of the week

	Spanish	Catalan
Monday	lunes	dilluns
Tuesday	martes	dimarts
Wednesday	miércoles	dimecres
Thursday	jueves	dijous
Friday	viernes	divendres
Saturday	sábado	dissabte
Sunday	domingo	diumenge

Numbers

	Spanish	Catalan		Spanish	Catalan
			19	diecinueve	dinou
1	un/uno/una	un(a)	20	veinte	vint
2	dos	dos (dues)	21	veintiuno	vint-i-un
3	tres	tres	30	treinta	trenta
4	cuatro	quatre	40	cuarenta	quaranta
5	cinco	cinc	50	cincuenta	cinquanta
6	seis	sis	60	sesenta	seixanta
7	siete	set	70	setenta	setanta
8	ocho	vuit	80	ochenta	vuitanta
9	nueve	nou	90	noventa	novanta
10	diez	deu	100	cien(to)	cent
11	once	onze	101	ciento uno	cent un
12	doce	dotze	102	ciento dos	cent dos (dues)
13	trece	tretze	200	doscientos	dos-cents
14	catorce	catorze			(dues-centes)
15	quince	quinze	500	quinientos	cinc-cents
16	dieciseis	setze	1000	mil	mil
17	diecisiete	disset	2000	dos mil	dos mil
18	dieciocho	divuit			

Glossary

Albufera Lagoon (and surrounding wetlands).

Altar major High altar.

Ajuntament Town Hall.

Avinguda (Avgda) Avenue.

Badia Bay.

Barranc Ravine.

Barroc Baroque, the art and architecture of the Counter-Reformation, dating from around 1600 onwards, elements of which – particularly its ornate gaudiness – remained popular in the Balearics well into the twentieth century.

Basílica Catholic church with honorific privileges.

Cala Small bay, cove.

Camí Way or road.

Can At the house of (contraction of *casa* + *en*.

Capella Chapel.

Carrer (c/) Street.

Carretera Road, highway.

Castell Castle.

Celler Cellar or a bar in a cellar.

Churrigueresque Fancifully ornate form of Baroque art named after the Spaniard José Churriguera (1650–1723) and his extended family, its leading exponents.

Claustre Cloister.

Coll Col, mountain pass.

Convent Convent, nunnery or monastery.

Correus Post office.

Església Church.

Estany Small lake.

Festa Festival.

Finca Estate or farmhouse.

Font Water fountain or spring.

Gòtic Gothic.

Illa Island.

Jardí Garden.

Llac Lake.

Mercat Market.

Mirador Watchtower or viewpoint.

Modernisme (Modernista) Literally "modernism" ("modernist"), the Catalan form of Art Nouveau, whose most famous exponent was Antoni Gaudí.

Monestir Monastery.

Mozarabe Christian subject of medieval Moorish ruler; hence **Mozarabic**, a colourful building style that reveals both Christian and Moorish influences.

Mudéjar Moor subject to medieval Christian ruler. Also a style of architecture developed by Moorish craftsmen working for Christians, characterized by painted woodwork with strong colours and complex geometrical patterns; revived between the 1890s and 1930s and blended with Art-Nouveau forms.

Museu Museum.

Nostra Senyora The Virgin Mary (lit. "Our Lady").

Oficina d'Informació Turística Tourist office.

Palau Palace, mansion or manor house.

Parc Park.

Passeig Boulevard; the evening stroll along it.

Pic Summit.

Plaça Square.

Plateresque Elaborately decorative Renaissance architectural style, named for its resemblance to silversmiths' work (*platería*).

Platja Beach.

Pont Bridge.

Port Harbour, port.

Porta Door, gate.

Puig Hill.

Rambla Avenue or boulevard.

Rei King.

Reial Royal.

Reina Queen.

Reixa Iron screen or grille, usually in front of a window.

Renaixença Rebirth, often used to describe the Catalan cultural revival at the end of the nineteenth and beginning of the twentieth centuries. Architecturally, this was expressed as *Modernisme*.

Retaule Retable or reredos, a wooden, ornamental panel behind an altar.

Riu River.

Romeria Pilgrimage or gathering at a shrine.

Salinas Saltpans.

Salt d'aigua Waterfall.

Santuari Sanctuary.

Sant/a Saint.

Serra Mountain range.

Talayot Cone-shaped prehistoric watchtower.

Torrent Stream or river (usually dry in summer).

Urbanització Modern urbanization or estate development.

Vall Valley.

CONTEXTS

Index

DIRECT ORDERS IN THE UK

Title	ISBN	Price
Amsterdam	1858280869	£7.99
Andalucia	185828094X	£8.99
Australia	1858281415	£12.99
Bali	1858281342	£8.99
Barcelona & Catalunya	1858281067	£8.99
Berlin	1858281296	£8.99
Big Island of Hawaii	185828158X	£8.99
Brazil	1858281024	£9.99
Brittany & Normandy	1858281261	£8.99
Bulgaria	1858280478	£8.99
California	1858280907	£9.99
Canada	185828130X	£10.99
Classical Music on CD	185828113X	£12.99
Corsica	1858280893	£8.99
Costa Rica	1858281369	£9.99
Crete	1858281326	£8.99
Cyprus	185828032X	£8.99
Czech & Slovak Republics	1858281210	£9.99
Egypt	1858280753	£10.99
England	1858281601	£10.99
Europe	1858281598	£14.99
Florida	1858280109	£8.99
France	1858281245	£10.99
Germany	1858281288	£11.99
Goa	1858281563	£8.99
Greece	1858281318	£9.99
Greek Islands	1858281636	£8.99
Guatemala & Belize	1858280451	£9.99
Holland, Belgium & Luxembourg	1858280877	£9.99
Hong Kong & Macau	1858280664	£8.99
Hungary	1858281237	£8.99
India	1858281040	£13.99
Ireland	1858280958	£9.99
Italy	1858280311	£12.99
Jazz	1858281377	£16.99
Kenya	1858280435	£9.99
London	1858291172	£8.99
Malaysia, Singapore & Brunei	1858281032	£9.99
Mexico	1858280443	£10.99
Morocco	1858280400	£9.99
Moscow	185828118 0	£8.99
Nepal	185828046X	£8.99
New York	1858280583	£8.99
Nothing Ventured	0747102082	£7.99
Pacific Northwest	1858280923	£9.99
Paris	1858281253	£7.99
Poland	1858280346	£9.99
Portugal	1858280842	£9.99
Prague	185828015X	£7.99
Provence & the Côte d'Azur	1858280230	£8.99
Pyrenees	1858280931	£8.99
Romania	1858280974	£9.99
St Petersburg	1858281334	£8.99
San Francisco	1858280826	£8.99
Scandinavia	1858280397	£10.9
Scotland	1858281660	£9.99
Sicily	1858281784	£9.99
Singapore	1858281350	£8.99
Spain	1858280818	£9.99
Thailand	1858281407	£10.
Tunisia	1858280656	£8.9
Turkey	1858280885	£9.9
Tuscany & Umbria	1858280915	£8.9
USA	185828161X	£14.
Venice	1858281709	£8.9
Wales	1858280966	£8.9
West Africa	1858280141	£12.
More Women Travel	1858280982	£9.9
World Music	1858280176	£14.
Zimbabwe & Botswana	1858280419	£10.

Rough Guide Phrasebooks

Czech	1858281482	£3.5
French	185828144X	£3.5
German	1858281466	£3.5
Greek	1858281458	£3.5
Italian	1858281431	£3.5
Spanish	1858281474	£3.5

Rough Guides can be obtained directly in the UK* from Penguin by contacting:
Penguin Direct, Penguin Books Ltd, Bath Road, Harmondsworth, West Drayton,
Middlesex UB7 0DA; or telephone our credit line on 0181-899 4036 (9am–5pm) and
ask for Penguin Direct. Visa, Access and Amex accepted. Delivery will
normally be within 14 working days. Penguin Direct ordering facilities
are only available in the UK.

The availability and published prices quoted are correct at the time
of going to press but are subject to alteration without prior notice.

DIRECT ORDERS IN THE USA

Title	ISBN	Price
Amsterdam	1858280869	$13.59
Andalucia	185828094X	$14.95
Australia	1858281415	$19.95
Barcelona & Catalunya	1858281067	$17.99
Bali	1858281342	$14.95
Berlin	1858281296	$14.95
Big Island of Hawaii	185828158X	$12.95
Brazil	1858281024	$15.95
Brittany & Normandy	1858281261	$14.95
Bulgaria	1858280478	$14.99
California	1858280907	$14.95
Canada	185828130X	$14.95
Classical Music on CD	185828113X	$19.95
Corsica	1858280893	$14.95
Costa Rica	1858281369	$15.95
Crete	1858281326	$14.95
Cyprus	185828032X	$13.99
Czech & Slovak Republics	1858281210	$16.95
Egypt	1858280753	$17.95
England	1858281601	$17.95
Europe	1858281598	$19.95
First Time Europe	1858282101	$9.95
Florida	1858280109	$14.95
France	1858281245	$16.95
Germany	1858281288	$17.95
Goa	1858281563	$14.95
Greece	1858281318	$16.95
Greek Islands	1858281636	$14.95
Guatemala & Belize	1858280451	$14.95
Holland, Belgium & Luxembourg	1858280877	$15.95
Hong Kong & Macau	1858280664	$13.95
Hungary	1858281237	$14.95
India	1858281040	$22.95
Ireland	1858280958	$16.95
Italy	1858280311	$17.95
Jazz	1858281377	$24.95
Kenya	1858280435	$15.95
London	1858291172	$12.95
Malaysia, Singapore & Brunei	1858281032	$16.95
Mexico	1858280443	$16.95
Morocco	1858280400	$16.95
Moscow	1858281180	$14.95
Nepal	185828046X	$13.95
New York	1858280583	$13.95
Nothing Ventured	0747102082	$19.95
Pacific Northwest	1858280923	$14.95
Paris	1858281253	$12.95
Poland	1858280346	$16.95
Portugal	1858280842	$15.95
Prague	1858281229	$14.95
Provence & the Côte d'Azur	1858280230	$14.95
Pyrenees	1858280931	$15.95
Romania	1858280974	$15.95
St Petersburg	1858281334	$14.95
San Francisco	1858280826	$13.95
Scandinavia	1858280397	$16.99
Scotland	1858281660	$16.95
Sicily	1858281784	$16.95
Singapore	1858281350	$14.95
Spain	1858280818	$16.95
Thailand	1858281407	$17.95
Tunisia	1858280656	$15.95
Turkey	1858280885	$16.95
Tuscany & Umbria	1858280915	$15.95
USA	185828161X	$19.95
Venice	1858281709	$14.95
Wales	1858280966	$14.95
West Africa	1858280141	$24.95
More Women Travel	1858280982	$14.95
World Music	1858280176	$19.95
Zimbabwe & Botswana	1858280419	$16.95

Rough Guide Phrasebooks

Czech	1858281482	$5.00
French	185828144X	$5.00
German	1858281466	$5.00
Greek	1858281458	$5.00
Italian	1858281431	$5.00
Spanish	1858281474	$5.00

THE LOWEST PRE-BOOKED CAR RENTAL OR YOUR MONEY BACK.

AS RECOMMENDED BY **ROUGH GUIDES** *AS RECOMMENDED BY*

Holiday Autos is the only company to actually guarantee the lowest prices or your money back at over 4000 worldwide rental locations in Europe, USA, Canada, and Australasia.

All our rates are truly fully inclusive and FREE of any nasty hidden extras. Also available in the USA and Canada are our range of luxury motorhomes and campervans. Don't waste money - book with Holiday Autos - guaranteed always to be the lowest on the market.

Holiday Autos.
NOBODY BEATS OUR PRICES.
0171- 491 1111